ACHIEVING HUMANE ORGANIZATION

ACHIEVING

HUMANE

ORGANIZATION

Robert H. Simmons

Department of Political Science
and Public Administration
California State University
Los Angeles

Daniel Spencer Publishers
Malibu • California

Dedication

To my children: Richard, Karolyn, Drew and Rachael,
and to my many students, and clients
—each a source of inspiration, support, critique and nurture.

Copyright ©1981 by Robert H. Simmons

Printed in the United States

International Standard Book Number: 0-936496-01-0

Library of Congress Catalog Card Number: 80—85447

PREFACE

The technological urban cultures of the world may be characterized as involving complex arrangements of groups and organizations which range from a wide variety of small groups to immense, complex and interdependent organizations which are called bureaucracies. The people and their leaders in these countries have selected these arrangements for the conduct of their most important business. Yet these groups, organizations and bureaucracies frequently fail in fulfilling effectively their tasks and missions even while striving to survive. They are often viewed as frustrating the very purpose for which they were created. Oppression is a pervasive condition within the groups and organizations which make up these bureaucracies. Likewise, oppression characterizes the relations with the citizens and clientele they are designed to serve. Humane bureaucracy, seemingly a contradiction in terms, seems impossible to achieve. Power plays, conflict, boredom and destructive competition characterize the interpersonal life of these human arrangements. How long can we contain these destructive forces? How long will we tolerate them?

Elliot Jaques suggests that "A humanitarian society depends upon the humanity of its social institutions." He further suggests that bureaucracy is the "inevitable handmaiden of large-scale technology…" Human progress in industrial societies, Jaques avers, essentially rests upon the attainment of "requisitely humanitarian bureaucratic systems."[1]

Sir Geoffrey Vickers, a perceptive English social analyst and management specialist, suggests that the primary concern of our children will be to establish sufficient authority, i.e., establishing safe constraints, within which aggression can be expressed so as to create access to their liberties. He suggests that this is a challenge to both innovate and conserve. He suggests this will require our children to widen their sense of human obligation so that it extends not only across the frontiers of nations but also across the temporal boundaries of the generations including the unborn.[2]

Achieving requisite innovation and conservation encompasses the responsibility of utilizing organizations and technology to enhance the quality of human life. This in turn depends upon a deeper and more effective understanding of humankind. Such knowledge and responsibility involve an awareness in each human being of his or her own consciousness and personal competence. It involves, as well, a sharpened awareness and insight into our own unconscious and the relationship of our unconscious to how we present ourselves in groups. Erik Erikson suggests the last century has dramatically expanded our awareness of unconscious motivation rooted in our animal ancestry, in our economic history and formed by our inner estrangements.[3]

Access into a vast and diverse variety of self-awareness and growth activities is evermore available. Self-conscious awareness of the crucial importance of our own inner life, the relationship of our early childhood to the kinds of choices of action that each of us perform in our daily lives, and how we interact with one another is essential for the full emergence and survival of humanity. It is no longer the province of psychiatry alone; social scientist, organizational developer, group process analyst are all vitally concerned. Human survival depends upon a more complete understanding of ourselves, our groups and our organizations.

Bureaucracy is a collectivity of groups and organizations. Its existence is an ever present reminder that human society is dependent upon the regulation, control, manipulation and production characteristic of such complex organizations. Henry Jacoby observes that the overpowering anonymity, control and impenetrability of such organizations produces fear and discontent. He suggests the voices which complain are the same as those demanding the regulations, the controls and the productivity which are their daily fare. Further, he observes that the disintegration of the old feudal order and the rise of modern industry has thrown a multitude of individuals together, bereft of social ties, except for those of family, and these persons were without local authority to whom they could turn. Because they needed some system of authority they invested centralized bureaucracy with more and more authority. For these and other reasons he fully explores, we have utilized and continue to rely upon large organizations to perform needed social tasks.[4]

The United States has turned to large public and private organizations to regulate private sector organizations when they seem to run amuck. Large public and private organizations deliver crucial social values to great numbers of people. These large complex organizations are all too frequently a source of threat to those very values they are supposed to sustain and deliver. Observing this as characteristic of complex organizations Rosabeth Moss Kanter aptly rephrases Lord Acton's dicta as a distinct characteristic of large organizations, "Powerlessness corrupts. Absolute powerlessness corrupts absolutely."[5] This work examines the many corruptions of powerlessness associated with bureaucracy and organization which may be indeed as dangerous or more dangerous than the excessive concentration of power at the top of organizations of which this study is concerned as well. It is the fundamental premise in this effort that organizations rooted in management practice which perpetuates human alienation and powerlessness cannot deliver the humane values with which they are entrusted and are expected to deliver to our society.

Public bureaucracy and private sector organizations do deliver important social values into an everchanging social process. This function must be exercised in a civilized and responsible manner. The emphasis needs to be placed upon the revision of our understanding and use of power, cooperation, intimacy and work in groups and organizations. What is needed is an ethic of good public and private management, an ethic of good planning, and an ethic of intentional change intervention which responds wisely to the dilemmas, limitations and possibilities of the modern organization, formulates humane options and implements humane alternatives. It is toward this end that this book is written.

This book began to take shape during the writing of an earlier book co-authored with my colleague Eugene P. Dvorin, *viz. From Amoral to Humane Bureaucracy.*[6] The need to write it became more compelling with my experiencing several "Tavistock Events" sponsored by the A.K. Rice Institute. The power drama of that process was of such significance to me that I at once moved to pursue and develop tools to explore that process.

I pursued, applied, tested, modified, re-applied and re-tested the ideas utilized here over the four-year period these materials have been developing. They were utilized, applied, tested and modified by public administration practitioners, corporate managers, supervisors, students, clients and client groups. Through this process much of the material here received significant validation, thus tentative support was provided for the underlying hypotheses and theoretical observations made in this effort.

The overwhelming majority of my students are public service practitioners and a goodly number, too, are from the private sector. They never hesitated to try, apply, use, critique, and provide crucial feedback concerning the materials presented. Where I am certain of my ground, at least three practitioners validated it through disciplined observation and application. Of course, these are, for the most part, hypotheses; there still remains much to be elaborated, empirically tested and pursued. The responsibility for the material, the errors of omission, commission and judgment are fully my own.

Some recent developments concerning power and behavior within and among groups are exceptionally useful and are distinctly applicable to our understanding, *viz.*, the work of Wilfred Bion and Eric Berne among others. Berne's superb conceptual work on groups has been largely ignored and Bion's important contributions are quite distinctive and on the surface somewhat mystifying. Both of these men represent different perspectives in their approaches to groups, yet each is immensely helpful in providing tools to help better understand group processes. Both men, psychiatrists, observed and theorized about the distinctive aspects of group behavior. Berne particularly noted the integral relationship between human behavior in groups and the outcome of what happened in that group or organization.[7] Elliot Jaques provides the broad theoretical context into which this effort is linked.

No comprehensive review of group and organization literature is attempted in this effort. Rather, the goal of this work is to plumb some of the recent conceptual developments and the results of experience and practice which have emerged within recent years and examine their significance for analysis, application and change within groups and organizations.

The preoccupation of the traditional organizational behavior literature is with competition, conflict and the motivation (frequently manipulation) of human beings so they will produce more. It frequently ends up being a profound betrayal of the human personality in the service of "the larger" cause, i.e. the organization. The tremendous explosion recently in organizational development has moderated this trend, but certainly not reversed it. Rensis Likert, Warren Bennis, Douglas McGregor, Abraham Maslow and others have done much to focus on human need within groups and organizations as it relates to organizational change and management style.

A tremendous literature is being developed on power, conflict and its resolution; yet there is little understanding of the operations of power. Not very significant progress has been made into studying the role and function of groups, especially within the larger organization. Morton Kroll has observed that the study of groups offers possibilities for research in large organizations.[8] These groups have a profound impact upon the organization and bureaucracies of which they are a part. Power within groups and power among inter-linked groups has, as yet, never been systematically examined.

It is important to identify the fundamental and underlying assumptions within the context of this effort. It is assumed here that there are significant parallels between behavior among small groups and the behavior within and among large organizations. These are represented in the transactions of those persons involved. Specifically, it is assumed here that what holds true in the micro-social unit also pertains to the macro-social unit. With this in mind, examples are utilized drawing from interpersonal transactions at the micro and macro levels of group and organizational life as illustrative of the concepts and hypotheses offered here.

Part I focuses upon the oppression and alienation in groups and organizations and includes the first two chapters. The first chapter identifies and explores the nature of power and alienation within modern groups, organizations and bureaucracy. The second chapter examines the human milieu, i.e. the daily world of organizational work and the nature of the oppression which exists there.

Part II suggests some conceptual tools for demystifying group and organizational structure, dynamics, and process with particular regards to power and includes chapters 3 through 7. Chapter 3 explores and revisions the structure, authority and dynamics of bureaucracy with particular attention given to the nature of the groups within the larger organization. Chapters 4 and 5 attend to identifying private structure, group processes and covert role differentiation. The power scenarios which characterize organizational group life are the focus of Chapter 6. Chapter 7 is concerned with the nature and interrelationship of stress, cohesion and development within a group.

Part III centers upon the problems involved in obtaining a productive and humane bureaucracy and encompasses the remaining chapters in the book. Chapter 8 outlines an intentional change sequence which is responsive to the aspects of the organization identified in the earlier chapters and focuses upon the problem of a more effective and humane delivery of the organizational mission while attending to the needs for a humane internal arrangement and establishing and maintaining humane treatment of those served by the organization. Chapter 9 focuses upon the nature and attainment of cooperative work. Finally, Chapter 10 deals with making the change to an effective, productive and humane bureaucracy. Developing constitutional responsibility for modern organization is essential. Chapter 10 identifies some interim steps which might be utilized to begin the transition. A glossary and summary of the hypotheses are included for the convenience of the reader.

This is only an initial effort and is designed to bring to those concerned the first fruits of this perspective and approach to understanding group process. The approach defined and presented here may be appropriately designated group process analysis and those who pursue it certainly may be designated group process analysts. It is a field ripe for further development and pursuit. The goal intended here is to encourage, through the use of group process analysis, further interest in learning about the uses and abuses of power in modern organizations and implementing humane cooperative activity in groups and organizations. It is hoped, too, that this effort will spur the confrontation and subsequent conversion of our groups and organizations to support and sustain more humane, compassionate behavior within their boundaries and without as they link into their service environment. It is with hope of supporting such confrontation and humanization that this book is written.

Robert H. Simmons
Los Osos, California

PREFACE NOTES

1. Elliot Jaques, *A General Theory of Bureaucracy*, N.Y., Halsted Press, John Wiley & Sons, 1976, pp. 376-377.

2. Sir Geoffrey Vickers, *Value Systems and Social Process*, N.Y., Basic Books, Inc., 1968, p. 66.

3. Erik H. Erikson, *Insight and Responsibility*, N.Y., W.W. Norton and Co., Inc., 1964, p. 243.

4. Henry Jacoby, *The Bureaucratization of the World*, Berkeley, Calif., University of California Press, 1973, pp. 1-8; for an insightful presentation for the reasons for the growth and continued reliance upon bureaucracy, see pp. 9-35 and pp. 61-112.

5. Rosabeth Moss Kanter, *Men and Women of the Corporation*, N.Y., Basic Books, 1977, pp. 164-205.

6. Eugene P. Dvorin and Robert H. Simmons, *From Amoral to Humane Bureaucracy*, San Francisco, Canfield Press (a division of Harper & Row), 1972.

7. Eric Berne, *The Structure and Dynamics of Organizations and Groups*, N.Y., J.B. Lippincott, 1963. Wilfred Bion, *Experiences in Groups*, N.Y., Basic Books, 1961.

8. Morton Kroll, "Understanding Large Organizations – The Group Field Approach Revisited," *Public Administration Review*, November/December, 1976, pp. 690-694.

ACKNOWLEDGMENTS

Writing a book is a singularly lonely effort yet it cannot be accomplished without help. When the final manuscript for a previous effort was submitted for publication, a friend and colleague suggested that a chapter on intentional change be deleted from the book and form the initial efforts of a new book as there was much to commend giving special attention to intended and creative change. This effort emerged from that counsel and for this I am indebted to John Crow, University of Arizona. He has carefully read most of what I have ever written and in this case, as in the past, his careful, insightful and sensitive contributions considerably enhanced the result. Morton Kroll, University of Washington, read the manuscript with professional care. His exceptionally thorough critique provided important and significant alterations. His enthusiasm for the project was a constant and vital support. His suggestions were of especial value to the design and outcome of the effort. To each of these good friends I express my very great appreciation.

Claude Steiner, author of *Scripts People Live*, provided salient feedback and helpful suggestions. Bernard J. Somers and Joseph Phelan, valued colleagues in the Department of Psychology, California State University Los Angeles, each provided very special advice and counsel. Garrett O'Conner, psychiatrist and Lars Lofgren, Staff Psychiatrist, Brentwood Veterans Administration Hospital in Westwood, Los Angeles, were both instrumental in introducing the work of Wilfred Bion into my experience. The creative and original work of Bion on group process provides important roots for the materials developed here. Adam Tom Kohler, Psychologist and Clinical Program Evaluation Specialist, Brentwood Veterans Administration Hospital in Westwood, Los Angeles, provided important conceptual information concerned with the transition to humane organization. To each of these men I express my gratitude.

The work of Eric Berne on organizational and group structure and dynamics has not received the full scholarly attention it deserves, largely perhaps because it has been overshadowed by the developments stemming from his work on transactional analysis in psychotherapy. His largely ignored efforts to conceptualize organizational and group processes, dynamics and structure are of great importance. An overzealous commercialism by a few of his well intentioned followers has, unfortunately, fogged the deserved scholarly recognition of his efforts. Much of the conceptual material developed in this effort is rooted in his work. He was a profoundly creative, productive and careful scholar whose published efforts warrant primary academic concern. I did not have the good fortune of his counsel during his lifetime, yet my intellectual and emotional debt to him is great.

Lauren Oliver, formerly a psychologist with the Brentwood Veterans Hospital, Westwood, California, now a candidate for a PhD in Clinical Psychology at the University of California Los Angeles, provided valuable counsel and research support throughout. I am especially indebted to her for the materials concerned with small group process. She was a full research partner and her help in a myriad of special ways was an immeasurable contribution to this effort.

Kate Perry gave generously of her time and her considerable skill to thoroughly enhance the quality and presentation of the conceptual material.

Virginia Walter, Regional Librarian, City of Los Angeles, and candidate for a PhD in Public Administration, University of Southern California, carefully read the manuscript and provided a valuable and detailed critique. Her practiced and skilled review salvaged many paragraphs from obscurity and set aright many an awkward sentence. These women, together with Susan Edelstein, Ronald Farwell and Mary Coleman, were a continuous source of support and encouragement, leavening the moments of downheartedness and impasse and frequently providing intelligent and sensitive resolutions of troublesome quandries.

Jackie Holley provided distinctive and valuable insights concerning the material on cooperative work. Her contributions, together with those of Renan Sercarz, Annette Greene, Deane Lange and Allen Lange were most consequential in the evolution of the chapter concerned with covert role development.

My dear friend, co-author and colleague, Eugene P. Dvorin, provided help, inspiration and encouragement, counseling a judicious mixture of boldness and caution.

John Maulding, former Superintendent of Buildings, County of Los Angeles, and Don Galloway, Director, Department of Community Development, City of Los Angeles, carefully read the manuscript. Each of their contributions to the development of the material were detailed and extremely useful. Each man is a skilled, competent, humane manager.

Lenore Dowling, formerly Director, Special Programs, Immaculate Heart College, Los Angeles (now no longer operating) was particularly helpful in providing opportunities to explore these materials.

There is another special burden which cannot be fully met here. I wish to express my very profound gratitude to the hundreds of practitioners, students and clients who tried, experimented, wrote, reported, enthused, despaired, criticized, responded, cultivated, honed, used, discarded, fostered, adapted, modified and contributed to the ideas and methods presented. These persons came from all levels of government; federal, state and local, as well as from the private sector. The space is simply insufficient to list the names of all those persons truly deserving of mention.

The concepts, ideas, procedures, methods and materials utilized in this work were not only tested and re-tested by these students, clients and practitioners, but several business institutions and public agencies supported this effort by providing opportunities for special classes, seminars and workshops. My own California State University Los Angeles, provided modest support through the offering of experimental classes based upon the use of these materials. Additionally, the Photography and Graphics section of the Audio-Visual Department were particularly helpful in preparing materials relevant for classroom use which demonstrated these concepts and ideas. Yo Yamasaki, who prepared the graphics and Yuri Watanbe deserve a special note of recognition.

The McKenzie River Conference on Political Science sponsored by the Department of Political Science, University of Oregon, offered a very useful forum to present particular materials. John Orbel, Chairperson, Henry Stevenson, Gayle Keiser, and L. Dallas Hardison were all helpful. Rachel Starr and Ward Ching contributed important information. The Danforth Foundation, which provided important nurture and assistance to me in the past, encouraged my interest because their very organization exemplified a devoted concern for things humane. Presley C. McCoy is an old friend to whom much is owed and who has a sustaining concern for achieving the humane.

Some of the initial thought underlying this effort grew from the rich dialogue provided while I was a Senior Research Scholar under the Fulbright Exchange Program at the University of Tasmania, Hobart, Tasmania, Australia. Here Ralph Chapman and Bruce Davis of the University of Tasmania, Michael Wood, now of the University of Western Australia, Perth, and Roger Wettenhall, Director, School of Administration, Canberra College of Advanced Education, challenged, explored and criticized in helpful and skillful ways the material I presented. I am particularly indebted to Roger Wettenhall for the help, encouragement, opportunities and the support he provided throughout.

James D. Carroll, formerly Chairman, Department of Public Administration, The Maxwell School, Syracuse University, now of Brookings Institute, Washington, D.C., encouraged pursuing humane and ethical concepts in bureaucracy and organization. Through his careful reading of this manuscript, he made a considerable contribution. My colleague, Steve Blumberg, Mayor of Manhattan Beach, California, and the Center for Public Policy and Administration, California State University, Long Beach, provided enthusiastic and appreciated support for this effort in addition to an important and detailed critique. Donald Mathews, Chairperson, University of Washington, Department of Political Science, was most encouraging, especially in the initial stages of this effort.

My colleagues at California State University Los Angeles, Robert Callahan, Jack Misner, Virgil J. Stevens, George C. Littke, Addison Potter, Tom McEnroe and Ed Malecki provided important information and support at critical junctures in the effort.

My daughter Karolyn and my son Richard supplied key energy at crucial times.

Frances Dickson, Ann Montegari and Jeanne Harlan took the manuscript through many drafts with competence, patience and care. I am very grateful for their help. Mary Lou Ochoa, former Graduate Secretary of the Public Administration Program, California State University Los Angeles provided information, backup, support and attended to a myriad of detail. She is an invaluable and special friend.

John Stout, my editor during the crucial stages of the effort, furnished sensitive, able, competent assistance.

My wife, Mia Mitchell Simmons, provided everpresent support in a thousand ways, all of which were essential. I gratefully and lovingly thank her for those important contributions.

My publisher, William Knowles, from the very beginning provided enthusiastic support, prudent suggestions and unwavering faith and energy. His involvement in this effort has been distinctive, unique and invaluable.

To each of these persons and to the many more who helped, I am very appreciative. I give my earnest and profound thanks for each gave to this effort in a special, distinctive and unique way. Each, however, must be absolved of any errors of omission and commission. Full responsibility for the final product is completely my own.

Robert H. Simmons
Baywood Park
Los Osos, California

FORWARD

Our society needs humane organizations. This is the statement which Robert Simmons has made with this book.

It is a statement which has been gestating in the minds and the writings of a number of scholars for some time. Professor Simmons has brought that statement to life. It is now our responsibility to nurture that life, allow it to thrive, and stimulate its most luxuriant growth. *Achieving Humane Organization* needed to be written; it now needs to be read. This volume should be required reading for anybody in a position of management or supervision.

The concept of humane organization emerges in these pages not as an unrealistic ideal, but rather as attainable reality. The author brings to us the avenues and the tools for the achievement of this vital goal.

This extremely well-documented book, reflecting extensive research and some six years of painstaking labor and unrelenting effort, makes a significant contribution to the literature. But even more importantly, it makes an essential contribution to society. Members of organizations want to feel that they are a part of a humane institution; people being served by our institutions must be served by humane ones. And upon reading Simmons' Characteristics of an Ideal Cooperative Work Group, one is struck by a feeling of, "Oh, yes. How wonderful to be able to work and produce in a setting like that." Indeed, it may be an ideal setting, but Professor Simmons correctly tells us that it is possible As a start he suggests sincere "caring about oneself, caring about others with whom one is working and caring about what is accomplished within the work situation." Experience has demonstrated that this caring is not typical organizational *raison d'être*. Heeding Professor Simmons' message will assist in making more manifest this elusive concept.

The message of this book is timeless. It stimulates our interest in "implementing humane cooperative activity in groups and organizations." Who amongst us cannot support and enthusiastically endorse that goal? If this book enhances our ability to actualize this goal, it surely must be regarded as a potential classic.

A constant theme throughout the book is the need to achieve organizational productivity. The message, quite simply, is that achieving humane organization is the requisite "prelude to effective production."

Those of us in positions of organizational leadership know that our responsibility is awesome. Professor Simmons tells us that "to achieve humaneness and effective production within modern organizations is a profound challenge." We accept that challenge. We know that any technical competency which takes no account of the individual humanness of every person involved stands self-condemned.

This important book serves to focus our attention on this dual role of producing organizational results by achieving humane organizations. For this accomplishment Robert Simmons deserves our everlasting gratitude.

Stephen K. Blumberg
Associate Professor and Assistant Director
Center for Public Policy and Administration
California State University, Long Beach
Mayor, Manhattan Beach, California

TABLE OF CONTENTS

**PART III: ACHIEVING HUMANE, COOPERATIVE AND PRODUCTIVE
GROUPS AND ORGANIZATIONS**

PART I

THE ORGANIZATIONAL ENVIRONMENT

Chapter 1

ORGANIZATIONS AS INSTRUMENTS OF SOCIAL PURPOSE AND PRODUCTIVE EFFORT

Organizations are an ever present concomitant of modern life. Their productive contributions to the improvement of human material existence are highly valued and urgently sought. Bureaucratic organizations in the developed world pervade and dominate human existence and those in the less developed and non-developed world seek its mixed blessings with a driving passion. Large organization is a crucial provider of work and provisions essential physical and social needs of those who receive its services and products. Yet frequently the consequences of organizational activity are costly and destructive to the human personality, traditional society and the earth's life support system.

Organizations as Instruments of Purpose and Accomplishment

Organizations are collective aggregations of people who utilize their skills, competence and energy to perform coordinated activity designed to achieve particular goals. Organizations have been utilized to accomplish purposes which are vital, useful and even sublime. The research and maintenance contributions to human life and health, the production of energy and energy distribution networks, the establishment and maintenance of great national parks and forests, the construction of vast road systems and great bridges, space exploration, education of the vast and diverse public to read, to write and perform numerical operations, and many other achievements are phenomenal accomplishments derived from organizational effort.

Yet organizations have been utilized for the accomplishment of corrupting, hurtful, nefarious and even dreadful purposes. The carnage at My Lai in Vietnam, Lockheed Corporation's bribery of high political executives in other nations, most notably Japan, the revelations of great numbers of civil rights violations by the Federal Bureau of Investigation and the tragic abuses disclosed concerning the activities of the Central Intelligence Agency—all occurring in the late 1960's and the 1970's—are stunning examples of this organizational propensity.[1]

Even where, presumably, effective restraints exist within the political process, the secrecy available in bureaucracy, together with its claim of legitimacy, may result in significant abuses. No better example of this variety of bureaucractic arrogance may be found than the disclosure by the United States Army that it conducted 239 germ warfare tests in the open air between 1949 and 1969 including a secret air-launched simulated attack of San Francisco with a bacterium which was suspected later of causing pneumonia.[2] Management within private bureaucracy (large corporations) and public bureaucracy alike all too often succumb to the temptations that accompany the accumulation of vast amounts of power with the concomitant harvest of fear, abuse and corruption.

When the survival of an organization is perceived as threatened, humane values may give way to survival demands. In the public sector the drive for survival feeds a hunger for power which often leaves corruption in its wake. Where profit is the measure, manipulation, deceit and exploitation are frequented on employee, client and customer.

The accomplishments of organizations have been many, frequently significant and sometimes great; yet life inside an organization is strained, power-oriented and laden with fear. The urgency behind the organizational thrust for survival is matched by the personal urgency of its members themselves to survive. Excessive fear is a pervasive aspect of life inside large organizations. This fear is ever present and it may be recognized or unrecognized, acknowledged or unacknowledged, real or imagined. It may be fear of losing one's job or fear of hurting one's career. It may be fear of failure, fear of criticism, fear of making an error, fear of a negative evaluation, fear of punishment, fear of getting caught, fear of consequences, fear of being made a scapegoat, fear of getting blamed, fear of not doing a good job, fear of doing too good a job, fear of another's displeasure, fear of being ridiculed, fear of disapproval, fear of not being competent, to identify only a few of the sources of such fear.

This condition is endemic, Guy Benveniste suggests, and underlies organizational uncertainty, elicits defensive personal behavior, poisons the wellsprings of mutual trust, jeopardizes friendships and careers, spawns uncertainty, powerlessness and resentment, and provokes discontent, dissatisfaction and criticism in management, employee, client, customer and citizen. In a word, it supports the human alienation which is today so characteristic of much of the life within an organization.[3]

Elliot Jaques writes that the human alienation spawned by paranoiagenic institutions seriously disrupts social relations and contributes to the violence of society. He proposes significant alternative institutional structures which are rooted in empirically validated theory. His contributions cannot be ignored and can serve as a basis for reordering modern organization.[4]

Organizations are places of fear in varying degree. As long as fear resides there the creative and fully productive human spirit cannot unfold but rather it remains to some degree mean, venal, selfish and vulnerable to corruption.

Management and worker alike must confront the conditions of their own alienation and "front up" to their own responsibility for its rectification. Citizen, student, scholar, client, manager and worker concerned with the organization and its impact must raise their own consciousness concerning the alienated context of life within the organization. Then responsibility and action must be taken for developing and maintaining in those organizations conditions conducive to human dignity. With my colleague, Eugene P. Dvorin, we have written:

> Bureaucracy can no longer ignore the centrality of human dignity, either in its theory or in its operational aspects... The crucial development must be recognition that the practicing bureaucracy cannot administer toward the goal of human dignity unless the bureaucracy embraces it.[5]

A first step is to face up to the reality that corporate and bureaucratic organizations are not persons! This is an insidious idea which has done much mischief. The organization conceived as a person becomes vulnerable to the protective mechanisms characteristic of human transactions. Public organizations are powerful in a different way. Public organizations have the clout of sovereignty. They are "creatures" created by the state and this makes them enormously powerful or can do so. Internally, they reflect the same vicissitudes characteristic of most large organizations. Thus it is easy to set the organization "above" the human being and empower the organization as humans themselves empower one another.

The Organization as a Person: An Historical Sketch

In the late Roman Empire, a corporation was an association developed by patrician families which possessed legal status separate and distinct from the members which made it up. It was a fictional legal "body." It had legal rights and it was, in a word, "immortal." Through this immortality the capacity was gained to own property even after all its founders had died and been replaced. This provided continuity of power and ownership through generations. In medieval Europe the use of the corporate form evolved to include universities, cities and significant segments of the Catholic Church. It remained for the United States to empower the corporation as a secular, private "legal person" and give it legal protection. Chief Justice John Marshall, writing the decision in the Dartmouth College case, observed a corporation is ". . . an artificial being, invisible, intangible and existing only in contemplation of the law."[6]

As a person, the corporation may own property, make contracts, sue and be sued, and enjoy what human beings cannot, *viz.*, immortality. The stage was set in the American jurisdiction to extend the rights available to human beings to a non-human entity which could do anything a human being could do at law and exist forever as well.[7] An important advantage in the emergence of the corporation in the American jurisdiction was forged.

After the Civil War, the Fourteenth Amendment was ratified in 1868 which, among other things, stated ". . . nor shall any State deprive any person of life, liberty, or property, without due process of law; nor deny to any person within its jurisdiction equal protection of the laws." Here the corporation becomes further advantaged as "due process of law" and "equal protection of the law" become available legal rights to the corporation as a "person at law" under the meaning of the Fourteenth Amendment.

In the post-Civil War United States, three separate traditions come together to form the basis for the emerging dominance of organizational society. First, the full fruition of bureaucratic hierarchical forms within the governing tradition of European nations. This is best articulated in the work of Max Weber.[8] Second, the emergence of the corporation as the singular, most significant institution dominating industrial, particularly American, society.[9] Finally, the emergence of the scientific management movement which had an incredibly significant impact on the evolution of management within both the corporate structure and public bureaucracy as well.[10]

These three forces come together and provide the thrust necessary for the ultimate dominance of the bureaucratic organizational form within American society. It is the distinctive aspect of this conjuncture that the secular corporation has gained in the American political tradition the "upperhand." Professor John Davis labored with considerable prescience when he wrote in 1897 that the present tendency was for corporations to become ". . . essentially governmental bodies." He observed more and more the individual citizen of this country finds ". . . citizenship in his country has been largely metamorphosed into membership in corporations and patriotism into fidelity to them."[11] This work of John P. Davis stands as a most significant study of the origin and development and emergence of corporations in their relationships to the authority of the State.

Anthropomorphizing Organizations: Attributions and Consequences. The attribution of personhood to corporate organizations is unfortunate in its consequences.

It is a legal fiction which is significant in differentiating public and private organizations, but it has pernicious if sometimes useful results. The secular corporation today has emerged as a dominant institution in the world. Corporations, in increasing frequency, assault the life-sustaining environment of the planet. The emergent corporate system is more and more viewed as a serious challenge to the preeminence of the nation-state on the planet.[12] The method of rendering such corporations responsible and accountable are not at all adequate. Empowering the "private" corporation with personhood, i.e. personality, separate, legal and distinct, is the unique contribution of American legal history.

The distinction between private corporate organization form and public bureaucratic form seems to become evermore vague. Jaques observes, "Whether they like it or not, and whether or not they care to recognize the fact, those who manage employment organizations bear a heavy responsibility for the well being of the nation."[13]

Large organizations have emerged upon the scene to evermore dominate human life and times. This process of personalizing organization simultaneously impersonalizes people. The organization is empowered and placed above its members and clients. These human beings then are frequently dealt with as dehumanized objects.

One young woman in her late twenties fought many years against the debilitating disease of muscular dystrophy. Confined to a wheelchair she had nevertheless, with the help of public funds available to the handicapped, prepared herself educationally to contribute to her own maintenance and support. In 1978, Ms. Lyn Thomas took her own life after receiving a computer prepared notice from the Social Security Administration that her earnings exceeded income limits and this required the termination of her attendant care and in addition the letter informed her she owed the U.S. Government $10,000 for her previous training. Under a recent state law her earnings, of about $500 per month, were well under the limit of $675.00 per month such persons could qualifiedly earn. The federal notice was indeed incorrect. This incident triggered a self-destructive impulse in this young person who had valiantly struggled against the increasingly pernicious results of her debilitating disease.[14]

This incident raises serious questions concerning intergovernmental agency relationships and responsibility. Even more, it demonstrates the horrendous inhumanity of a public administration which is solely "objective" and "efficient." The notice sent by the Social Security Administration was routine and automatic, justified on the basis of efficiency and productivity. The many public servants involved each were doing their job correctly without sympathy, enthusiasm or compassion. The result was tragic, indefensible, avoidable and certainly inhumane.

Yet there is a tradition in American public administrative experience which is deeply rooted in the humane and markedly contrasts with this absence of humanity, compassion and sympathy. The aristocratic federalist fathers were very much concerned with the individual. The government they foresaw and its administration, as well, was predicated on this value. This contrasting tradition may well be a source of dysfunction and dissidence when an organization administers without sympathy and without enthusiasm.[15]

The disenchantment of the public with agencies established to accomplish humane objectives, for example, education, welfare, social security, to identify a few, is reflected by the growing hostility each of these agencies face in the increasingly difficult struggle for public support and public monies to operate their programs. The increasing disenchantment of the public with the public service and the public servant is reflected in their growing unwillingness to "foot the bill." This may be in part attributable to the unanticipated consequences flowing from the absence of sympathy, compassion and enthusiasm in their dealings with their client sector.[16] Additionally, the clients of such agencies frequently face hostility and rejection by agency personnel. This, from the very people chosen to carry out programs born of public policy which was itself a response to articulated needs seated in the public's concern, compassion, sympathy and enthusiasm to solve the tough problems which create human suffering. Such programs were designed to alter and to change situations in a way which enhanced the dignity and survival needs of the recipients. Client, student, recipient are all too frequently turned into victims at the delivery level of an agency's program.

Programs born of compassion, concern, sympathy and the urge to enhance the human condition may well have to be delivered in that same manner by the public servants concerned to fully achieve the desired result. A public service which fails to understand this may well face the loss of the support required to sustain their efforts. Efficiency, productivity, honesty and accountability are all essential—alone they are sterile, inadequate, and insufficient.

Organizations: The Role of Key Historical Figures. The assertion organizations ought to be treated as persons and given rights needs and careful reexamination in view of more recent understandings. Organizations need not and ought not be dealt with as persons, but as structures of powers capable of immense possibilities for good or ill. It is the people in organizations who, through their coordinated and cooperative efforts, have the ability and capacity to use the power available in organizations. The inhuman blocks, buildings, symbols, telephones and wires that make up the physical characteristics of the organization are not a distinctive, viable entity. To conceive the organization as a person leads to the attribution of human characteristics to the organization *per se*. Consider this statement written by a prestigious and well-respected writer:

> *To achieve the minimum degree of necessary cohesiveness in the personality of an organization, its leaders must in some way affect the personality of its members. They must bring about a situation in which some of the purposes of the organization become a part of the purposefulness of members. This often leads to elaborate systems of disciplinary measures and indoctrination. At times it produces a high degree of conformance pattern of behavior, thought, habit, dress and speech.[17]*

In this writer's description the difference between public and private are minimized. All organizations have fictional personalities extended to them. This is a jarring note in a fine two volume work. No doubt sometimes awesome alienating conformity is achieved within organizations but it is through oppressive management, not through "cohesiveness in the personality of the organization." The organization has no personality; people have personalities. To see it differently empowers the organization to become something it is not.

The mischief has been carried even further. Recently, in the context of organizational development programs in utilizing, for example, transactional analysis concepts, one writer observes, "Just as individuals have scripts, so do organizations. The lifeline of many organizations resembles the lifeline of a person."[18] This writer suggests organizational scripts include the same kind of things that make up a personal script. Eric Berne, the founder of Transactional Analysis, observed that a script is a life plan based on a decision made in childhood, reinforced by the parents, justified by subsequent events, and culminating in chosen behavior alternatives.

In no way does an organization fit this definition. Founders, early organization leaders, may have profound impacts on the culture of the organization. Such a culture may among other things encompass, (1) the nature of the physical world of the organization, (2) the authority system, (3) the injunctions and attributions of key founders, (4) laws, rules, rituals and courtesies and (5) a distinctive social system. Any social aggregation will have specific and distinctive characteristics which some may label "personality." This has little to do with corporate legal status. The idea that the organization is a person is a mischievious one and contributes to deceiving us into perceiving them as being something they are not. Organizations do not think. Organizations do not feel. Organizations have no conscience. People have these qualities. They are characteristic of human beings, not of groups or organizations.

It is therefore important to understand how people behave inside the organization in management positions and in membership positions. Certainly, founders and key significant historical figures may be more important than living members and living leaders who operate within the context of the organization. The historical figure or founder may have a unique impact on the group but he or she does not supply an agency script, nor does an agency "choose" a script as Berne suggests a child does.

A case in point is the Federal Bureau of Investigation where the key significant founder, J. Edgar Hoover, who built an effective crime-fighting organization, in his later years used secret files to accumulate power to intimidate congressmen and congresswomen and then utilized such power to manipulate their behavior and obtain their support in Congress for the FBI. There is emerging evidence that Hoover condoned violations of the law by his agents. Those agents by their unquestioning loyalty to Mr. Hoover gave away their power, thereby abandoned their capacity to make autonomous decisions and submitted to his definition of what was lawful and necessary. Agents thus became involved in break-ins, mail openings, and wire-taps.[19]

In this instance, the personality of the founder and the founder's script is significant. Yet it is insufficient to understand the organizational behavior and processes within the Federal Bureau of Investigation; alone it is not enough. The FBI is a public safety agency with considerable impact beyond the script of its first director, yet the impact of Hoover on the agency is of distinctive importance because founders do have special significance for an organization.

Key figures in the history of an organization may and frequently do have an important impact on the ongoing culture, society, traditions and rules which develop within an organization. This impact may at first glance seem to be reflected in the behavior of organizational members. The temptation is to attribute this to an "organizational personality." Such personification belies a more accurate perception of the organization.[20]

The Confounding of Public and Private Organization, Purpose and Meaning

This confusion of the person with the organization together with the even more murky distinction between public and private organizations confounds our understanding, particularly concerning the uses of power within organizations and the exercise of power by organizations. This is so because hierarchy is utilized by both the public and private organizations to achieve organizational goals.

The fragmentation of the public executive was strongly influenced by the post-Civil War dominance of the Presidency by an active Congress. The progressive movement of the late 1800's further encouraged such fragmentation and this period in U.S. history is characterized by an increase in numbers of public executive-administrative entities. The elaboration and fragmentation of the public executive is characterized by the elaboration of independently elected executives for a variety of public agencies, the development of autonomous and semiautonomous governmental entities at the state and local levels of government and the emergence of vast and broad administrative hierarchies in the executive of the the federal government as well. An unanticipated consequence of this concerns administrative responsibility. Public accountability of private corporations is a distinctive and, as yet, unmet challenge since those public agencies charged with their supervision are dominated by those very same segments of the economy they are charged with supervising.

The distinct line between public and private organizations more and more recedes into insignificance, yet there remain important and significant differences. Public organizations more and more market their particular competencies through the contract device as does the private organization.[21] This disintegration of the difference between public and private is a characteristic which has emerged in the post-World War II period as whole sections of American industry have become evermore dependent upon public expenditures.[22] Public organizations such as water and power authorities, research agencies and the like are often precluded from competing in the private sector. Public agencies are frequently charged with programs designed to funnel money into the private sector when some facet of that sector is economically threatened.

The fragmentation of the American public executive at the federal and state and local level encourages the growing autonomy of American public organizational structures.[23] This tendency is represented in many ways today, but in particular it is most noticeable in management theory. This view asserts the managing of organizations, whether public or private, has no significant differences. Problems of accountability, public interest and implications of the action of these organizations are thus obscured.

One example of how confused the public interest question can become involves the problem of public accountability regarding the ozone layer protecting the surface of the planet from the deadly ultraviolet rays of the sun. The federal government in 1976 was spending about 14 million dollars with an additional 3 million dollar support from industry to understand the complex chemistry of the upper atmosphere. This money partially goes to support research in a variety of universities as well as funding the National Academy of Science's research efforts. The Academy's report confirms that aerosol spray propellants are, in fact, gradually depleting the earth's protective shield of ozone and this may lead, they indicate, to an increased risk of skin cancer. The report noted regulation of fluorocarbon propellants "is almost certain to be necessary." Yet in an astonishing retreat from responsibility, the report recommended that the government delay imposing any regulations for up to two years until further research clarifies the degree of threat to life on earth.

The considerable impact of the ozone layer upon the totality of the earth's life support system was not adequately assessed within the report of the National Academy of Science. A dermatologist at Harvard Medical School and a member of the committee noted that the incidence of melanoma had been rising 5 to 10 percent annually in the United States since the use of aerosols was introduced, granting the existence of other fluorocarbon sources of pollutants as well. With limited vision reflecting the implicit value orientation of industry, this Harvard dermatologist suggested that educational programs should alert Americans to the special dangers of melanoma and ways to prevent sunburn might be a more effective means of preventing the disease than shoring up the ozone layer by banning fluorocarbons.

The narrowness of this orientation is perplexing for the implications of the elimination of the ozone layer has a far greater implication than simply the increased factor of skin cancer in human beings. Traces of ozone are formed in the stratosphere by solar radiation acting on oxygen molecules. The resulting gas shields the earth's plants and animals from approximately 99% of the most damaging wave lengths of ultraviolet light. In addition, the ozone of the upper air helps to maintain the earth's atmospheric heat balance and thus influences the planet's climate. This has an incredibly significant impact on the agricultural cycle on the planet and, as yet, is not fully researched.

Knowing full well fluorocarbons contained in aerosol are depleting the earth's protective shield of ozone, under these conditions the National Academy of Sciences recommended a two-year delay. E. I. DuPont Corporation, a major producer of fluorocarbon, had urged a delay of 18 months to two years.[24] Fortunately, upon hearing the news, the public made considerable inroads on the use of aerosol sprays through the voluntary reduction in their use. Here the line between public and private blurs as the interests of a major industrial corporation dominates the consideration of public concern.

This story is repeated in other ways as in the forest industry where the struggle is reflected in relations between the forest service and the large lumber interests or, as with the grazing interests in the great Southwest and Midwest and where these tensions are reflected in relationship of the Bureau of Land Management to the great cattle ranch interests. The once powerful independent regulatory commissions themselves are more and more captured by the very industries they are supposed to regulate; thus definition of a broader public interest recedes in the face of emerging, bureaucratic and corporate power and interests.[25]

Public and Private Organizations: Differences and Similarities. As the line between public and private vanishes a special field of study concerned with management has emerged. This new "field" is divorced from concerns of whether an agency is public or private and is rather focused on problems of how to maintain and obtain full and efficient production and under these circumstances problems of accountability and public interest recede as considerations for the technique of management *per se* increase.[26] Yet important differences remain. Some of the more distinctive aspects of public administration may be summarized as follows:

1. In public administration, mission, financing, organizational structure and operations are all vested ultimately by constitutional statutory authority.
2. Public administration is disciplined by, accountable to, and responsible to the citizenry through the political process.
3. Public administration is charged with the responsibility and task of fulfilling the public interest.

Public bureaucracy or private corporate organizations today tend to encompass the following similarities: First, the business or task of the organization is continuous. Second, such business is conducted in accordance with stipulated rules and orders. These rules and orders relate to the duty of each person to perform particular kinds of work, the authority necessary to carry out the assigned work, and the kind of organizational compulsion and control available which may be legitimately employed in carrying out such work. Third, each person in the organization functions within a hierarchy of authority with higher offices being assigned on the basis of technical competence. Fourth, the buildings and resources utilized by the workers as well as the managers to perform their assigned function are not owned by those persons. Fifth, the offices which they occupy are occupied by appointment or contract and cannot be sold or inherited. Sixth, much of their business is conducted on the basis of written documents.

In such organizations human competence, human energy and human activities are specialized and then coordinated into productive effort. This productive effort is seen as machinery to run smoothly without interference from human foibles. In governmental administration this is often referred to as "the machinery of government." In private organizations it is often referred to as "sound management." Thus speed, certainty, decisions supported by documentary records, continuity, discretion, uniformity of operation, systematic forms of subordination, and the reductions of conflict and friction are seen as advantages to get and obtain productive work.

Bureaucractic organizations functioning in this manner operate efficiently. Under these circumstances the individual is seen as a unit of machinery to be designed and managed to fit neatly into a smooth-running and functioning machine. Bureaucratic organization, Weber asserts, "is ... technically the most highly developed means of power in the hands of the man who controls it ...." He suggests that under normal conditions, "... the power position of a fully developed bureaucracy is always over-towering."[27] Indeed, he observes, in every bureaucracy there is the urge to increase the superiority of the professionally informed by keeping knowledge and intention secret. Bureaucratic organization always tends to be administered behind a veil of secrecy. It hides, insofar as it can, its knowledge and action from criticism. Knowledge, when combined with secrecy, becomes a primary means for the exercise of power and, when housed within the confines of a bureaucratic organization, it may become awesome.

An Urgent Task: To Understand Organizational Power and Process. Hierarchical organization is a process of institutionalization within a culture and society which relates human beings one to another on the basis of unequal power relationships based upon role expectations utilizing corresponding sanctions and rewards to obtain behavior that is consistent and predictable.

The stage for the transformation of the social order is set by defining bureaucratic structure as vulnerable to domination. Rinehart Bendix, in examining "bureaucracy and the problem of power," noted "... the indispensibility of skilled administrators make it a subservient tool."[28] In such a situation, human beings are seen as actors in a context of interaction. Harlan Cleveland suggests this is a very distinctive aspect of organization. As actors they are alien from their personhood and reflect a value pattern which is institutionalized within the organization and the group within which they work. These reflect the survival needs of the organization, the tasks incumbent upon the organization to perform and the implicit values within the authority of the group itself.[29] Cleveland suggests too that organizations in the future will not be hierarchical pyramids with most of the actual control at the top. He indicates they will be "... *systems* — interlaced webs of tension in which control is loose, power diffused, and centers of decision plural."[30] The uncertainty which Benveniste suggests is the root of many organization ills would, in Cleveland's view, become even further extended and remain an ever present characteristic of organizational life. To examine the origin and nature and effective responses to such uncertainty is imperative.

Traditionally in organization, power, prestige and wealth are distributed in ever-diminishing amounts downward through a pyramidal (hierarchical) structure. Power within bureaucratic organizational structure is undemocratic even anti-democratic, elitist, and in scarce supply. It is a profound paradox within democratic systems of government that the very instruments used to administer the business of government are undemocratic in their operation and conduct. Democratic political theory supports that as long as an agency remains accountable to the democratic electorate, all is well. This dubious tenet has been explored elsewhere.[31] It is important here to notice the citizens in the most advanced democracies today frequently spend the greater part of their waking day working within an essentially undemocratic and frequently anti-democratic organization.

It is undemocratic in the sense that the worker or employee has little control over working hours, conditions or pay. Where the contrary seems to be the case it is often simply a matter of the employee giving power up to a union, and thus, through strength in numbers, matching the power of the organization. In public jurisdictions the use of employee unions is increasing although it is still the exception rather than the rule. Even in 1978 public employees were still being thrown in jail in their efforts to effect some control over their working conditions. In Normal, Illinois 22 firemen spent 42 days in jail in an effort to get union recognition and a negotiated contract.[32]

Organizations are anti-democratic as well, in the sense that the worker, after spending the better part of his or her day within the "gentle care" of a large organization, is ill-prepared to exercise the power and responsibility required of a citizen in a modern democratic industrial nation where effective citizen involvement requires a politically literate and participating electorate. Many organizations discourage, suppress or penalize dissent through a variety of intimidations, threats and punishments. When this is not the situation, dissent is inhibited by organizational domination of the time, attention and loyalty of the employee-citizen. This is in marked contrast with the public ethic of the United States and many other western nations where dissent is a strong part of the public behavior of many people. Where this situation exists constraints upon organizations exist regardless of how tenuous and inadequate they may be. Certainly, the American political context cannot be understood apart from this. An ethic and process for constraint and redress of organizational abuses do exist even if rudimentary or poorly used.

Organizations *per se* are not immoral, yet they are often effectively immoral. This is a crucial aspect of the present moral crisis in bureaucracy. Effective contrary responses by citizen and scholar in the United States today have not been forthcoming. It is the legacy of the Vietnam War which was perhaps the greatest, and as yet unassessed, example of that unique aspect of organizational life which justifies organization choices and actions, and then rigorously suppresses dissent internally and externally up to the limit of its available resources and power. Organizations are blind for the simple reason that they are not persons and organizational process is different than personal process. Consequently, organizations must be responsive to some person or group of persons who control their resources and power. In addition, organizations are in unique ways affected by the drama of human existence which occurs every day within their confines.

Process, Power and Alienation

Process. Perhaps the key idea in our technological-bureaucratic age is the idea of process. Human history may be seen as a stream of events which are neither random nor provident, but rather occur according to patterns of human behavior and strivings. These are imperfectly understood but they are discoverable and when once discovered can accept intentional intervention through intelligent human action. Today is for-ever spawning tomorrow. Tomorrow is necessarily different and change is embedded in the process.

Progress, in contrast, is thought to be a progressive bettering of the conditions of human beings on the planet. Progress is seen as an effort to maintain and to improve and to survive. When it goes awry, disintegration, oblivion and elimination of the nation, organization or species occurs. The modern organization has special access to science and technology and they are coordinated by management to serve organiza-tional purposes. The modern organization today grows more and more unrestrained, yet limitation is a requirement more and more imposed by nature's limitations on organization's uses of nature's resources. Freedom means today often the choice of our own limitations rather than freedom from limitation.[33]

Process is a fundamental component within the public organization. The idea of process concerns interaction involving a number of steps or operations which are linked together in some way. Arthur F. Bentley focused on the concept of process and eliminated all distinctions among groups inside government and outside govern-ment. He observed a governing body is of no value except as one aspect of the process. It cannot be described adequately except in reference to the deep-lying interests which function through it.[34] David Truman centers upon the development and functioning of political groups within the political process as an essential con-comitant of that process. Herbert Simon narrows his study of these processes to the decision-making processes which lie at the heart of administration.[35]

A very useful way of examining these ongoing processes is to center upon the char-acteristics of human interaction. Vickers observes that a full understanding of human interaction is still wanting.[36] Yet our understanding of human behavior and inter-action has proceeded exponentially in these closing decades of the 20th century from origins in the psycho-analytic work of Sigmund Freud proceeding to the elaborate collection of growth and awareness experiences available today across a broad spec-trum of theory and related experience. The meaning of human interaction and its relation to organizational process was disclosed in the early productivity experiments conducted by Bell Telephone Laboratories and described in the writing of Chester I. Bernard. These experiments known as the Hawthorne Experiments determined that, where human beings felt special and important, productivity increased. Status was, in this instance, more significant in productivity than remuneration.[37]

Processes may be revealed by the patterns of interaction specific to them. The patterns of interaction may be disclosed by the transactions between and among the participants. These transactions are overt manifestations of social intercourse. Eric Berne conceived this process in a series of linkages, i.e., a chain of related stimuli and responses. A transaction initiated by X elicits a response in Y. This response in turn becomes a new stimulus for X. These are transactional linkages or chains of transactions which provide distinctive analytical units for examination. This analyt-ical tool may be applied to groups and within groups as well as individuals to derive better understanding of personal, interpersonal, infragroup and intergroup behavior.[38] Analysis of this kind has been utilized in examining personal and organizational decision processes.[39]

Power. Hate, greed, aggression, envy and love operate covertly as well as overtly in most human groups. These forces impact upon group processes in distinctive ways with important consequences for the group and for the broader organization. Melanie Klein and Joan Revere note that aggression can be linked to hate or to love which springs from the life sources of the human being. Revere writes each person knows from experience that bad temper, selfishness, meanness, greediness, jealousy and enmity are felt and expressed all around every day by others, although one may not appreciate their existence so well in one's self.[40] Aggression is closely linked to what Revere calls the love of power or more particularly the will to power. She suggests it derives from the attempt to "control the dangers" in oneself more directly than by the methods of projection and of flight. She observes, "It is always the controllable character of one's desire and aggression, and one's helplessness in the face of these impulses, that is most dreaded."[41] She notes in further clarification:

> One way of reaching security is by aiming at omnipotent power in order to control all potentially painful conditions and have access to all useful, desirable things, both within oneself and without. In phantasy, omnipotence shall bring security.[42]

Revere suggests power is not necessarily even indirectly aggressive, but it has a strong tendency to become so. Omnipotence may mean seeking security by fleeing or gaining total power over another. She observes, "People in whom the will to power as a method of attaining security is over-developed may, of course, become dictators; but they may also become criminals, gangsters, roadhogs, and so on."[43]

This drive for omnipotence is the mark of the authoritarian personality. In contrast, to be powerful within one's own being, with one's own skills, with one's own capacity, with one's own emotions, is an internal power. In the authoritarian personality love, admiration and readiness for submission are automatically aroused by the presence of power, whether of a person or of an institution. Power holds a captivating fascination for those seduced by its siren call.[44] Eric Fromm suggests:

> ...freedom has a twofold meaning for modern man: that he has been freed from traditional authorities and has become an "individual," but at the same time he has become isolated, powerless, and an instrument of purposes outside himself, alienated from himself and others; furthermore, that this state undermines his self, weakens and frightens him, and makes him ready for submission to new kinds of bondage. Positive freedom on the other hand is identical with the full realization of the individual's potentialities, together with his ability to live actively and spontaneously.[45]

Fromm suggests this is rooted in our effort to escape from aloneness and powerlessness and the human individual is ready to abandon, or has abandoned, selfhood either by withdrawal, submission to some form of authority, or by blind compulsive conformance to accepted patterns.

In the modern organization this is more frequently neither dramatic nor intense. The question is more "how much of myself must I relinquish in order to keep my job?" Yet it does, on occasion when combined with the urge to succeed, provide for the organization manager or employee a significant moral choice, as when Jeb Magruder, Herb Porter and others of the "President's Young Men" in the Committee to Re-elect the President decided, under the urgings of their organizational superiors, to commit perjury. This, in one sense, is relinquishing power to another, i.e. empowering another and rendering oneself powerless.[46]

Fromm identifies some of the roots when he suggested the idea of work for the sake of accumulation of capital is of enormous value. Yet it has made humans work for extrapersonal ends and made them servants to the very machines they built. This feeds the feeling of personal insignificance and powelessness which contributes to a distinctive form of human corruption. Fromm proceeds to explore the idea of powerlessness. The human being has the capacity to reason and to imagine. Because of this we become aware of our aloneness and our separateness, of our powerlessness and our ignorance, and of the accident of our birth and of our death. In an attempt to transcend this separateness, he suggests the human being can "attempt to become one with the world by submission to a person, to a group, to an institution, to God ...."[47] Often a person is said to "give his life to the organization." This is spoken affirmation of this observation of Eric Fromm.

A common element in both submission and domination is the symbiotic nature of the relationship. Both persons involved have lost their integrity and freedom; they live on each other and from each other, satisfying their craving for closeness and suffering from the lack of inner strength and inner self-reliance which require freedom and autonomy. Furthermore, they are constantly threatened by the conscious or unconscious hostility which is bound to arise in this dependent relationship.[48] Organizations house this relationship and the attendant stress is severe on all members of the organization.

Power is a pervasive part of organizational existence. It is essential to understand what it is, how it is used and what purpose and function it serves. Power relationships occur within a group or among several groups. The uses of power may range from mild to awesome in consequence. Power is the capacity to cause people to do something or not to do something, i.e., perform an action or refrain from action or more subtly to avoid, restrain or fend off some action on the part of others. It can be exerted in a moment or it can be averted over a long period of time.

This concept of power is consistent with that of Elliot Jaques. Jaques notes that power is "... the quality of an individual (or a group). . . to influence other individuals either singly or collectively by channeling and directing their behavior in such a way as to help him fulfill his aims."[49] Jaques notes that when the use of power is in some way legitimated it is authorized and this grants to the user the right, i.e., the authority to use and exercise it within established limits. Power unregulated by sufficient constitutional restraints favors those who are strong, hard, and self centered, undermines the will to social cohesion, and finally corrodes and erodes the social fabric.[50] The uses of power, personal or organizational, may range in intensity from suggestion, persuasion, manipulation and threats to overt coercion involving tissue damage, torture and death. The exercise of power may be subtle and intimidating, manipulative, persuasive or charismatic.

Alienation. Alienation is the process where a human being is unable to experience himself or herself as the active bearer of one's own power and one's own human potential. We feel ourselves as impoverished "things," utterly dependent upon powers outside ourselves upon whom we project our most precious feelings. In return for security, i.e., allaying the fears attendant to personal survival we are often tempted and sometimes do lay our personal power at the feet of sometimes anonymous, invisible and alienated authority. Sometimes we do this to "succeed."[51] Frequently, we do not feel and are rarely conscious of, and often deny our dependencies upon the organization in which we work. Yet in times of stress we may well be driven to that realization, even if reluctantly. At that point, the emerging awareness may be accomplished with deep-seated resentment because dependence is often felt to be dangerous and threatening since it involves the possibility of deprivation.[52]

Yet we fear more than anything else the destructive forces that operate within ourselves. Sometimes these forces are repressed, i.e., "shoved out" of view and arise at odd times to cause embarrassment and sometimes great difficulty. It is these forces about which we are gaining more awareness that hold the key to our understanding of human behavior in groups and organizations. A clearer understanding of the forces leading to creative and productive participation within the significant groups where one lives and works can be gained if a clear view is obtained of the prohibitions to the full unfolding of the human personality and potential within those groups.

The alienated person is disempowered—in a word, powerless. Actions are experienced as under the influence or control of another. The person who is alienated thinks of herself or himself as a thing, as an investment to be manipulated by one's own consciousness or by other people. There is a lack of a sense of self. It is a profound feeling that one has no control over one's life. The fact is, Eric Fromm observed:

> ... man does not experience himself as the active bearer of his own powers and richness, but as an impoverished "thing," dependent on powers outside of himself, under whom he has projected his living substance.[53]

Alienation pervades almost all human relationships at work. Organizational settings frequently reinforce human alienation. Both manager and worker do not relate to the final product or organizational output as something concrete, valued and useful. For the manager, production is an end to be obtained through the sophisticated manipulation and control of human beings. Frequently social science, psychology and psychiatry are exploited to serve those ends.

A behavior modification program conducted by Ohio Bell Telephone Company responded to concerns over low employee morale and production. "Future shock" was applied. Groups of 15 to 20 employees were ushered into a small meeting room, the lights were dimmed and projected onto a television viewing screen where a simulated television news broadcast showing the complete economic collapse of their company right before their very eyes. Worker productivity jumped 10% and the plant utilizing this technique estimates savings of $29 million during the first year of the experiment.[54]

The human being succumbs to the oppressive social structures created out of alienation and these frequently are bureaucratic administrative structures, be they private or public. An example of this occurred in a food processing plant on Chicago's southside. This plant installed 35 television monitors on the factory floor so the activities of the 450 workers there could be observed. At a central command station, management keeps detailed records of every move the workers make. Slow workers, slackers, small talk is all detected as are phone calls and trips to the toilet which require management passes.[55]

The overwhelming impact of many management processes on the worker is to strip the worker of his right to think and to move freely, to control not only his actions but his creativeness, his curiosity and his independent thought. The inevitable result is the urge of the worker to flee or to fight, to dissolve into apathy and dependence or destructiveness, and indeed even regression into childhood dependence.[56]

The tendency of the worker to succumb to the more oppressive aspects of the organizational environment is deeply rooted in the physiological and physical needs of human beings since most persons require protection from danger, threats, and deprivation. These are the bottom levels of Abraham Maslow's concept that human beings have an hierarchy of needs and when the lowest are met, the needs at the next level up require satisfaction. He suggested the higher needs at the top of the hierarchy only become activated to the extent that the lower needs become satisfied. He identified these five basis needs as follows:

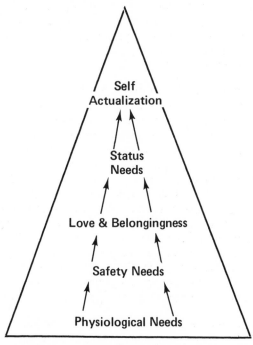

Figure 1-A. Maslow's Hierarchy of Needs

1. Physiological needs, such as hunger, thirst, the activity-sleep cycle, sex, and evacuation.
2. The safety needs for protection against threats and danger and deprivation.
3. Love and belongingness needs encompassing requirements for satisfactory association with others, for belonging to groups, in giving and receiving friendship and affection.
4. The esteem needs, for self-respect and for the respect of others, often identified as status needs or ego needs.
5. The self-actualization or self-fulfillment needs to achieve the potential within one's self for the maximum development and creative self-expression.[57]

When the needs of a level below fail to be satisfied individual concern and attention will move at once to attend the problems of satisfying those needs. This is graphically portrayed in Figure 1-A.

The life available inside most organizations provides satisfaction for most workers of only the first two need levels, viz., satisfaction of the physiological and safety needs and these are often meagre and supplied grudgingly by a reluctant public or private sector management under the duress of union threats, legislative investigation and enactments or pressure from special and interested publics.

The roots of alienation, Erik Erikson suggests, may be in the failure to face early repressed and unspoken childhood fears.[58] These fears are seated in the intentional or unintentional deprivation in childhood of the needs characterized by Maslow. As the stages of growth proceed, so does the sense of separation, aloneness, isolation and powerlessness. It is a trading off of risks for the seductive and spurious comfort of what appears riskless. Autonomy is traded for security. When an organization is the vehicle for such a trade or surrender, personal potency is resigned in favor of the requirement of organizational hierarchy. Under these conditions fear becomes an endemic concomitant of organizational life.

Organizational Hierarchy as an Aspect of Alienation

Organization with its modern industrial and scientific techniques seems to be indispensable, yet it is certainly threatening to the human dignity and freedom which is a necessary condition of rewarding human existence.[59] Frederick Thayer has discerned a unique historical connection between hierarchy and alientation. Thayer notices the pervasive, tacit assumption that hierarchy is accepted as inevitable, desirable and necessary. This underlies the belief that no organization (family, church, corporation, public agency, nation-state) can achieve its social purposes except through the interaction of persons denoted as "superiors" and persons defined as "subordinates."[60] Thayer asserts that the mainstream of contemporary democratic thought starts with the assumption that all social organizations, which include the family as well, are and ought to be hierarchically structured and that governmental structures as well must be consistent with such concepts of hierarchy. The validity of hierarchy as a way of organizing human affairs has not undergone serious question since the emergence of modern corporate and public bureaucratic forms.

Competition and Alienation. Thayer notices "Competition, hierarchy and alienation are closely related to each other..." He points to the fear that attends the small businessman, or the corner grocery or the family farmer, who really does not want to face stiffer competition, since he may wake up the morning after and find himself out of business and branded a failure. The mere thought of this is discomforting and even though he may be frightened of overwhelming corporations the size of General Motors or public organizations the size of the Department of Defense, he is frequently willing to trade employment for security in such massive organizations. In these instances, the strength that comes with security is the ability to stave off threats of competition, fears of failure and the like. Thayer suggests the more competitive the market, the more hierarchical the corporate response must become, and the more impersonal or nonpersonal managers and workers responses then become. In consequence, they are more efficient. The ideal of competition cannot be fully defined unless it is understood as someone going out of business, losing out on a good position for which one is qualified, etc., being thrown out of work, even though we do not want this to happen to us, to our friends, or to very many others.[61]

In this inexorable sequence hierarchy initially creates alienation and competition reinforces both; then alienation reinforces both itself and hierarchy and competition. Thayer observes:

> *Only the removal of competition will enable individuals and organizations to discover*

how humanely they can behave toward one another. The logic of competition is one of fear, being driven out of business, of losing out on promotions, of being fired, of losing status. This dictates the military model of organization, and the resultant combination of hierarchy and competition only accelerates alienation.[62]

Hierarchy and Powerlessness. The key to understanding power in the hierarchical organization is the pervasive feeling of powerlessness. Each person in the organization sees himself or herself as powerless *vis a vis* the one up (above) him and powerful, *vis a vis* the one down (below) him or her. Thus in submitting to hierarchy, one becomes powerful sometimes and powerless at other times. Yet this is not authentic personal power; it is "borrowed" organizational power. The individual still remains powerless in his or her own reality. It is a distinctive system of oppression whereby the desired individual behavior is achieved by manipulation, pressure, threats, and coercion.

The isolated and powerless person in an organization is blocked from realizing emotionally and intellectually his or her creative potential. Such a person lacks the inner security, self constraint, personal responsibility and spontaneity required to overcome the unbearable nature of such powerlessness. He or she may then seek to destroy the world around him or her as well as himself or herself in a desperate attempt to defend against being crushed by it. Behavioral overlays such as apathy, indifference, compulsive behavior or withdrawal disguise this potential from view. Fromm identifies this urge as a lingering tendency within a person which waits for an opportunity to be expressed. News items, from time to time, demonstrate the tragic consequences of this "lingering tendency:"

SAN FRANCISCO (AP) — A city employe (sic) apparently angered over a bad evaluation of his work was arrested after two of his coworkers were killed and a third was wounded during a shooting spree at a water pumping station....

"We didn't know he was holding a grudge," said...[the] security director for the city water department. "We thought we had solved his problem. A meeting with him yesterday broke up on good terms."

. . . .

Co-workers described [him] as "moody" and "unhappy about his evaluation." But they said he was "easy to get along with, normal and definitely not morose."[63]

This man is fully responsible for his actions yet the organization set the stage for the emergence of this behavior. This pathological response is indicative of his alienation and oppression and a symptom of the organizational context of such alienation and oppression.

Hierarchy, Oppression and Alienation. Oppression among other things is the maintenance of the condition of human alienation. Oppression is maintained by lies, deception, and power plays. Oppression is the manipulation or coercion of human behavior by intimidation, force, or threats of force. In a democracy this oppression may be assumed "voluntarily" by the worker and manager who, out of necessity for survival or to fulfill the psychological strivings for prestige and success, are "blind" to its existence.[64]

The lies are verbal communications which, among other things, involve the tissue of rationalizations concerning how things are done in the organization. For example, fabrications designed to explain who gets promoted, how personnel and work assignments are made and how organizational rewards are parceled out. One glaring example of this is the Civil Service "rule-of-three" where the person desired by the selection board is frequently not the person found on the rule-of-three list. In this instance, as well as when the desired name is not on the list, a great deal of bending and twisting is done to obtain the "right" selection or avoid a "wrong" one.

One city in the western United States, for example, had the opportunity three times to select an exceptionally competent, sensitive, community-oriented, administratively capable police chief. He was head of their highly successful and innovative community relations function and was considered humane in his orientation to the department as well. Each time this particular associate chief took the promotional exam to become chief the Police Commission found him unacceptable under the "rule-of-three" even though each time he passed the written promotional exam with the highest rating. He was found "wanting" on the oral exam! He was seen by influential public safety people as "soft on crime," yet he was one of the most highly respected associate police chiefs in the nation. This was a subtle deceptive strategem designed to achieve the covert goals of those charged with making the choice.

Deceptions are actions which involve, among other things, spurious strategems for the accomplishment of organizational objectives. Deceptions may contain partial truths which make them more easily believable by the dependent worker who is just trying to make it through the day and provide for himself or herself and any dependents involved. Thus the establishment of a state park in one area may be a ploy to throw the conservationist "off the trail" while logging quotas are increased around the area meanwhile, and state park service employees are told only "half" the story. Thus unwittingly they are deceived and lay the lie on the public in the course of their daily work.

Power plays in organizations revolve around the struggles for resources, greater budgets, more prestige, and control of organizational programs and mission. They may involve personal grudges or be a part of the life-striving of the concerned persons. Competition for a real, presumed, or intentionally created scarcity is an essential part of the power play. This may involve power, prestige or resources and is a pervasive part of modern organizational life.

A power play is a transaction whereby a person, group, or organization obtains from another person, group, or organization something which is wanted against the opposition of the concerned person, group, or organization. In the face of a required budgetary reduction, one might find an urban police chief struggling with the fire chief and city librarian for scarce property tax funds in an effort to keep their branch district services open to serving the public. Each may escalate his or her use of power to gain control of the funds until the ultimate goal is achieved and the public is thus denied a decision resting on the merits of satisfactory alternatives.

Mystification and Oppression. This oppression must not be experienced as such. R. D. Laing suggests this must be seen as benevolence and experienced as kindness.[65] Thus organizational explanations frequently misrepresent and discount the validity of a worker's perception. Explanation, manipulation, threat and the use of force and coercion so as to obtain the worker's denial of his or her own sense of reality, obscure the validity of his or her perceptions and secure his or her commitment to group and organizational truths. This is the process of mystification wherein the worker ends up colluding with and supporting his or her own oppression, even, on occasion, explaining to others why such (oppressive) conditions are necessary. Phrases such as "at least" and "if only" or "something worse could have happened" are all language clues to the existence of such mystification. They are indicative of a behaviorial submission to implicit and explicit organizational requirements.

The Consequences of Alienation. Human organizations are filled with men and women who are alienated, mystified, and oppressed, who have no comprehension or understanding of themselves or the processes in which they are involved. It is this alienated, mystified and oppressed condition in which human beings move and work and have their being in the modern technological industrial world. Within the organization, group structures and social systems maintain and continue the oppression. Under these circumstances too many human beings continue to be alienated from their work, from their emotional life, from their intelligence, from their pleasures, and from the world which surrounds them. Many are also alienated from the social forces which determine the nature of society and the character of every person living in it. This kind of alienation encourages feelings of helplessness before the forces which govern us and inhibits responsible individual decisions and discourages individual action to respond creatively and effectively to change it.

Under these circumstances disasters seem to appear evermore frequently, as if they were natural catastrophes rather than what they really are—that is, occurrences aided by human beings without intention and without awareness. The following incident was created by human beings, yet it takes on the aura of a "natural catastrophe." In Northern Italy, a factory owned by Swiss businessmen using technology created by the American chemical industry, using Italian workers, experienced an escape of highly poisonous and hazardous chemical defoliant into the atmosphere which fell on hundreds of square miles of Northern Italy. This chemical dropped on people and animals with the capacity to inflict profound genetic damage on any children or adults who will have the ability to procreate in the future.[66]

Most of the human beings involved in the manufacturing process knew of the danger. Most of the human beings made choices to participate in the process. Most of the human beings, including the scientists who created this profoundly toxic chemical, to the human beings who did the work in the factory, all made conscious and unconscious daily choices concerning its production. All seemed powerless to stop the event, yet all along the way, each one is responsible for contributing to the event. The human person who continues this process of abandoning his or her own responsibility and autonomy up against seeming technological imperatives and necessities may well be abandoning future generations, if not to oblivion, to a lifetime of crippled, tragic, physical distortion and personal unfulfillment, let alone bear the responsibilities for even greater catastrophes.

Less spectacular yet equally insidious is an incident involving the poisoning of a community water source which resulted from illegal waste dumping by Occidental Chemical Company (a subsidiary of Occidental Petroleum) in Lathrop, California. In 1979 company management conceded that laws were violated when pesticides were secretly dumped by the plant into nearby waste ponds which eventually percolated into community drinking water wells. Confidential internal memos disclosed this was occurring at least four years prior to 1979 and that by June 1976 this company had been dumping five tons of pesticide per year into the ground. The situation was disclosed early in 1979 by state pollution officials who found traces of DBCP (dibromochloropropane) pesticide in the nearby wells used for drinking water. As early as 1958 studies indicated this pesticide would cause, at least, testicular atrophy, male sterility and chromosomal damage linked to birth defects. These results showed up in a significant number of the workers in the Occidental plant in Lathrop in 1977. Company culpability was compounded in that management was aware and troubled by the problem, yet took no action to resolve it and, indeed, deliberately misled the Regional Water Quality Control Board concerning the extent and scope of the hazard.[67]

It is the alienation and mystification concerning power which makes behavior inside organizations in a democratic society so difficult to comprehend, primarily because it belies the democratic rhetoric of the system. For most of us who spend our daily lives inside an organization, democracy is a myth where the substance and reality are absent. The freedoms which we aver exist in the political sphere are not available within the organization which dominates the best hours of our waking daily lives. Any expression of our distinctive humanness such as tenderness, compassion, empathy, vulnerability; any expression of personal identity, if not suffered or tolerated, is penalized, ridiculed, or exploited. What remains is individual cynicism and despair hidden behind the mask of the happy worker, who seems alternatively compulsive, apathetic, unquestioning and eager to please or angry, snarling, frustrated and caged.

Roles and Alienation. In American organizational and bureaucratic practice the subordinate is expected to submit with a smile to superior authority and even participate in determining the conditions of his or her subordination. The relationship should be informal, friendly and personable. This neatly conceals the harsh authoritarian nature of bureaucracy, while maintaining a facade of near-friendliness—a special kind of non-intimate courtesy. In organizations, men and women give up their power to roles, but people can only play roles by detaching themselves from their real feelings and therein lies the core of alienation within modern organization.[68]

In organizations, we are not free and equal; we are ordered and unequal. We are actors in roles. We are non-persons. We are programmed in our relationships one to another and alienated from ourselves. Hierarchy involves ruling and being ruled, issuing commands and orders, and obeying commands and orders, submitting to organizational and group demands and calculating how to survive and succeed within the intricate matricies of the group and organization. Ralph Hummel suggests that bureaucracy is fundamentally a replacement of society and that it has produced a "... dehumanized human fragment—socially crippled, culturally normless, psychologically dependent, linguistically mute, and politically powerless...."[69]

Each employee must seemingly internalize the following ethical imperatives:

- Don't think, don't feel, just perform.
- Don't move without permission.
- Compete! (your co-worker is your adversary).
- Don't talk unless it's job related.
- Accumulate what is in scarce supply.
- Don't question rules and orders.
- Succeed at all costs (failure is oblivion).
- Produce at the pace established by one's peers.
- Don't challenge the organization.
- Don't question your supervisor's judgment.

Human qualities like friendliness, courage, courtesy, kindness, are transformed into commodities, into personal assets that will bring a higher price on the personality market or an upgraded position in the hierarchy. If an individual fails to make a profitable use of one's self, her or she is a failure and if one succeeds, one feels successful.

A person's sense of value is dependent upon the forces outside of one's self. As such the alienated personality loses a good deal of his or her sense of self-worth because the sense of self stems from one's own experience, one's own thinking, one's own feeling, one's own decisions, one's own judgment, and one's own actions.

The antidote to this is to establish conditions in which there is freedom for human beings to fully realize themselves in an uncompromising way. This freedom involves the activity of a totally integrated personality. This is not activity to which a person is driven by isolation, fear, and powerlessness. It is responsible activity. It is activity which values one's self as well as others. It permits and encourages cooperative relationships and brings intimacy and achieving personal potential within reach.

If this activity is within group or organizational confines it may be designated as work. Jaques defines work as that aspect of "... human activity in which the individual exercises discretion, makes decisions, and acts, in seeking to transform the external physical or social world in accord with a predetermined goal."[70] The difference between Maslow's "self-actualized" individual and the worker in an employment setting is that the worker is using his unique capacity to relate cooperatively to the work that others are doing as well. The worker who is working up to his full capacity within an organization operates within a time-frame for the accomplishment of his/her task. This accounts for individual differences that allow for an effective arrangement of tasks, specialization of labor and variable levels of responsibilities.

An Urgent Need: To Demystify Life Inside Groups and Organizations

There is an urgent and compelling need to demystify the internal context of organizational life. Then to proceed and examine some available tools which could be utilized to bring effective change. Finally, to propose additional possibilities for altering the context and output of modern organization so it may become more responsive to human needs while achieving greater productivity as well. A concern here too will be with public bureaucracy as these are the distinctive mechanisms which the public has selected, not only for the delivery of their most needed services, but public organizations have often been selected to provide supervision of the private sector when the abuses there have become so great as to require public regulation.

Organizational productive effort and efficient operation of organizational affairs must submit to and utilize measures of humanness. Efficiency and production must be disciplined by humane requirements. The whole organization needs to become involved in the conversion to a more humane context, culture and process. Where only a part or segment of the organization is involved and management is unsupportive, then alteration of only a segment of the organization to a more humane organizational life renders those involved in such changes vulnerable to power plays, hostility, and envy and easily becomes a set-up to eliminate the sensitive and conscientious workers and the more sensitive and humane managers. Thayer suggests that new approaches assume that individual human needs can be satisfied and the resources for doing so are available and that competition is not necessary and meaningful work is available. He calls for an unalienated future and suggests that those wedded to "the ethic of individualism" will have difficulty grasping the meaning of his words. Yet he suggests in clear, powerful language:

> ... the unadorned ethic legitimizes the repression of some citizens by other citizens. It presumes that those designated "superior" by virtue of talent, organizationally assigned role, or wealth are turned loose to dominate others. Those who cling to the ethic often forget that the game they play cannot be defined other than in terms of "winners" and "losers." The successes of one individual can be described only by the failure of others. Most people understand this, if only subconsciously, and "success" is uncomfortable;

those who win are damaged psychologically by what they must do to win, or they know *they inflict costs upon others.* [72]

It is essential to develop some conceptual tools for use in the task set out here. Once this is done, it will be possible to proceed, first by exploring the context of organizational life, then by examining how organizations may be effectively changed and productivity ultimately enhanced and finally exploring how greater human dignity may be developed and maintained within modern groups and organizations.

SUMMARY

Bureaucracies may be characterized as including a variety of groups and organizations involving processes of human interaction located in a variety of hierarchical arrangements where human beings have access to power, prestige and resources distributed in ever-diminishing amounts downward through a pyramidal structure. This spawns and contributes to a wide degree of alienation, paranoiagenisis, and atrophy which are distinctive aspects of human existence within modern organizations. This ambience is maintained by lies, deception and power plays which vary in intensity from subtle cues, persuasion, intimidation, to outright force. It is all the more insidious because group and organization members are so separated from their own humanness that they are blind to such alienation. Under these circumstances the aphorism, "What you don't know can't hurt you," is false since in these groups and organizations what you don't know could well hurt you. Understanding of these aspects of group and organizational process is essential if the ends of human dignity are to be served.

NOTES

1. Regarding My Lai see e.g., U.S. Department of the Army, *The My Lai Massacre and its Cover Up: Beyond the Reach of the Law?* (The Peers Commission report with a supplement and introductory essay on the Limits of the Law by Joseph Goldstein, Burke Marshall, Jack Schwartz), N.Y., Free Press, 1976; William R. Peers (Lt. Gen.), *The My Lai Inquiry*, N.Y., Norton, 1979; Mary Therese McCarthy, *Medina*, N.Y., Harcourt, Brace, Javanovich, 1972; Seymour M. Hersh, *Cover-up: The Army's Secret Investigation of the Massacre at My Lai 4*, N.Y., Random House, 1972; Seymour M. Hersh, *My Lai 4: A Report on the Massacre and its Aftermath*, N.Y., Random House, 1970; Richard Hammer, *The Court Martial of Lt. Calley*, N.Y., Couard, McCann & Geoglegan, 1971; regarding Lockheed Corporation bribing see e.g., Berkeley Rice, *The C-5A Scandal; An Inside Story of the Military-Industrial Complex*, Boston, Houghton Mifflin, 1971; David Boulton, *The Grease Machine*, N.Y., Harper Row, 1978; regarding the F.B.I. see e.g., Fred J. Cook, *The F.B.I. Nobody Knows*, N.Y., Macmillan, 1964; Morton Halperin, *The Lawless State: The Crime of the U.S. Intelligence Agencies*, N.Y., Penguin Books, 1976; Cathy Perkus (ed.) *Cointelpro: The F.B.I.'s Secret War on Political Freedom*, N.Y., Monad Press, (distributed by Pathfinder Press), 1975; Pat Watlers and Stephan Gillers (eds.), *Investigating the F.B.I.*, N.Y., Doubleday, 1973; David Wise, *The American Police State: The Government Agencies Against the People*, N.Y., Random House, 1976; Sanford J. Ungar, *F.B.I., An Uncensored Look Behind the Walls*, Boston, Little, Brown and Co., 1975; regarding the unlawful behavior of the C.I.A. see e.g., *Report to the President* by the Commission on C.I.A. activities within the United States, Nelson A. Rockefeller, Vice-President, Chairman, U.S. Govt. Printing Office, 1975; Philip Agee, *Inside the Company: C.I.A. Diary*, N.Y., Stonehill, 1975; Morton Halperin, *The Lawless State: The Crimes of the U.S. Intelligence Agencies*, N.Y., Penguin Books, 1976; Harry Paul Jeffers, *The C.I.A., A Close Look at the Central Intelligence Agency*, N.Y., Lion Press, 1970; Victor Marchetti and John D. Marks, *The C.I.A. and the Cult of Intelligence*, N.Y., A.A. Knopf, 1974; Leroy Fletcher Prouty, *The Secret Team: The C.I.A. and Its Allies in Control of the*

United States and the World, Englewood Cliffs, N.J., Prentice-Hall, 1973; Harry House Ransom, *The Intelligence Establishment*, Cambridge, Mass., Harvard University Press, 1976; Christopher Robbins, *Air America*, N.Y., Putnam, 1979; David Wise and Thomas Ross, *The Invisible Government*, N.Y., Random House, 1964.

2. *L.A. Times*, March 9, 1977.

3. Guy Benveniste, *Bureaucracy*, San Francisco, Boyd and Fraser Publishing Co., 1977, pp. 3-26, for helpful critical review of job satisfaction measures see James C. Taylor, "Job Satisfaction and Quality of Working Life: A Reassessment," *Journal of Occupational Psychology*, Vol. 50, pp. 243-252, 1977, (Printed in Great Britain), and also see Rick Jacobs and Trudy Solomon, "Strategies for Enhancing the Prediction of Job Performance from Job Satisfaction," *Journal of Applied Psychology*, Vol. 62, No. 4, pp. 417-421, 1977.

4. Elliot Jaques, *A General Theory of Bureaucracy*, N.Y., Halsted Press, John Wiley & Sons, 1976, pp. 6 *et. seq.*

5. Eugene P. Dvorin and Robert H. Simmons, *From Amoral to Humane Bureaucracy*, San Francisco, Canfield Press (a division of Harper & Row), 1972, p. 60.

6. 4 Wheaton 627, see also Carl Brent Swisher, *American Constitutional Development* (2nd. ed.), Cambridge, Mass., Houghton-Mifflin Co., 1954, pp. 157-167.

7. See generally Melvin Anshen and Francis D. Wormuth, *Private Enterprise and Public Policy*, N.Y., The Macmillan Co., 1954, pp. 136-169; A.B. Levy, *Private Corporations and Their Control*, London, Routledge and Kegan Paul, 1957; for historical perspective see Sir Henry Maine, *Early History of Institutions*, 1875, and his *Ancient Law*, 1885, republished, Boston, Beacon Press, 1963; also A.V. Dicey, *Introduction to the Study of Law and the Constitution*, 8th ed., London, Macmillan, 1927; see also Jaques, *op. cit.*, p. 19.

8. Max Weber, *Essays in Sociology*, H. Gerth and C. Wright Mills (eds.), N.Y. Oxford University Press, 1946; Max Weber, *The Protestant Ethic and the Spirit of Capitalism*, Talcott Parsons, tr., N.Y., Oxford University Press, 1947; Max Weber, *The Theory of Social and Economic Organization*, A.M. Henderson and Talcott Parsons, trs., N.Y., Oxford University Press, 1947.

9. There is a plethora of literature available. Here are some representative examples: John P. Davis, *Corporations, A Study of the Origin and Development of Great Business Combinations and of Their Relation to the Authority of the State*, written in 1897 and published in 1904 and republished by Capricorn Books, N.Y., 1961; Adolph A. Berle and Gardiner C. Means, *The Modern Corporation and Private Property*, N.Y., Macmillan, 1932; A.A. Berle, Jr., *The 20th Century Capitalist Revolution*, N.Y., Harcourt-Brace, 1954; Peter F. Drucker, *The Concept of the Corporation*, N.Y., John Day, 1946; G. William Domhoff, *Who Rules America?*, Englewood Cliffs, N.J., Prentice-Hall, Inc., 1967; *Higher Circles*, N.Y., Random House, 1970; Richard J. Barnet and Ronald E. Muller, *Global Reach: The Power of Multinational Corporations*, N.Y., Simon and Shuster, 1974; John Kenneth Galbraith, *The New Industrial State*, Boston, Houghton Mifflin Co., 1967; Daniel Bell, *The Coming of Post-Industrial Society*, N.Y., Basic Books, 1973.

10. Kenneth E. Boulding, *The Organizational Revolution*, N.Y., Harper, 1953; Henri Fayol, *General and Industrial Management*, Constance Storrs, trs., London, Pitman, 1949; Mary Parker Follett, *Dynamic Administration: The Collected Papers of Mary Parker Follett*, Henry C. Metcalf and Lyndall Urwick (eds.), N.Y., Harper, 1942; Frederick W. Taylor, *The Principles of Scientific Management*, N.Y., W.W. Norton, 1967; Luther Gulick and Lyndall Urwick (eds.) *Papers on the Science of Administration*, N.Y., Institute of Public Administration, 1937; Woodrow Wilson, "The Study of Administration," *Political Science Quarterly*, 1887, pp. 197-222.

11. Davis, *loc. cit.*, p. 280.

12. W.H. Inge, *The Idea of Progress*, Romanes Lecture, Oxford, Humphrey Milford, 1920; see also Sir Geoffrey Vickers, *Value Systems and Social Process*, N.Y., Basic Books, Inc., 1968, pp. 3-26; and see Note 7 above, Daniel Bell, "The Corporation and Society in the 1970's," *Public Interest*, No. 24 (Summer) 1971, pp. 5-32.

13. Jaques, *op. cit.*, p. 21.

14. *L.A. Times*, March 8, 1978.

15. I am indebted to Morton Kroll for this insight. The defense of this point concerning the

federalists may be found in Leonard D. White, *The Federalists: A Study in Administrative History*, N.Y., The Macmillan Co., 1956, *passim*, but e.g., see esp., pp. 284-290, for a comprehensive American public administrative history see also his *The Jeffersonians: A Study in Administrative History, 1801-1829*, N.Y., The Macmillan Co., 1961, *The Jacksonians: A Study in Administrative History, 1829-1861*, N.Y., The Macmillan Co., 1963, and *The Republican Era: A Study in Administrative History, 1861-1901*, N.Y., The Macmillan Co., 1963.

16. cf. Victor A. Thompson, *Without Sympathy or Enthusiasm*, University, Ala., The University of Alabama Press, 1975, *passim*, and Robert H. Simmons, and Eugene P. Dvorin, *Public Administration, Values, Policy and Changes*, Alfred Publishing Co., Inc., 1977, pp. 639-655 and Dvorin and Simmons, *op. cit.*, *passim*, and generally William L. Morrow, *Public Administration, Politics, Policy and the Political System*, second edition, N.Y., Random House, 1980.

17. Bertram M. Gross, *The Managing of Organizations*, Glencoe, Ill., The Free Press (a division of Macmillan Co.), 1964; see also generally Vol. I, pp. 32-315, and Vol. II, p. 489.

18. Dorothy Jongward, *Everybody Wins: Transactional Analysis Applied to Organizations* (revised ed.), Reading, Mass., Addison-Welsey Publishing Co., 1976, pp. 7-8. This is an unfortunate use of the script concept developed by Eric Berne who developed the concept and in addition developed some very precise tools to both understand organizational dynamics and utilize transactional analysis in "treating" the "ailing" organization. Berne himself did not apply the concept of scripts to organization even though he had plenty of opportunity in his *The Structure and Dynamics of Organizations and Groups*, N.Y., J.B. Lippincott Co., 1963, cf. Lyman K. Randall, "The Transactional Manager: An Analysis of Two Contemporary Management Theories," in Jongward, *op. cit.*, pp. 275-313.

19. *L.A. Times*, March 31, 1977, p. 1; see also Note 1 above.

20. See Berne's concept of euhemerus and euhermerization where a primal leader becomes greater in death than in life in *Structure and Dynamics of Organizations and Groups, op. cit.*, pp. 98-100.

21. Clarence H. Danhoff, *Government Contracting and Technological Change*, Washington, D.C., The Brookings Institution, 1968; and see also my review in the *Western Political Quarterly*, September 1968, pp. 678-680.

22. See Harlan Cleveland, *The Future Executive*, N.Y., Harper & Row Pub., 1972, pp. 48-62.

23. Simmons and Dvorin, *loc. cit.*, pp. 41-71; for an excellent discussion of the complexities of public administration see Dwight Waldo, *The Enterprise of Public Administration: A Summary View*, Novato, California, Chandler and Sharp Publishers, Inc., 1980.

24. *L.A. Times*, September 14, 1976, p. 1.

25. To identify just a few of the materials available in the literature on this subject. Louis M. Kohlmeier, Jr., *The Regulators: Watchdog Agencies and the Public Interest*, N.Y., Harper & Row Publishers, 1969; Harold Koontz and Richard W. Gable, *Public Control of Economic Enterprise*, N.Y., McGraw-Hill, 1956; Emmett S. Redford, *Ideal and Practice in Public Administration*, University, Ala., University of Alabama Press, 1958, pp. 107-137. See also generally his *Administration of National Economic Control*, N.Y., The Macmillan Co., 1952; Pendelton Herring, *Public Administration and the Public Interest*, N.Y., McGraw-Hill Book Co., Inc., 1936, pp. 377-399; John F. Winslow, *Conglomerates Unlimited, the Failure of Regulation*, Bloomington and London, Indiana University Press, 1973; Francis E. Rourke, *Bureaucracy, Politics and Public Policy*, Boston, Little, Brown and Co., 1969; Eugene P. Dvorin and Robert H. Simmons, *From Amoral to Humane Bureaucracy*, San Francisco, Canfield Press (a department of Harper & Row Publishers, Inc.), 1972, pp. 36-46; Ashley L. Schiff, *Fire and Water*, Cambridge, Mass., Harvard University Press, 1962.

26. Gross, *loc. cit.*, Vols I & II (see Note 13 above). This is a most comprehensive effort by Bertram Gross. The management of organizations locates the origin of management deep within the history of the public sector. Public and private concerns fade within the pages of Professor Gross' book as management theory and practice move to dominate the book's focus.

27. Gerth and Mills, *loc. cit.*, pp. 196-244 and pp. 232-235, cf.; Jaques Ellul, *The Techno-*

logical Society, N.Y., Alfred A. Knopf, 1964, pp. 248-249.

28. Reinhard Bendix, "Bureaucracy and the Problem of Power," *Public Administration Review*, Vol. V, 1945, pp. 194-209, the roots of organizational power may reach deep into Platonic Tradition cf. Karl R. Popper, *The Open Society and Its Enemies*, Vols 1 & 2, fourth edition (revised), 1962, N.Y., Harper & Row Publishers, Inc., 1963 by arrangement with Princeton University Press, *passim.*

29. Talcott Parsons, *The Social System*, Glencoe, Ill., The Free Press, 1951, pp. 38-39, see also generally Talcott Parsons, Robert Bales and Edward A. Shils, *Working Papers in a Theory of Action*, N.Y., the Free Press of Glencoe, 1953.

30. Cleveland, *op. cit.*, pp. 13-29.

31. Simmons and Dvorin, *op. cit.*, pp. 41-76.

32. *L.A. Times*, April 16, 1978.

33. Vickers, *op. cit.*, p. 21.

34. Arthur F. Bentley, *The Process of Government* (new ed.), Cambridge, Mass., Harvard University Press, 1967, p. 300, first published in 1908.

35. Herbert A. Simon, *Administrative Behavior*, N.Y., Macmillian, 1948, *passim*; see also David B. Truman, *The Governmental Process*, N.Y., Alfred A. Knopf, 1960.

36. Vickers, *loc. cit.*, p. 15.

37. Chester I. Barnard, *The Functions of the Executive*, Cambridge, Harvard University Press, 1938, *passim*; see also F.J. Rothlisberger, *Management and Morale*, Cambridge, Mass., Harvard University Press, 1941, pp. 24-25; Elton Mayo, *The Social Problems of an Industrial Civilization*, Boston, Mass., Graduate School of Business Administration, Harvard University, 1945; Elton Mayo, *The Human Problems of an Industrial Civilization*, Boston, Mass., Harvard Business School, 1933; F.J. Rothlisberger and William J. Dickson, *Management and the Worker*, Cambridge, Mass., Harvard University Press, 1939.

38. Eric Berne, *Transactional Analysis in Psychotherapy*, N.Y., Grove Press, Inc., 1961, Ballantine Books, p. 82; see also his *What Do You Say After You Say Hello?*, N.Y., Grove Press, Inc., 1972; pp. 42-42; and posthumously under the editorship of Claude Steiner with the assistance of Carmen Kerr, *Beyond Games and Scripts*, N.Y., Grove Press, Inc., 1976, pp. 16-17.

39. Fremont J. Lyden, George A. Shipman, Robert W. Wilkinson, Jr., "Decision-Flow Analysis, A Methodology for Studying the Public Policy Making Process," in Preston P. LeBreton (ed.) *Comparative Administrative Theory*, Seattle, University of Washington Press, 1968, pp. 156-157; see also Talcott Parsons and Edward A. Shils (eds.), *Toward a General Theory of Action*, N.Y., Harper & Row, 1951, *passim*, Irving L. Janis and Leon Mann, *Decision Making, A Psychological Analysis of Conflict, Choice and Commitment*, N.Y., The Free Press, Inc., 1977.

40. Melanie Klein and Joan Revere, *Love, Hate and Reparation*, N.Y., W.W. Norton Co., Inc., 1964, pp. 4-5; see also generally Karen Horney, *The Neurotic Personality of Our Time*, N.Y, W.W. Norton, 1937.

41. Klein and Revere, *op. cit.*, pp. 38-39.

42. *Ibid.*

43. *Ibid.*

44. Eric Fromm, *Escape From Freedom*, N.Y., Holt, Rinehart & Winston & Co., Inc., 1941, p. 168. For an exhaustive study of the authoritarian personality and the social implications flowing therefrom, see T.W. Adorno, Else Frenkel-Brunswik, Daniel J. Levinson, R. Nevitt Sanford, *The Authoritarian Personality*, N.Y., W.W. Norton, 1950, *passim.*

45. Fromm, *Escape From Freedom, op. cit.*, p. 270.

46. Irving Janis and Leon Mann, *Decision Making, op. cit.*, pp. 243-277; John Dean, *Blind Ambition*, N.Y., Simon and Shuster, Inc., 1976, *passim*; and Carl Bernstein and Bob Woodward, *All the President's Men*, N.Y., Simon and Shuster, Inc., 1974, *passim.*

47. Fromm, *Escape From Freedom, op. cit.*, pp. 111-112; see also generally pp. 103-206.

48. Fromm, *Escape From Freedom, op. cit.*, pp. 34-36.

49. Jaques, *op. cit.*, p. 39, see also p. 228 and 239.

50. *Ibid.*, see also Bertrand Russell, *Power*, London, George Allen & Unwin Ltd., and New York, Barnes & Noble, Inc., 1962, p. 9; see also Chapter III, pp. 25-34, Who Suggests The Analytical Possibilities of the Concept for the Social Sciences.

51. Fromm, *Escape From Freedom, op. cit.*, pp. 114-138.

52. Klein and Revere, *Love, Hate and Reparation, op. cit.*, pp. 7-8; see also Emile Durkheim, *Suicide*, N.Y., The Free Press, 1951, *passim*; on the social impact of aggression see Sigmund Freud, *Civilization and Its Discontents*, N.Y., W.W. Norton & Co., Inc., 1961.

53. Eric Fromm, *The Sane Society*, N.Y., Holt, Rinehart & Winston, Inc., 1955, reprinted by Fawcett Publications, Inc., Greenwich, Conn., p. 114. On the roots of alienation and anomie, see also Emile Durkheim, "On Anomie," selected from his writings in C. Wright Mills, *Images of Man*, N.Y., George Braziller, Inc., 1960. pp. 449-485, and Karl Marx and Friedrich Engels, "On Alienation," selected from their writing in C. Wright Mills, *ibid.*, pp. 486-507.

54. *New Times*, November 12, 1976, p. 18.

55. *Ibid.*

56. William James, *The Principles of Psychology*, Vol. 2, London, Henry Holt & Co., 1890, this is an early recognition of fight/flight reaction when threat is perceived.

57. A.H. Maslow, "A Theory of Human Motivation," *Psychological Review*, July, 1943, pp. 370-396. See also his *Toward a Psychology of Being*, Princeton, N.J., D. Van Nostrand Co., Inc., 1962; and his *Motivation and Personality*, N.Y., Harper & Row Publishers, Inc., 1954, cf. F. Herzberg, *Work and the Nature of Man*, Cleveland, Ohio, World Publishing Co., 1966.

58. Erik H. Erikson, *Childhood and Safety*, (2nd ed.), N.Y., W.W. Norton & Co., Inc., 1963 (1st ed. 1950), pp. 209-274.

59. Bertrand Russell, *Freedom vs. Organization*, N.Y., W.W. Norton & Co., Inc., p. 450.

60. Frederick C. Thayer, *An End to Hierarchy! An End to Competition!*, N.Y., New Viewpoints (a division of Franklin Watts), 1973, p. 44, copyright 1973 by Frederick C. Thayer. Used by permission of the publisher, Franklin Watts, Inc.

61. Thayer, *loc. cit.*, p. 82.

62. Thayer, *loc. cit.*, p. 134.

63. *L.A. Times*, February 17, 1979, Part II, p. 1.

64. Irving Janis and Leon Mann, *Decision Making, op. cit.*, pp. 243-308, and John Dean, *Blind Ambition, op. cit., passim.*

65. R.D. Laing, *The Politics of Experience*, N.Y., Ballantine Books (Random House, Inc.), 1967, pp. 57-76. See also Stanley Milgram, "Behavioral Study of Obedience," *Journal of Abnormal Psychology*, Vol. 67, 1963, pp. 371-378, for obedience seated in anomie and the unquestioning acceptance of even tenuous authority as a way of escaping personal responsibility for a decision; see also S. Milgram, *Obedience to Authority*, N.Y., Harper & Row, 1974, *passim.*

66. *L.A. Times*, July 31, 1976, see also Thomas Whiteside, *The Pendulum and the Toxic Cloud*, New Haven, Conn., Yale University Press, 1979.

67. *L.A. Times*, May 11, 1977, June 19, 1979; an editorial June 9, 1979; and a recent report indicating the Environmental Protection Agency will ban all further use of DBCP pending a full investigation of the health hazards it poses, July 19, 1979.

68. Joseph Bensman and Arthur J. Vidich, *The New American Society*, Chicago, 1971, pp. 22-23; Robert H. Simmons and Eugene P. Dvorin, *Public Administration: Values, Policies and Change, op. cit.*, pp. 620-629; see also R.D. Laing, *The Politics of Experience*, New York, Ballantine Books, 1967.

69. Ralph P. Hummel, *The Bureaucratic Experience*, N.Y., St. Martin's Press, Inc., 1977, p. 221 and *passim.*

70. Jaques, *op. cit.*, p. 99.

71. *Ibid.*, pp. 171-178.

72. Thayer, *op. cit.*, p. 196, see Note 61.

RELATED READING

Barnett, Richard J. and Miller, Ronald E. *Global Reach: The Power of Multinational Corporations*. New York: Simon and Shuster, 1974. This book focuses upon the growing power of a few hundred multinational corporations. It identifies the emergence of new transnational managers for whom corporate loyalty transcends national loyalty and how they project corporate power on a global scale.

Berle, Adolph A. and Means, Gardiner C. *The Modern Corporation and Private Property*. New York: Macmillan, 1932. The classic study on the rise of modern corporations and their emergence to dominate private property and social purpose.

Domhoff, G. William. *Who Rules America?* Englewood Cliffs, N.J.: Prentice-Hall, Inc., 1967. This book identifies an American governing class rooted in corporate ownership who are the beneficiaries of the new industrial state.

Fromm, Eric. *The Sane Society*. New York: Holt, Rinehart & Winston, Inc., 1955. This effort suggests that modern human beings are alienated from the world they created, from one another, from the things they produce, the things they are, the things they consume and their government. He suggests important steps that can be taken to change this.

Galbraith, John Kenneth. *The New Industrial State*. Boston: Houghton Mifflin Co., 1967. This effort suggests the decline of capitalism and the emergence of a new industrial state. This new state is dominated by a few hundred corporations which subordinate social purpose to their needs through monopolies on advanced technology, specialized manpower and information.

Gerth, H.H. and Mills, C. Wright. *From Max Weber. Essays in Sociology*. New York: Oxford University Press, 1958. This book is a collection of writings from the German sociologist Max Weber whose creative effort is essential to an understanding of modern bureaucracy.

Maslow, Abraham H. *Toward a Psychology of Being*. 2nd edition. Princeton, N.J.: D. Van Nostrand Co., Inc., 1962. This effort indicates human beings can be loving, noble, and creative and are capable of pursuing the highest values and aspirations.

Mayo, Elton. *The Social Problems of Industrial Civilization*. Boston: Graduate School of Business Administration, Harvard University, 1945. This important book identified the need to stress the importance of groups and the necessity of understanding their behavior if effective cooperation is to be secured.

Revere, Joan and Klein, Melanie. *Love, Hate and Reparation*. New York: W.W. Norton Co., Inc. This book identifies and explores the roots of alienation using traditional psychoanalytic theory with particular reference to the origin of aggression.

Vickers, Sir Geoffrey. *Value Systems and Social Process*. New York: Basic Books, Inc., 1968. This book emphasizes the importance of developing new value systems which are rooted in the appreciation of the humane as essential to more effective social management and regulation.

Chapter 2

THE HUMAN ASPECT OF GROUPS AND ORGANIZATIONS

In our predominantly urban-technological society the overwhelming majority of men, women and children spend the greater part of their waking day within the confines of a small face-to-face group. These groups are frequently linked with large, often complex, organizations. These organizations, in turn, may be viewed as composed of a variety of small groups linked together in a variety of patterns and relationships. The focus of most of these groups is a variety of tasks usually identified as work, yet they may also involve activity which is thought to be play.

We, as children, more often than not begin our pre-school days in a "play group," where the line between work and play seems undifferentiated. Gradually, at home and at school, the differences between what is work and what is play is learned. Work tends to become associated with the absence of joy and care, with loss of control of one's own life; body and mind are in the "hands of" a parent, teacher or supervisor; smartness is converted into performance. The worth and value of a person depends upon the quality of his or her performance. Joy, care, anger, risk-taking, and the use of authentic personal competence and power is available only in play or in brief structured respites from the classroom or work situation. Under these conditions the full authentic development of the whole human personality is usually inhibited, even precluded.

Occasionally, and for some even more often, persons are able to work at what they enjoy and therefore enjoy their work. This experience is usually rooted in a group which is supportive of such effort. Some individuals in these fortunate circumstances gain access to the development of at least part and occasionally all of their full potential. Work which has personal meaning, social purpose, and is valued by others within the work group and by others outside the work group, as well, is what a substantial proportion of the population seeks. Such work brings joy, reward and satisfaction to the worker. Most persons strive for this kind of work and they strive also to seek the work situation which supports that possibility. It is one tragedy of the organizational work group, as presently constituted, that this possibility is all to often frustrated, defeated and unavailable.

A fully developed human being is in command of his or her intelligence, able to express fully and safely feelings of anger, sorrow, joy, and love and has access to his or her own power, capacity and competence. Some of the behavior associated with this is reflected in a developed awareness around the options one has available and the choices one has to make. This includes, as well, access to broad use of the bodily expressions which are concomitants of one's own emotional life. This means tears, rage, laughter, shaking, perspiring, a full vocal expression from shouting to singing and other related bodily expressions are available for appropriate use.

A fully developed human being is aware of his or her own rage, anger, joy, sorrow, envy, hate, etc. and has understanding and mastery as to how these are delivered to another human being or into a group. A full command of these is necessary, a full awareness of how they function is required and appropriate places for their expression need to be available.

Human beings in the work situation generally have no access to these personally nor do they have permission for their use and safe expression. Indeed, if these are openly expressed the reactions range from hostility to threats, ostracism and removal for such direct expression of feelings. The result is that life for many is lived out in unrewarding, unsatisfying work groups. In the work group mindlessness, joylessness, lovelessness, powerlessness, inequality and competitiveness replace human awareness, spontaneity, creativity, and intimacy. This defeats most cooperative work efforts. Most persons in the work group transact their "psychological business" from this alienated personal psychological place.[1] The individual reflecting his or her own alienation links up with other individuals reflecting similar alienation. The group, in unspoken reciprocal collusion, becomes mindless, joyless, loveless and powerless as well.

The Daily World of Organizational Work
Banal Groups

These groups are the "everyday garden variety" of groups. Banal groups are not noticeable; they are unimportant, melodramatic, humdrum and boring. Persons who live and work within them generally are "shut down," "tuned out, " and "turned off." The substance of interaction in these groups is common, routine, with only a glimmer of life occasionally surfacing, which, when it becomes too noticeable, brings the immediate retribution of higher authority. These groups are seen as "normal." Membership in these groups is seen as necessary. People whom we care about and respect (parents, teachers, counselors) tell us this is what life is really all about — being the "nice" person, functioning adaptively in a work group, being a good worker. To depart from this work situation except for another, more lucrative "higher status" job in a different work group might label one who leaves as unstable, undependable and even a "failure."

One public adminstrator practitioner who is an exceptionally capable investigator for the State of California Contractors' Licensing Board tells of his being an animal tender at a well-known zoological garden. His assignment was to care for the elephants and hippopotamuses. It was a good job and well paid. His involvement with these animals was filled with joy. He left this "pedestrian job" with no future to take a "better opportunity." For him the "roses" of "success" and "promotion" do not begin to compare with the joys associated with the earlier job, yet the disapproval of his co-workers and tensions produced in his family for not "getting ahead" produced sufficient personal stress that the choice he made to change jobs was based on those factors rather than what it was that he, in reality, wanted. Part of the personal harvest was the loss of joy in his work for what seemed like "success" but felt bad! It may be that the same troubles would have overcome him had he remained at the zoo, yet the choice he made was based on what he was told was good for him and what he ought to do, viz. "succeed" and "get ahead." He did not make the choice based on what he actually wanted. If he had, he may have still chosen to leave the zoological gardens but he would have avoided playing "if only I had" and taken better care of himself in later choices.[2]

Banal work groups are extraordinarily unsatisfying, yet most people gain some awareness of this only after they have spent a lifetime of trying to live "according to the rules." As a result, people in their older years frequently feel their lives to be senseless, useless, wasted.

Here our efforts are primarily concerned with banal work groups. It is helpful to identify two other groups, both may develop separately or they may emerge out of the dynamics of a banal group,[3] the hamartic group and the cooperative group.

Hamartic (tragic) Groups

An hamartic life plan is one which brings the person usually blindly and compulsively to a self-destructive and tragic ending. Eric Berne has identified this life plan as a script. A script is based upon a decision made in childhood, reinforced by the parents, justified by subsequent events and culminates in chosen behavioral alternatives. In contrast to banal groups, tragic groups are characterized as groups where individuals bent on their own destruction are able to usurp group process and carry the group with them onward to destruction.[4]

Hamartia is an accurate word to use. In ancient Greek tragedy, it is an error in judgment generally resulting from a flaw in the character of a tragic hero which compels the hero onward to destruction. Thus an hamartic group may be conceived as a group blindly involved in determined activity leading to destructive consequences. Stories about such groups may reflect noble or ignoble behavior. The noble ones become a source of inspiration, hope and encouragement. The ignoble ones generally end up in the courtroom, the prison, the hospital or the morgue.

Sometimes banal group process may become hamartic (tragic) in its consequences. At other times groups are formed where the deliberate purposes are violent, self-destructive and tragic. Hamartic groups often end "with a bang" dramatically. Their members may decide to kill, rob, maim, wound or steal. Examples of such tragic groups are those connected with the "dirty tricks" section of the C.I.A. during the decades of the 1950's, 1960's and the 1970's, Lt. Cally's platoon at My Lai in Viet Nam, the group of men involved in the Committee to Re-elect former President Richard Nixon who participated in activities which led ultimately to their own demise, the "Manson Family" or the Peoples Temple in Jonestown, Guyana.[5]

Sometimes groups get caught up in the mystique of their own mission. For example, groups of agents in the Federal Bureau of Investigation became involved in a number of illegal activities, including such things as mail openings and wire taps, to pursue their perceived mission during the Viet Nam war and during the intense days of the Civil Rights Movement of the 1950's and 1960's. Indictment of a number of these FBI agents conducting such illegal activities occurred. Thus these men were caught in the trap of violating the law in order to uphold the law. More subtle is the issue of an organization knowingly placing a segment of the public at risk while pursuing organizational objectives. In April 1979 Senator Edward Kennedy (D. Mass) at a Joint Congressional Committee hearing in Salt Lake City, Utah presented documents indicating the Atomic Energy Commission in the early 1950's, within the vicinity of the Nevada Test Site for atomic weapons in southern Utah, knowingly exposed people to large amounts of radiation and publicly minimized any serious health risks.[6] These are not unknown problems in Anglo-American legal history and are, in part, the reason for the development of the tremendous restraints placed on executive power by the United States Constitution. What causes the transition of a banal work group into an hamartic one remains to be determined.

Banal and Hamartic Groups Compared. A banal group may go on for years and dissipate or die with no one giving any particular notice. It frequently looks and feels like a melodrama or a soap opera. The banal group has no clear ending or clear beginning. A banal group may alternate from bad to worse but it is not memorable. It has no sudden reversals, no suspenseful moments. It looks good on the surface but it is devastatingly boring. Hamartic groups, on the other hand, are more visible;

they are sharper; they are dramatic; they have a definite progression from prologue through climax to catastrophe.[7] A psychological leader can be identified in such groups as one who, in the minds of the members, seems the most highly endowed with superior, sometimes superhuman, qualities the group ideology expresses. Thus membership attributes leadership qualities to the person selected and then depends on that person for leadership. This process of attribution and dependency spawns irresponsibility on the part of both the leader and the group.

When a banal group becomes involved in hamartic consequences the group may become destructive, notorious and spectacular, sometimes with banner headlines on the front pages of the local newspaper and reported on the evening television news. These groups sometimes are dominated by individuals who themselves lead spectacularly tragic lives. Tragic work groups can emerge in hospitals, prisons, or even unexpectedly in other places such as a business corporation, an educational institution or a department of employment. Pathological groups may not always end in a spectacular manner, and may revert once again to a banal group. They may, of course, continue over a long period of time. There is much to be learned about internal aspects of group conditions and behavior which generate hamartic consequences.

Cooperative Groups

There is a third variety of a group which may be identified where the processes and outcomes are very different from the previous two. Almost every person at one time or another in his or her life has experienced membership in a group which has felt really good, from which a great deal of satisfaction is derived, a sense of a "job well done" occurs, and the person feels good about his or her own contributions and the contributions others make. It feels rewarding, intimate, satisfying. Members can be vulnerable without fear and powerful without having to "trash" or "put down" another member. A sense of joy and care pervade the group and each person is treasured and valued. This is a setting in which a full human being may flower and develop. It may derive in a banal group and last only a few moments, or extend for days, weeks, or months, perhaps years, and then revert into banality once again. It may be achieved intermittently, alternating between banality and cooperative endeavor.

Barry Collins and Harold Guetzkow offer a number of studies with evidence that when work group members are motivated by their personal, self-centered needs, their group's task effectiveness is reduced. Two studies emphasized the disruptive character of competitive, individualistic motivation. One found that group members operating with the competitive reward structures did not establish interpersonal relationships which encouraged them to increase productivity. Another study presented a task requiring the group members to make a choice among a variety of motivational orientations, specifically cooperative, individualistic and competitive. Generally, the cooperative choice produced greater task accomplishment scores. The competitive choice resulted in the poorest performance and the individualistic choice produced intermediate results.[8]

The cooperative group can provide the basis for the emergence of a humane organizational setting. It behooves us to learn more of this, how it emerges, what are its characteristics and how it may be achieved and developed within modern organizations and bureaucracy and if that is possible at all. For the present, it is important to identify it and note that is is possible for attainment.

Banal groups, hamartic groups and cooperative groups are phenomena of group life which are relevant to the understanding of the uses and abuses of organizational and bureaucratic process. Hamartic groups are beyond the intended scope of this effort. Attention here centers upon the context of the banal work group and how its conditions may be altered to encourage and develop a cooperative, productive group responsive to the need for a dignified and humane life.

Banal Work Groups: Family Origins

Max Weber identified the household as the most "natural" of the closed and bounded social action systems. He writes, "The earliest substantial inroads into unmitigated . . . authority proceed not directly from economic motives but apparently from the development of exclusive sexual claims of the man over women subjected to their authority." Weber continues:

> The domestic household is the fundamental basis of loyalty and authority, which, in turn, is the basis of many other groups. This "authority" is of two kinds: (1) the authority derived from superior strength and (2) the authority derived from practical knowledge and experience. It is, thus, the authority of men as against women and children; of the ablebodied as against those of lesser capacity; of the adult as against the child; of the old as against the young . . . it becomes a part of the relationships originally having a domestic character. [9]

Eric Berne focuses on how this is learned in childhood and responds to the possibility of its alteration:

> Parents, deliberately or unaware, teach their children from birth how to behave, think, feel and perceive. Liberation from these influences is no easy matter since they are deeply ingrained and are necessary during the first two or three decades of life for biological and social survival. Indeed, such liberation is only possible at all because the individual starts off in an autonomous state, that is, capable of awareness, spontaneity and intimacy, and he has some discretion as to which parts of his parents' techniques he will accept. [10]

Steiner suggests that the "basic training" we all receive in life encompasses a "systematic attack" on three essential human potentials: the potential for intimacy, the potential for awareness, and the potential for spontaneity. This is achieved through the scripting for lovelessness, joylessness, mindlessness, and powerlessness which occurs in childhood and are essential components in what he identifies as banal scripts. [11] The process underlying such scripting is explained further on in this chapter. It is this process which prepares the future workers for membership in banal work groups and boring organizations. The mood and the spirit of a traditional work group reflects such lovelessness, mindlessness, joylessness, powerlessness and unequal interpersonal relationships which were learned in childhood and today characterize human interaction in organizational and bureaucratic culture.

Weber identified the origin of hierarchical power, and the implication of this for sex-role scripting in the domestic household and work assignments in bureaucratic organizations is immense. [12] Ronald Sampson, in exploring *The Psychology of Power*, writes that Sigmund Freud failed to see any possibilities for human development through cooperative equality and peace. Sampson suggests this was due to Freud's own inability to challenge the accepted views of the relations which more appropriately ought to obtain between men and women. For Freud, the social relationship between a man and a woman was inevitably one of dominance and subjection. Sampson suggests Freud's view of the impossibility and undesirability of equality between the sexes, while purporting to be a scientific hypothesis, was little more than the contemporary prejudice of his class and time. [13]

John Stuart Mill, writing in 1869 in his essay *The Subjection of Women,* observed the dominance of men over women in the conjugal family had unfortunate consequences for the men, the women and the children involved. He observed in his essay, for which he was held in much contempt at the time, that the power to hold others in servitude was essentially morally corrupting, especially for men; and that such powerlessness engendered in women created profound frustration and resentment. He stated the family itself became a "school of despotism" in which the children learned the weapons of the struggle for power. Thus early on, children learn the arts and weaponry of self-deception, oppression and evasion. Although this is morally debilitating, it is often the only recourse available to children to survive within the family.[14]

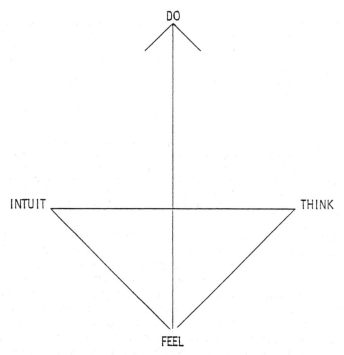

Figure 2-A: The Whole Person

Sex-role scripting in the American family has been explored by Hogie Wyckoff. Wyckoff states:

> The definitions of male and female roles are, from day one, intensively socialized into children and these same definitions are constantly reinforced throughout our lives. Classically, a man is "supposed to be" rational, productive and hardworking, but he is not "supposed to be" emotional, in touch with his feelings, or overtly loving. On the other hand, a woman is not supposed to think rationally, be able to balance the checkbook, or be powerful. She can supply the man she relates to with the emotional feelings functions that are missing in him, and he can take care of business for her. These... are the extreme characteristics of male/female sex roles. Obviously all people do not completely fit into these roles.[15]

The implications of this for traditional roles and expectations assigned to men and women in bureaucratic organizations is obvious. Men are the "managers" and women are the "secretaries." Men "think" and women "do." Men chair the meetings and women prepare the coffee and the minutes. Men and women surrender their competence and authentic personal power in organizations and groups to roles, but people can only play roles by "detaching" themselves from their real feelings. Sex-role scripting contributes to this.[16] As children we are whole people, containing the potential of developing into whole, mature adults, capable of thinking, intuiting, doing and feeling. Male-female roles learned early in life split this wholeness. Child rearing practices among other things frequently and specifically circumscribe and inhibit boys' feelings and intution, while girls specifically are circumscribed and inhibited concerning doing and thinking. Boys are supported to think and do. Girls are supported to feel and intuit. Yet all four of these human characteristics are available for each person to use and develop except where physical damage precludes it. Figure 2-A is a graphic summary of the whole person.

These messages are delivered to children every day, sometimes hourly, often with severe penalties, certainly with accompanying approbation and disapprobation. Thus are children taught to ignore and often deny their own feelings. Consequently, as adults in bureaucratic settings, they are "split" and divided from their real feelings. Here there is no need to face one's own emotions. If indeed a glimmer of feeling rears its head, it is embarrassing and causes consternation and one seeks to immediately regain "control." The human being now becomes an "actor" and finds a degree of "safety" in his new role. In this process formal authority is protected from challenge and personal "freedom" is conditioned on good behavior which, in turn, rests upon powerlessness. Fully trained by family and school, young men and women are ready to take their places in the loveless, joyless, mindless organization laden with the dynamics of power, unaware of what lies ahead. Now the stage is set to explore the context of life in a banal work group.

Banal Work Groups: Lovelessness

"The Wicked Witch"

She thought of a new way to kill my love
for the beautiful Munchkin maiden, and made
my axe slip again, so that it cut right through
my body, splitting me in two halves. Once
more the tinner came to my help and made me a
body of tin, fastening my tin arms and
legs and head to it, by means of joints, so
that I could move around as well as ever.
But, alas! I had now no heart, so that I
lost all my love for the Munchkin girl, and
did not care whether I married her or not.[17]

[Spoken by the Tin Woodman in *The Wizard of Oz.*]

Lovelessness is taught and maintained through carefully delineated cultural and social imperatives which may be designated the "stroke economy." Berne defined a stroke as "a unit of social recognition." They are essential to individual human survival or, as Berne averred in their absence, "your spine shrivels up," and he meant it in the literal sense. Strokes can be positive or negative, purchased or freely given, verbal, nonverbal or through touching. In the "stroke economy," strokes are in scarce supply. Since this is so, they must be earned. This is taught in the home and maintained on the job. The rules of the stroke economy are:

(1) Strokes may be only rarely given and then only under special circumstances;

(2) No strokes may be requested;

(3) No strokes may be accepted (they must be discounted);

(4) All strokes received must be humbly and quickly discounted.

The word "stroke" is less emotionally loaded than the word "love." In groups and organizations the word "love" is often ignored, ridiculed and put down in conversation on the job and in the academy. Rather, words such as very competent, greatly admired, fine scholar, revered professor, superb craftsman, respected colleague, a fine engineer, etc. are disguised substitutes quite acceptable for the expression of sensitive and caring feelings. When the word love is used it becomes a subject embarrassing to speak of, frequently evoking cynical comments and sarcastic derision. This drives out the possibility of tenderness within the work group and successfully evades dealing in an overt, straightforward level with the underlying sexual connotations which occur often in work groups and are frequently ignored to the subsequent peril of the group. Sometimes covert sexual signals are used manipulatively, thus souring trust and putting off caring relationships.

Nurture and care are different than an explicit sexual relationship, yet frequently in a group or organization nurture and care are mistaken for sexual overtures. Since this is risky, an environment is created where neither genuine nurture or care are available. Frequently, this is done through ridicule, put-downs, sarcasm and the like, which makes risking care for another group member easier to avoid. In actuality, if dealt with openly and in a straightforward manner, nurture, tenderness and care could become available and arrangements concerning sexual attractions and wishes put aside and dealt with at a more appropriate time and in more effective ways. Steiner observes, "Strokes are necessary for human survival, and when people can not obtain positive strokes, they will settle for negative strokes because they too, even though they feel bad, are life supportive."[18] Thus the tin woodman performed his group task and got his "strokes" from time to time from an oil can!

In the work situation, "organizational strokes" becomes translated into an elaborate fabric of rewards and punishments that relate to pay, space allocations and furnishings, and a host of other factors that are specific to each particular work situation. The goal is to control, manipulate, manage easily and guarantee a steady worker who performs with little resistance all assigned tasks in efficient ways. Thus a worker interested in being good and pleasing his supervisor and doing well will be neither recalcitrant nor questioning of the tasks and roles assigned. This makes for good employees but irresponsible human beings.

The stroke econony is a characteristic of a typical (banal) work group. When the rules are "broken" the group reacts to the "violator" with embarrassment, discomfort, sometimes anger, and behavior which increases the social-psychological "distance" between. This is a primary aspect of a banal work group.

Banal Work Groups: Joylessness

> When Dorothy, who was an orphan, first came
> to her, Aunt Em had been so startled by the child's

> laughter that she would scream and press her hand
> upon her heart whenever Dorothy's merry voice reached
> her ears; and she still looked at the little girl
> with wonder that she could find anything to laugh at.[19]
>
> [Nonverbal communication from Auntie Em, *The Wizard of Oz*.]

Joyfulness is sometimes accompanied with loud talk, laughter and raucousness. These are considered an anathema at the work place. They are frequently discouraged and often penalized. They are thought to be disruptive of the work environment. Here again, the lessons of childhood are continued and reinforced in the banal work group. Primary "basic training" for joylessness is obtained through injunctions and attributions. Attributions are ascribing behavior and actions of someone to another person. These can be negative or positive: "You will end up a drunk like your Uncle Harry," "You're going to be a doctor, just like your father." On the job they might sound like, "You're as bad as George, you never get anything done on time," or "Kathryn, this is a superb analysis, you are going to end up a department chief just like Helen." Injunctions include such commands as: "Don't be playful," "You're stupid," "Don't jump," "Don't cause trouble," "Be seen and not heard," "Sit still." The words ought to and should have also accompany injunctive training statements which are continued in use within the work environment. Expectations around "ought to" and "should have" are soon learned and reinforced by gesture, word and action. Being "sent to coventry" in a British factory would deny a worker any verbal involvement from his fellow workers. Silence here is full of meaning and it is a clear message: "Shape up or ship out." Auntie Em successfully communicated to Dorothy the dangers of being joyful by the gesture to her heart which she made with her hand. Sometimes injunctions are reinforced through a wide variety of home remedies falling in the general category of punishment. The goal is to develop and maintain a compulsive, ritualistically oriented person who will behave, keep his or her eyes down on the desk and the "nose to the grindstone."

The natural curiosity and wonder felt about ourselves and our environment and the natural propensity to explore everything with awe and wonder is turned aside and the good, efficient, compulsive worker becomes the ideal toward which we are taught to strive. Organizations and the work groups therein reflect aspects of the basic training in lovelessness and joylessness that the worker learned at home as a child, had reinforced in school, and now continues within the banal work group. Two other components of the banal work group remain to be identified: mindlessness and powerlessness.

Banal Work Groups: Mindlessness

> ...but the old crow comforted me, saying:
> "If you only had brains in your head you would
> be as good as any of them, and a better man than
> some of them. Brains are the only thing worth
> having in this world, no matter whether one is
> a crow or a man.
>
> (and later)
>
> "If this road goes in, it must come out," said
> the Scarecrow, "and as the Emerald City is at the
> other end of the road, we must go wherever it leads us."

"Anyone would know that," said Dorothy.
"Certainly, that is why I know it," returned
the Scarecrow. "If it required brains to figure
it out, I should never have said it."[20]

[Of the Scarecrow – *The Wizard of Oz*.]

Curiosity, the urge to learn and to know, intuition, the ability to perceive and to know things without conscious reasoning, and reasoning, the intellectual use of inference and deduction, have all at one time or another been considered part of the "black arts" and witchcraft and, periodically throughout history, have been circumscribed and condemned. Those individuals brave enough to pursue them have been hounded, reviled, persecuted and killed. Socrates was given the choice of hemlock or exile for misleading the young; Galileo had to recant his theory of astronomy because it went against the popular, conventional wisdom of the times; Anne Hutchinson, a serious thinker about religious matters, questioned some of the Puritan beliefs held as truth by the Puritans of the Massachusetts Bay Colony. She was tried as a witch and exiled and finally killed in an Indian uprising. All these persons pursued truth; all were thwarted by those who held power and held sway over the conventional wisdom of the time.[21]

Gaining awareness and pursuing the frontiers of knowledge have been almost steadily opposed in history by the frightened masses of people who attributed magic and wizardry to the scientist and scholar and opposed, too, by the leading and powerful governing authorities of the time who see threats to their control in the pursuit of the unknown. Anne Hutchinson was guilty because she had not learned her sex role very well. Women were expected to attend church, raise children, and keep the home. Here is a dramatic example of the social consequences of behavior which falls outside the scripted sex role. In girls and women, rational thinking is attacked in the crucible of the home; and in boys and men, their feelings and intuition suffers the same fare. Each one of these is an essential component of personal authentic power. Their full development in each human being is generally discouraged and thwarted.

Rationality and intuition are defeated through discounting, lying and the accompanying punishment for misbehavior in their use. Discounts are directed toward intuition, emotions and rationality. Discounting is revealed by such phrases as, "You're stupid," "Dummy," "That's nothing to be frightened of," or when, "No, I'm not really mad at you," is sharply contradicted by behavior. If the facts are investigated and the perceptions and understanding of the person called as stupid, it would rebut the epitaph. When the phrase, "There's nothing to be frightened of," is used, the listener's genuinely felt fear is essentially ridiculed. A denial of anger may be said with teeth and fists clenched and the body taut in a manner which gives the lie to the words and thereby discounts the valid perception of the person to whom it is spoken. In this instance, body language betrays the words. In the quote from the scarecrow in *The Wizard of Oz*, the crow observed the absence of any brains in the scarecrow's head, a full discount – yet as the story proceeds the group's survival depends upon the "brains" of the scarecrow. Dorothy also participated in discounting the perceptions and statements of purpose voiced by the scarecrow.

Lies, half-truths, partial truths, and omissions of truth are a fundamental part of every person's childhood. Media advertising specializes in half-truths, politicians court us with lies of omission and commission, parents frequently tell their children blatant, bold-faced lies about what they do, where they go, Santa Claus, childbirth and sex. Steiner observes:

> *Lying and secrecy are powerful influences in scripting for Mindlessness, and lies along with discounts are capable of producing the kind of mental confusion which is called "schizophrenia" and which I prefer to call madness.* [22]

In organizations, discounting and lying occur in varying intensity and the pathology related to this within governmental organizations led us and kept us in an unwanted war, *viz.,* Viet Nam. It brought a president's resignation, it led competent public safety organization officials to violate the very law they took an oath to uphold, to the relocation of Japanese-Americans into concentration camps, and the Germans under Hitler to the ominous attempt at total genocide of the Jewish population under its control.

The impact of Mindlessness on organizational life is insidious, as the compulsion to "succeed" frequently blinds those who pursue it to the moral implications of their choices. Most work groups may reflect some degree of mindlessness. The depths and dimensions of mindlessness within a work group have been expressed recently in the Watergate affair and in some of its more elaborate consequences. Young men found it easy to commit perjury — to lie. Respectable agents of the C.I.A. and the F.B.I. found it convenient to violate the laws they were sworn to uphold. [23]

The systematic attack on intelligence, intuition and feelings continues into the great majority of work situations. People are told not to feel, what to feel, what to believe, what to think, not to trust one's own feelings, not to trust the fact one sees, not to trust anything but the facts that are presented. Secrecy and "the official reason" explain away the final vestiges of humanness in the work situation. Thus through injunctions and attributions, particularly those which seem to be in friendly banter, such as "You're stupid," "What's the matter, Dummy?" continue the effective discounting and sustain the message of mental incompetence. The goal is to obtain a docile, disciplined, powerless worker capable of manipulation without question and control without concern. In short, a worker who will do as he is told, no questions asked. The rules for the maintenance of mindlessness in the organization are (1) Don't think; (2) Don't feel; and (3) Don't say what you think. Thus the third component in the banal work group is complete.

Banal Work Groups: Powerlessness

"Don't you dare bite Toto! You ought to be
ashamed of yourself, a big beast like you, to
bite a poor little dog!"

"I didn't bite him," said the Lion, as he
rubbed his nose with his paw where Dorothy had
hit it.

"No, but you tried to," she retorted. "You
are nothing but a big coward."

"I know it," said the Lion, hanging his head
in shame; "I've always known it. But how can I
help it?"

(and later)

So he sprang into the water, and the Tin Woodman

caught fast hold of his tail, when the Lion began
to swim with all his might toward the shore.[24]

[About the Lion in *The Wizard of Oz*.]

Sometime ago while standing in a checkout line in a local supermarket ready to
have my groceries costed so that I could depart, I was standing behind a young,
harassed mother. She had a full basket of groceries and in the little place where you
could put a babe in arms in the grocery basket was a child in diapers and at her feet
was a little girl about eight and a little boy about age four, perhaps three. The little
boy was pursuing his natural curiosity, checking out at his level all the various things
on which his eyes rested. Then he reached for them, making an attempt to feel and
discover their nature. The girl, about eight, had been assigned the task of caring for
her younger brother, and she was exasperated at having to chase this little boy all
over the store and prevent him from creating havoc of the supermarket shelves.
Finally, exasperated, she hauled off and hit her little brother. Upon seeing the incident, the mother turned around, reached back as far as she could and gave the little
girl a swift, hard slap across the face with the back of her hand, uttering the following
words: "There, that'll teach you to hit your little brother." My response was, "Yes,
Madam, indeed it will!" In that simple little story is told how the family teaches
powerlessness.

Steiner identifies the process involved in this incident The Rescue Game.[25]
Steven Karpman identifies this process as The Drama Triangle, i.e., there are three
basic positions: Victim, Persecutor, Rescuer, arranged around a triangle in which the
persons involved switch from one role to another.[26] In the story, several roles and
quick switches in positions on the drama triangle are apparent. The little daughter
"rescues" the mother from taking care of her little brother; the daughter, out of
resentment and exasperation, persecutes the little brother; and thereby becomes
the victim of her mother's exasperation (her mother's own feelings of victimization)
at having to shop and simultaneously care for three under school-age children.

In the opening vignette to this section from *The Wizard of Oz* the lion is a Victim
subject to a Persecution transaction from Dorothy. Later he is involved in a Rescue
of his fellow sojourners to Oz who are caught in a raft in rough water. Figure 2-B
is a graphic representation of the Rescue (Drama) Triangle.

Within organizational work groups the drama triangle is acted out in many ways
and many times with a variety of participants, sometimes including fairly elaborate
alliances. Each person may play one of these roles at one time or another as it relates
to peers, subordinates, supervisors, or themselves. The family creates a propensity
in most human beings to be comfortable in relationships where they are either
"one-up" or "one-down" to other human beings.[27] Specifically, the family teaches
powerlessness to some of its members and techniques of power to others through
the use of the Rescue or Drama Triangle. Later the destructive consequences of this
Drama (Rescue Game) are infinite and repeated daily within the context of the
organization and within the banal work groups that perform the activity of the organization. Steiner suggests that most of the "games people play" comprise the bulk
of their daily transactions with each other and are simply "power plays." Furthermore, he suggests, the particular types of power plays in which each person engages
are pathetic repetitions of the games one once learned and was forced to use for
survival as a child in the arena of the family power struggles.[28]

The Rescue Triangle

Barbara Brown

Figure 2-B: From Claude Steiner, *Scripts People Live*, New York, Grove Press, Inc., 1974, p. 148

Powerlessness within the organization is continued by controlling the social and work context in which each person is involved; controlling the nature, variety and quality of the decisions a person makes on the job; and denying individual participation in the design of his or her work and the time-frames involved. The careful prescribing of work boundaries and tasks isolates the worker from situations that would enable him or her to risk, to learn and to grow other than within the prescribed manner of the organization. When secrecy is added to the context of power and renders additional information crucial to full understanding unavailable to the individual, powerlessness is sustained. This kind of one-up and one-down relationship with one's fellow workers and supervisors is encompassed in hierarchy but goes beyond it and sustains a primary cultural value, *viz.* competition.

This experience of being one-up and one-down to a whole variety of people is so common to us that we think it is natural and to be expected, and that we should react to it by trying as hard as we can to succeed and to get ahead. The truth is most persons dislike competitive struggle and are more easily enthused and more safely motivated through cooperative endeavors. Yet competitiveness and individualism are so highly touted that they interfere with the capacity for people to develop cooperative and equal relations.[29]

Persons who occupy "one-up" roles to someone else look more powerful, frequently feel more powerful (while at the same time harboring doubts about it) and are within the organization more powerful. This power, however, is the facade of power; it is connected with role; it is temporary and not authentic, genuine, personal power. Sometimes occupants in these roles confuse such a role with their own identity and merge with it in such a manner as to be synonymous with it. The authentic human personality is lost in the role. The characters of the *Oz* story represent a "work group" which has a specific task, *viz.*, to get to Oz. Each has a banal script which limits the skills available for each. Yet together they pool their limited scripted resources and develop a whole work group utilizing all of their skills cooperatively to accomplish their task, e.g. the cowardly lion, scripted into powerlessness, nevertheless uses his courage to which he is blind to aid the group to achieve its goal. It is now possible to see more clearly and more precisely the nature of the work in the modern organization.

Banal Work Groups: Mood and Ambience

In the organizational, technological, industrial society of today, the overwhelming number of persons involved spend the greater part of their waking life and day within the confines of a "work group." Such groups exist for the purpose of conducting organizational tasks. They vary in size from small, perhaps three to five persons, to somewhat large, involving "pools" of people such as clerk-typists, assembly line workers and the like.

The banal work group in a modern industrial society is mystified, alienated, and oppressed. This is reflected in group interaction and the transactions of group members. Interpersonal relationships of group members are generally competitive, calculated to avoid intimacy and laden with the drama of power plays. Transactions with authority and authority figures are characterized by fear, criticism, negative responses, resentments. Organizational rules and orders reinforce the alienating nature of the work environment, and management is seen more often as rigid and insensitive. Most groups are subject to more or less rigid controls relating to monitoring standards, job performance and evaluation, and personnel reviews.

These banal work groups generally range through the organizational hierarchy and exist for the purpose of conducting organizational tasks. They reflect a matrix of power specific to the group and organization. Each worker and manager brings his or her own individual conscious and subconscious psychological paraphernalia, personal skills and competence to the group and to the task assigned. On one level, organziational members perform tasks; another level, they act out hidden psychological agenda — sometimes conscious — more often below their own consciousness. The tone, the mood and the context of power within the group and organization reflect an everchanging matrix within which covert and overt transactions and processes take place.

The daily world of work seems to alternate between barren, arid, boring and empty, routinized work, ritualistic interaction and a real world jungle of feeling hidden from view, full of anger, disappointment, fear, sorrow, suffering and sometimes poignant caring. The feelings and capabilities associated with awareness, spontaneity and intimacy which comes with most human beings at birth are generally out of view and out of reach for most members of a work group. Men and women in banal work groups grow dull and the consciousness of other alternatives seems beyond their awareness and understanding. When a group or individual is presented an opportunity to change it is no surprise to observe the members of a work group struggle to defend the fetters of their own alienation. To risk the unfamiliar is very fearful, and people often prefer the spurious comfort and blindness of the familiar situation.

The payoffs for the participants are, first, pay in return for labor to earn their daily bread; second, ritualized management of very fearful feelings; third, turning away the wrath of the authority figure by being a good worker; and, finally, obtaining some feeling of security and identity, however self-deceptive that is in actuality. The payoffs for management are thought to be steady labor, no conflict and dependable production. The banal work group itself is alienated, rigid, controlled, and without creativity or enthusiasm.

The Context of Alienation and Oppression

Each person carries to his or her adult tasks childhood patterns concerning the use of these human capacities, i.e., joy, love, mindfulness, sorrow, powerfulness, etc. How each person expresses these in a group and how they are received by a group in which one is a member has important implications for the kind of roles which develop within such groups.

Federal, state and local employees who have been my students over a period of several years were asked to identify aspects of their work situation where they felt oppressed and they articulated observations which expose the mindlessness, joylessness, lovelessness, and powerlessness which characterize their work situation and reveal the transactions which maintain such scripting in existence. The following are some selected examples of their observations:

1) Discounting = Mindlessness

"Decision making has to go through so many channels which make matters more difficult and when I ask why, they reply, 'I have to make my own decisions,' when in reality I have recommended that decision and get no credit for it."

"I feel oppressed on my job when my superior tells me to write a report or perform a project in a certain way and forgets his original instructions and gives me entirely new instructions which are different a few weeks later. Not only does this cause a lot of extra work, but it usually includes a mild reprimand for not doing it correctly the first time."

"I feel oppressed on my job when there's no work to do."

"I feel oppressed on my job when I am assigned a task without knowing for what the results will be used and I find out later that I took the wrong approach because I did not know."

2) Injunctions = Joylessness

"I feel oppressed when I am told what to wear on my job and how to fix my hair. I have no say in what affects my lifestyle, including the punch card record, my clocking in and out and I am called a troublemaker when I don't go along with the boss's petty instructions on dress and behavior."

"When I make a suggestion about a better way of doing a particular procedure and I am looked at as though I have made waves and I am told that I should not make waves."

3) Stroke Economy = Lovelessness

"I feel oppressed on my job when I feel that my efforts are not supported by the administrators and end up feeling like I'm making empty motions in the air."

"I feel oppressed on my job when no one appreciates the work I have done and the effort I have put into it."

4) Rescue Triangle = Powerlessness

"I feel oppressed on my job when fellow employees criticize my decisions or actions after the fact and say, "You should have done such and such...""

"I feel oppressed on my job when I discover that my superiors have discussed at length assignments involving my skills. I am the last to know and usually do not have a choice as to whether I'd like to perform the work."

"I am oppressed on my job when certain employees who are unhappy with their jobs turn on those of us who have taken additional training in order to improve our job performance and conditions."

"I feel oppressed on my job when I hear through the grapevine that we're going to have some sort of change and the administration won't or doesn't talk about it."

"I feel oppressed on my job when information related to my job is witheld from me, not only from the management within my own agency, but from other city departments as well, with which we interface under normal circumstances."[30]

These responses from public employees at the federal, state and local levels of government reflect the conditions characteristic of banal work groups in the public service.

Members of groups such as these, like the sojourners to Oz, labor under mystified oppression. Each person reflects his own scripting and articulates his own unique variety of oppression. The Scarecrow, e.g., constantly engages in self-discounts and self-deprecation while, at the same time, exhibiting remarkable intelligence and reason in the conduct of his assumed task. Each seeks to obtain from a source outside himself the very thing each has within but has hidden from his own consciousness. Is it not so with persons in most groups, including work groups?

Sometimes this oppression is so comfortable members do not seek a release from it, but rather seek to maintain it! The most extreme example is shown by the men who, upon being released from prison soon return, pounding on the prison doors (or commit a crime again) to get back in so they may enjoy the "freedom of their chains." It is so painful for these men to be "on the outside" that the seductive security and seeming comfort of being one-down draws these men to return to the illusory comfort of their own unique oppression.

Perhaps the most insidious and pervasive characteristic of the banal work group is not the nature of the task a worker performs or the task of the group but rather the matrix of power and the power plays, games and scenarios which occur within such groups and within the organization as well. This is the most dramatic activity within the banal work group and reflects the ongoing nature of power relationships among the various levels of the hierarchy and the membership and among group members themselves. The most ominous implications of this is that under these conditions a considerable proportion of persons within groups, organizations and bureaucracy do what they are told to do with little heed to the moral implications of conscience, so long as they perceive the order of command comes from "legitimate authority."[31] An understanding of these power relationships is crucial to the reduction, modification and elimination of worker oppression and achieving in the long run effective productivity in a humane way.

Rosabeth Moss Kanter suggests a variation to Lord Acton's axiom, "Power tends to corrupt and absolute power corrupts absolutely," *viz.*, powerlessness tends to corrupt and absolute powerlessness corrupts absolutely. Kanter, e.g., has observed that the relatively powerless in positions of organizational authority use more authoritarian control, discipline, coercian and threats which, in turn, provokes resistance and aggression which then prompts such managers to be even more coercive, controlling and restrictive. Thus the drama triangle is maintained in this manner inside the organization between powerful feeling managers and employees who feel powerless. Elliot Jaques observes "In hard reality... manager subordinate relationships are two-way reciprocal relationships and not just one-way downwards coercive relationships."[33] This realization has rather profound implications for organizational design.

The many corruptions of powerlessness associated with groups, organizations and bureaucracies may be dangerous as an excessive concentration of power at the "top" of such organizations. Indeed, it may be suggested that absolute power at the top of an organization requires reciprocal absolute and total powerlessness at the bottom of an organization. Thus as power increases in concentration at the top it is ever more diluted and subordinated at the lower levels. In organizations where there is still available energy and where there are still low levels of fear and high levels of frustration among those who occupy the lower levels of the organizational pyramid there will be a tendency to develop rules, regulations and delaying strategies and tactics. These are generally expressions of frustration, fear and the urge to survive on the part of people who feel powerless and seek to make others heed them, if only through delays and protectionist tactics. Thus it is important to understand more fully the structural concomitants and the behavioral sources of personal powerlessness as a necessary requisite to rectify human alienation within groups or organizations or bureaucracies.

The travelers to Oz were each alienated from a part of themselves. Each one internalized and "believed" he did not have the missing piece he sought. Each had special skills which could be utilized by the group which the others seemingly did not have. Each was uniquely blind to his own power. Paradoxically, within the group each member could use that part of themselves in the interest of the group which they otherwise had to deny. Thus by cooperating together in a group they were able to effectively use what each had to give in order to successfully complete their task. So it is with most work or task groups; the somewhat alienated members (through specialization, coordination and supervision) are able to accomplish work. Certainly, there are advantages, gains and payoffs from such efforts. Yet such a group is not intrinsically satisfying. The human alienation and the pathology of such groups is continued, internalized and remains unsolved.

Persons blind to their own emotional processes become irresponsible in how his or her emotions then are delivered or transacted within a group. It behooves the members of a group to become aware and responsible, to elevate to a conscious level the emotional interactions which occur within the context of the group and gain awareness as to how this links and enmeshes with the larger organization.

SUMMARY

The daily world of organizational work occurs in a setting which reflects the love-lessness, joylessness, mindlessness and powerlessness which were learned in childhood within the family and to which sex role scripting has contributed significantly to the outcome. Cooperative groups and hamartic (tragic) groups have infrequently issued from banal work groups to influence profoundly the quality and productivity of the group, and, in the case of hamartic groups, altering the very nature of the group in awesome ways.

Power is the primary currency of relations within an organization. Supervision and subordinate/superordinate relations in organizational settings reflect to a varying degree a panorama of power relationships. Such relationships are fraught with difficulty in practice and spawn a variety of irresponsibilities when the urge to power waxes and personal integrity and competent judgment wanes. This is the shadowy side of organization which damages the human psyche and requires ratification if we are to fully enjoy the benefits to the person and to society organization can bring.

NOTES

1. Claude Steiner, *Scripts People Live*, N.Y., Grove Press, 1974, p. 70 & pp. 97-98.

2. Interview with a District Supervisor, State of California Contractor's Licensing Board, March 16, 1977 conducted by the author.

3. The concepts of banal work groups and tragic or hamartic work groups are related to the way individuals are prepared to live their lives. My use of the terms here is directly linked to the work of Claude Steiner, *op. cit.*, pp. 97-160; cf. Peter M. Newton and Daniel J. Levinson, "The Work Group Within Organization: A Sociopsychological Approach," in *Psychiatry*, Vol. 36, May 1973, pp. 115-142.

4. Eric Berne, *Transactional Analysis in Psychotherapy*, N.Y., Grove Press, 1961, p. 4; Steiner, *op. cit.*, pp. 69-70, 97-104; Muriel James and Dorothy Jongeward, *Born to Win*, Reading, Mass., Addision-Wesley Publishing Co., 1971, pp. 69-95.

5. On the Jonestown ending of the Peoples Temple, see *Newsweek*, December 4, 1978, and Arthur Janou, "For Control Cults Must Ease the Most Profound Pains," *L.A. Times*,

December 10, 1978, Part VI, p. 3; see also Marshall Kilduff and Ron Javers, *The Suicide Cult: The Inside Story of the Peoples Temple Sect and the Massacre in Guyana*, N.Y., Bantam, 1979; Charles A. Krause with Lawrence M. Stern, Richard Harwood and Frank Johnston, *Guyana Massacre: The Eyewitness Account*, Berkley Press, 1979; John Maguire and Mary Lee Dunn, *Hold Hands and Die: The Incredibly True Story of the Peoples Temple and the Rev. Jim Jones*, N.Y., Dale Books, 1979; Jeannie Mills, *Six Years with God: Life Inside Reverend Jim Jones' Peoples Temple*, N.Y., Avon Publishers, 1979; Diane Johnson, "Heart of Darkness," *New York Review of Books*, April 19, 1979; on My Lai see Note 1, Chapter 1; on the Committee to Re-elect the President (Nixon) see among others Carl Bernstein and Bob Woodward, *All the President's Men*, N.Y., Simon and Schuster, Inc., 1974; John J. Sirica, *To Set the Record Straight: The Break-in, The Tapes, The Conspirators, The Pardon*, N.Y., Norton, 1979; Leon Jaworski, *The Right and the Power: The Prosecution of Watergate*, N.Y., Readers Digest Press, 1976.

6. For the published report on F.B.I. activities see the *L.A. Times*, April 26, 1977, Part I, p. 4; see also Note 1, Chapter 1; concerning the published report on the A.E.D. see *Newsweek*, April 30, 1979.

7. See Steiner, *op. cit.*, p. 68, pp. 98-103, and p. 233; and Eric Berne, *What Do You Say After You Say Hello?*, N.Y., Grove Press, 1972, pp. 225-229.

8. Barry E. Collins and Harold Guetzkow, *A Social Psychology of Group Processes for Decision Making*, John Wiley & Sons, Inc., pp. 89-90.

9. Max Weber, *Economy and Society*, edited by Guenter Roth and Claus Wittich, Bedminster Press, N.Y., 1968, p. 359, pp. 363-4.

10. Eric Berne, *Games People Play*, N.Y., Grove Press, 1964, p. 183.

11. Steiner, *op. cit.*, p. 105; for a psychoanalytic analysis of the uses and consequences of fear and anxiety in childhood see Erik H. Erikson, *Childhood and Society*, (2nd ed.), N.Y., W.W. Norton Co., Inc., 1963, pp. 48-108 and pp. 403-424 but *esp.* pp. 405-413.

12. Weber, *Economy and Society, op. cit.*, pp. 359-364, *et. seq.*

13. Ronald B. Sampson, *The Psychology of Power*, N.Y., Vintage Books, 1965, p. 29.

14. John Stuart Mill, "The Subjection of Women," in John Stuart Mill, *Three Essays: On Liberty, Representative Government, The Subjection of Women*, London, Oxford University Press, 1975, pp. 427-549. For more on this aspect of J.S. Mill's thought, see Sampson, *op. cit.*, pp. 45-113; cf. Claude Steiner, *op. cit.*, pp. 165-6; and Adrienne Rich, *Of Woman Born*, W.W. Norton, N.Y., 1976, *passim*.

15. In Steiner, *op. cit.*, p. 165. See also Dorothy Dinnerstein, *The Mermaid and the Minotaur: Sexual Arrangements and the Human Malaise*, N.Y., Harper-Row, 1976, *passim.* Dinnerstein examines with great clarity the origins and maintenance of this split of human wholeness into sex role differentiation with males expressing mastery, enterprise, worldmaking, while women represent the body, immediate feeling and experience, and a direct connection with the physical and social environment. Further, she explores the way men and women have collaborated in creating this situation.

16. It may be thought that the recent women's movement has changed this. Such is not the case, although inroads have been made. See Eleanor Brantly Schwartz, *The Sex Barrier In Business*, Atlanta, Ga., Publishing Services Division, Georgia State University, 1971, p. 50 *et. seq.*, Rosalind Loring and Theodora Wells, *Breakthrough: Women into Management*, N.Y., Van Nostrand Reinhold Co., Inc., 1972, p. 29 *et. seq.*; and *esp.* Harold H. Frank, *Women in Organization*, Philadelphia, University of Pennsylvania Press, 1977, pp. 273-275.

17. L. Frank Baum, *The Wizard of Oz*, Chicago, Ill., Reilly and Lee Co., 1900, copyright renewed, 1956, p. 58. See also Loren Eiseley, *The Unexpected Universe*, N.Y., Harcourt, Brace Jovanovich, 1964, pp. 124-146.

18. Steiner, *op. cit.*, p. 107.

19. L. Frank Baum, *The Wizard of Oz, op. cit.*, pp. 10-12; on the importance of joy see especially W. Shutz, *Joy: Expanding Human Awareness*, N.Y., Grove Press, 1967.

20. *Ibid.*, p. 45, 47.

21. For information on Socrates' choice see Plato, *The Trial and Death of Socrates*, trans.

from the Greek, Benjamin Jowett, N.Y., Heritage Press, 1963 and Alfred Edward Taylor, *Socrates*, Garden City, N.Y., Doubleday, 1953; for information on Galileo see Tommaso Campanella, *The Defense of Galileo*, (trans. and edited with introduction and notes by Grant McColleg), N.Y., Arno Press, 1975 and George de Santillana, *The Crime of Galileo*, Chicago, University of Chicago Press, 1955; for information on Anne Hutchinson see Deborah Crawford, *Four Women in a Violent Time: Anne Hutchinson (1591-1643) Mayer Dyer (1591-1660) Lady Deborah Moody (1600-1659) Penelope Stout (1622-1732)*, N.Y., Crown Publishers, 1970 and Helen Augur, *An American Jezebel: The Life of Anne Hutchinson*, N.Y., Brentano's, 1930.

22. Steiner, *op. cit.*, p. 133. See pp. 118-138 for a full development of this concept.

23. For some variations on this theme see Irving Janis, *Victims of Groupthink*, Boston, Houghton-Mifflin Co., Inc., 1972, *passim*; William H. Blanchard, *Aggression American Style*, Santa Monica, Ca., Goodyear Publishing Co., Inc., 1978, *passim*; and Lewis Yablonski, *Robopaths: People as Machines*, Baltimore, Md., Bobbs-Merrill Co., 1972, *passim*.

24. L. Frank Baum, *The Wizard of Oz*, *op. cit.*, p. 63 and 82.

25. Steiner, *op. cit.*, pp. 146-154.

26. Stephen B. Karpman, "Script Drama Analysis," *Transactional Analysis Bulletin*, 7, 26, 1968, pp. 39-43.

27. Steiner, *op. cit.*, p. 151; see generally Erik H. Erikson, *Childhood and Society*, *op. cit.*, pp. 48-108.

28. Steiner, *op. cit.*, pp. 212-222.

29. *Ibid.*, p. 156; see also D. Kaplan, "Power in Perspective" in R. Kahn and E. Boulding (eds.), *Power and Conflict in Organization*, London, Tavistock Publications, 1964, pp. 11-32.

30. These self-revealing statements were collected from Public Administration Practitioners in my graduate seminars through the years 1975-1977 at California State University of Los Angeles; see also generally F. Herzberg, *Work and the Nature of Man*, Cleveland, Ohio, World Publishing Co., Inc., 1966, *passim*, and F. Herzberg, F. Mausner, and B. Snyderman, *The Motivation to Work*, N.Y., Wiley, 1959, *passim*.

31. Stanley Milgram, "Behavioral Study of Obedience," in the *Journal of Abnormal and Social Psychology*, 1963, Vol. 67, pp. 371-378; see also his *Obedience and Authority*, N.Y., Harper & Row, 1974.

32. Rosabeth Moss Kanter, *Men and Women of the Corporation*, N.Y., Basic Books, 1977, pp. 164-205, but particularly pp. 186-197.

33. Elliot Jaques, *A General Theory of Bureaucracy*, N.Y., Halsted Press, John Wiley & Sons, 1976, p. 294.

34. I am indebted to James D. Carroll for the particular focus of concern in this section.

RELATED READING

Berne, Eric, *What Do You Say After You Say Hello?* New York: Grove Press, 1972. An excellent and clear presentation of the original, fertile and exciting advances of Eric Berne in understanding human behavior.

Dinnerstein, Dorothy. *The Mermaid and the Minotaur: Sexual Arrangements and the Human Malaise*. New York: Harper & Row, 1976. Dinnerstein charts the split of human wholeness into sex-role differentiation and examines the distinctive manner in which women and men have collaborated to maintain unresolved that central ambivalence toward enterprise and self-creation which lies at the heart of the human malaise.

Fromm, Eric. *Escape from Freedom*. New York: Holt, Rinehart & Winston Co., Inc., 1941. An important exploration of alienation as it works between the individual and the social system with special attention to the flight of humans from personal responsibility and human wholeness.

Goldberg, Herb. *The Hazards of Being Male: Surviving the Myth of Masculine Privilege*. New York: Nash Publ., 1976. A most significant contribution to understanding today's men. Men have been anesthetized and robotized through a socialization process which requires them to repress and deny an almost total range of emotions and human needs so as to succeed and be masculine. This effort explores the costs of this to men.

Kanter, Rosabeth Moss. *Men and Women of the Corporation*. New York: Basic Books, Inc., 1977. A rich and perceptive book concerning the integral relationship of organizational structure and human problems with particularly valuable contributions centering upon powerlessness, roles of men and women and the opportunities and barriers to needed change and alternate organizational structures.

Laing, R.D. *The Politics of Experience*. New York: Partheon Books, 1967. A truly important book in helping to understand the relationship of alienation, power and projection. An important theoretical underpinning of the conceptual ideas presented in this book.

Rich, Adrienne. *Of Woman Born*. New York: W.W. Norton, Inc., 1976. With great incisiveness and passion, Rich examines the polarity between motherhood as an institution defined and restricted under patriarchy and motherhood as the potential nurturing relationship. Motherhood as an institution is analyzed as the keystone of diverse social and political systems.

Sampson, Ronald B. *The Psychology of Power*. New York: Vintage Books, 1965. An excellent presentation on the corrupting aspects of power and the implication of this for men, women and society. This is a truly important book.

Steiner, Claude. *Scripts People Live*. New York: Grove Press, 1974. This is a superb book. An innovative and creative extension of transactional analysis. This book provides the germinal ideas which underlie much of the work presented in this volume. This is a very special book.

PART II
GROUP AND ORGANIZATIONAL STRUCTURE, AUTHORITY AND PROCESS

Chapter 3
STRUCTURE, AUTHORITY AND DYNAMICS WITHIN GROUPS AND ORGANIZATIONS

To achieve humaneness and effective production within modern organization is a profound challenge. John Stuart Mill, over a century ago, noted the receding liberty of the individual in the emerging industrial democratic society. Mill observed, "Individual spontaneity is hardly recognized by the common modes of thinking as having any intrinsic worth, or deserving any regard of its own account." Mill observed:

> *Supposing it were possible to get houses built, corn grown, battles fought, causes tried, and even churches erected and prayers said, by machinery – by automatons in human form – it would be a considerable loss to exchange for these automatons even the men and women who at present inhabit the more civilized parts of the world... Human nature is not a machine to be built after a model and set to do exactly the work prescribed for it but a tree which requires to grow and develop itself on all sides, according to the inward forces which make it a living thing.*[1]

Mill sought to preserve the liberty of the individual through free and open discussions. Yet the forces threatening the individual continued unabated.

The Organizational Milieu and Alienation

The reduction of human beings into "automatons" presaged the modern concerns articulated so well in the novels of George Orwell, Aldous Huxley and the writing of Jaques Ellul.[2] Lewis Yablonsky identifies the classic disease of organizational life as "robopathology." He identifies robopaths as efficient functionaries and bureaucrats cut off from their feelings, exhibiting robot-like behavior. Specifically, he states, "This dehumanized level of existence places people in roles where they are actors mouthing irrelevant platitudes, experiencing programmed emotions with little or no compassion or sympathy for other people."[3] Herbert Marcuse has identified this condition as one of "perfect alienation" in a one-dimensional society.[4] Yablonsky and Marcuse, among others, warn that where human beings care not for one another, violence easily reaches monstrous proportions.

Rollo May suggests that our survival depends on whether human consciousness can be surfaced, with sufficient strength, to stand against the oppressive, dreary and stultifying consequences and pressures of technological progress. He warns, "We must find ways of sharing and distributing power so that every person in whatever realm of our bureaucratic society can feel that he too counts, that he too makes a difference to his fellows and is not cast out on a dunghill of indifference as a non-person."[5]

In the United States the language of equal rights and the friendly smile disguise the harsh power of bureaucracy. Modern democracy, which nurtured technological bureaucracy, becomes itself captured and made prisoner of that same bureaucracy. The American bureaucrat obscures the authoritarian style of bureaucracy with friendly egalitarian euphemisms. "Casual, seemingly warm, friendly, personal, and non-officious" styles mask American bureaucratic practice.[6]

This spawns an invidious hypocrisy which becomes implicit in bureaucratic relationships. Bensman and Vidich observe:

> In actual bureaucratic practice the subordinate is expected to agree voluntarily with his superior and to suggest the conditions for his subordination without ever openly acknowledging the fact of his subordination. The rhetoric of democracy has become the sine qua non of bureaucratic authoritarianism. [7]

Secrecy, deception and maneuver (fundamental characteristics of power plays) replace clear meaning, honest, direct language and complete the process of mystification. With intriguing elaboration, this drama proceeds amidst an organizational structure which ranges from very simple to very complex in arrangement.

Organizational Structure and Authority

Bureaucratic organization is a system of arranging authority, responsibility, power, prestige and wealth in ever diminishing amounts downward through a pyramidal arrangement of persons and groups. Those entrusted to deliver the organization's mission on the line have the least power, authority and responsibility. Those who have the most power, authority and responsibility are the most remote from the primary (front line) tasks which deliver the organization's purpose. This perspective, however, does not explain the deviations, modifications, and alterations which characterize bureaucratic organizations. A more comprehensive analysis is essential. Bureaucracy may be viewed as an organization or a collectivity of organizations characterized by ordered hierarchical arrangements which contains an established system of authority, described rights and duties; an ordered communication and decision-making system; orderly and systematic recordkeeping; general rules and orders; and established full-time workers.[8] This definition reflects the initial and singular perspective of Max Weber on bureaucracy.

Anthony Downs suggests a somewhat different criteria and observes that Weber's criteria may be comprehended within his own definition, viz. "A bureaucracy is large (where the highest in rank know less than half of all the other members), a majority of its members are full time; hiring, retention and promotion are based on assessment; and the major portion of its output is not evaluated in any markets external to the organization...."[9] Elliot Jaques suggests that "Bureaucracies are systems of work in which people are responsible for using their judgment and discretion in carrying out tasks on behalf of a manager who is accountable for their work."[10] Further Jaques supports that bureaucracy refers to all employment systems whether public or private where a stratified employment hierarchy exists with at least one manager who in turn has a staff of employed subordinates.

Organization is essential to bureaucracy. An organization is a system of consciously coordinated specialized activities, forces and behavior, involving one or more groups, designed and created to achieve specific and determined purposes. This definition is very similar to that of Anthony Downs. If differs in that it adds behavior to the definition and focuses upon groups rather than persons per se.[11] An organization may also be perceived as a collection of fully differentiated persons and groups located within defined or understood boundaries.

All bureaucracy comprehends organizational forms within its network, yet not all organizations are bureaucratic. However, all organizations and bureaucracies are made up of two or more persons which may be called groups. A group is an aggregate collection of people aware of their common relationships and sharing significant boundaries which may, among other things, be spatial and psychological in form.

Bureaucracy, complex organization and small groups have become the subject of great concern and careful study. There is a fertile, abundant and growing literature centering upon the significance, structure, function, and behavior of bureaucracy, organizations and groups.[12]

A fundamental problem of modern organization is its rigidity and its lack of ability and responsiveness to change in order to meet the constantly changing urgencies of the times. Michel Crozier suggests that, "a bureaucratic system of organization" is not able to correct its behavior in the face of its errors and that it is too "rigid to adjust without crisis to the transformations that the accelerated evolution of industrial society makes more and more imperative."[13] It is this conservative, unyielding propensity of organizational behavior which must be more fully addressed and remedied. To this end, further analysis is required.

It is possible to enhance and advance our understanding of bureaucracy, organizations and groups through a systematic analysis using a series of analytic categories which provide a comprehensive view not generally accessible through the more traditional approaches. Five distinctive perspectives may be utilized to disclose organizational arrangements, dynamics and process. **First**, there are the *manifest structures* which are the parts of the organization in public view and are easily ascertainable from both public and organizational record sources. The use of the word *manifest* here is deliberate and intentionally avoids the use of *formal* in reference to organizational structure. It is used here as Jaques uses it, *viz.*, to identify the role relationships as set out in the organization chart.[14] **Second**, there are the *authority matricies* which establish the legitimacy and support of the organizational leadership functions. **Third**, there are the *organizational dynamics* which focus on the forces leading to the cohesion, integration, disintegration and decay, i.e. the survival or death of the organization. Specifically, this involves activity relating to organizational boundaries. **Fourth**, is the *private structure* by which individual group members are integrated into the ongoing organizational and group processes. This is accomplished through linkages which include the way a person perceives such processes and then the way he or she is actually experienced by other members in the concerned group. **Fifth** and finally, *group process* which is concerned with promoting and maintaining the orderly procedures of the concerned group.[15] These conceptual materials are partially derived from some of Eric Berne's less known materials.[16] His work on the structure and dynamics of groups and organizations is a highly useful and precise set of conceptual tools which are of considerable help and provide a distinctive and innovative approach to groups and organizations. Berne offers a systematic, but not fully developed, framework for the "therapy" of ailing groups and organizations. It has not yet been accorded deserved recognition and, consequently, has not come into the full and effective use to which it can be made. The tools and analytical constructs which Berne provides are important, although not completely articulated, advances in analyzing, exploring (in a comprehensive manner) and understanding the behavior and dynamics of groups—healthy, ailing or pathological. Berne's categories begin with *Public Structure*. This is his least well developed category and is not adequate as he presented it because it lacks the sophistication, research, support and insightful understanding he brings to the remaining analytical categories he developed. The phrase manifest structure is more appropriate to express his meaning without getting into the difficulties of dealing with the vagaries, obscuries and historical-legal aspects of the word public. The phrase manifest structure encompasses the expression of an organization and group structure which is publicly ascertainable, distinctive and defined with relative clarity.

The Manifest Structure

The information and data relevant to a full understaning of the structural arrangements of public organizations are generally available to the public. In private organizations this information is less accessible. Limited access even in the public sector may exist where public safety or national defense organizations are involved. There are at least five aspects generally manifested by the formal organizational structure: first, the policy-making aspects; second, the strategic aspects; third, the tactical aspects; fourth, the operational aspects; and fifth, the performance aspects where the work of the organization is actually done.[17]

Policy-making Level. The policy-making level involves design, planning, generalizing and decision concerning the course and direction of an organization's future as well as an accounting for on-going results. These are the boards, and top management in the private sector and the Cabinet level positions in the public sector and involve persons who can abstract policies, set strategies and plans related to the growth and survival of the organization or system of organizations. This level will link into the political and economic context of the social system at the highest policy-making levels. The development, design and application of technological, social and economic theory is of great concern at these levels. An understanding of power which is deeply rooted in experience is essential to success at this level. This level too is deeply concerned with altering and changing social values.

Strategic Level. The strategic aspects of the organization are those functions which generally concern among other things, designing organizational structure and goals, developing the budget, crucial participation in budgetary support decisions affecting the organization and its purpose and developing and maintaining organizational power resources. In the case of policy and budget processes, the public organization frequently initiates and defines the basic materials on which the executive and the legislative rely for their consideration and review. Thus the strategic levels of an organization focus upon planning, programs, and goals, and includes the development and management of the support budget which must have executive and legislative approval prior to implementation. Strategic level structure and activity are disclosed by the formal and nonformal meetings established to conduct the tasks required at this level.

Legislative debates, budget documents, organizational schedules, flow charts, materials prepared for advisory board discussions provide relevant information revealing the specific structure at this level. Key management personnel and the official role they occupy within the organization can be identified. Organizational structure at this level usually responds to the particular skills and competence of the specific person with defined responsibilities. Frequently, the structure and title will be altered to conform to the perceived need to use the full competence available in such a person.

The decision process at this level involves the identification of policy, program development and strategies which relate the organizational program to the information received and deemed significant. Value concerns, public interest concerns, alternatives, options, survival threats, payoffs in losses and gains, and a variety of other considerations are analyzed to derive effective organizational responses which ultimately relate to the survival requirements of the organization.

Tactical Level. The focus here is upon the middle-range of the organization's authority, status and power structure and concern is with integrating and coordinating the total organizational effort, supervision of the myriad groups and organizational subdivisions conducting the work of the organization and communication of the essential information needed to conduct organizational activity. Work at this level is concerned with the programs being implemented throughout the organization. Specifically, management at this level is concerned with implementing and coordinating the activities and tasks necessary to carry out organizational policies and programs. When it is more narrowly conceived it is involved with monitoring expenditure levels, program costs, projected costs, data processing, record keeping, accounting and payroll coordination, and the personnel decision system which identifies work force projections, personnel, staffing, training and review. It is the artifacts of this level which are the subject of organization and management concerns. Here is where the organizational chart, manning tables, and flow charts concerned with the conduct of organizational affairs are articulated. Organizational charts, of which there are an overwhelming variety, indicate the official organizational roles prescribed by management processes. In addition, a roster of the persons occupying these positions is generally available. This gives some idea of the power relationships of the persons involved in an organization. Frequently, such charts and the public revisions reflect ongoing or concluded power struggles within the management.

Operational Level. The focus of this level generally includes front-line supervision separating management from worker. This is the primary task focus of management, linking the management to the worker. In public safety, it is the sergeant in charge of patrol officers; in public welfare, it is the eligibility supervisor in charge of the eligibility workers who actually work the cases; in the hospital, it is the supervising ward nurses, etc. This level identifies the unique aspect of the organization where the work and mission of the organization come into clear view. The activity at this level concerns three functions: the technical function which matches program requirements, priorities, and projections to program operations concerned with programming, scheduling, work performance and work evaluation. Second, the administrative function which conducts the routines related to budget, finance, records, clerical procedures, maintenance, mail and personnel services. Finally, operations which are concerned with material, equipment, space, and supply requirements, and relate their availability to determined organizational needs. Organizational structure at this level is disclosed by space and seating charts and schedules which additionally give clues to power and process within the organizational structure. The operational level is thus concerned with the conduct of administrative supports, technical supports and program operations.

Performance Level. The focus here is upon the collectivity of persons and groups usually, but not always, indentified at the bottom of an organizational chart. These generally are groups of people who accomplish the designed task of the organization. These groups may range from quite small in number to include scores of persons. The process which occurs in these groups link organizational authority to group performance. These groups are charged with the task of getting the work (i.e. purpose) of the organization accomplished. It is at this level where powerlessness and alienation become readily apparent.

Organizational structure identifies the arrangements designed for the accomplishment of the organization's purpose. The primary function of such a structure is to provide an orderly framework within which to conduct the work of the organization. In its simple form it is a social aggregation of people defined by an external boundary separating the members from other persons in the social system and one major internal boundary separating the leader from the rest of the members. It becomes compounded if a modest hierarchy is added. It evolves to a complex form when horizontal differentiation is formally added to an elaboration of the hierarchical structure.[18]

In summary, these are the public aspects of the organizational structure and are respresented visually by organization charts which arrange identified formal roles in relationship one to another and determine as well the number of positions available for each role. This manifest (public) structure, Berne suggests, among other things, identifies the formal role, function, and relationship within each organizational segment. it includes as well a roster of the persons involved in the organization who occupy the roles. This includes indentification of role titles and the incumbent who occupies each of those positions. It involves space and location arrangements which give clues to status and power relationships as well as the task relationships. Schedules, flow charts, procedures involving formal communication systems and record keeping practices are all contained within the manifest structure.

The Authority Matrix

There are two aspects to the organizational authority matrix. The first includes leadership and the second involves canon.[19] Leadership includes the powerful persons who are effective or symbolic determinants of the group's process. Canon is the accumulation of written and unwritten rituals, laws, and custom which regulate the attitudes, behavior and, not infrequently, the dress of the organizational membership. These are primary influences within organizational process which lend purpose and identity to the group and organization.

Organizational authority thus involves not only the explicit aspects of current leadership, but includes the expression and implicit characteristics of a group which are characterized as the traditional influences, unwritten, formal and informal traditions and the rules, regulations and laws which overlay behavior and decision within the organization.

Leadership. Chester I. Barnard suggests that leadership in this context is "an indispensible social essence" that gives common meaning to common purpose, creates incentives, infuses decisions with consistency and inspires personal conviction which produces the cohesiveness to do cooperative work.[20] "Leadership," Philip Selznick suggests, "is a kind of work done to meet the needs of a social situation." He further suggests the institutional leader needs to be fundamentally concerned with the promotion and protection of values.[21] Chester I. Barnard earlier focused on the value orientation of executive leadership:

> *Executive responsibility... is that capacity of leaders by which, reflecting attitudes, ideals, hopes, derived largely from without themselves, they are compelled to bind the wills of men to the accomplishment of purposes beyond their immediate ends, beyond their times.*[22]

This early concern for the relations of value to organizational leadership has become more a facet of policy and decision making studies. Efforts concerned with organizational leadership *per se* center attention upon the search for leadership traits and identification of leadership style. The search for leadership traits and the identification of leadership styles has characterized traditional scholarly approaches to leadership. The search for traits that distinguish leaders from the crowd has not been wholly successful. Some scholars have identified a number of characteristics which have been associated with effective leadership in a variety of situations. Specifically, the following have been suggested:

1) capacity (intelligence, alertness, verbal facility and judgment);

2) achievement (knowledge and athletic accomplishments);

3) responsibility (dependability, initiative, persistence, aggressiveness);

4) participation (activity, adaptability);

5) status (socio-economic postion and popularity).[23]

Whether these result from leadership experience or are distinctive precedent traits is moot. They seem to be at least culturally specific to urban technological civilization, if not universal. Collins and Guetzkow suggest each of these personal characteristics could contribute to overcoming task, environmental and interpersonal obstacles. The importance of a particular characteristic would depend upon the nature of the task or obstacle.[24] The specific meaning and expression of these characteristics within each person is so varied and complex that they are uniquely and distinctively expressed in each leader. This difficulty combined with the psychological aspects of leadership seem to diminish considerably the usefulness of this approach.

Attention to leadership styles has had considerably more impact and more useful results. There have been four styles of leadership which have been predominant in the concerns of the students of leadership. These are: 1) charismatic leadership; 2) autocratic leadership; 3) laissez-faire leadership; and 4) democratic or participative leadership.[25]

The charismatic leader emerges within periods of social distress among groups of people who need to empower such a leader with qualities that transcend things human and temporal, e.g. performing miracles, receiving revelations, performing heroic feats, experiencing baffling success. Powerful myths follow their death and failure in their efforts while alive will bring opprobrium and ruin. The charismatic leader is born with a group where the feeling of powerlessness and dependence are shared. The charismatic leader opposes rational and bureaucratic leadership or management and there is an uneasy tension where the charismatic leader dominates bureaucratic social systems.[26]

The autocratic leader uses power which ranges from coercion and force to benevolent paternalism. Fear, threats, force and intimidation are the measure of this person's authority. An autocratic leader may be a charismatic leader as well. The laissez-faire leader gives free rein to the group and encourages individualistic and competitive behaviors. Participative leaders encourage group-member participation in the design, assignment, decisions and fulfillment of the tasks required.

Recently far more sophisticated approaches have developed toward understanding organizational leadership. Robert Blake and Jane Mouton have developed a "managerial grid" where management style is located on a grid which relates management style to concern for people and concern for production. They demonstrate that the most effective management style is where the manager has great interest in both people and production.[27] Rensis Likert presents a continuum of management styles ranging from a totally job-centered perspective to an employee-centered perspective. This was linked to the quality reflected in the organization's management system. He identified four systems, *viz.*, 1) exploitive-authoritative; 2) benevolent-authoritative; 3) consultative; and 4) participative. Each of these reflect a particular style of motivation, communication, decision, goals and controls.[28] Douglas McGregor rests his analysis to leadership upon the assumptions a manager makes about people. A coercive management style assumes people dislike work and must be coerced, controlled, and directed toward management goals. This he identified as a theory X management style. An integrative management style emphasizes the intrinsic worth of the worker and validates a person's desire to be self-directed and responsible. This he identified as theory Y management style. These are only a few of the more advanced approaches to group and organizational leadership.[29]

Another useful way of focusing on a leader is to notice the organic function such a person has within the group or organization. Examining the function and nature of a leader's position and influence may yield useful and additional knowledge. The studies indentified here have focused only upon the formal or responsible leader. It is at least as important to observe the nature and composition of leadership as leadership within a group.

The Leadership Mix. Each group has an ever evolving leadership mix which is distinctive and specific to the group itself. It emerges out of the group process and includes more than formal leadership alone. Leadership in groups and organizations is reflected through the personal influence, quality and nature of the power available to those who lead. Of especial relevance is the degree of vigor which the followers of a particular leader stand ready to obey and the tenacity the followers use in defending the leader, for these reveal significant tensions and dystentions within the group or organization.

Berne suggests there are three distinct aspects or varieties of personal leadership within an organization. The responsible leader reflects the offical organizational structure and role. The effective leader may or may not have an official position but his or her competence is respected and generally recognized. He or she is a most powerful figure in shaping the actual decisions concerning group tasks. The psychological leader symbolizes and expresses behaviorally the implicit and shared emotional aspects of the group.

The responsible leader is the front man, the official head of an organization. The effective leader is the person who makes the actual decisions. He or she may be the person in the back room or, on the contrary, be very visible. She or he may be the executive officer aboard a ship or the political boss of a major city. This is the most significant person in the traditional structure. A psychological leader is a person whose ideas are followed in times of stress. He or she may be the most powerful person within the group. Who this leader is depends upon the dynamic processes within the group. The personal powers of such leaders are usually exaggerated. This role may vary among a number of persons and different times. At times this leader has almost a mystical hold on the response of the group members. The members demand specific and certain qualities of the psychological leader. He or she is the one who is likely to survive as a revered and honored forebear. This leader is frequently imbued with superhuman qualities. Such a leader is supposed to be omnipotent, omniscient, immortal, invulnerable, irresistible, incorruptible, unseductible, indefatigable and fearless. Lasting charisma may attach to this person.

All of these leadership functions may be located in the same or separate persons and change over time. The psychological leader tends to emerge into visibility in times of stress or over long periods of time. A group under profound distress may tend to forward a leader who represents the pathological nature and unspoken shared wishes of the group itself. Such a leader is a focal point symbolizing the group's underlying and shared fantasies and needs. If he is successfully attacked, recedes from view, or weakened somehow in his capacity to lead through disease or internal stress, this undermines the group's capacity to carry on. The group constantly, often restlessly, seeks a leader who reflects the underlying implicit needs of the group at the time.[30]

Canon. The canon consists of three aspects, the basic charter of the group, the definitive laws, and the history and culture of the group. The basic charter (constitution) flows from the activity of the group and the nature of the responsibility system among the group members. The responsibility of leaders and members are usually defined and the activity in broad outline is defined. The purposes and goals of the group or organization are identified and the structure for making decisions and regulating behavior is outlined. Generally, there is also a procedure for changing the constitution.

The object of the canon is to regulate group work and manage the internal processes of the organization. Enforcement is maintained by the commitment and restraint of the members with unacceptable variations in etiquette and behavior punished by mild disapproval, rejection, ostracism, or confinement. Relaxation of these regulatory activities are contained in permissive, sometimes ritualized deviations from the accepted norms, e.g. humorous "spoofing" of a leader may be a way of delivering effective criticism which, if delivered in a different manner in violation of the acceptable group norms, would lead to rejection or removal of the critic.

The legal aspect is the specific collection of laws, rules and orders, written procedures which officially link together persons within the organization. These may be established rules and orders or corporate instructions that guide how to purchase supplies, how to write technical reports, what is legally possible, etc. This tends to make up the guiding orthodoxy which is utilized to justify the day-to-day activities of the group or organization.

Cultural influences are the traditional organizational beliefs recognized as orthodox within the language and communication of the group or organization and considered binding on the membership. These are the shared beliefs and the "sacred" literature which provide the orthodox canon of the organization or group. These may involve key philosophical writings, sacred text from religious and spiritual literature and a variety of testaments and documents which support the orthodox tradition and are recognized as binding within the group. These are used in the struggles within the group to rationalize and justify action. They, in fact, serve as a basis for the ideology which the group articulates as the reason for its existence.

Group culture includes (1) the rational aspects of an organization which encompasses physical equipment; (2) the governing structure, things of that order. In addition, it includes (3) the etiquette and the rituals and procedures of the organization. Finally, it includes (4) the emotional and behavioral context of organizational life.

The historical aspects are reflected by the key individuals who provide the basic canons of orthodoxy under which the group and organization functions. Thus from the canon flow the cultural, legal and historical influences, written and unwritten, which guide and regulate the attitude and inner workings of the group. All groups tend to imbue their deceased canon-makers with greater than human characteristics. These ancient leaders are often recipients of attributions that are more god-like than human. Living leaders always have lesser prestige than departed ones. Sometimes special rules are articulated for particular people in the group who become specialists in interpreting, amending and elaborating the early canonical authorities. The behavior of individual members of the group sometimes cannot be understood separate from the nature of the deceased leader.

Berne identifies this process as euhemerization after the Greek philosopher Euhemerus who observed this process whereby ancient kings and heros took on mythical attributes in the popular imagination until they became larger-than-life and then ultimately god-like with the original reasons for this emergence lost in the haze of the past. After the death of a primal leader euhemerization occurs as has happened to a number of the founders of the United States. Later leaders who change the constitution or basic charter may undergo this process as well.[31]

Power Resources. Leadership and canon are reflected in the power resources of the organization. Human beings within an organization use the power available within the organization for the conversation of demands for survival and/or change into their possibility. This is done by using humane energy, psychological ability, social prestige, collective action, competence, physical resources, information and social, political and economic supports. This provides the setting for reassessing the nature of organizational power and resources. Organizational management must be concerned not only with the internal aspects of the organization but it must also be concerned with the environment from which it draws its resources. The context of organizational power varies and relates to the unique characteristics of the jurisdiction in which it is set. Amitai Etzioni provides a perspective on power which is relevant in an organizational or group setting. He suggests, "Power is a capacity to overcome part or all... resistance, to introduce changes in the face of opposition (this includes sustaining a course of action or preserving a status quo that would have otherwise been discontinued or altered)."[32] Leadership and canon are an essential aspect of management's ability to engender the power and resources necessary to perform the mission of the agency. Organizational power and power within an organization may be derived from the following sources:

1. the nature and design of executive leadership;
2. the fiscal and budgeting practices and relationships;
3. the context of program activity;
4. the federal, legislative, judicial, administrative and clientele relationships;
5. the traditional historical patterns;
6. the nature of the social system within the organization and the nature of the social system into which the agency is linked;
7. the nature of the personnel systems and patterns within the organization; and
8. the nature of competence and expertise available in the agency.

The nature and activities in each of these categories within a public organization may serve as resources of power on which an organization may draw to better effect its survival and its mission.[33] Kenneth J. Meier suggests that the power of public organizations is rooted in and a function of the policy environment in which the organization functions, the relative balance of public support to opposition, the special knowledge and expertise available within the organization and the cohesion of the organizational membership; and the quality of the available leadership.[34]

This list is undoubtedly incomplete for each group or organization has specialized "currencies of power" specific to which relate to such things as tradition, position and status, location, communication, etc. The capacity of the leadership to identify and draw upon resources of power to assure agency survival and mission accomplishment is a crucial aspect of the cohesive force within the agency. The fundamental unit of an organization which is a singular focus of leadership and through which survival needs and organizational goals are effectuated is the small group.

The Small Group: Development, Significance and Function

An aggregate collection of people becomes a group when, through the transactions among the members, an awareness of their common relationships develop and significant boundaries can be identified. This is usually associated with the emergence of a common task and purpose or focus. This is the fundamental unit for the conduct of organizational work. They are more frequently intentionally created by the organization but they may emerge randomly and voluntarily within the organization as well.

A variety of forces may operate to produce a group—an external threat, requirements to satisfy needs for security, safety, affection, status, belonging, etc. Additionally, collective regressive behavior in response to a pervasively shared, often unspoken, emotion may create a group. This is the specific concern and focus of the work of Wilfred Bion which is explored below. Once formed, it may be hypothesized that the ultimate goal of any group or organization is its own survival, and, in pursuit of this shared and unarticulated purpose, the group behaves as a system. It is distinct and separate from the individual members who make it up. This urge for survival is frequently masked or disguised, yet survival as a group becomes the primary concern and preoccupation of the group, motivating the energy of the members. Each member, in the face of this, is torn between his or her personal needs and the needs he or she senses for the group and those needs which only the group's survival could satisfy, e.g. status, belonging, strokes, etc.[35]

When individuals become members of a group, individual behavior alters and a distinctive, unique, and collective indentity emerges. A task group, a lynch mob, a football team, a specialized religious community, a police force, a fire-fighting unit, a school, a university, etc. are all phenomena in which the group becomes the vital focus. Membership in such a group may be thrilling, exciting, frightening, rewarding, dull, boring, sorrowful, anxious, satisfying, or an ambiguous collage of these feelings. Membership implies a perimeter or boundary which has a very distinctive significance to such a group or organization.

Organization and Group Boundaries: Their Crucial Significance

Robert Ardrey identified the importance of the link between territory and species survival. He suggested the maintenance of, and dominance over, a piece of territory is essential to the safety, security and survival of any species. The essential concept of territory includes the idea of a heartland and a border. The border identifies the heartland and is maintained against encroachment by other members of the same species.[36]

A boundary distinguishes different classes of membership within a group, as well as distinguishing the group from its external environment. Boundaries may be distinguished in constitutional, physical, psychological, social and spacial terms. Boundaries may be open, closed, or sealed. An open boundary may be crossed in either direction. A closed boundary limits entry in certain ways. A sealed boundary limits exiting except in certain ways. The individual, the small group and the more larger groups are increasingly complex manifestations of the heartland/border principle. Each can be described as having an inner world and an outer world and the boundary function indicates transactions across these boundaries.[37] Boundaries imply the existence of limits and parameters. This raises two fundamental questions: 1) What may be the the location of the boundary? and 2) What may be the nature of the boundary?

A group boundary may be distinguished by the differentiation of the interaction among group members in the environment within which the group is sited or exists. Patterns of interaction develop and may be seen as contributing to the interdependence and cohesiveness of the group concerned. A physical boundary is a factor or set of factors delimiting a significant region. This defines a boundary in a concrete geographical or material sense and, alone is insufficient. The idea of a boundary describes the parameters or limits of action which apply to the energy and activity of the group members and distinguishes that activity and membership from the environment as a whole.

Group order, ritual and regulation generally involve establishing orderly procedure for entry and exit at the major external and internal boundaries. Tasks of the group are likewise the subject of group procedures which define and delimit their function, as such, task boundaries are generally defined with some precision. Role boundaries develop, emerge, and are specifically defined and once these boundaries are defined, there exists a shared understanding concerning them and the appropriate ways they may be crossed. Finally, all organizations have time boundaries which are significant to the group's operation. The concept of boundary may be utilized as an analytical unit applied by an observer in limiting concern and focus upon the patterns of interaction within the group. It thus provides an accessible empirical phenomenon which is observable.[38]

Boundaries are often made in terms differentiating the power of the system, as between a President and the Legislature and the Courts. Boundaries may be defined functionally as between electrical and mechanical engineers. A boundary is often elastic and sometimes imprecise, but it is also tangible and may be impervious if properly maintained. Indeed, one of the main functions of any group is to maintain its boundaries against encroachments from persons or other groups within the environment within which it exists.[39]

Manifest Structure and Time Span Boundaries

Elliot Jaques has identified significant and profound time frame boundaries which can order organizational structure and link that structure effectively to the work capacity of the individual. His work is perhaps the most profound advance in organizational theory since the work of Max Weber. Jaques would organize work so as to reflect the following propositions:

1. A universally distributed "depth-structure" within each bureaucracy which reflects the natural lines of stratification at the three month time span level, the 12 month level, the two year level, the five year level, the 10 year level, an tentatively 20 years and beyond. Managerial strata of an organization can be designed so as to reflect these empirically valid divisions.

2. The existence of the stratified depth structure of bureaucratic hierarchies is

reflective of the social arrangements reflecting the existence of discontinuity and stratification characteristic of human capacity. The level of work capacity, Jaques expresses, can be denoted as the longest time-span with which a person can cope. These activities involve, among other things, problem solving, goal directed behavior, doing, working, and creating.

3. The rate of growth of the work capacity of individuals follows regular and predictable paths.[40]

If the context of work in an organization is sufficiently differentiated to provide roles which allow freedom of individual expression i.e., self actualization, with respect both as to interest and level of ability, then the social system and the individual personality can be mutually reinforcing.[41]

Traditional organizational theory does not take cognizance of time frame boundaries in the design of organizational structures. The efforts of Jaques have profound implications for the design of organizational structure and work. There is, thus, an optimal number of organizational levels depending upon the time-frame requirements of the work to be done. Utilizing the manifest organizational levels identified earlier and relating this to Jaques time-span concept organizational structure may be arranged accordingly:[42]

Stratum 1: The **performance level** involves work-capacity time spans below three months in duration. In this instance the persons fulfilling the manifest role functions are assigned to tasks in concrete terms and these are carried out in direct physical contact with the output task of the organization. This level involves activity and task design limits up to three months in duration.

Stratum 2: The **operational level** usually involves front line supervision separating management from the worker. Tasks at this level are characterized by new qualities not found below the three month time span. The goal no longer can be completely specified and some imagination must be exercised in the construction or definition of the project, yet the task is still concrete in the sense that the output can be imagined in concrete terms. Individual work capacity operates within a 12 month time span boundary and organizational activity and task design encompass goals up to one year.

Stratum 3: The **tactical level** is focused upon the middle range of the organization's manifest structure where it is too remote to physically oversee or imagine at once a person's entire area of responsibility. Thus a kind of "imaginal scanning" must continually occur so that progress can be guided by coherent instructions particularly to the operational level supervisor. Individual work-capacity operates within the 1-2 year time-span and the level of the organization involves 1-2 year task and activity design.

Stratum 4: The **strategic level** of an organization is concerned with, among other things, defining policy goals, budget and organizational design. Direct command of the day to day operations are lost. Innovation and change can be intuited and designed. This involves abstract work focused upon "conceptual modeling." Here the total form of the project cannot be grasped but rather it is intuitively sensed. The work capacity boundary is 2-5 years and involves a level of abstraction which operates within a 2-5 year time frame.

Stratum 5: The **policy-making level** of an organization may be separated from the strategic function and involves generalizing about the future directions of the organization(s). This evolves from intuitively developed theory which is deeply rooted in experience. Concern here is with the survival of the organization. This involves the capacity to abstract significance from policies, strategies, plans and information generated from below. It involves work capacity which can organize projects up to five years in duration and a level of organizational task and activity management which accounts for a five year time span.

Stratum 6 & 7: Jaques adds two more levels concerned with 10 and 20 year time-span boundaries. These are tentative and seem to be related to the capacity and involvement with institution building and elaboration as well as the design and creation of new institutions.

Although Jaques does not indicate this, these may well link in significant ways to the political and cultural context of the social system and in some way grow from the needs, wants, fears, angers and concerns which exist there. He suggests that these are tentative yet there is emerging support for their existence.[43]

Jaques has noted a profoundly significant link between work capacity and organizational depth structure, *viz.*, the higher level of abstraction a person can manage, the longer the tasks or projects which he will be able to plan and further into the future.[44] The level of work which a person does results not from activity but rather from the time-span goal of the activity. Given these observations it would appear much organizational design in traditional organizations is inappropriate and frequently quite oppressive, as Jaques suggests: "Forced under-employment through lack of availability of adequate levels of work in the bureaucratic sector of industrial societies has effects akin to imprisonment."[45] Thus for the sake of human survival and humane employment opportunities, organizational redesign is imperative.

Organizational and Group Dynamics: A Concern for Boundaries

Organizational and group dynamics encompass the influences affecting the boundaries of the organizational and group structure. This specific aspect of organizational phenomena may be identified as organizational dynamics concerned with anything related to the disturbance, securing, stabilization or destabilization of the key boundaries within organizations and groups. Key boundary concepts relating to organizational and group analysis may be identified as follows: the major external boundary between the group and its external environment. The major external boundary which separates leadership from other categories of membership. Minor boundaries within the membership may occur within leadership region or within the membership region as distinct from leadership. Minor internal boundaries can also occur within the leadership region itself.[46] These can be diagrammed accordingly. Figure 3-A, Major Group Structure, is a graphic representation of these concepts. Berne suggests group and organizational dynamics include three basic components. First, are the influences acting upon the major and minor boundaries of the group structure. These are primarily outside pressures and internal agitation. Second, are the individual proclivities which is a group member's propensity to express himself or herself in unique and characteristic ways. An individual proclivity that is in harmony with group forces tends to strengthen such a group. Berne identifies this as a syntonic procliv-

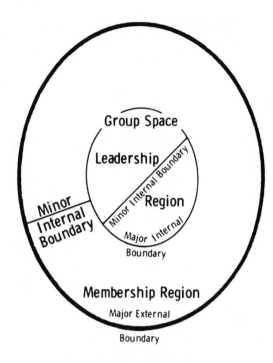

Figure 3-A: Major Group Structure.

Adapted from Eric Berne, *The Structure and Dynamics of Organizations and Groups*, New York, Grove Press, Inc., Evergreen Edition, 1966, copyright J.B. Lippincott 1963, pp. 54 and 58.

ity. An individual proclivity opposed to the forces of the group tends to weaken the group. Berne identifies this as a dystonic proclivity.[47] Group members are frequently torn between their own proclivities and the need to maintain the group's ongoing existence. Finally, group cohesion which is an operative force derived from the need of members to maintain an orderly existence of their group.

Perceiving small groups in this manner is helpful to an understanding of the nature and impact of stress upon such a group.[48] Stress is introduced into a group or organization when there is any unusual, unexpected, or unanticipated information or event which threatens (as perceived by the members) or disrupts the major group or organizational boundaries. The function of stress across time-frame boundaries and understanding the impact of such stress remains to be fully investigated.

Organizational and Group Dynamics When Stressed

Stress may occur within a group as a result of an unexpected, unprogrammed, non-traditional, extraordinary, or unusual disturbance of the major external or major internal boundaries of the group. Even the anticipated possibility of such an occurrence can give rise to unusual stress within the group. Wilfred Bion observed stress such as this could drive a group to certain basic assumptions, i.e. a group would behave "as if" it could achieve survival by pairing, fight/flight, and dependency.[49] These emerge, he suggested, as a response to an underlying, unspoken, shared fantasy among the group members. To this Turquet has added a fourth — oneness.[50] Margaret

Rioch has related these basic assumption modes to specific but unspoken emotional sharing.[51]

Basic Assumption Groups

When a group is stressed, the emotions associated with the basic assumptions can be described by the usual designations of anxiety, fear, hate, love, etc. Feelings associated with the pairing group express hope, optimism in contrast to feelings engendered in a fight/flight group where hatred, destructiveness and despair tend to be the order. Feelings evoked in a dependency group reflect despair, even despondency. Pairing groups tend to be open to new ideas for its basic canon, but when the dependent group or the fight/flight group is active, a struggle takes place to suppress the new idea and often those who make them, because it is felt that the emergence of a new idea interferes with the seeming cohesive force of the group, i.e., the *status quo*.

A group under severe stress may move through each one of these positions rapidly. Under prolonged stress a group may get "locked into" a particular position. The idea of a pairing group seems to encompass safety through shared fear, encompassing as well the hope for some resolving option to appear and occur in the future. The fight/flight group rests on the response to an internalized fear involving unspoken perceptions concerned with the safety of the group and the need to be a part of it. The fear of threatened dissolution may give rise to a dependency group. The group which emerges out of dependency may be temporary or long term and may be authoritarian, either political or religious or secular. In this latter instance, independent thought is stifled, heresy and treason righteously hunted and obedience and loyalty demanded. Bion suggests that if left to itself the dependent, fearful group will choose as its leader its least "healthy" and most pathological member; for example, a paranoid schizophrenic, a severe hysteric or delinquent.[52]

When the basic assumption is intensely felt, a group member may feel either in danger of being victimized or lost or extruded from the group. Personal identity is lost through the anonymous unanimity of group feeling. Margaret Rioch observes:

> In the naive or unconscious fantasy, the leader of the dependency group has to be omnipotent; the fight leader has to be unbeatable and the flight leader uncatchable; the leader of the pairing group must be marvelous but still unborn. But in the mature work group which is making a sophisticated use of the appropriate basic assumption, the leader of the dependency group is dependable; the fight/flight group is courageous; and the leader of the pairing group is creative.[53]

Rioch suggests that the work task is akin to a serious parent and the basic assumptions are like a fun-loving or frightened child. This suggests important linkages to Berne's conceptual work. Bion suggests the basic assumption group exists without any seeming effort, whereas the work group requires all the concentration, skill, creative and organizational forces that can be mustered by the group and brought into full flower. Bion suggests that a group, like an individual, may be stupid, cruel or intelligent and concerned. Margaret Rioch cites the interrelationship of human relationships. She notes the ease with which human beings give away their power:

> For there seems to be a tendency in human beings which becomes aggravated when they are isolated or faced with unfamiliar situations, to find the exercise of their own powers to mind and will extremely burdensome.[54]

She focuses upon a perplexing paradox required of all participants in any human group:

> *Competence and talent, whether in music or interpersonal relations or in anything else are marvelous sources of gratification to the person who exercises them. The dissatisfaction that so many people feel in their working lives often stems from not finding a way to put their talents, large or small, in the service of the task.*[55]

She identifies specifically the fundamental contradiction facing all participants in a group. "A group cannot function so long as each one insists upon his autonomy. But paradoxically neither can a group function if each individual abdicates his autonomy." She suggests this can be resolved by a person facing clearly his freedom to belong or not to belong to a group and making a choice specifically about that and, secondly, the individual needs to perceive the essential unity of himself and his or her group.[56]

The work or task group focuses outwardly toward the mission of the organization. The basic assumption group focuses upon itself, the problems of survival and the more archaic aspects of dealing with authority. The reversion to the basic assumption modes is the response of groups when stressed by unanticipated or anticipated, but unsuccessful, defense against unwanted penetrations of its major external boundary or any untoward incidents occurring across the major internal boundary.

Bion perceived that particular institutions in any society reflect the collective basic assumption strivings and provide the structure and vehicle to channel these archaic feelings. The church, for example, attempts to respond to and satisfy dependency needs, military and industrial organizations employ the strivings related to fight/flight motivations. The maintenance of an upper class and a political system is linked to the pairing mode which is reflected by their emphasis upon breeding, appropriate family life and succession. The re-emergence in our society of groups concerned with mysticism and cosmic consciousness reflects the basis assumption mode of oneness and seems to reflect the sense of loss which accompanies the alienated existence in the fragmented organizations of modern technological society.

Leadership in Basic Assumption Groups

The leader in basic assumption groups is "unborn" and the leadership matrix is the focus as the group seems in constant need and in search of a leader on whom it can rely to provide nurture, safety, support and material well-being. In a pairing group the shared pervasive emotion focuses on the hope for a new leader. But if a new leader is produced he or she is soon rejected. Rioch observes, ". . . in order to maintain hope, he must be unborn."[57] Thus, when the leader of a group fails to meet the group's expectations, and this is inevitable, the group will rid itself of him or her and seek another alternative. When this temptation is accepted by another ambitious member, his or her fate will be exactly the same as the previous one.

A group functioning in a dependency mode tends to use as a leader a member who expresses the deeply felt anxieties of the group and thus expresses the pathology of the group, i.e., the leader defines by behavior the underlying dimensions and causes spawning the fear and acts for the group. The leader of this group dramatizes the group's shared emotion in an intensity required by the group process. It is in this instance, Bion suggests, the group chooses its least healthy member. The emotions which tend to predominate the dependency group are greed, jealousy and resentment. In the absence of a leader, the group feels deserted and tends to forget its squabbles and often "cuddle up like little birds in a nest."[58]

The predominantly shared emotion of the fight/flight group focuses on panic and rage. The leader tends to emerge within the context of this group as a person

BION'S "BASIC ASSUMPTION" GROUP MODES: SURVIVAL AND DISSOLUTION UNDER STRESS

SITUATION	BASIC (TACIT) ASSUMP-TION (GROUP BEHAVES)	CHARACTERISTICS	PROCESS	CONSEQUENCES
PAIRING	**As If:** The group has met to bring forth a Messiah or a Savior.	Two people get together on behalf of the group to carry out the task of pairing and creation (sex of the two persons is of no matter).	— The group appears to give its responsibility for survival to two of its members.	**Leadership:** No actual leader needs to be present. The group, living through the pair, hopes for a new idea, creation, etc. will emerge and be born to solve old problems.
	Goal: To solve problems and avoid hatredness, destructiveness, and despair.	The group is not bored; an atmosphere of hope and expectancy pervades the group.	— The group focuses on the future.	— To maintain hope, the idea, or leader, etc. must remain unborn. If born or produced he/she(it) will be soon rejected.
	Effect: To bring forth a new leader, new creation, new hope.	The hope must always be unborn.	— Simple "truths," cure-alls, and simplistic alternatives will solve all difficulties.	**Membership:** The group enjoys an air of optimism and hopefulness. It brooks no exception to the "expected" deliverance which is "morally" correct. The group seems soft, pliant, agreeable, easy. New ideas, new leadership, new creative suggestions will be "put down" for the destructiveness and anger (hatred) in the group have not been reduced or dealt with.
			— The everpresence of hope is the key to the existence of this group.	

Table 3:1. Bion's "Basic Assumption" Group Modes

BION'S "BASIC ASSUMPTION" GROUP MODES: SURVIVAL AND DISSOLUTION UNDER STRESS

SITUATION	BASIC (TACIT) ASSUMPTION (GROUP BEHAVES)		CHARACTERISTICS	PROCESS	CONSEQUENCES
FIGHT/FLIGHT	As If:	Self-preservation is the reason the group exists and this can only be done by fighting or running from someone or something.	Action is essential. The individual member is expendable and in battle or in flight may be abandoned for the sake of the survival of the group. Confrontation or flight are expressed in a variety of group behaviors.	— Anti-intellectual, hostile to self-study, self-searching and self-knowledge called nonsense. Leadership in this direction is blocked and avoided. — The group flees from the task of examining all the options available.	Leadership: The leader is empowered and experiences ease in directing the group from fearful flight in panic to headlong blind attack in rage. — The leader is crucial in this mode and is chosen as appropriate because he/she is seen as one who can "mobilize the group for attack or lead it in flight."
	Goal:	To attain preservation of the group by opposing or avoiding a threat.		— The group girds for struggle rather than confront the difficult task of dealing with stress.	Membership: The group is volatile, easily moved to panic or rage. Needs instantaneous satisfaction of its felt emotions. Hostile to leadership which offers no quick alternatives.
	Effect:	To become the vehicle for the expression of panic (rage and fear).		— The group readies itself for rebellion, defense or flight rather than confront its own process.	— Contains a great deal of rage and fear which has been frustrated or blocked in expression.

Table 3:2. Bion's "Basic Assumption" Group Modes

BION'S "BASIC ASSUMPTION" GROUP MODES: SURVIVAL AND DISSOLUTION UNDER STRESS

SITUATION	BASIC (TACIT) ASSUMPTION (GROUP BEHAVES)	CHARACTERISTICS	PROCESS	CONSEQUENCES
DEPENDENCY	**As If:** A super-being exists who will care for, provide and make the group safe.	The members act in a powerless, mindless, know-nothing manner, implying the leader is all powerful and all-knowing.	— The group looks to one person to solve its problems and who will see that the irresponsibilities of the members will not go too far as to be harmful and disastrous in their consequences.	**Leadership:** No leader can meet group's requirements. All fall from power as the group searches for the super being.
	Goal: To attain security thru and have members protected by one person.		— Squabbling, pettiness, little jealousies emerge.	Euhemerization of the leader occurs after a period of time.
	Effect: To constrain the operation of fear.		— Resentment at being dependent with the wish to remain so accompanying.	**Membership:** — The process group dominates the work group and the relationship between members and leader looks more and more like a religious group or cult.
				— When deserted by a leader the group may forget their internal squabbles and close ranks, seeing the outside world as hostile, cold and unfriendly. To confront this in the group is "heresy."

Table 3:3. Bion's "Basic Assumption" Group Modes

BION'S "BASIC ASSUMPTION" GROUP MODES: SURVIVAL AND DISSOLUTION UNDER STRESS

SITUATION	BASIC (TACIT) ASSUMPTION (GROUP BEHAVES)	CHARACTERISTICS	PROCESS	CONSEQUENCES
ONENESS*	**As If:** The group has met to join or merge with a higher universal force. **Goal:** To survive through commitment to a cause greater than and transcendent to the group itself. **Effect:** To achieve a higher level of consciousness and experience a lost sense of unity and wholeness.	Group members seem to join in union with an all powerfull, higher "cosmic" force. Surrender, passive behavior, a loss of individual identity, a merging with the group so as to "disappear" into the whole characterize this response. The group surrenders to a higher force through seemingly passive participation.	— Group responds to leaders who offer methods for attaining a mystical union with a higher power outside the group. — The group commits itself to a cause or movement as a way of survival. — The reliance on mystified expectancy and higher consciousness is the key to this group. — Some members promise access to enlightenment through special processes, knowledge and ritual.	**Leadership:** Leaders who offer one philosophy of life or methods for attaining higher levels of consciousness emerge in the group. **Membership:** Contemplation, meditation, wonder, awe are words that describe group behavior in this mode. Members succumb or surrender to a "real" or momentary "guru."

*This was not in Bion's original basic assumption grouping but was suggested by P. M. Turquet in 1974 (See Note 18).

Table 3:4. Bion's "Basic Assumption" Group Modes

who can mobilize the group for an attack or lead it in flight. The members of a fight/flight group are volatile and easily moved into rage or panic. They need instantaneous satisfaction of the deeply felt emotional life. Survival is seen as requiring aggression which may involve scapegoating, physical attack, snide remarks, etc. or flight which may include withdrawal, passivity, avoidance, examining past events, etc. The leader who can mobilize these forces is selected but will not last too long because the bickering, infighting, suspicion, and competition make most leadership bids short-lived because they are high risk situations.

The predominant emotion in the oneness basic assumption mode is a sense of loss and the need to restore a feeling of wholeness and completeness not available in earthly groups. Leaders emerge in this mode who articulate a philosophy of life or distinctive methods for achieving higher levels of consciousness. Surrender is a characteristic aspect of behavior in this group. Tables 3:1-4 display the data developed concerning each basic assumption group. Each table indicates the basic assumption situation, the basic assumption goals and the effect sought, the characteristics, process and consequences for the leadership and membership when the group operates in each mode. These tables are not definitive nor ought they be considered to be complete. They rather display relevant, observable aspects of basic assumption group life.

Group Behavior: Basic Assumption Transitions Under Stress

These basic assumption modes may have been functional to survival in the past. Today, these modes tend to reflect an archaic part of human behavior functional to survival under immediate physical threat, which may on occasion, even today, be crucial. Yet in the developed society of today, they become, at the least, a dysfunctional aspect for solving problems relating to survival in a post-technological age, and, at the most, a condition precedent to the annihilation of all human life on the planet. These basic assumption transitions when the group is stressed are summarized in Figure 3-B. The basic assumption oneness has not been included in this figure. It is still too recent an hypothesis to be fully accepted as a basic assumption and added to those observed by Bion. Yet there is good supportable evidence for its existence and availability to the group. It seems to be generated by a sense of loss, disillusion and isolation—a kind of estrangement among the members of the group where behavior in pursuit of other basic assumptions has been of no avail. The circumstances engendering it are not fully assessed. Oneness as a basic assumption has, however, been included descriptively and in Tables 3:1-4.

When laid out as in Figure 3-B, it is possible to begin to glean some understanding of the rescuer-victim-persecutor triangle which is such a pervasive aspect of most human relationships and is an important concomitant of group behavior. When Rescue (drama) Triangle activity is linked to basic assumption life within a group, the group members are blind to its operations. When it fuses to a high degree of intensity, it leads to witch hunts, inquisitions, lynchings, air hijackings, etc. or new religions, social change and reform movements. This process may well be effectively explained by focusing on Berne's concept of individual games and how they may link into the group process. This offers a rich harvest for study.[59]

Group Boundaries and Basic Assumption Modes

It may be stated with assurance that minor and major disturbances across primary boundaries in groups and organizations successfully interrupt group work activity

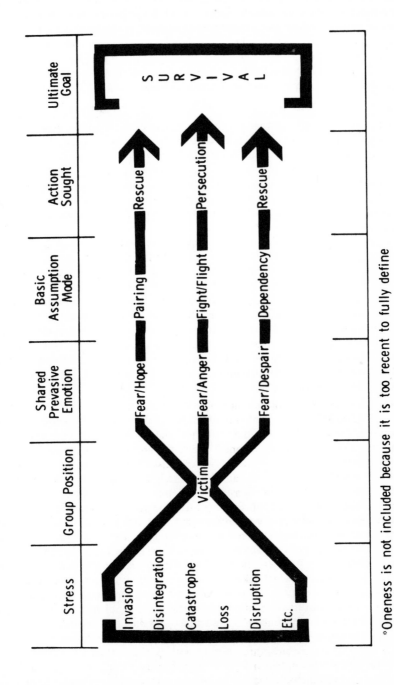

Figure 3-B: Basic Assumption Transitions Under Stress

while group members attend to the repair and management of the unanticipated occurrence and its consequences. When this occurs, work, which is the primary focus, goal, or activity of the group, gives way to process, rather than these concerns. The energy put forth by each member is unrelated to the primary task with which he or she is concerned or to which he or she is assigned. The group members' attention and energy are rather directed toward the structure and dynamics of the group itself, although not the only response, is not an unusual one.

Organizational and Group Forces: Survival and Termination

When it is understood that survival is ultimately an individual goal and the mystified goal of the group, it is possible then to identify two sets of forces which threaten the group. First, disruptive forces from without; and, second, disorganizing forces from within. Survival of any group is dependent upon two aspects of group dynamics, first, the ability to do organized work; and, second, the requirement of the group to maintain an established structure within which to do the work.[60] Consequently, any group must attend to three primary forces threatening the disintegration of a group.

The first is decay (agitation) from within; the second is disruption (pressure) from without, such as an attack or a reorganization; the third, destruction, which may result from a physical phenomenon such as tidal wave, flood, earthquake and fire, etc. Unless these processes are hindered and interrupted, the death of the group will result. Occasionally, groups, particularly in the public sector, undergo such actions as annexation, incorporation, consolidation, loss of funding and other forms of alteration and change. Additionally, some functions may be thrust upon them, all of which disrupt and alter the major boundaries and introduce a varying degree of stress. Little scholarly attention has been given to the intentional termination of a group or organization. This certainly merits further concern in view of the increasingly limited resources available.

Pressure, Agitation and Cohesion. Forces which impact the major external boundary deliver outside pressure upon it and across it. The internal forces of decay operating with consequence upon the major internal boundary are those which may be identified as agitation. The responses which the group gives to these are indicative of the forces of internal cohesion which exist to thwart decay and disruption. Pressure, agitation and cohesion are the dynamic forces affecting the survival of the organization at its most critical aspects, *viz.*, its major internal and external boundaries.[61] Figure 3-C presents this conceptual schematic in graphic form. When these boundaries are stressed in any variety of ways, they bring to life through the transactional proclivities of the members and may spawn the latent basic assumption modes. It is the primary objective of any group to maintain its own orderly existence. This is a primary concern of the emotional life of the group. It is the emotional aspect of the group under stress which takes precedence over work. Once the existence of the group is assured it can turn to the activity which is its primary focus and task. The group may set aside its own internal dissention and problems and set aside its own work when the primary concern is thwarting or fending off serious threat from without. This is especially true if it is a cohesive and goal-oriented group.

Group survival may be of three distinct varieties. First, there is ideological survival. Here the group no longer exists as an organized and significant force in the community. It retains the potential for resurgence but it simply exists in the minds of its members long after it has lost a significant geographical or physical base. Second,

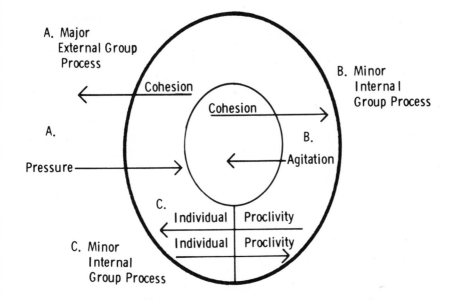

Figure 3-C: Organizational and Group Forces

From Eric Berne, *The Structure and Dynamics of Organizations and Groups*, New York, Grove Press, Inc., Evergreen Edition, 1966, copyright J.B. Lippincott, 1963, p. 70.

there is a physical survival. In this instance, the ideological aspects may have lost intensity yet the group hangs on, maintaining its physical properties and symbolic existence long after it serves any functional purpose toward achieving effective survival. Third, there is effective survival. This is the effective combination of the physical aspects of the group which support the ability of the group to carry on organized work.[62]

The underside of survival is termination. This occurs when the group is no longer meeting the specific needs and wishes of the individuals who make it up. The members put forth no emotional energy for its preservation. The group decays and this is generally accompanied by disintegration of its physical properties. If the membership is wiped out regardless of the cohesive ideology, the group cannot function—that is, it is effectively destroyed. A group or organization may be destroyed as an effective force by violating the major group structure itself. This may be done through erosion of its ideology by, among other things, attacking its validity. It may be accomplished through attrition, i.e., through gradual attack bringing partial or full destruction of the properties and funding sources as well as the membership. Finally, the major group and organizational boundaries may be penetrated through disruption. If it is gradual, it could be achieved through infiltration of its boundaries over a long period of time. If sudden, it could lead to panic.[63] It is the unanticipated penetration or agitation or the perceived threats of such penetration or agitation (real or imagined or feared) which spawn the existence of the basic assumption group modes and bring them into life within the group.

A Small Group Survival Problem: "Live is Evil Spelled Backwards"

One autumn evening in 1975, my colleague, J. Holley, was leading a small seminar concerned with group process and power.[64] The seminar consisted of eight members. During this particular evening a distinctive event occurred which demonstrates the existential validity of Bion's theorem. The seminar was gathered in a room on a second floor of an older building located in a section of Los Angeles where foot traffic is moderately heavy. There were no elevators and there was only one walk-up stairway. This was the only exit except for fire escapes which were quite difficult to activate except under extreme emergency conditions.

The process of the seminar involved lecture discussion for the first half, a break, and then a structured experience relating to the material during the second half. The first three seminars were uneventful, covering the material and relating it to experiential learning. This evening was to be different. This was the only class in the building that evening. No administrative staff was present and the room itself was remote from the administrative section of the building. Additionally, there was only one entrance and exit to the room. The seminar was gathered in a circle on sofas and conducted in a relaxed atmosphere.

Fifteen minutes into the evening a man climbed heavy footed up the stairs and walked through the door. His manner was unusual. He was unkempt, and his appearance seemed sinister. He placed himself between the group members and the only exit door available. Only half of the seminar members could see him. The others had their backs to him. His manner and appearance were so threatening that Ms. Holley intuitively decided not to challenge his entry. She spoke of the need for strokes which underlie human behavior, and the consequences when persons do not seem to get enough.

The time for the break period (usually 10 minutes) came and went but the seminar members sat, seemingly "enthralled" with the stimulating presentation of the material by Ms. Holley. Suddenly, the stranger stood up, took a few steps toward the door, turned to the group, and spoke clearly so all could hear, "Remember, live is evil spelled backwards," and strode out the door.

There were loud sighs of relief accompanied by body motions appropriate to the verbal and nonverbal release of great tension. The room had been immersed in fear and its stimulus was now gone. Ms. Holley questioned the group concerning their reactions and responses. All had listened to her presentation. None had heard the material presented or the discussion which followed. Each had, nevertheless, participated in the discussion! The psychic energy and attention of each group member was riveted on the intruding stranger. Ms. Holley herself was positioned so she could continuously observe him. She intuitively felt the intruder was somehow involved in the discussion and even sensed through monitoring his bodily movements that, just prior to his leaving, he made a significant but unspoken decision. She asked each group member to share what they thought and felt during the time the intruder was present. At times the group expressed they were certain that, as the person in authority, Ms. Holley knew what to do and everything would be "all right." At other times, they glanced almost furtively about to assess how to get out and found their exit blocked because the stranger had interposed himself between them and the only door. Others had carefully looked for implements of defense—varieties of which might be available—assessing chairs and nearby implements for possible use. At other times, they had spoken in whispers to one another. At one time, Ms. Holley's presentation was interrupted while two members seemingly spoke of "strokes" they each had needed within their family and had not received.

Here are the ingredients for the unexpected penetration of the external boundary in a manner as to give rise to the fears of the membership for their own person and for the survival of the group. The hidden, yet observable, responses of the membership recapitulate Bion's basic assumption modes moving among them as they evoked behavior expressing fear and concern. All attention to the group task stopped while the group dealt with the intrusion, even while it seemed the task was proceeding.

The foregoing event involved a "temporary group" with a time certain in the future for its demise. More apropos of an ongoing group or organization would be a serious threat to its essential resources. In the spring of 1978 in California the funding of an overwhelming number of local governmental services was seriously threatened by a property tax initiative, known as Proposition 13, which placed a limit on the amount of property taxes available for support of those programs. In particular, the initiative considerably reduced the funding available to supply those services. They included, among other things, fire and police protection, water and sewer service, libraries, public schools and federal funding of local programs requiring matching funds. The proposition, if passed, threatened a layoff, statewide, of over 400,000 local government and public school employees and a considerable reduction of some of these services and the closure of others. During the time the proposition was a viable political choice and as the election date neared these agencies in their various communities were dominated by survival concerns. Educating the public as to the specific nature of the impact, defeating the proposition, trying to locate other sources of funding, planning organizational reductions in services and personnel, and a variety of related tasks dominated the concerns of those in these programs. Employees, even some with as much as eight and 10 years of seniority who might be affected, were scrambling for other jobs all over the nation. Still others were too paralyzed to act. An incredible number of organizations and the family units dependent on the wage-earner therein were threatened with disruption and loss. In these families and agencies the overwhelming proportion of time and attention on the job and off, within the agency and within the work groups, was spent talking in pairs and small groups of their fears. Individual, group, and organizational survival became primary concerns in the face of this impending threat. Some groups were girding for battle. Others were helping their members flee to other employment. Still others were resigned to the inevitable feeling that "they" could not let that happen and the money would come from "somewhere" to keep the organization in service. This is a dependency mode. Each of the basic assumption modes emerged at various times in a variety of circumstances in a number of threatened agencies. Ritualized routine matters were handled but planning, problem-solving and decision-making concerned with the long run organizational mission were interrupted to deal with this threatened loss of substantial financial support. The organizational task became, in effect, its own survival in the face of these serious threats to its funding sources.[65] Task activity is responsive to the constituency of group membership and the pressures and agitations affecting it. This task may coincide with management goals or it may be in conflict with management purposes.[66] In these two illustrations, constituent task focus coincided with management goals.

Some Hypotheses Concerning Group Behavior

These observations are presented in the nature of initial formulations. They have not been empirically verified and a more systematic analysis is required to sustain their ultimate validity. Yet there is enough experiential support for them to warrant and merit further investigation. In these situations, pressure across the major external boundaries spawned stress which initiated basic assumption behavior in operational situations.

These events demonstrate the availability of basic assumption responses when perceived threats to organizational or group existence operate within the life of the group. Each response exists because, in the dim past of human existence, these archaic survival modes were essential to the actual survival of human groups. They are activated today when perceived, real or fantasized threats impact on the group process. Miller and Rice observe:

> The members of any group. . . inevitably in a dilemma: On the one hand, safety lies in the preservation of its own boundary at all costs and the avoidance of transactions across it; on the other hand, survival depends upon the conduct of transactions with the environment and the risk of destruction.[67]

It is now possible to identify some useful hypotheses concerning group behavior utilizing the information from Berne and Bion. The hypotheses underlying the conceptualization of group life presented here may be summarized as follows:

1. The transcendent task of any group is to survive and it will do what it must to accomplish this.

2. Group behavior is expressed through transactions deriving from the distinctive fantasies and projections of its members.

3. The contributions and transactions of the members are made in the service of the primary task, viz., survival.

4. The behavior and transactions of any member at any one moment express the unique linkage between a member's own needs (script strivings, hidden agenda, etc.) and the needs of the group in the service of its primary task.

5. Whatever is happening or spoken in the group is an expression of the member cum-group, i.e., it reflects an aspect of the group itself.

6. The membership of a group which has, or is threatened with, unstable major internal or external boundaries is predominantly concerned with stabilizing such boundaries. Task work is generally interrupted until such stability is assured.

7. When a group is stressed it does not function rationally, but rather the unconscious fears, wishes, anger, defenses, fantasies, impulses, introjections and projections operate and become a significant aspect of group dynamics and process.

8. The underlying rituals, pastimes and games among the membership reflect the tensions among the individual adjustments to the group and the acceptance by the group of individual members.

9. Group cohesion is an operative force deriving from the need of members to maintain an orderly existence of their group.

10. Raising the consciousness of the group member concerning group processes provides the opportunity for group members to observe their own transactions, expand the spoken and behavioral choices open to them, and enhance their personal effectiveness in the group as a whole.

SUMMARY

Bureaucracy can be examined utilizing five categories which reveal its full dimensions. These include: 1) the manifest structure; 2) the authority matrix, 3) organizational and group dynamics; 4) private structure; and 5) group process.

The manifest structure centers attention upon the strategic, tactical, operational and performance aspects of the organization.

The authority matrix centers on the nature of organizational leadership with specific attention directed toward a leadership matrix involving the responsible, effective, and psychological leaders. In addition, it includes concern for the organizational canon. Organizational canon includes the basic charter, legitimizing organizational activity, the legal aspects including laws, rules, orders, etc., which provide for orderly procedure as do the cultural influences and historical aspects affecting organizational activity.

Organizational and group dynamics center on the forces related to pressure, agitation, and cohesion expressed in activity concerning the significant boundaries of the organization. These forces are concerned with the survival and termination of the organization. Unanticipated, unexpected or unusual behavior concerning major organizational boundaries spawn on occasion basic assumption behavior within the affected group or groups.

When these aspects of an organization are more fully revealed, greater comprehension of the organization is accessible and individual and group behavior within an organization is more readily understandable. Also the possibility of developing more humane interpersonal relations within an organization may be enhanced and likewise a more humane and effective delivery of the organizational mission may be achieved.

NOTES

1. John Stuart Mill, *On Liberty*, (1859), edited by Alburey Castell, Arlington Heights, Ill., A.H.M. Publishing Company, 1947, p. 59, copyright 1947 by A.H.M. Publishing Co.

2. See e.g., George Orwell, *Nineteen Eighty-Four*, N.Y., Harcourt Brace, 1949; Aldous Huxley, *Brave New World*, N.Y., Harper, 1932; and his *Brave New World Revisited*, N.Y., Harper, 1958; Jaques Ellul, *The Technological Society*, N.Y., Alfred A. Knopf, 1964.

3. Lewis Yablonsky, *Robopaths: People as Machines*, Bobbs-Merrill Co., Penguin Books, 1972, pp. 6 and 15. For further discussion see Michael P. Smith, "Alienation and Bureaucracy: The Role of Participatory Administration," *Public Administration Review*, Nov./Dec., 1971, p. 660; see also Michael Maccoby, *The Gamesman: The New Corporate Leaders*, N.Y., Simon and Schuster, 1976.

4. Herbert Marcuse, *One-Dimensional Man*, Boston, Beacon Press, 1964; see also, generally, Robert Townsend, *Up The Organization*, N.Y., A.A. Knopf, 1970.

5. Rollo May, *Power and Innocence*, N.Y., W.W. Norton & Co., 1972, p. 23.

6. Joseph Bensman and Arthur J. Vidich, *The New American Society*, Chicago, Quadrangle Books, 1971, pp. 22-23.

7. *Ibid.*

8. Max Weber, "Bureaucracy," in *From Max Weber*, H.H. Gerth and C. Wright Mills (eds.), N.Y., Oxford University Press, 1946 (Galaxy Edition), pp. 196-240. See also a fine summary and discussion of Weber's concept and definition of bureaucracy in Ralph P. Hummel, *The Bureaucratic Experience*, St. Martin's Press, Inc., 1977, pp. 73-83. Robert Boguslaw calls attention to Weber's observation that bureaucratic power is always overpowering and suggests, like Weber, that secrecy is one of the most powerful tools of bureaucracy. He suggests the normally overpowering position of bureaucracy in modern society is considerably enhanced by computer-based systems management and computer-

stored record-keeping. Robert Boguslaw, *The New Utopians, a Study of System Design and Social Change*, Englewood Cliffs, N.J., Prentice-Hall, Inc., 1965, pp. 187-196, cf. B. Guy Peters, *The Politics of Bureaucracy*, N.Y. and London, Longman, Inc., 1978, pp. 2-3, and Alfred Diamant, "The Bureaucratic Model," in *Papers in Comparative Administration*, ed. Ferrell Heady and Sybil L. Stokes, Ann Arbor, Mich., Institute of Public Administration, 1962, pp. 79-86.

9.   Anthony Downs, *Inside Bureaucracy*, Boston, Little, Brown & Co., Inc., 1967, pp. 24-31, cf., Richard Hall, "The Concept of Bureaucracy, An Empirical Assessment," *American Journal of Sociology*, Vol. 69, (1963), pp. 32-40.

10. Elliot Jaques, *A General Theory of Bureaucracy*, N.Y., John Wiley & Sons, 1976, p. 62, see also pp. 49 and 52.

11. Downs, *op. cit.*, p. 24; see also generally Charles Perrow, *Complex Organizations: A Critical Essay*, Glenview, Ill., Scott Foresman and Co., Inc., 1972.

12. The literature includes such broadly respresentative materials as Chris Argyris, *Interpersonal Competence and Organizational Effectiveness*, Homewood, Ill., The Dorsey Press, Inc. Richard D. Irwin, Inc., 1962; Chris Argyris, *Personality and Organization*, N.Y., Harper, 1957; Chris Argyris, *Understanding Organizational Behavior*, Homewood, Ill., Dorsey Press, Inc., 1960; E. Wight Bakke, *Bonds of Organization*, N.Y., Harper, 1950; Reinhard Bendix, "Bureaucracy and the Problem of Power," *Public Administration Review*, Vol. 5 (1945), pp. 194-209; Warren G. Bennis, "Leadership Theory and Administrative Behavior: The Problem of Authority," *Administrative Science Quarterly*, Vol. 4 (1959), pp. 260-301; Adolph A. Berle, Jr. and Gardiner C. Means, *The Modern Corporation and Private Property*, N.Y., Macmillan, 1932; Peter M. Blau, *Bureaucracy in Modern Society*, N.Y., Random House, 1956; Peter M. Blau and W. Richard Scott, *Formal Organizations*, San Francisco, Ca., Chandler Publishing Co., 1962; Amitai Etzioni, (ed.) *Complex Organizations: A Sociological Reader*, N.Y., Holt, Rinehart and Winston, 1961; George C. Homans, *The Human Group*, N.Y., Harcourt Brace and World, Inc., 1950; Elliot Jaques, *Changing Culture of the Factory*, N.Y., Dryden, 1952; Daniel Katz and Robert Kahn, *The Social Psychology of Organizations*, N.Y., John Wiley & Sons, 1966; Albert Lepawsky, *Administration*, N.Y., Alfred A. Knopf, Inc., 1955; Norton Long, *The Polity*, Chicago, Ill., Rand McNally Co., 1962; Norton Long, "Public Policy and Administration: The Goals of Rationality and Responsibility," *Public Administration Review*, Vol. 14 (Winter 1954), pp. 22-31; Alexander H. Leighton, *The Governing of Men*, Princeton, N.J., Princeton University Press, 1945; James G. March and Herbert Simon, *Organization*, N.Y., John Wiley & Sons, Inc., 1958; James A. Medeiros and David E. Schmitt, *Public Bureaucracy: Values and Perspectives*, North Scituate, Mass., Roxbury Press, 1977; Robert K. Merton, *Social Theory and Social Structure*, N.Y., The Free Press of Glencoe, 1963; Robert Merton, Alisa P. Gray, Barbara Hockey, and Hanan C. Selvin (eds.), *Reader in Bureaucracy*, Glencoe, Ill., The Free Press, 1952; James D. Mooney and Alan C. Reily, *The Principles of Organization*, N.Y., Harper & Bros., 1939; Charles Perrow, *Complex Organizations*, Glenview, Ill., Scott-Foresman, 1972; Robert Presthus, *The Organizational Society*, N.Y., Alfred A. Knopf, 1962; Francis E. Rourke, *Bureaucracy, Politics, and Public Policy*, Boston, Little, Brown, 1959; Edgar H. Schein, *Organizational Psychology*, Englewood Cliffs, N.J., Prentice-Hall, 1971; Philip Selznick, "An Approach to the Theory of Bureaucracy," *American Sociological Review*, Vol. 8 (1945), p. 49; Philip Selznick, "Foundations of the Theory of Organizations," *American Sociological Review*, Vol. XIII (Feb. 1948), pp. 25-35; Philip Selznick, *Leadership in Administration*, Evanston, Ill., Row-Peterson, 1957; Herbert A. Simon, *Administrative Behavior*, Second Edition, N.Y., Macmillan Co., 1961; James D. Thompson, *Organizations in Action*, N.Y., McGraw-Hill Book Co., 1967; Victor A. Thompson, *Modern Organization*, N.Y., Alfred A. Knopf, 1961; Gordon Tullock, *The Politics of Bureaucracy*, Washington, D.C., Public Affairs Press, 1965; Dwight Waldo, *The Administrative State*, 1948; William Foote Whyte, *Organizational Behavior: Theory and Application*, Homewood, Ill., R.D. Irwin, 1969; Michael Young, *The Rise of Meritocracy*, N.Y., Random House, 1959.

13. Michel Crozier, *The Bureaucratic Phenomenon*, Chicago, Ill., University of Chicago Press, 1964, p. 198; see also Richard Hall, *et. al.*, "Organization Size, Complexity and Formalization," *American Sociological Review*, Vol. 33, (1968), pp. 903-912.

14. Elliot Jaques, *op. cit.*, pp. 32-33, structure is used in this effort to refer to particular patterns of role relationships within bounded social nets, cf., Jaques, *op. cit.*, p. 25.

15. These categories differ in emphasis from Jaques' concepts. Jaques concept of assumed social structure centers upon the role relationships understood by each of the participants. These varying perspectives on the part of each participant are functional aspects of the organizational dynamics. Jaques also identifies extant social structures which he denotes as the actual context of particular behavior. This is more explicitly delineated here as a significant aspect of the private structure, cf. Jaques, *op. cit.*, pp. 32-35.

16. This five-faceted construct is deeply rooted in Eric Berne, *The Structure and Dynamics of Groups and Organizations*, N.Y., Grove Press, Inc., Evergreen Edition, 1966, copyright J.B. Lippincott Co., pp. 28-81. I have chosen to use manifest structure to more accurately express the nature of the overt structural relationships to the total context of bureaucracy. I have made every effort to retain the essential core of Berne's ideas.

17. For a more complete discussion of the aspects of the manifest structure, see Robert H. Simmons and Eugene P. Dvorin, *Public Administration: Values, Policy and Change*, Port Washington, N.Y., Alfred Publishing Co., pp. 395-609.

18. Jaques, *op. cit.*, pp. 258-276.

19. cf. Berne, *The Structure and Dynamics of Organizations and Groups, op. cit.*, pp. 32-37 and pp. 105-115. Berne uses the phrase "group authority" to identify these sets of organizational influences. I have selected a phrase which seems to me to be more specific and precise. The phrase "authority matrix" specifically calls attention to the complex setting which indicates the origin, setting and maintenance of legitimacy for the group or organization. It is more precise in that it suggests a variety of sources for the group's legitimacy and validity are utilized to support and justify organizational tasks and mission.

20. Chester I. Barnard, *The Functions of the Executive*, Cambridge, Mass., Harvard University Press, 1962, p. 283.

21. Philip Selznick, *Leadership in Administration*, Evanston, Ill., Row, Peterson and Co., 1957, pp. 22 and 23-38.

22. Barnard, *op. cit.*, p. 283.

23. See Herbert A. Simon, *Administrative Behavior*, N.Y., Macmillan, 1948, Morton Kroll, "Hypotheses and Design for the Study of Public Policies in the United States," *Midwest Journal of Political Science*, Vol. 6, 1962, pp. 363-83; Dwight Waldo, *op. cit.*, Fremont J. Lyden, George A. Shipman and Morton Kroll, *Policies, Decisions and Organization*, N.Y., Appleton-Century-Crofts, 1969; Robert Dubin, George Homans, Floyd C. Mann, Delbert C. Miller, *Leadership and Productivity*, San Francisco, Ca., Chandler Publishing Co., 1965, Wendell Bell, Richard J. Hill, Charles R. Wright, *Public Leadership*, San Francisco, Ca., Chandler Publishing Co., 1961; Eugene P. Dvorin and Robert H. Simmons, *From Amoral to Humane Bureaucracy*, San Francisco, Ca., Canfield Press (Harper-Row), 1972.

24. B.E. Collins and H. Guetzkow, *A Social Psychology of Group Process for Decision Making*, N.Y., Wiley, 1964, p. 212.

25. For further information on the meaning and origin of the concept of charismatic leadership see Weber's essay on the sociology of charismatic authority in H.H. Gerth and C. Wright Mills, *From Max Weber: Essays in Sociology*, N.Y., Oxford University Press, (Galaxy Edition), 1958, pp. 51-55; for further information on the other three styles of leadership see Robert T. Golembiewski, "Three Styles of Leadership and Their Uses," *Personnel*, Vol. XXXVIII, No. 4 (July-August 1961), pp. 34-45; Ralph Waite and Ronald Lippitt, "Leader Behavior and Member Reaction in Three Social Climates," in Dorwin Cartwright and Alvin Zander (eds.) *Group Dynamics: Research and Theory*, 3rd Edition, N.Y., Harper & Row, 1968, pp. 326-334, and Edward A. Shils, "Charisma, Order and Status," *American Sociological Review*, Vol. 30, No. 2, (April 1965), pp. 199-213.

26. Gerth and Mills, *op. cit.*, p. 52 and pp. 245-251; see also Shils, "Charisma, Order and Status," *op. cit.*, pp. 199-213, for a helpful discussion on Max Weber's concepts of charismatic leadership see Reinhard Bendix, *Max Weber, An Intellectual Portrait*, Garden City, N.Y., Doubleday & Co., Inc., Achor Books, 1962, pp. 298-328.

27. Robert Blake and Jane. F. Mouton, *The Managerial Grid*, Houston, Texas, Gulf Publishing

Co., 1964, *passim.*

28. Rensis Likert, *New Patterns of Managment*, N.Y., McGraw Hill, 1961, *passim.*

29. Douglas McGregor, *The Human Side of Enterprise*, N.Y., McGraw Hill, 1960; see also, e.g., F. Hertzberg, *Work and the Nature of Man*, Cleveland, Ohio, World Publishing Co., 1966.

30. Berne, *Structure and Dynamics of Organizations and Groups, op. cit.*, p. 106, *et. seq.*, cf. Carl G. Jung, "The Concept of the Collective Unconscious," in Joseph Campbell, (ed.) *The Portable Jung*, N.Y., Penguin Books, 1976, pp. 59-61.

31. Berne, *Structure and Dynamics of Organizations and Groups, op. cit.*, pp. 98-99.

32. Amitai Etzioni, *The Active Society*, N.Y., The Free Press, 1968, p. 314; see also Elliot Jaques, *A General Theory of Bureaucracy*, N.Y., John Wiley & Sons, 1976, p. 39 and p. 293 for a psychologically oriented definition of power *viz.*, as influencing others to fulfill specific personal aims.

33. Robert H. Simmons and Eugene P. Dvorin, *Public Administration: Values, Policy and Change*, Port Washington, N.Y., Alfred Publishing Co., 1977, p. 574, for a more complete development on this point refer to the material in pp. 559-608; see also Robert H. Simmons, "The Washington State Plural Executive: An Initial Effort at Interaction Analysis," *The Western Political Quarterly*, Vol. XVIII, No. 2, June 1965, pp. 363-381.

34. Kenneth J. Meier, *Politics and the Bureaucracy: Policymaking in the Fourth Branch of Government*, North Scituate, Mass., Duxbury Press, 1979, pp. 55-67; see also Francis E. Rourke, *Bureaucracy, Politics and Public Policy*, Boston, Little, Brown and Co., Inc., 1969, pp. 11-86, and Anthony Downs, *Inside Bureaucracy*, Boston, Little, Brown and Co., Inc., pp. 44, 58, 211-222, these organizational power resources may be contrasted with the resources within a social situation that may be used as a basis of power. This includes, among other things, access to rewards, punishments, information, knowledge, legitimacy, expertise, experience, referent power (admiration and imitation) and reputation. The particular mix used will depend upon the situation, circumstances and people involved, see J. R. P. French and B. Raven, "The Bases of Social Power," in D. Cartwright and A. F. Zander (eds.) *Group Dynamics* (2nd ed.), Evanston, Ill., Row-Peterson, 1960, pp. 607-623.

35. Berne, *The Structure and Dynamics of Organizations and Groups, op. cit.*, pp. 227-236 and pp. 116-120. For his definition of a group, see pp. 26 and 67-77 for his suggestion that the ultimate goal of a group is its own survival, cf. Morton Kroll, "Understanding Large Organization—The Group Field Approach Revisited," *Public Administration Review*, Vol. 36, No. 6 (Nov./Dec. 1976), pp. 690-694.

36. Robert Ardrey, *The Territorial Imperative*, N.Y., Athenenum, 1966, *passim*; but especially pp. 169-173. cf. Berne, *Structure and Dynamics of Groups and Organizations, op. cit.*, pp. 116-117.

37. Berne, *Structure and Dynamics of Groups and Organizations*, pp. 116-117; Eric J. Miller and A.K. Rice, "Individuals Groups and Their Boundaries," in Arthur D. Colman and W. Harold Bexton, (eds.), *Group Relations Reader*, Sausalito, Ca., Grex, 1975, pp. 52-62 and also pp. 43-57.

38. Robert A. Dahl, *Modern Political Analysis*, Englewood Cliffs, N.J., Prentice-Hall, 1963, p. 23.

39. David Easton, *A Framework for Political Analysis*, Englewood Cliffs, N.J., Prentice-Hall, 1965, pp. 63-68, cf. Jaques, *op. cit.*, p. 23, pp. 40-41 and pp. 117-124 for important distinction concerning the sociological use of boundaries.

40. Jaques, *op. cit.*, pp. 100-160.

41. *Ibid.*, p. 101.

42. This presentation of some of Jaques' primary ideas cannot possibly do justice to the thorough, meticulous, careful, comprehensive, integrated theory of bureaucracy which he has developed. His efforts promise an incredibly fruitful harvest for those who pursue it, Jaques, *op. cit.*, pp. 99-301.

43. Jaques, *op. cit.*, pp. 144-152.

44. *Ibid.*, pp. 156-158.

45. *Ibid.*, p. 160, he also suggests that our employment produces symptoms of anxiety or disquiet. Such a condition will exist, he suggests, if a person is employed at a level of work beyond his capacity, *ibid.*, p. 185.

46. Berne, *Structure and Dynamics of Groups and Organizations, op. cit.*, pp. 67-78.

47. Berne, *Structure and Dynamics of Groups and Organizations, op. cit.*, p. 75.

48. Anthony G. Banet, Jr. and Charla Hayden, "A Tavistock Primer," in John E. Jones and J. William Pfeiffer, *The Annual Handbook for Group Facilitators*, La Jolla, Ca., University Associates, Inc., 1977, pp. 155-167, particularly pp. 156-159.

49. Wilfred Bion, *Experiences in Groups*, N.Y., Basic Books, 1961, *passim*; see also generally E.J. Miller and A.K. Rice, *Systems of Organizations*, London, Tavistock Publications, 1967.

50. P.M. Turquet, "Leadership: The Industrial and the Group," in G.S. Gibbard, J.J. Hartman and R.D. Mann (eds.) *Analysis of Groups*, San Francisco, Jossey-Bass, 1974, p. 357.

51. Margaret J. Rioch, "The Work of Wilfred Bion on Groups," in Arthur D. Colman and Harold Bexton (eds.) *Group Relations Reader*, Sausalito, Ca., Grex, 1975, pp. 21-34.

52. Wilfred Bion, "Experiences in Groups," *Human Relations*, Vol. 3, pp. 395-402, 1950; see also Vol. 1, 1948, pp. 487-496, Vol. 2, 1949, pp. 12-22, and pp. 295-303, Vol. 3, 1959, pp. 3-14, Vol. 4, 1951, pp. 221-226; see also the summary of his ideas in a clear and specific manner in Berne, *Structure and Dynamics of Groups and Organizations, op. cit.*, pp. 212-215.

53. Margaret J. Rioch, "The Work of Wilfred Bion on Groups," in Colman and Bexton, *op. cit.*, p. 30.

54. Rioch, "All We Like Sheep (Isaiah 53:6): Followers and Leaders," in Colman and Bexton, *op. cit.*, p. 162, and see the same article in its original source *Psychiatry*, Vol. 34, 1971, pp. 258-273.

55. Rioch, in Colman and Bexton, *op. cit.*, p. 176.

56. *Ibid.*, p. 177, cf. Bion in Colman and Bexton, *op. cit.*, pp. 14-20, cf. also Berne's concept of *Proclivities*, in Berne, Structure and Dynamics, *op. cit.*, pp. 158, *et seq.*

57. *Ibid.*, p. 27.

58. *Ibid.*, p. 28.

59. For Berne's concept of games, see his *Games People Play*, N.Y., Grove Press, Inc., 1964, and his *What Do You Say After You Say Hello?*, N.Y., Grove Press, Inc., 1977.

60. Berne, *Structure and Dynamics of Organizations and Groups, op. cit.*, pp. 67-71, see also D.W. Organ, "Some Variables Affecting Boundary Role Behavior," *Sociometry*, 1971, pp. 524-537.

61. Berne, *Structure and Dynamics of Groups and Organizations, op. cit.*, pp. 71-72.

62. Berne, *Structure and Dynamics of Groups and Organizations, op. cit.*, pp. 67-72.

63. Berne, *Structure and Dynamics of Groups and Organizations, op. cit.*, pp. 68-71.

64. This event occurred during a seminar concerned with power and authority held at Antioch College/West, Los Angeles, California, October 1975, and was related by the students and J. Holley to the author. The session was also recorded.

65. These preliminary observations were made by the author and his graduate students in April, May and June prior to the passage of a property tax limitation initiative (known as Proposition 13, the Jarvis Initiative) on June 6, 1978. Subsequent to its passage, local governments and California state government along with public education in the state faced a broad range of funding and survival problems. It may be hypothesized that drama triangle activity and basic assumption behavior will occur within the social milieu reflected in varying degrees of intensity. It is too early at the time of this writing to fully assess these events.

66. Miller and Rice in Colman and Bexton, *op. cit.*, pp. 62-68.

67. Miller and Rice in Colman and Bexton, *op. cit.*, p. 61.

RELATED READING

Bion, Wilfred, *Experiences in Groups*. New York: Basic Books, 1961. This is the effort which formulates Bion's basic approach to understanding group behavior. It is a distinctive and innovative approach.

Colman, Arthur D. and Bexton, Harold. *Group Relations Reader*. Sausalito, Ca.: GREX, 1975. A very helpful collection of readings exploring and expanding the work of Wilfred Bion as it relates to group behavior.

Deutsch, Karl. *The Nerves of Government*. New York: The Free Press, 1963. A truly important effort which examines the governing system as a complex and intrictate communication system. Power and conflict are minimized or simply responsive to managed responses.

Downs, Anthony. *Inside Bureaucracy*. Boston: Little, Brown & Co., 1967. This effort develops a theory of bureaucracy which reflects the present theoretical orientation toward bureaucracy. It takes bureaucracy seriously as an important force but raises no moral question. It centers primarily upon the internal aspects of the bureaucratic process.

Ellul, Jaques. *The Technological Society*. New York: Alfred A. Knopf, 1964. An important, even landmark, book examining the impact of technique and efficiency upon society. Ellul propounds an important challenge that cannot be ignored.

Jacoby, Henry. *The Bureaucratization of the World*. Berkeley, Ca.: University of California Press, 1973. A very significant study which examines the emergence of the administered world, explores its problems and suggests that the future of democracy is up against the engine of powerful bureaucracies and dependent upon the restoration of a politically aware public.

Medeiros, James A. and Schmitt, David E. *Public Bureaucracy: Values and Perspectives*. North Scituate, Mass.: Duxbury Press, 1977. An excellent effort indicating the need for an approach to bureaucracy which integrates machine, humans and political values as essential and legitimate within the social and bureaucratic processes.

Merton, Robert K.; Gray, Ailsa P.; Hockey, Barbara; Selvin, Hanan C. *Reader in Bureaucracy*. Glencoe, Ill.: The Free Press, 1952. A classic collection of readings centering attention on the many facets of bureaucracy which affect human existence within them.

Miller, Eric J. and Rice, A.K. *Systems of Organization*. London: Tavistock Publ., 1967. This book, of Tavistock socio-technical model, uses field examples to illustrate their attempts to reconcile two often contradictory views: 1) the view that the only purpose of organization is to insure efficient task performance; and 2) that the primary task of any enterprise is to satisfy the need of those who are employed in it.

Redford, Emmette S. *Democracy in the Administrative State*. New York: Oxford University Press, 1969. This singular effort keeps in view the essential need for a democratic and humane morality in the administrative state and focuses upon the problem of achieving it.

Rourke, Francis E. *Bureaucracy, Politics, and Public Policy*. 2nd Edition. Boston: Little, Brown & Co., 1976. This is a book which is sensitive to the role of bureaucracy in public policy making. It has a particular sensitivity to the roots and uses of bureaucratic power.

Simon, Herbert A. *Administrative Behavior*. 3rd Edition. New York: The Free Press, Inc. (a division of Macmillan), 1976. This is Simon's classic study of administrative behavior as decision-making and assumes that decision processes are the key to understanding organizational phenomena.

Chapter 4

BEHAVIOR AND PROCESS WITHIN GROUPS

Groups and organizations may be established deliberately through a legislative enactment or through appropriate administrative procedures in the public sector and in the private sector through a variety of ways ranging from voluntary and business groups to corporate forms. Groups may arise as well through more subtle, yet equally effective, processes. These are the results of the conscious choice of the individuals to band together to perform particular tasks.

Groups as Distinctive Entities

An aggregate cluster of persons becomes a group when: (1) through the transactions among the members, mutual awareness develops a common relationship, and there emerges a common group task, and (2) such a group, or social aggregation, has a definable external boundary with at least one major internal boundary. Where the major internal boundary is absent, it remains unstructured with only an external boundary and resembles a party. Groups are created in a variety of ways: through external threat, collective regressive behavior, as Bion suggests, or through attempts to satisfy needs for security, safety, dependence, affection, etc.

Thus it is, when individuals become members of a group, their behavior alters and a collective identity emerges around the task focus of the group itself. This can be a soccer team or a pickup baseball or basketball team on a recreation field or playground; it can be a lynch mob or a mob to stone witches; it can be a specialized combat unit (such as the Green Berets or the Marine Corps); it can be a religious commune (such as the Amish or the Mennonites); it can emerge to be a corporate organization (like Bell Telephone or IBM). It may evolve into a configuration where the groups or complex organizations become the focal point and the individual member fades into insignificance. Membership in such groups is attractive, often exciting, frequently ambiguous, and invites involvement, participation and engagement from the members of the group. The group becomes its own distinctive process. Much of the observable behavior in groups and organizations has been "lumped together" and identified as "informal" in contrast with the "formal" organization.

The Informal Organization: A Deceptive and Inadequate Concept

Some behavior which occurs in groups and organizations, in a manner not officially sanctioned, has been called informal organization. Ever since the Hawthorne experiments were conducted (approximately 1927-1937) by the Bell Telephone Company under the leadership of Chester I. Bernard, scholars of administration, organization and group process have been struggling to understand group and organizational behavior, which is, seemingly, distinct from the official organization. In the Hawthorne experiments, the women in the bank wiring room at Western Electric Corporation in Cicero, Illinois produced at a high level, regardless of any variation in the physical environment, e.g., raising or lowering of temperature or brightness of lights, etc. Finally, it was determined that these women thought they were special and therefore put out an extraordinary amount of extra work to get their production quotas met, regardless of the pleasantness or austerity of the circumstances. This event challenged profoundly Frederick W. Taylor's concepts of efficiency and, when combined with the findings of Mary Parker Follet concerning conflict during the same period, focused concern on group process which continues down to the present.[1]

All groups have manifest, latent, overt and covert aspects. The overt aspects are concerned directly with task performance and the manifest aspects are expressed in the official structure and procedures and are easily identified. It is the latent and covert aspects of group and organizational life which seem encompassed in the meaning of "informal organization." The latent aspects, among other things, include the emotional nature of the members, which becomes available when the group is under stress. The covert aspects are part of the private or hidden structure and process within the group itself which is not publicly sanctioned by group authority.

Group members each have hidden agendas or patterns of striving which are parts of themselves derived from their scripts. These hidden strivings are consciously or unconsciously witheld from the group, yet are powerful determinants of individual behavior within the group. The combined hidden agendas of group members constitute the latent aspect of group life. In contrast to the "rational, civilized, task-oriented" work group, the latent aspects of a group comprise the unconscious wishes, fears, defenses, fantasies, impulses, introjections and projections of the group members. It is these which surface and control the dynamics of the group and the processes of the group when the external boundaries are stressed.

The word "informal" fades into insignificance as the most recent developments in our understanding of human behavior and group process are utilized to enhance our understanding. It is no longer an adequate term to identify those aspects of organizational and group behavior which are essential to the survival of the group and a prelude to the productivity of the group. A brief survey of some of the variety of perspectives concerning the effort to fully understand group behavior will help identify the difficulty and complexities involved.

Perspective on Small Group Studies

The literature on groups issues from both the sociological and psychological traditions. Sociological contributions have been more concerned with the patterns of social structure which are independent of the particular individuals comprising the group at any one point in time. Psychological investigation has generally emphasized individuals and their psychological makeup rather than structural patternings. Early theorists within these approaches are readily identifiable. More recent approaches represent a closing of the hiatus between these two perspectives.

There are a variety of theoretical approaches to the analysis of groups, each offering a distinctive perspective. It is useful to identify some of the more helpful approaches. Field theory holds that behavior is the result of a field of interdependent forces. This approach utilizes the dynamics of relationship within a system of interrelative events and emphasizes the properties of a given structure, no matter what its history. This perspective developed by Kurt Lewin still has as its primary focus for addressing problems of organization, the individual. Important as this is, it has not led to a systematic theoretical formulation of group processes.[2]

Interaction theory views the group as a system of interacting individuals. Three basic components are usually identified, viz., activity, interaction and sentiment. This perspective supports that all aspects of group behavior can be accounted for by understanding the interdependent relations among these elements. This approach has frequently emphasized the recording and measuring of interaction in small group discussions and has guided a good deal of reasearch on group process.[3]

The empirical statistical orientation relies on the determination and identification of group characterisitics through the use of such empirical techniques as factor analysis and uses data such as population characteristics, aspects of internal structure such as roles and status gradients and syntality variables which relate the group acting as a whole.[4]

The sociometric orientation developed by J.L. Moreno focuses upon the network of interpersonal preferences and choices among group members. Group morale and performance are viewed as dependent upon the choices of the members and this is discerned through sociometric analysis. This approach has been helpful in elucidating interpersnal attraction and some aspects of group cohesiveness and compatability. It has stimulated very helpful research, although its effect on the development of systematic theory has been minimal.[5]

The psychoanalytic tradition derived from Freudian psychology is generally concerned with the motivational and defensive processes of the individual in group life. The work of Melanie Klein and others departs from a conception of the inner world of id-drives and instincts to develop an understanding of the highly personal inner world of ego-object relationships. This more interpersonal theory underlies the group analytic theory of Wilfrid Bion as well as the subsequent open-systems approaches of E.J. Miller and A.K. Rice and Daniel Katz and R.L. Kahn. This is a theoretically fertile orientation based upon observational data, yet it has not stimulated a great deal of empirical research to date.[6]

The general psychology orientation attempts to expand the theoretical formulations about individual behavior, e.g., learning, motivation and behavior, to the analysis of group behavior. Marvin Shaw suggest that this is perhaps not actually an approach but seems rather to be a denial that there is anything unique about group behavior. Certainly, the difficulty of shifting the level of analysis from the individual to the group presents great difficulty for empirical analysis.[7]

The open-systems approach to human organizations stresses the dependence of such enterprises for growth and viability upon their processes of transactions with the larger environment. A system in the meaning presented here is defined as a set of elements, or event structured units, which are actively interrelated, involving input, conversion and output activity and operating as a bounded unit. This theoretical approach is useful across different levels such that the individual, the group and the organization may be seen as progressively more complex manifestations of a basic structure field. This offers a great opportunity for research. The work of Katz and Kahn and Miller and Rice, identified earlier, are excellent examples of this dynamic open-systems approach. The great strength of this approach is indicated by its practical applications in the field to group and organizational problems, particularly in the efforts to reconcile the technology of the task with human social needs.[8]

It is important to note another more eclectic model of group process. Barry Collins and Harold Guetzkow have developed a group process model incorporating the broad range of theoretical and empirical approaches. The model includes the concept of interaction between task and interpersonal systems and the emphasis on the survival and maintenance of the group. They show that the task potential of the group, once interpersonal aspects are dealt with, can often exceed the resources of the group members working individually in isolation. These researchers found that interpersonal rewards are vital to maintain effective task activity.[9] This emphasis upon taking human needs into account dovetails with the open-systems model and with the orientation developed within this effort. These approaches support that a group or organization cannot be understood without constant study of the forces which impinge upon that system.

Morton Kroll has suggested the importance of the group field approach to organizational research.[10] Field studies allow the observation of groups over a period of time, thus availing the researcher of the developmental changes in the group. It is the observation of naturally occurring, enduring, ongoing groups which informs the theory of this volume.[11]

The ongoing relationships within a group may be characterized among other things as competitive, hostile, conflicted, compliant, submissive, cooperative, etc. Group and organizational outcomes are significantly related to small group process. The role of management and leadership in the intentional ordering of a group to achieve a specific purpose, goal or end is an important role to assess and understand. For management qua leadership has the responsibility to provide for the regular conduct of business, to respond to extraordinary internal events, and respond to unanticipated external crisis which impinge upon group and organizational boundaries.

The reconciliation of the two different orientations toward groups, *viz.*, the psychological approach with its emphasis upon the individual and the sociological approach with its emphasis upon group structure, may be found by focusing upon the aspects and nature of role. The glue between the individual and social structure of the group and organization may be found in the concept of role. Elliot Jaques notes that role is the dynamic aspect of status and this means "…what a person does, how he behaves as a result of social position or status." More particularly he suggests that role may be defined "…as the sociological context of individual behavior." Roles, he observes, are always parts of role relationships and that relationship is an integral part of the role itself.[12]

Group Structure and Role Development

Organizationally or group prescribed role demands may be distinguished from personal role definition. The manifest structure of an organization prescribes for each member a formal office or, as D. Levinson suggests, a social position. This formal position embodies the organizational demands and behavioral expectations that confront the occupant of such a position. These expectations may vary in explicitness, clarity and coherence. Such variability is a source of uncertainty and conflict. Personal role definition can be distinguished into two levels of adaptation: at the ideational level, role conception; and at the behavioral level, role performance. Both may be considered separately and both are influence by personal history, values, personality characteristics and script strivings, education, etc.[13] Each person occupying such a role in his or her various interactions inside an organization or task group tends to present herself or himself in a particular and distinctive way. This is called the persona. This is the way a person presents himself or herself to the group. It is, in particular, the way he or she chooses to be seen, the way he or she wants to be seen. The private structure places a group member into a particular covert role and this covert role is the way the person is actually seen, perceived and experienced by other members of the group.[14]

Jaques provides the conceptual setting which identifies the importance of role behavior, "Role relationships…constitute a field within which behavior occurs."

Persons occupying specific roles are part of a contextual net. The behavioral context at any given point in time is the resultant of the personalities of the role occupants, their perceptions and understanding of one another, their attitudes to the constraints imposed by the role relationships, their degree of socialization, and their ability to inhibit and control the nature of their transactions.[15] In this context the covert role may well be as important or more important than the formal organizational role.

The organization with its complex of groups provides a many-faceted emotional climate which tends to"demand" of the participant members varied forms of interpersonal allegience, friendships, deference, intimidation, ingratiation, rivalry and the like. Such groups provide the opportunity for stimulation, for structured interpersonal relationships, and for leadership. It is these aspects of organizational life which may be identified as reflecting the private structure of a group.

The Private Structure of Groups

The private structure of a group provides the "territory" within which, among other things, basic assumption behavior occurs. It provides the power play activities, drama triangle transactions and covert role development. The productivity and task of a group is dependent upon the outcomes and nature of the ongoing processes of the private structure.

The private structure reflects what is going on in the minds of group members with respect to their relationships with each other and to the various activities, processes and expectations within and of the group.[16] The image that each person carries in his other mind of himself or herself in relation to each of the other members of the group, the group as a whole, and his or her relationship to the leadership and/or authority is significant in relation to how a person behaves and transacts his or her own business with the group. Eric Berne identifies this as the imago and defines it as, "any mental picture, conscious, preconscious, or unconscious, of what a group is or should be like."[17] He suggests that this is any mental picture held by individual group members about what the group is like or what it should be like. These are often experienced as expectations.

Any difference between what a member anticipates, hopes for, or wants a group to be and what he or she perceives the group actually is gives rise to individual dissatisfaction and increases individual psychological tension. This determines how a person will adjust and relate to a group and work with other members of the group. As group members alter their mental picture of what the group is like, they increase the intesity of their transactions within the group. Each person in this sense creates his or her own ongoing history within the group.

Group Imagos

The mental image or imago each person carries in his or her mind undergoes alteration as one becomes an ongoing participant within a group. Berne identifies four basic adjustments in an individual's view of the group within which he or she participates. These may be identified as follows:[18]

1. **Provisional Group Imago.** As membership in a group is impending, one begins to form an initial mental image of what a group is going to be like for oneself and what one may hope to get out of it. This picture soon changes. Individual and group interaction in this phase is light and polite. It is specifically a blend of childhood fanasies and adult expectations based on previous experiences about what to expect

within a group.

2. **Adapted Group Imago.** This follows a superficial appraisal of other members of the group, usually done on the basis of observations made during one's own participation in the ritual and activity of the group. Other members become a little more defined with their personalities becoming a little more distinct in one's own mind. At this point an individual is a little more willing to become involved in group interaction in order to fulfill more readily his or her own needs for time structure, stimulation and stroking. He or she in this stage is selecting other members with whom he or she may become more closely involved. One is generally content here with recognition of a modest variety.

3. **The Operative Group Imago.** Before a person becomes fully engaged in the activities of the group, his or her idea of the group must undergo fundamental alteration. A person does not become a fully engaged member of a group until that person thinks he or she knows his or her own place in the leader's image of the group. This full participation remains wobbly and uncertain unless there is constant and repeated reinforcement of that judgment from the leader.

It is important to realize a member's own guess of what the leader thinks of him or her must be validated through experience with the leader from time to time, if that person is to remain a fully engaged member within the group process. Berne selects the phrase operative principle to identify this leader-member event. It means that a group member does not initiate action or become actively involved in the group process until he or she "knows" how he or she stands in the group imago of the leader. This judgment and a member's continued involvement required continual existential reinforcement. Specifically, this is a personal judgment a group member makes in the privacy of his or her own mind about how one stands in the eyes and mind of the leader and one's behavior hinges upon such a judgment made concerning what the leader thinks of one.

This operative principle is of substantial importance in understanding individual and group behavior. A considerable amount of all group behavior is spent in assessing, reassessing, evaluating, altering, testing, reacting, and readjusting one's inner judgment of what the leader thinks of one. This is perhaps the least understood and the most sensitive of all group links. It is the nexus which subtly, uniquely and distinctly affects performance, achievement, and advancement, as well as satisfaction.

Behavior is always rebounding off the silent judgments being made and tested by the individual group members as they assess their positions *vis-a-vis* the leader's. There may also be a self-fulfilling aspect to the operative principle, *viz.*, the group member acts out syntonically or dystonically in relation to the group based on his or her perception of the leader's judgment. The leader's reaction (thus invited) may be specifically responsive to the act and thereby reinforce existentially the member's perception. For example, a member perceives the leader does not like her. So she makes an error in her work. The reprimand is not long in coming. The judgment of the group member is existentially supported and the drama triangle in underway.

4. **Secondarily Adjusted Group Imago.** At this stage an individual gives up his or her own individual patterned strivings in favor of playing the group's way, i.e., conforming to its culture. In a small group, Berne observes, this may lead to "game-free intimacy." This is a relinquishment of a "script" pattern while at the same time retaining personal moral integrity.

A new member then enters a group with his own individual propensities, needs

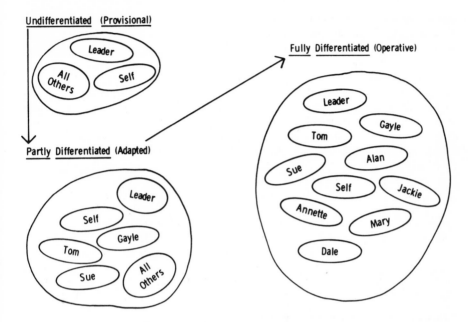

Figure 4-A: Stages in Imago Differentiation

and proclivities which he or she is willing to modify in order to gain some of the benefits of group membership and satisfy his or her own needs. Each member starts with a provisional imago and proceeds through a series of adjustments — adaptive, operative and sometimes secondarily adjusted — that permit him or her to ultimately become fully engaged in group activity and process. Figure 4-A is a graphic display of the progression of the first three stages of imago differentiation. Activity may be carried out regardless of the stage of an individual group imago. In order for a group to be fully engaged or the members of the group to be fully engaged, the imagos of each of the members must be differentiated so that each has an idea and a set of expectations concerning the behavior of others.

Member Transactions: Levels of Intensity

Knowledge of this progression in the mental image of a group member in relation to a group in which he or she is a member makes it possible, Berne suggests, to define with some exactness the intensity of the transactions of an individual within the group. The intensity level concerning member transactions may be identified as follows:

1. **Participation.** Initially, as a new group member, one casts the image by which one would like to be seen by other group members. This is "putting one's best foot forward." The tacit, unspoken agreement among the group members at this stage is, "if you don't disturb my persona, I won't disturb yours." It is the way a person wants to present himself or herself to the group. The transactional stimuli at this level are expressed in words or gestures, or even eye movements, which indicate that a person has some awareness about what is going on within the group process.

2. **Involvement.** As a group member develops greater awareness of the group

process and becomes "better acquainted" with some of the other members, he or she will play a passive role in relation to the activities of those members. In this instance, the group member's perception or imago of the group have undergone secondary judgment.

3. **Engagement.** When a group member has elaborated his or her view of the other members and made a tentative decision concerning the leader's perception of him or her, then this group member takes the initiative in starting activity to achieve his or her own overt or hidden purposes within the group. The purpose of initiating such action is to influence the course of another person's activity to one's own advantage. This occurs only after the member's group imago is operative.

4. **Belonging.** A person belongs to a group when he has met three primary conditions: a) he is eligible; b) he is adjusted into the group process; c) he is accepted into the group. Eligibility refers to meeting the requirements for membership within the specific group. Adjustment occurs when a person is willing to resign some of his or her own personal proclivities and propensities in favor of behaving the group's way. Acceptance means that other members recognize that a person has given up some of his or her own individual needs, desires, and proclivities in favor of group cohesiveness. Such an individual group member has signaled that he or she will abide by group rules, written and unwritten understandings. There is some evidence that this involves a critical event in group life.[19]

Stages in Group Time Structuring

These intensity levels of group member transactions link the group process in progressive stages which themselves reflect a parallel intensity in the group process. Not every group member moves or invests into the group at the same rate but, as a greater proportion of individual members increase the intensity of their transactions, the intensity of the group process reflects this added degree of vigor. Thus the degree of intensity through time within the group process itself refects the stages of imago development of its members and the degree of intensity of their energy inputs into the group process. These stages in group time structuring, Berne identifies as follows:

Rituals. A predictable series of member transactions related to group process in that they reflect acceptable, established courtesies and understood ceremony.

Pastimes. Mutual and complimentary transactions dealing with the light, personal activities or some aspect of the environment. These exchanges are basically unrelated and irrelevant to group process.

Games. Berne identifies these as a series of covert (ulterior) transactions leading progressively to a well-defined climax in which there is a hidden advantage or payoff to the players.

Intimacy. A direct expression of authentic, meaningful emotion between or among individual members and/or the group without covert or ulterior motives or secretly held reservations. It is certainly possible to achieve this in a work situation. Persons engaged in cooperative, meaningful team work, or as collaborators on the same task or project, may experience this sense of closeness, yet not see one another socially.

These are Berne's specific concepts and are very useful in helping to understand the dynamics of group process within the private structures.[20] Figure 4-B summarizes these differentiated stages of imago development and levels of intensity within the group process.

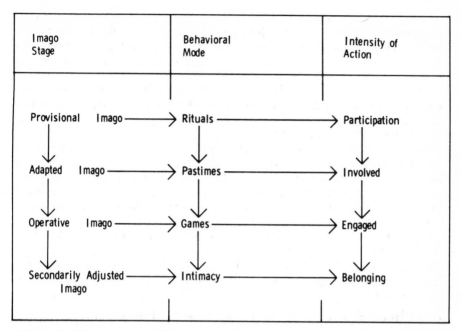

Imago Stage	Behavioral Mode	Intensity of Action
Provisional Imago ⟶	Rituals ⟶	Participation
Adapted Imago ⟶	Pastimes ⟶	Involved
Operative Imago ⟶	Games ⟶	Engaged
Secondarily Adjusted Imago ⟶	Intimacy ⟶	Belonging

Figure 4-B: Private Structure Differentiation in Group Members: Imago, Behavior and Action

Exploring Process and Structure in Groups and Organizations

Before task activity can proceed, the organization or group must overtly or covertly, intentionally or unintentionally, provide for the satisfaction of certain basic needs which each individual brings to the group and on which continuous participation in the group depends. These are as follows: first are the physical needs. This relates to creating an environment that is safe, is comfortable enough to work in, and has rudimentary sustenances, moderate temperature, food, water, and other basic essentials to the survival of the group. In addition, there must be available the basic opportunity for interaction among the members. An alternative to loneliness for group members must exist. Second, structuring the time of the members is required to deflect the fear and anxiety involved in which would otherwise be chaos and disorder. Time structuring promises the opportunity of order and the safety which order brings. Third, the opportunity to achieve authentic intimacy within the context of the group is an essential provision.

This urge for intimacy may be hidden or open, it may be simple or quite complicated, yet underlies many intense and important transactions that occur within group process. Members generally discourage its expression. It is often penalized by official authority. The pursuit of intimacy, therefore, generally requires independence of action, thought and personal responsibility which interpenetrates the private structure and is not well suited to situations which may be imminently public or may become public.

Individual drives toward intimacy achieve a variety of expression. This is because of (1) the requirements and compromises individual members must make to insure group survival, (2) the disguises in individual behavior which result from the fear of intimacy itself or fear of public exposure, and (3) the individual variations in the meaning of intimacy.[21] Berne identifies this process as stroking. It is a concomitant of many group transactions. All persons seek strokes and negative strokes are better than no strokes at all. Negative stroking is frequently sought unknowingly as a substitute for positive affirmations.[22]

These needs are achieved through social intercourse which includes stimulation, time structuring, and stroking. The fulfillment of these are among the reasons why individuals are willing to resign part of their individual propensities in favor of the needs of the group and group survival.

The group must also provide an opportunity for the individual member to forward his or her own life plan which is generally unconscious or hidden from personal view and understanding. This hidden agenda or script is an unconscious design each person has for his or her own life which is formulated in one's earliest years. Each group member takes the opportunity to forward that life plan as much as possible in any given situation. These may be identified as patterns of striving, or anacasm.[23]

These patterns of striving have been generally learned in early childhood and reinforced in later childhood and are used in transacting one's own emotional business with other people. These are the pervasive concomitants of all transactions inside a group and are usually acted upon in some manner by group members whether it be in pursuit of a task, combat or process.

Group Modalities: Task Group, Combat Group, Process Group

Individuals participating together in a manner that forms a group with a definable external boundary and at least one or more major internal boundaries, either created within the dynamic processes of individual interaction or imposed, creates a situation where the individual in the group exists in an association of mutual interdependence.[24] This association of the individual with the group may be identified as a symbiotic relationship; as such it is important here to pursue further the nature of the linkage between the individual group member and the group process.

Three basic group modes are identified by Eric Berne. The first may be identified as a task group or work group. In this instance, the boundaries of the group, both the external and the major internal boundaries, are in a state of well-established and understood order. They are in harmony. They are in equilibrium. In the task group mode most of the group's energies may be devoted primarily to work tasks. The environment is non-threatening and the group can focus on the work which it has chosen or is assigned to do. Here the energy of the members is extended and devoted to productive effort.

A second group mode which Berne identifies is the combat group. Here the group faces a serious and immediate threat from the external environment and attention is focused upon the maintenance of the group boundaries and the protection of the energy and resource supports. The goal of this group is the conquest or dissipation of the external threats or disruptive forces.

The final modality that may occur within an established group is the process group. When the group is operating in this mode the concern of the group is the internal interpersonal, emotional aspects of group behavior. The environment outside the external boundary may be threatening or not threatening. An unanticipated, unexpected rupture of the major external boundaries or any unusual loss, rupture or disruption of the major internal boundaries will produce a group process. Here the group focuses on itself in order to maintain and promote, achieve or reclaim the or-

MODE	EXTERNAL ENVIRONMENT	FOCUS	GOAL
TASK	Non-Threatening	Task Oriented	Productivity
Combat	Threatening	Surmounting External Disruption	Reduction, Dissolution, or Elimination of External Threats
Process	Either Threatening or Non-Threatening	Group Interaction	To Further Internal Order and Safety

Figure 4-C: Group Modalities

derly existence of the group.[25] It is under such stress that the basic assumption behavior, identified in the previous chapter, may emerge. It is a shared, pervasive sense that the survival of the group is at stake in this instance. Thus the goal of the internal process of the group is the promotion of its own border and safety. These group modalities are summarized in Figure 4-C. These group modes, task, combat and process, are aspects of group behavior (in any group) in response to or in the absence of varying degrees of stress upon the group.

Survival: The Ultimate Purpose

Three varieties of group survival were previously identified. The first is ideological, the second is physical, and the third is effective. Ideological survival is simply the survival of an organization in the minds and fantasies of the members and descendants long after it has any significance as an organized force in a community or a nation. Even though the group has physically ceased to exist it may spawn sentimental or even terrorist acts in its name.

An attempt to maintain cultural significance may spawn organizations that tend to capture the culture of the "old country" and there seems to be ever present the continuous hope for a renewed existence of the group. Sometimes the hope for renewed existence is actually sustained. The land of Israel was an ideological fantasy for many centuries and in this century was reestablished as an actual national state. The Irish, Swedish, eastern European communities that became established in American cities with the waves of immigration from Europe are examples of ideological survival. The physical survival of the group is necessary if it is to exist and thrive. On the various Indian reservations North American Indians such as the Zuni and Hopi in their pueblos, the Navajo on their reservation, though their lands have been to an extent redefined, have achieved a modest degree of physical survival.[26]

Groups may survive with ideological remnants along with redefined physical boundaries and still not achieve effective survival. The effective survival of a group rests on the membership's capacity and ability to carry on the organized productive activity that it deems essential to such survival. If the interpersonal relationships, belief systems and psychological ties which support the ideology of the group become tenuous or weak, members then feel little need to keep the group going and it falls apart from lack of love, care and commitment as they drift away. Here the group decays physically as well as ideologically and is rendered ineffective. If the formal structure of the group is eliminated or seriously weakened in a manner where the group is unable to fulfill its task, the group is effectively destroyed. Where the organizational mission is achieved and it is unable to redefine that mission successfully to its support and resource community, that organization will decay. Reorganization, reassignment of the group or organization's mission, or a successful attack on the group or organization's resources and supports will affect the ability of the group or organization to survive.

Even though the ideology may be strong and the formal structures intact, the internal dynamics of the organization may be in such disarray that it can be effectively disrupted from within. The avoidance of decay tends to be a problem of commitment and morale. The avoidance of destruction is the fundamental purpose of the combat group and the elimination and avoidance of disruption is one of the main concerns of the process group. Berne observes:

> ... in attempting to destroy a group as an effective force, the ususal procedure is to attack it ideologically to induce decay (erosion), to attack it physically to bring about partial destruction (attrition), and finally to penetrate the major boundaries in order to disrupt it (infiltration). [27]

The ultimate purpose then of each of the three group work modes, task, combat and process, is to assure the survival of the group, avoid decay, disruption and destruction and provision the order and safety of the group so work may be accomplished. The energy utilized by group members when combined make up the work of the group and is focused on productivity, maintaining internal and external structure or the conduct of group activity. Combat and process problems take precedence over task productivity insofar as any disturbance of its capacity to survive externally or any disturbance of its internal order immediately stops work task activities until the external threats are eliminated and internal order is achieved. Thus a group's capacity to do productive work rests on the maintenance of a stable environment and the resolution of internal stress. [28]

The first concern of any group is its orderly existence. Survival of the group is connected to the individual group member's idea of his or her own personal survival. Thus the possible termination of a group raises fears within the membership for their own personal survival. Group survival thus becomes the primary concern of the organization. Where survival is not an issue and it seems assured in the minds of the members, mission and task objectives become a primary concern, particularly in the tactical structure of the organization. Under these conditions survival is left to the policy-making and strategic levels of an organization.

The dysfunctional consequences of survival as the singular transcendent goal of individual and group survival has been explored elsewhere. [29] If this problem could be effectively addressed, this overriding concern for survival could diminish and concern for effective task performance increase. A significant approach to remedy this situation is forwarded by Elliot Jaques. There is an urgency in his writing when he suggests that the concerned political-social system needs to assume responsibility for creating and maintaining abundant employment opportunities. This he states is a primary employee right. It is, he states, the right of every person who seeks employment to be able to find work reasonably consistent with his interests, experience and capacity.[30]

Symbiosis in Group-Member Interaction: Combat Group

The combat group coalesces around an anticipated or existing threat from the external environment. When the threat is perceived as imminent and the group is a cohesive group, individual dissension is reduced or set aside and the group coheres in response to the external threat. Thus the group coalesces around a pervasive shared fear and/or frequently anger. This is reflected in a special closeness, cohesiveness, and dedication which supports group action to produce group survival, avoid disintegration of the group and relieve the threat to the internal structure of the group itself. Individual members each experience the fear and anger which comes in anticipation of the disruption or invasion and expresses these emotions with behavior reflecting, for the most part, commitment and dedication.

Individual group members through their own actions participate in activities calculated or felt to lead to individual and group survival which avoids group disintegration. The action taken may paradoxically risk that possibility as well. This combat group process is to be distinguished from the Bion fight/flight basic assumption mode by the quality and intensity of the group cohesion available to the group in answering to the external threat. Group cohesion relates to the work already done to assure the orderly existence of the group.

In a cohesive group, group members have most of their energy already engaged in the common goals of the group and the group has developed its capacity to deal with these in a direct, conscious and orderly fashion. This is reflected in a combat group which can "call up" the cohesive energy within the group and focus upon real survival threats. A fight/flight group finds little cohesion available to it and integration and coordination of individual energy in pursuit of the task is weak and generally not available. It moves rapidly between the fight/flight alternatives. The focus of a combat group is outward toward the actual threat across the external boundary. The focus of the fight/flight group is inward toward the internal aspects of the group. The fight/flight group is operating out of a "basic assumption." The combat group is facing an actual threat to its survival. Planning action, taking action or the immediate anticipation of taking action relieves tension and stress on the individual derived from the fear of death or economic disruption.

In a combat group individual members feel fear and anger which is expressed through commitment and dedication to the group purpose and supports their participation in risk-taking action which they feel will hopefully lead to a reduction or relief of the threat to themselves and the group. The group coalesces around a perceived external threat and develops a distinctive cohesiveness and dedication which is designed to support risk-taking action in a coordinated way so as to reduce or relieve the perceived threat to the group. The ultimate goal for both the individual and the group is survival of both. This symbiosis in group-member interaction in a combat group is summarized in Figure 4-D.

Symbiosis in Group-Member Interaction: Task Group

Individuals within a task group are primarily concerned with performing tasks specifically related to the "business" or purpose of the group. In the task group, individual emotional life is hidden and the individual is concerned with accomplishing

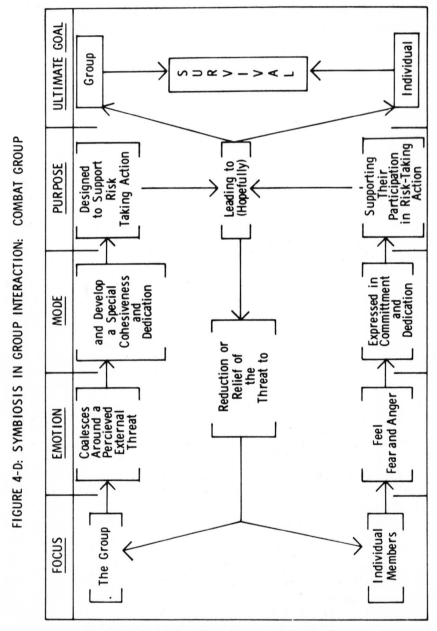

Figure 4-D: Symbiosis in Group Interaction: Combat Group

his or her work task. Dissembling is a characteristic reaction to dealing with emotions in a task group, i.e., emotions frequently are disguised, ignored, feigned and concealed and "split away" within this group. Rituals are maintained and routine procedures followed. These are designed to provide structure and orderly process to

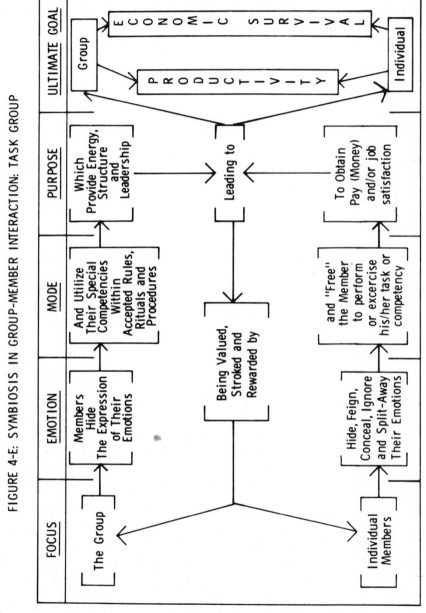

Figure 4-E: Symbiosis in Group-Member Interaction: Task Group

forward the productivity goals of the group.

Group members may be viewed as avoiding or hiding expression of specific emotions, utilizing the special competencies within the membership and organzing these special competencies according to accepted rituals and procedures in a manner that provides stimulation, structure and leadership. This, in turn, leads to coordinated group accomplishment. It also relieves and avoids the tension that comes from unfocused group activity and unstructured group process. Individuals with an activity or work group tend to "split" their emotions away and project then onto other members of the group and thus deny their own emotional life. Thus emotional life in a group is expressed in overt and covert behavior which may on occasion surprise group members who are blind to such processes. The goal in this instance in denying one's emotional life in a group is to achieve economic payoffs required for personal survival. In the task group individual members split and project their emotions and give expression to their emotional life in covert and overt behavior so as to free the individual member to do his or her own special task. From this is derived the strokes and payoffs necessary to provide for an individual member's needs.

In the task group individual members hide, feign, conceal, ignore and split-away personally felt emotions and thereby "free" themselves to perform or exercise their own special task or competency. This is done to obtain pay and satisfaction which leads to being valued, stroked and rewarded by the group as a whole and by members of the group individually. When the group becomes the focus, members are seen as hiding the expression of their emotions and utilizing their special competencies within accepted and established rules, rituals and procedures which provide energy, structure and leadership leading to being valued by the group. This then contributes simultaneously to the group goal of survival through productivity and the membership goal of fulfilling individual needs for economic survival and stroking. This symbiotic process linking an individual member to the group task is summarized in Figure 4-E.

Symbiosis in Group-Member Interaction: Process Group

Individual members within this group mode feel particular specific emotions of which they may or may not be aware and these are expressed in overt or covert transactions which are designed to obtain particular psychological payoffs or express in some manner deeply felt but recognized or unrecognized emotions. Effective performance of tasks within the group ultimately rests upon successfully dealing with the special nature of these relationships within the group. Berne observed that the successful conduct of group work (task) rests upon the successful resolution of these matters within the group. This observation is of such immense significance that it is fair to characterize it as Berne's Law:

...the effectiveness of the work group depends upon the success of the process group. [31]

Group activity cannot be understood, examined or intentionally changed without critical attention to the operations implicit in this characteristic of group life.

The effective survival of any group can be determined by the ability of the members to carry on organized work. The effectiveness of the work group depends ultimately on the success of the process group. [32] Any unexpected, unprogrammed, accidental or intentional disruption of the major internal boundaries or the major external boundaries will immediately interrupt that group's task activity until the threat to orderly group process or survival is resolved. The implicit or explicit attention of the group is immediately focused upon the rupture. Responses may reflect basic assumption modes previously explored, unless it is a combat group. When this occurs the group behaves in a manner expected to evoke particular varieties of action which relieve stress of the group and leads to survival of the group.

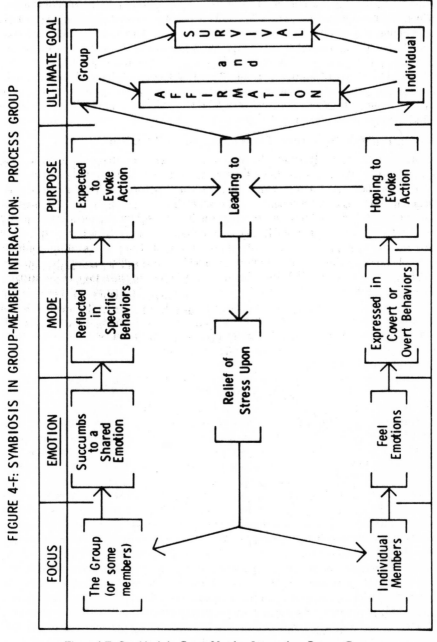

Figure 4-F: Symbiosis in Group-Member Interaction: Process Group

In the process group individual members feel emotions which are expressed in covert or overt behaviors in the hopes of evoking action which leads to the relief of stress, fear, anxiety, etc., of the individual member. Where the group is the focus either the group as a whole or some of its members succumb to a shared emotion which is then reflected in specific behaviors expected to evoke action which reduces or eliminates a variety of stresses within the group. This process simultaneously contributes to the divergent yet compatible goals of orderly process (affirmation) and survival. Figure 4-F illustrates this symbiosis in group-member interaction within the context of a process group. The effectiveness of the work and productivity of the group depends upon success of the process group at resolving group process events. It is the structure, transaction, and interaction of group process which next receives attention.

Group Process: Structure, Transaction and Interaction

Before proceeding, it is useful to differentiate between group process and a process group. Group process centers upon the variety, meaning, patterns and consequences of the transactions and interaction linkages and networks which characterize the ongoing processes of human behavior in organizations and groups. As such it involves the boundaries, procedures and routines established within the manifest structure and centers on the impacts and linkages encompassing the whole, as well as the many diverse structural parts of the group and organization. The focus is on the conflicts and struggles resulting from attempts to organize, disorganize, reorganize, modify or change or otherwise alter the structure of a group or organization. If the struggle is focused outward and it is a struggle involving outside pressure and the cohesion of the group it may be external group process, as it takes place at the major external boundary. If it results from conflicts and problems arising among the leadership it is major internal group process. If the struggles and conflicts arise from transactions and interaction patterns involving individual members of the organization minor group process results.

A process group is one where the group is primarily engaged in internal group process. It involves the aspects of group behavior and the behavior of individual group members as they struggle through their transactions in the group to respond to real or imagined threats to the survival of the group and to meet their own emotional strivings as well. Specifically, the process group deals with the emotional aspects of group life. A group process is a specific event or series of connected on-going events in response to stress arising from events related to the major boundaries of the group. There are two aspects to a process group. First, a process group is brought into being when a group is processing the emotional fallout spawned by stress-producing events which threaten or actually penetrate major group boundaries. This is intermittent in its occasion. Second, a process group occurs when a group is dealing with ongoing projections, splits and other emotional aspects of group life and these transactions peak and dominate the concern and attention of the group. This includes, among other things, the drama of power plays, rescues, persecutions, drama triangle operations, covert role differentiation and basic assumption behavior. These are generally hidden, frequent and often continuous. They amplify and recede in intensity, waxing and waning in response to their own internal patterns.

Groups are processing all the time, since the emotional life of the members does not abate while the members are present in the group or the work situation. If work tasks are being performed with any effectiveness, the processing of group emotional life is successful. This may occur with or without the blessings of legitimate authority and occurs even in the face of hostile authority. The process group mode becomes operative when these concerns dominate the group attention. These are prior and transcendent concerns which must be attended and resolved if task is to proceed with any effectiveness. It is not possible to avoid, ignore, repress, penalize, or eliminate the necessity of dealing with this aspect of group life. It is a condition precedent to achieving effective task performance. In groups process (work) precedes task (work). Task and performance and group survival rest upon the successful resolution of the emotional aspects of life within the group.

Leadership in Process Groups

In the previous chapter it was observed a responsible leader within an organization and group is a person with a legal and organizational authority to exercise the assigned attributes to such a position. The effective leader is the one who may make the actual decisions and have the decisive influence in decision making that may or may not have a formal role within the organizational structure. The psychological leader is one who is the most powerful within the private structure of the group members.

The psychological leader serves as model and mold for the individuals transacting business within the private structure. This person may not be articulated, identified or understood in the operational context of the group; nevertheless, he or she is a powerful determinate of behavior because of his or her ability to impact on the emotions flowing within the private structure. The psychological leader, in contrast to the effective leader, is the one whose questions are most likely to be answered and whose suggestions are more likely to be followed in situations of stress.

Hidden Group Processes

Established processes which exist in the manifest structure are open to view and review, are easily accessible, and may be readily assessed. Yet the operations and success of these overt processes rest upon the underlying and dynamic interpersonal world of the group members. This world is generally hidden from view, frequently unconscious and often unrecognizable from the explicit behavior seemingly readily observable in the organization. This behavior which is hidden from view, difficult to observe and understand, may be identified as hidden group processes. These processes are an expression of the covert emotional dynamics which accompany any human involvement in group and organizational life. It is the outcome of these processes within the process group which determines the outcome of the task and mission of the group or organization. Berne's Law applies: The effectiveness of the work (task) group depends upon the success of the process group.[33]

Dealing with human emotions within the organizational and group context in ways other than through the typical means of denial, discipline, routines and punishment is an absolute essential change which must be brought to human groups and organizations if the dysfunctional consequences of these hidden processes are to be diminished and even avoided. If alienation is to be abated, reduced and eliminated and human potential restored, provisioning the organization for creative and healthy responses to human emotions is required. If productivity, output and accomplishment of the organizational goals and mission are to be achieved, the process group phenomenon must be responsive to the needs of the whole human being in healthy and straightforward ways. When a process group is underway no task work is done. The group is dominated by concern for establishing, or reestablishing, equilibrium and boundaries. The effectiveness and survival of an organization or group depends upon the dynamics within the private structure. This relates to the satisfaction of the needs, experiences, wishes and emotions of the group members.

SUMMARY

A group is a specialized social situation set within physical, geographical, psychological, spatial and temporal boundaries which may be open, closed or sealed where there is a particular and distinctive group culture and process. Any specific organization or group may be analyzed through its manifest structure, authority matrices, its private structure which involves the adjustment of each member into the group, group process which involves group and individual responses to stress and in relation to boundaries, and finally by examining interpersonal transactions.

The private structure reflects the evolution and development of the group imago of each member. Thus the provisional imago gives way to the adopted imago which gives way to the operative imago and this, when intimacy and belonging are achieved, gives way to the secondarily adjusted imago. Each of these in turn reflect a specific intensity, the transactions ranging from involved participation through engagement and belonging. These in turn are reflected in the rituals, pastimes, games and intimacy which occur in the group.

Group process is the work required of the group in order to promote and continue the orderly existence of the group. When the boundaries are in a state of well-established equilibrium, most of the group's energy will be exerted upon its work tasks. Any unusual event within the group affecting the major external boundary, its major internal boundary or major events among the members of the group itself will spawn a process group, wherin attention to task activity immediately recedes until such disruption is resolved. As such, the group becomes a process group dealing with the emotional aspects of the group until the problem is resolved.

When the major external boundaries are intruded in a disorderly and disruptive way it may, if sufficient cohesion is present, be called upon to defend itself, in which case it may be called a combat group.

A group must, as well, continuously process the ongoing emotional life of its members as that links into the group as a prior condition to effective group performance. This is a fundamental corollary of Berne's Law, i.e., the effectiveness of the work group depends upon the success of the process group. This is essential to an understanding of group life.

NOTES

1. Chester I. Barnard, *The Functions of the Executive*, Cambridge, Mass., Harvard University Press, 1938; Mary Parker Follett, "Dynamic Administration," *The Collected Papers of Mary Parker Follett,* Henry C. Metcalf and L. Orwick, (eds.), N.Y., Harper & Row, 1942.

2. For a more detailed presentation of these perspectives see Dorwin Cartwright and Alvin Zander, (eds.), *Group Dynamics*, 3rd edition, N.Y., Harper & Row, 1968, *passim*; and Marvin E. Shaw, *Group Dynamics, The Psychology of Small Group Behavior*, N.Y., McGraw-Hill Book Co., Inc., 1976, *passim*; on field theory see Kurt Lewin, *Field Theory in Social Science*, D. Cartwright, (ed.), N.Y., Harper, 1951, for detailed presentation of information from social psychological research see Gardner Lindzer and Elliot Aronson, (eds.), *The Handbook of Social Psychology*, 2nd ed., Reading, Mass., Addison-Wesley Pub. Co., 1969, esp. Vol. IV, *Group Psychology and Phenomena of Interaction*, Chapters 1-4.

3. George Homans, *Social Behavior: Its Elementary Forms*, N.Y., Harcourt Brace and World, 1961; and Robert F. Bales, *Interaction Process Analysis*, Cambridge, Mass., Addison Wesley, 1950, see also A. Paul Hare, F. Borgatta and Robert F. Bales, (eds.), *Small Groups: Studies in Social Interaction*, N.Y., A.A. Knopf, 1961.

4.   R. B. Cattell, "Concepts and Methods in Measurement of Group Syntality," *Psychological Review*, 1948, Vol. 58, pp. 48-63; and his "New Concepts of Measuring Leadership," in Cartwright and Zander, *op. cit.*

5.   J. L. Moreno, *Who Shall Survive? A New Approach to the Problem of Human Interrelationships*, Washington, D. C., Nervous and Mental Disease Publishing Co., 1934.

6.   Melanie Klein, et al., *Developments in Psychoanalysis*, N.Y., Hillar House, 1952; Daniel Katz and R. L. Kahn, *The Social Psychology of Organizations*, N.Y., John Wiley & Sons, 1966; E.J. Miller and A.K. Rice, *Systems of Organization*, London, Tavistock Publications, Ltd., 1967; and Wilfred Bion, *Experience in Groups*, London, Tavistock Publications, Ltd., 1959; and Margaret J. Rioch, "All We Like Sheep —(Isaiah 53:6): Followers and Leaders," *Psychiatry*, Vol. 34, 1971, pp. 258-273.

7.   Marvin Shaw, *op. cit.*, pp. 16-17.

8.   Alvin Zander, *Groups at Work*, San Francisco, Jossey/Bass Co., Inc., 1977.

9.   Barry E. Collins and Harold Guetzkow, *A Social Psychology of Group Processes for Decision Making*, N.Y., John Wiley & Sons, 1964, pp. 88-139.

10. Katz and Kahn, *op. cit.*, p. 26; and Morton Kroll, "Understanding Large Organizations— The Group Field Approach Revisited," *Public Administration Review*, Nov/Dec 1976, pp. 690-694.

11. Shaw, *op. cit.*, pp. 403-405.

12. Elliot Jaques, *A General Theory of Bureaucracy*, N.Y., John Wiley & Sons, 1976, pp. 24-25, on detachability and permanence of roles see pp. 30-32; see also D. Levinson, "Race, Personality and Social Structure in the Organizational Setting," *Journal of Abnormal and Social Psychology*, 1959, Vol. 58, pp. 170-180.

13. Levinson, *op. cit.*, p. 176. Role expectation in the manifest structure is similar to the concept of "positional authority" in which the role expectation of authority is vested in any individual who happens to occupy a given position in the organization. This type of authority may be identified typically as "rational-legal" authority, see F.E. Kast and J. E. Rosenzweig, *Organization and Management: As Systems Approach*, N.Y., McGraw-Hill, Inc., 1970, (revised 1979).

14. cf. Jaques, *op. cit.*, pp. 30-37, the concept of covert role presented here may be seen to be an aspect of assumed social structure suggested by Jaques, p. 33; when the role occupants are actually behaving within the function of their actual roles Jaques terms this the extant social structure, p. 33.

15. Jaques, *op. cit.*, p. 29, see also his distinctive application of the concept of status in relation to role in hierarchy, pp. 29 *et. seq.*

16. Elliot M. Fox, "Eric Berne's Theory of Organizations," *Transactional Analysis Journal*, Vol. 5, No. 4, Oct. 1975, p. 349.

17. Berne, *Structure and Dynamics of Organizations and Groups*, N.Y., Grove Press, Inc., Evergreen Edition, 1966, p. 244.

18. Berne, *Ibid.*, pp. 163-166.

19. Berne, *Ibid.*, p. 165; see also pp. 79-81 notes.

20. Berne, *Ibid.*, pp. 237-250 and his *What Do You Say After You Say Hello?*, N.Y., Grove Press, Inc., 1972, pp. 3-26.

21. Eric Berne, *Games People Play*, N.Y., Grove Press, Inc., 1964, pp. 14-20.

22. Berne, *Games People Play*, *op. cit.*, p. 15, Claude Steiner, *Scripts People Live*, N.Y., Grove Press, Inc., pp. 20, 36-37, 77, 110-17.

23. Berne, *Structure and Dynamics of Organizations and Groups, op. cit.*, pp. 79 & 160-161.

24. Eric Berne, *The Structure and Dynamics of Organizations and Groups, op. cit.*, pp. 53-66. See especially pp. 227-236 for a useful classification of social aggregations (first published by J.B. Lippincott Co., 1963); also see Chapter 3, Rioch's "mature" basic assumption group compares to Berne's combat group, see her "The Work of Wilfred Bion," in Colman and Bexton, *op. cit.*, p. 30.

25. *Ibid.*, pp. 42-43.

26. For information on the Hopi see Laura Thompson and Alice Joseph, *The Hopi Way*,

N.Y., Russell & Russell, 1965; for information on the Zuni see Ruth Benedict, *Patterns of Culture*, N.Y., Houghton Mifflin, 1934 and Dorothea Leighton and John Adair, *People at the Middle Place: A Study of the Zuni Indians*, New Haven, Conn., Human Relations Area Files Press, 1966; for information on the Navajo see Clyde Kluckhon, *The Navajo*, Cambridge, Mass., Harvard University Press, 1951 and James F. Downs, *The Navajo*, N.Y., Holt, Rinehart and Winston, 1972.

27. *Ibid.*, p. 68.

28. There is an urgent propensity in established organizational leadership to support the status quo within and without the organization. A substantial body of literature addresses the question, e.g., Marilyn Gittell, *Participants and Participation*, N.Y., Center for Urban Education, 1967, Peter Marris and Martin Rein, *Dilemmas of Social Reform*, N.Y., Atherton Press, Inc., 1967, Robert Morris and Robert H. Binstock, *Feasible Planning for Social Change*, N.Y., Columbia University Press, 1966, and James A. Riedel, "Citizen Participation: Myths and Realities," *Public Administration Review*, May/June, 1972, esp., p. 215.

29. E.g., see Eugene P. Dvorin and Robert H. Simmons, *From Amoral to Humane Bureaucracy*, San Francisco, Ca., Canfield Press (Harper & Row Publishing Co., Inc.), 1972, pp. 8-10.

30. Jaques, *op. cit.*, pp. 181-189.

31. Berne, *op. cit.*, p. 76.

32. Berne, *op. cit.*, pp. 68-78.

33. Berne, *op. cit.*, p. 42 and p. 76.

RELATED READING

Berne, Eric. *Structure and Dynamics of Groups and Organizations*. New York: Grove Press, Inc., 1966. This is an important, innovative and original approach to the theory of group dynamics. The ideas presented by Berne here underpin much of the material in the present volume.

Berne, Eric. *Games People Play*. New York: Grove Press, Inc., 1964. This book was written for practicing clinicians but has had an immense impact in a variety of ways. It is the formulation and presentation of the ideas underlying transactional analysis which is a unique and distinctive approach to understanding human behavior and achieving creative and humane change as well.

Cartwright, Darwin and Zander, Alvin, editors. *Group Dynamics*. 3rd Edition. New York: Harper & Row, 1967. This is a useful collection of professional papers organized in a limited number of theoretically defined topics. Papers range from theoretical formulation to laboratory studies with emphasis upon empirical approaches to understanding group behavior.

Collins, Barry E. and Guetzkow, Harold. *A Social Psychology of Group Process for Decision Making*. New York: Wiley, 1964. This is a very clear presentation of the social-psychological view of groups, structurally designed to evolve general principles from existing empirical evidence for a model of group process.

Erikson, Erik. *Childhood and Society*. New York: W.W. Norton, 1950. This book is a true classic mapping the impact of childhood upon society with particularly skillful references to the operation of the personal psychological defenses and their cost to society as a whole.

Hall, Edward T. *The Hidden Dimension*. New York: Doubleday, 1966. This engaging book deals with the structure of experience as it is molded by culture and centers upon the uses of personal space, both public and private, as shared within cultural groups.

Janis, Irving. *Victims of Groupthink*. Boston: Houghton-Mifflin Co., 1972. Explores the distortion of the concept of consensus through the suppression of dissent and the requirement for a cohesive decision under pressure time frames by decision-making groups. This book explores the high social costs involved when this has occurred.

Katz, Daniel and Kahn, Robert L. *The Social Psychology of Organizations*. New York: Wiley, 1966. These authors use open system theory to define organization as a structure of human acts or events, as a system of roles. It is a notable theoretical advance in that it offers a framework to examine the multiple levels of individual, group and organization.

Shaw, Marvin E. *Group Dynamics, The Psychology of Small Group Behavior*. New York: McGraw-Hill Book Co., Inc., 1976. This book provides an excellent overview of the research findings on small group behavior. It emphasizes the results of controlled empirical studies. Each chapter concludes with a list of plausible hypotheses derived from the studies reported in each chapter.

Singer, David L.; Astrachan, Boris M., Gould, Lawrence J.; and Klein, Edward B. "Boundary Management in Psychological Work with Groups," *Journal of Applied Behavioral Science*, Vol. 11, No. 2, 1975, pp. 137-176. Using the socio-technical open systems model of organizations, a typology of group events is developed based upon two variables: 1) the task system; and 2) the psychological level at which task is pursued.

Truman, David B. *The Governmental Process*. New York: Alfred A. Knopf, 1960. This book uses a specialized conceptualization of process to develop and explore the formation, power and impact of "pressure groups" in the American political process.

Yablonski, Lewis. *Robopaths: People as Machines*. Baltimore, Md.: Bobbs-Merrill Co., 1976. An exploration of the impact of technology upon human beings and the conversion of the human being to a machine and the consequences this holds for society.

Chapter 5

ROLE DIFFERENTIATION WITHIN GROUPS

Men and women at work frequently give their power away to groups, organizations and bureaucratic structures represented by management. Characteristically, they detach themselves from their real feelings, as this is seemingly required for individual survival within the work situation. Yet for work to get done, that is, production to be achieved, the human dimensions of intelligence, joy, power and care must find their expression in overt straightforward and safe ways. Otherwise they will operate in covert, unexpected and ruinous ways. These human aspects of group life significantly affect the private structure of the group and have a profound effect on productivity and effectiveness of the group.

The Drama Triangle transactions, power plays, introjections, projections and their consequences, among other things, provide the dynamic aspects of the structure and processes of the private structure. These occur generally without the conscious awareness of the participating group members. Frequently the difficulties, pain and suffering which are the oft denied payoffs that accompany such activity are experienced as "inevitable" and "unavoidable." Often someone is "blamed" for a specific occurrence and there is a grain of truth to the accusation. When the result is exposed by one of the more vulnerable members who delivers feelings through tears, anger, rage or fear, the group seems close and the tensions seemingly relieved. Sometimes this overt expression of emotion is denigrated and seen as a "display," an exhibition of "weakness" where such a person is seen as a "loser" to be "rescued." It is important to examine these aspects of group process in greater detail.

The Banal Work Group: The Operations of Projection

The characteristic expression of the individual worker's own humanness in the organizational and work group setting is intriguing. The idea that an individual denies and represses his or her own feelings and then projects these feelings onto another human being or inanimate object and reacts to that other human being or object in distinctive ways is well known and is a fundamental explanation for such group phenomena as scapegoating. In this instance, the person denies, puts away "out of sight" that which he dislikes a lot in himself and then "finds" it in another person. Then he condemns or blames that person (who reflects the fault that exists in "the eye of the beholder") for having such a fault. The scapegoat is thus born.

When scapegoating becomes a group or even a national phenomenon it may be quite elaborate and focus on a whole ethnic subdivision or a particularly unpopular facet of the social system or national culture, the manner in which the Nazis used the Jewish population of Europe during the late 20's, 30's and 40's, ending in the awesome holocaust of the concentration camps. On a smaller scale this phenomena goes on inside families and work groups sometimes in rather sad and pathetic ways. Participants in bureaucratic settings split off their real feelings and project these feelings onto others. This seems to be a way individuals handle their own emotions when they must not express such feelings overtly. Thus splitting and projection become a way of handling humanness in the hidden levels of group process within the organization and in their own particular work group.

In the banal work group heavy managerial and peer pressure involving disapproval, humiliation, modification of pay and loss of job are on occasion brought to bear for "inappropriate" expression of such feelings as joy, anger, fear, sympathy, care or regret. Under these circumstances the individual worker becomes an "actor" hiding his or her "real" feelings behind the safety and security of a private structure role. In addition, for his or her own reasons, e.g. introjections or guilt, a group member selects or accepts the role that the group casts for him or her, for whatever those particular reasons might be. Additionally the group member may anticipate subtly in setting up the role so he or she may play it.

Under these circumstances management is protected from many significant challenges because they have a monopoly on affirmative personal approval and psychic and monetary rewards. An individual's "freedom" at work is conditionally based upon one's own powerlessness and the recognition of that on some level. The work situation then is joyless, mindless, and loveless and nearly everyone feels anger and fear consciously sometimes, but more often this is repressed and pushed out of one's own consciousness pending delayed delivery to another.

Over a period of time the members of a banal work group accumulate a reservior of deeply felt emotions, fears, resentments, angers, sorrows and cares. If these were safely, effectively and directly expressed they might be potent enough, even explosive enough, to spawn significant alteration of the oppressive work environment. However, the expression of anger, discontent and challenge is so fraught with danger inside the usual work group it is generally repressed and negated rather than safely dealt with by the individual experiencing it. It is consequently projected at some time onto someone else in the organization who, unable to effectively deal with it, is defensive or for some reason colludes in the process. Thus the debilitating, alienating, destructive network continues to be woven strand by strand, individual by individual, into the oppressive bureaucratic fabric.[1]

These are covert roles and their emergence within work groups and organizations may be identified as covert role development. Jaques observes, "Every person's behavior is influenced, bounded, pressed into place, not solely by whichever role he happens most immediately to be occupying but by his full complement of roles—one or more active, others latent, some overt, some covert, some consistent and some in conflict."[2] Here Jaques recognizes a covert role function and identifies other contingent roles pressing upon the participant as well.

Trigant Burrow observed projection has emerged as a universal reaction in humans. It "clutters the brains" of men and women and impairs their natural channels of social contact and communication.[3] Organizations and groups cannot escape the impact of this phenomenon. Yet they exist, are organized and operate on the basis that human emotions don't exist (or are a great inconvenience) and when they do it is embarassing, and they are something to be controlled, managed and rendered predictable. If Berne's Law (The effectiveness of the work group depends upon the success of the process group) were fully realized by organizational theorists and management, swift steps could be taken to develop healthy, creative responses to integrate human emotions into organizational and group life. Processing group emotional life is an essential component in work task outcomes and is universally ignored except either to impose negative management responses to the dysfunctional consequences or else management uses these emotional aspects manipulatively to betray the human personality and achieve organizational ends. This may seem harsh and deserves to be moderated on some occasions where management is genuinely attempting to implement humane conditions in their organizations.

Regularly, these deeply felt emotions are split off and projected into persons who play particular kinds of roles, e.g., someone in the work group takes on the clown role and acts out for the group the humor and joy felt within the group or to relieve the tensions through laughter or "gallows humor." A "crazy one" may rise to absorb the denied fears of the group members or a "crazy maker" may emerge where a shared perceived reality on the part of the group members may be denied by another member of the group or by the management, in which case the "reality" itself is discounted and the people who have experienced such reality experience crazy feelings.

A person accepts the projections of the other group members regarding his or her covert role out of his or her own needs for stroking and time structuring. In these instances individuals within the group collude in the process of role differentiation by selecting roles for themselves which are comfortable and reinforce their own personal ways of behaving. This may be done without any awareness of the behavior by those engaging in it.

A second form of collusion occurs when a group member silently experiences a particular feeling and withholds it, i.e., "sits on it," but relishes the delivery of the emotion, when it does occur, to the person to whom the anger, e.g., was felt. In a group this "weighty silence" is usually shared by more than one person. In this instance, they all wait in silence through gestures and often covertly or explicitly with words encourage someone to deliver the withheld feelings to the deserving member. If another group member says "You're afraid, angry" e.g., there is often a denial by the challenged member. Meanwhile, the member withholding the feeling is secretly enjoying the process.

Evidence of this occurred within a district office of the Internal Revenue Service. One revenue officer was promoted from the ranks of his peers to supervise his former "equals." It was accomplished according to the good order of formal procedures established to insure fairness in selection as well as quality. Higher management was seemingly unaware that he was the most disliked and disrespected member of the section. This was all well known to those who worked with him. As a supervisor he became a rigid, demanding, controlling, and "by the book" administrator. He was resented and this resentment was withheld and consequently built up to a very great intensity until one day one of the revenue workers who had previously been a peer walked into his office, punched him in the nose and quit. All the other officers enjoyed the drama, shared the resentment and secretly supported the delivered anger. The build-up of hostility which preceded the event was reflected in the transactions among the members within the private structure.[4]

These projections and collusions are endless repetitions of behavior learned in childhood. The innumerable individuals who deny and thus refuse to own their own innermost feelings give up their only source for real power to effect intentional change in their own lives and participate in significant change within their group and organization. All groups must provide for the expression of mindfulness, joyfulness, powerfulness, and caring to function regardless of how disguised these might be within the private structure. When the expression of these are frustrated, discounted and penalized, envy, anger, resentment and guilt find their way into the interplay of covert group processes.

There is an aspect of this projective process which mystifies the group members and contains partially the reason organizations, treated as artificial persons, are bound to be disappointing to those who empower them in that manner. Because they are not in reality human they can give nothing of humanness back when it is projected onto them. It would be the purpose as well as the goal of a humane organization to create the conditions which give each person safety and permission to be powerful, to be competent, to be smart, to be joyful, and to be caring and nurturing. For it is these qualities which are needed, even required, to provide individual access to his or her creativity and support personal responsibility sufficiently so one may make his or her own moral choices. It is only when human beings are in touch with these humane qualities they can know the quality and morality of their own transactions and interactions with their co-workers and with management.

Persons within groups who are in touch with their own humanness can take care of themselves better, make the moral choices required to protect their personal integrity, and participate more fully and meaningfully in the goals of the organization of which they are a part. With this in mind, the Socratic imperative "know thyself" takes on new significance. Organizations are an important component in providing the conditions which will nurture these attributes. It is essential that this responsibility be confronted within the organizational context. It is all the more necessary today because organizations are such an integral part of our existence.

Banal Work Group: Covert Role Differentiation in the Private Structure

In the private structure of a banal work group, covert role differentiation takes place involving splits and projections which reflect the way individuals within a work group express their own emotions. When the group is interacting and transacting with one another, these splits, projections and introjections spawn a unique system of collusions and alliances. Specific temporary or long term roles emerge which are the repositories of these collusions and projections. These roles are occupied by specific players. Alliances involve several participants in the group who "split-away" a specific aspect of their humanness and "pour" this aspect into one other member of the group who colludes or "buys into it" for his or her own reasons. The reasons may be guilt, resentment, fear and to get specific strokes, negative or positive, as well as existential recognition that the individual member does exist in fact. Thus a person takes on a role such as: the crazy one who acts out some of the "craziness" in the group, or a shaman who retains all the "special unwritten knowledge" about how to survive in the organization; an earth mother who becomes the ritual nurturer of members within the organization; the clown previously mentioned; the scapegoat; the critic; the psychological leader; or the assassinated leader. These and a number of other roles begin to emerge over a period of time in a work group and become a functioning part of the hidden group process within the work group. Figure 5-A is a graphic summary of these observations.

An organization critic may become the "conscience" of the group so other group members no longer need to make their own moral choices. They abandon such responsibility to the person who has for his or her own reasons accepted the critic role. It places a tremendous burden on the actor even though he is highly valued in the role because the others can then conveniently abandon their own responsibilities for the moral choice he or she articulates. In the U.S. Senate this role for many years was played by Senator Phillip Hart of Michigan.[5] Senator Hart, who died of cancer at the age of 64 in late 1976, was frequently called the conscience of the Senate. His colleagues, his peers had made him the Senate critic, the keeper of the Senate's conscience. As such he championed many of the Civil Rights and Anti-Trust

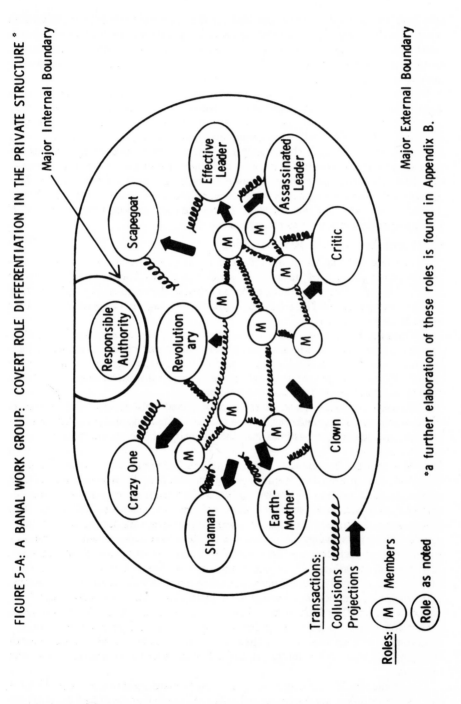

FIGURE 5-A: A BANAL WORK GROUP: COVERT ROLE DIFFERENTIATION IN THE PRIVATE STRUCTURE *

*a further elaboration of these roles is found in Appendix B.

Figure 5-A: A Banal Work Group: Covert Role Differentiation in the Private Structure

laws now on the books. He fought, and for the most part failed, in the Senate to break up oil companies and impose limits on corporate power. He fought the auto industry on a variety of fronts, even though it was his home state's employer. He fought organized baseball, even though his wife's millionaire father had once owned the Detroit Tigers.

He rarely gained that which he sought which is the true role of the critic, for in reposing such responsibility into one role occupied by one person it becomes a neat evasion of the responsibility of each other member to confront and take action on the very issues which the "group conscience" articulates. The covert aspect is the manner in which Senator Hart was "used" by the other Senators to avoid taking on their own responsibility for causes which they thought were "morally correct" but somehow could not bring themselves to articulate their own opposition. This vignette indicates the distinctive connection between the overt or formal role and the distinctive aspects of the covert role group and organization members play. This distinctive linkage needs further investigation.

Overt and Covert Role Relationships

Covert role differentiation takes place in the private structure. It occurs throughout the entire network of transactions within the group. These covert transactions link into the processes and structure characteristic of the manifest or public structure and the overt processes. There are four transactional stages in the manifest structure where these exchanges occur:

1. **Opening Exchanges**. These opening exchanges are accompanied by settled courtesies, polite words and gestures, gentle banter and expected responses each bounded by what is "acceptable" as defined by the specific organizational and group culture. Within the private structure ritual behavior dominates the transactional patterns and their intensity is that of participation.

2. **Routine Activities**. These activities are reflected in the accommodated arrangements which characterize the regularized routines of the organization. Private structure transactions reflect pastimes and the intensity of the transactions is that of involvement.

3. **Meetings and Conferences**. These are held to deal with future planning, budgets, immediate critical events concerning policy and the like. These events may involve routine decision making or involve decisions concerning exceptional situations relating to such matters as personnel, tasks, information, resources, policy, etc. The private structure transactions find the members engaged in serving their "hidden agendas" or script strivings, i.e, games. Transactions here are laden with the drama of power although such drama is not absent from the previous transactional patterns.

4. **Special Occasions**. These occasions are available but seldom occur. They happen, e.g., at holiday times, upon the celebration of a successful organizational achievement or the accomplishment of a particular goal. These may range from activities like an office Christmas or Valentines party to the successful landing of an exploration vehicle on the moon or Mars. Private structure activity centers upon the appreciation of each member for their unique contribution. Each feels a sense of belonging and there is the direct yet controlled expressions of intimacy among the members.

It is on the special occasions where the organizational rigidities, accommodations and role orientation are loosened and often mocked. For individual members on these occasions feel safe and authentic and involve, on occasion, non-sexual intimate encounters. Rank, prestige, and status are diminished in intensity and moderated in the responses as the members interact with one another. It is often a rare glimpse into what a safe and humane work group could be like.

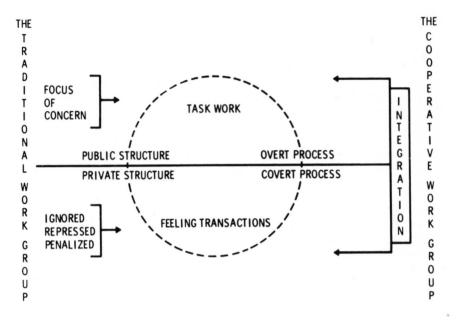

Figure 5-B: The Work World

The traditional world of work centers the concern upon the manifest or public structure and the overt transactional system. The feeling transactions of the private structure are generally hidden, ignored, repressed and all too frequently penalized and punished. When they are recognized they are, again all too frequently, manipulated into the service of organizational production in cynical and hypocritical ways. These feelings find their expression within the covert process. A cooperative work group would, however, seek to integrate these structures and processes in a way that creatively and humanely achieves the goals of the individual members, the group and organization and the clientele served. Figure 5-B is a conceptualization of these work world options. More knowledge and understanding is needed concerning the development of covert roles within the private structure. It is to the nature of covert role differentiation, the situation in which it occurs, and the characteristics of its occurrence which next gains our attention.

Covert Role Differentiation: Situation, Characteristics and Process

Earlier it was observed that (Berne's Law) the effectiveness of the work group depends upon the success of the process group. It was suggested also that the outcome of the process group depends upon the nature of the private structure. It was noted too that when the major or external boundaries are stressed work stops and a process group gets underway, since the impending threat to the group cohesion must be met in order for the group to proceed and return to work. The process group is concerned with reestablishing the equilibrium and securing the boundaries and this depends upon the dynamics of the private structure which relate to the satisfaction of each member's needs, experiences, wishes and emotions. The only exception to this phenomenon is a group or organizational response to a major invasion of the external boundaries which mobilizes the group into combat. In which instance, if there is sufficient cohesion and absence of decay in the group, it will coalesce to defend itself against such an imminent threat or actual penetration. So it has been observed that unanticipated, unexpected or anticipated and expected stressful incidents at the major boundaries raise issues of group survival.

Exchanges among the group members, both physical and verbal, disclose the nature of the internal group process within the context of the private structure. These transactions will generally reflect individual proclivities. A participant or an observer can perceive a group process event is underway in any particular group if more than one person joins in overt or covert activity focusing upon one or more other members of that group in a manner other than the orderly routines established or accepted by the group. Again, an observer or participant may perceive that a group process event is underway when either the major external or the major internal boundary is penetrated or invaded in a manner other than the orderly routines and procedures established and accepted by the group.[6] Transactions across the minor boundaries within the membership or within the leadership may contribute to or detract from group purposes. As such they involve a minor process and become indicative of a diversion. A closer look at the nature of these diversions begins to enable us to disclose the fabric of the covert processes of the group or organization concerned.

Henry Ezriel has observed that group members dealing with common group tension project unconscious "fantasy-objects" to various other members of the group and try to manipulate those members accordingly. He observes that each person stays in the role assigned to him by another person only if it happens to coincide with his own fantasy and if it allows him to manipulate the other persons into appropriate roles as well. Generally, a person will try to manipulate and move the discussion so that the real group conforms more closely to his own unconscious fantasy.[7] Against this background of projection, manipulation and collusion, Bion teaches that the group demands a structure consisting of a leader and the followers. He indicates that the group may well turn resentful and be constantly suspicious of a leader, always ready to diminish or dismiss him or her if he or she does not show the characteristics that they think appropriate or proper.[8]

The group puts subtle, often intense, pressure upon individuals who do not conform to the emerging basic assumptions held within the group. It is useful to know that a dependent group is a frequent characteristic of a banal work group under stress and that this phenomenon is particularly significant. When this occurs, Bion has observed that what emerges is something like a religious system. As it takes hold, independence of thought is stifled and heresy is righteously hunted and the leader of a small face-to-face group is often criticized because he or she is not a magician who can accomplish the magic requirements for the group to proceed undisturbed. In a large social system where the figure is elevated to a superhuman characteristics the results can be awesome indeed. Bion observed that if left to itself the dependent group will choose as its leader "the least healthy" member of that group.[9]

It is perhaps helpful to hypothesize that every group, organization or social system under stress forwards the leader (executive) who is most representative of the particular melange of shared fears, resentments, anxieties, anger, hopes and despairs among the members of the group or the social system. Richard Nixon in a fearful America threatened with internal decay resulting from an unpopular war abroad reflects such a possibility. In the larger political context we may identify this as the "politics of despair." Yet if the despair and the fear is linked to hope, the group, organization or social system is apt to forward a leader who best represents the possibility of healing and repair. Such was the case in depression-ridden America when Franklin Delano Roosevelt emerged. In these instances, the politics of hope do battle with the politics of despair in the unconscious of the members of a social system as they select the leaders to forward the programs of action that the citizen-member will support. To a much lesser degree, organizations and groups under stress reflect the same struggles.

Covert Group Role Differentiation: Role Assignments

Within the ongoing processes of the private structure of a banal group each member, regardless of the degree of involvement, that is whether he or she is participating, involved, or engaged in the internal processes of the group, is assigning covert roles to other group members and seeking his or her own covert role in the group. Each such role assigned to a group member involves some degree of his or her own collusion and involves tradeoffs with other group members. The following examples will suffice:

A. **Clown.** The clown gains approval and even affection (strokes) and trades off the possibility of having any impact or real significance when the "chips are down."

B. **Shaman.** Shamans gain strokes (that is, respect) of the group members by appearing to have some special knowledge which could be called wisdom within the context of the group. To achieve this role, the person must trade off the respect or approval of the more cynical and skeptical members and also forego the possibility of intimacy.

C. **Crazy One.** The crazy one gains attention strokes for recognition of his or her distinctive behavior and responses. The tradeoff here is resigning access to the group's respect and relinquishing any possibility of intimacy.

D. **Critic.** The critic is usually content with negative strokes for his or her pronouncements are usually not too popular. Here one must tradeoff the affection and even tolerance of the other group members for the "joy" of being "respected" from a "distance."

E. **Assassinated Leader.** The assassinated leader gains strokes by having risked greatly and lost greatly. As such he receives affection and to some degree immortality. The tradeoff is intimacy, career, and sometimes one's own life.

F. **Psychological or "Natural" Leader.** Gains strokes in terms of power, affection and admiration. The tradeoff is social and personal security.

G. **Scapegoat.** Generally receives negative strokes, resentments, deserved or undeserved, and trades off respect and security in the balance.

H. **Revolutionary.** Gains strokes for articulating the discontent of the group. The tradeoff is the risk of personal security and self-destruction, as well as one's own career and even perhaps one's own life.

These are but a few examples of the covert symbiotic relationships between a group member and the group and identifies the payoff which tends to motivate an individual into a particular covert role. The group itself supplies the kinds of psychological support the individual member needs and in return the individual members supply to the group a particular way of handling what the group and the members deny and blindly split away. All of this may occur against the ongoing background of a continuing banal work group. The tasks of the group get done unless the group is stressed. Where these roles may emerge as distinctive, clear and significant in any particular event, as such, they may be a signal for the emergence of a basic assumption mode. Likewise, each role is related to the power context, i.e. the role is assumed either from a one-up or a one-down position and the group's attitude toward the role's occupant is from a one-up or a one-down position.

The role situation itself can be located on the Drama Triangle, i.e. the group and the role can each be located as Victim, Rescuer or Persecutor on the Drama Triangle. Consequently, they reflect ongoing yet changing power arrangements. Each particular role situation involves, (a) characteristics that are specific to the group and (b) characteristics that are specific to the covert role. These characteristics can be identified at any time the role emerges within the dynamic processes of the group. Consequently, the process that goes on within the group is exposed by the nature of the personal transactions and group interactions that occur and can be identified and specified.

Covert Power Networks: Groups and Organizations

Covert networks of power may develop which, in their most awesome form, may link an entire social system together in the service of death and destruction as in Nazi Germany. Organizational games of power may result in personal strain, incidental and/or long term, leading to a variety of results such as absenteeism, illness, and reduced productivity and serious consequences for the organization may be involved.[10]

Covert power networks within organizations provide a background for the drama involved in struggles for power which may be unrelated to the task of the organization itself, but nevertheless reflect the covert nature of the power relationships within such organizations. An example of this is an incident at the Marine Corps Camp Pendelton at Oceanside, California where a group of black marines attacked a group of white marines on November 13, 1976 in a Marine Corps barrack on that base. Under the surface and within the interaction network lay the protagonists of the Black Panthers and the Ku Klux Klan. These black and white supremist organizations provided the ideology and the rationale for covert struggles of power within the involved Marine Corps units and impacted on the capacity of those units to ultimately fulfill their tasks.[11]

These consequences can only occur when the level of human existence within an organization or social system becomes so dehumanized that they really become actors mouthing irrelevant platitudes without feeling, experiencing only programmed emotion with little and no compassion, empathy or sympathy for one another or the persons involved in the task. In the absence of hamartic dimensions, these persons fit well into banal groups. These are the robopaths identified by Lewis Yablonsky.[12] These group members are sycophantic, conforming, approval seeking, manipulative group participants, fearful of peer disapproval. Under the impact of these there is a group atmosphere where there is no dissent, no permission to be different and the pressure to conform is very intense.

Where there exists at high policy making levels a strong concurrence-seeking tendency in such groups the emergence of effective consensus is precluded. There is rather a likelihood that inadequate process and defective decisions result. Irving Janis identifies this as groupthink.[13] Groupthink, in contrast to robopathic behavior, may occur within policy-making groups. Janis observes:

> *The more amenability and espirit de corps among the members of a policy-making in-group, the greater is the danger that independent critical thinking will be replaced by groupthink which is likely to result in irrational and dehumanizing actions directed against out-groups.*[14]

Robopathology and groupthink both reflect the existence of pathological and convert power transactions effectively sustained by a network of group processes which need to be investigated and assessed. Suitable responses need to be developed so as to avoid the dysfunctional consequences which flow from these conditions. These phenomena result from linkages among the group members and leadership in a manner which disempowers the participants, clouds personal responsibility and leads to dehumanizing decisions and consequences. These linkages among the individual group member transactions and group processes involved is difficult to understand, difficult to assess, and difficult to comprehend. Yet it is both necessary and possible to develop tools to understand and to assess this process.

Covert Role Differentiation: Analytical Possibilities

Thus it is possible to comprehend more clearly and develop specific understanding concerning group covert role differentiation within the covert or private structure of any banal work group. First, it is possible to identify the role situation, the characteristics, and the process (the transactional processes) involved in each specific covert role that may emerge within the dynamics of the group process. Each role situation may express a tentative basic assumption mode which may emerge as a primary group aspect. In groups exhibiting basic assumption behavior, covert role development will be a very visible and dynamic aspect of the process. Second, a power orientation can be identified for the group and the role itself and these positions located on the Drama Triangle. Specific characteristics can be identified as occurring within the group and for the covert role. The particular interaction process involved may be articulated and defined.

The covert roles that people select for themselves for their own reasons to play inside a group or an organization may be quite distinctive or may be a unique combination of one or a few. The time spent in such a role may range from a moment to a lifetime where an individual becomes identified and synonomous with the role itself. The intensity of role involvement may range from relatively mild to one of single continuous and conspicuous involvement. Over a period of time one person may be seen to perform a variety of roles. The roles that people select for themselves over the long run in the group or an organization relate to one's own deeper motivation, i.e. one's own "hidden agenda," game or script. These are related to the nature of the tradeoffs that each person makes to meet his or her needs.

So it was with our mythical friends who we encountered in Chapter 2. Dorothy, the cowardly lion, the scarecrow and the tin woodman made up the work group whose task it was to journey to Oz. Each denied a part of themselves and "loaded" this on another member who had "permission" to retain what the others seemed to have lost. Each had to deny what they intrinsically had contributed to the group. None were whole persons. Each had a part of what the whole group needed to get the job done. Each rediscovered his own humanness through the help of a wonderful old fraud who functioned by mystifying the others around his own uses of power. A whole society had been organized around this mystification. After being unmasked it was discovered what they all knew anyway—he was a bad wizard but a good man and each had what they had sought from him all along! The cooperation stemming from scripted human inadequacy is a set up for the operation of the Drama Triangle. It is counterfeit cooperation. It is fraudulent because it sets up expectations from one another which are difficult and often impossible to realize, are not fully articulated and seed resentment, guilt and hurt feelings. Genuine cooperation occurs when each participant is a whole person and the full potential of each is encouraged and shared and the competence and creativity of each valued in a conscious, intentional manner by other members of the group.

Covert role differentiation occurs within the private structure of a work group. The role situation, the characteristics of that role and the related group processes characteristic to the role is the focus of group transactions when that particular role "takes care of" the group's emotional business. There are significant payoffs for the member who somehow has elected to "play" the part as well as for the players who need that part played.

Awareness of that process by the players and by organizational leadership can lead groups and organizations to move effectively in response to integral human needs within the organization and avoid the high personal and organizational costs associated with these covert roles. Organization and group members can opt not to play this way and seek more authentic and personally rewarding behavior.

SUMMARY

The dynamics of banal work groups are laden and overlaid with the consequences deriving from the emotional needs of each person within the group. Each must satisfy his or her own needs and relate in the patterned responses learned and utilized for their satisfaction and for survival in childhood which are now hidden from view. There is a heavy investment in the survival of the group so the negative and positive payoffs which are felt to be needed and seem very comfortable can be maintained. Thus each person needs the group to survive as long as possible. If the task of the group nears completion, the thrust of the group is to seek another task so as to continue in existence. Individual and group survival become a fundamental aspect of understanding group dynamics.

Persons within a banal group, even a tragic (hamartic) group, almost always collude in the processes of role differentiation by selecting covert roles for themselves which are comfortable and provide payoffs which reinforce their personal ways of behaving. There is invariably silent acquiescence and unspoken approval, sometimes accompanied by overtly expressed denial, of behavior which expresses a shared feeling or fantasy within the group. The results from time to time are generally inane, occasionally embarrassing, and sometimes tragic for those individuals blind to their own innermost feelings who participate in the drama seemingly unknowingly. In their most awesome form these roles link together to form networks of power which lead to a variety of results which on occasion may produce profoundly detrimental consequences.

It is possible to develop analytical tools to better understand covert role differentiation within the private structure or groups by examining the specific role, the characteristics of the role, and the transactional processes involved in the emergence of the group and its selection by a member.

NOTES

1.   Arthur D. Colman, "Irrational Aspects of Design," in Arthur D. Colman and W. Harold Bexton, *Group Relations Reader*, Sausalito, California, GREX, 1975, pp. 313-328; see also Robert H. Simmons and Eugene P. Dvorin, *Public Administration: Values, Policy and Change*. Port Washington, N.Y., Alfred Publishing Co., 1977, pp. 611-634.

2.   Elliot Jaques, *A General Theory of Bureaucracy*, New York, John Wiley & Sons, Inc., 1976, p. 36.

3.   Trigant Burrow, "The Social Neurosis," *Philosophy Science*, Vol. 16, pp. 25-40, 1949, cf. Eric Berne, *Structure and Dynamics of Organizations and Groups*, New York, Grove Press, 1966, pp. 215-218.

4.   This incident was related by a practitioner/student during the course of a graduate seminar at California State University Los Angeles conducted by the author in the fall of 1977.

5.   *L.A. Times*, December 29, 1976, Part I, p. 5.

6.   It is possible to develop an analysis of individual transactions in groups through the use of the tools developed by Eric Berne. See particularly the materials previously indentified in earlier notes and in particular his *Games People Play: The Psychology of Human Relationships*, New York, Grove Press, Inc., 1964, *passim*; and Dorothy Jongeward, *Every-Body Wins: Transactional Analysis Applied to Organizations*, revised ed., Addison-Wesley Publishing Co., 1976, *passim*.

7.   Henry Ezriel, "A Psychoanalytic Method of Group Treatment," *British Journal of Medical Psychology*, Vol. 23, pp. 59-74, 1950.

8.   W.R. Bion, *Experiences in Groups, Human Relations*, Vol. 1, pp. 314-320, 487-496 (1948); and Vol. 2, pp. 12-22, (1949). See also his *Experience in Groups, op. cit.*, pp. 129-138.

9.   W.R. Bion, *ibid.*, Vol. 2, pp. 295-303 (1949); and Vol. 3, pp. 395-402 (1950). See also his *Experience in Groups, op. cit.*, pp. 138-150.

10. Hans Selye, *The Stress of Life*, McGraw Hill Book Co., N.Y., 1956; see also his *Stress Without Distress*, N.Y., J.P. Lippincott, 1974; cf. Robert Caplan, Sidney Cobbs, John French, Jr., R. Van Harrison, and S.R. Pinneau, *Job Demands and Worker Health: Main Effects of Occupational Differences*, National Institute of Safety and Health, Government Printing Office, 1975; see also Robert L. Kahn, Donald M. Wolfe, Robert P. Quinn, J. Diedrick Snock, and R.A. Rosenthal, *Organizational Stress in Role Conflict and Ambiguity*, N.Y., John Wiley & Sons, Inc., 1964; and Charlton R. Price and Harry Levinson, "Work and Mental Health," in *Blue Collar World: Studies of the American Worker*, Arthur B. Shostak and William Gomberg, editors, Englewood Cliffs, N.J., Prentice-Hall, Inc., 1965; Richard M. Michaels, "Driven Tension Responses Generated on Urban Streets," in *Public Roads*, Washington, Bureau of Public Roads, U.S. Department of Commerce, August, 1960.

11. *L.A. Times*, December 2, 1976, p. 3.

12. Lewis Yablonski, Robopaths: *People as Machines*, Penguin Books, Baltimore, Maryland, Bobbs-Merrill Co., 1976, pp. 6-31; forerunners to this orientation are William H. Whyte, Jr., *The Organization Man*, N.Y., Simon and Schuster, 1956; William Sloan, *The Man in the Gray Flannel Suit*, N.Y., Simon and Schuster, 1955 (fiction). See also Anthony Downs, *Inside Bureaucracy*, "Consensus: Holding on to What You've Got," Boston, Little, Brown & Co., 1976, pp. 96-101, 267-268.

13. Irving Janis, *Victims of Groupthink*, Boston, Houghton-Mifflin Co., 1972, pp. 11-13; cf. George Orwell, *Nineteen Eighty-Four*, N.Y., Harcourt, Brace & Co., 1949, pp. 303-314; see also generally Janis and Leon Mann, *Decision Making, A Psychological Analysis of Conflict, Choice and Commitment*, N.Y., The Free Press, 1977.

14. Janis, *Victims of Groupthink*, p. 13.

RELATED READING

Ardrey, Robert. *The Social Contact*. London: Collins, 1970. Observes the essential requirement for the survival of any society is order, an order which is responsive to the biological and social needs of such a society.

Arendt, Hannah. *The Origins of Totalitarianism*. New York: Harcourt, Brace & World, Inc., 1951 (3 volumes). This is a classic study of the uses of projection, power, isolation and loneliness in the service of totalitarian rule. What is true in small group behavior is relevant for larger social systems, including our own as well.

Berelson, Bernard and Steiner, Gary A. *Human Behavior: An Inventory of Scientific Findings*. New York: Harcourt, Brace & World, Inc., 1964. A systematic collection of the empirical data as it relates to human behavior.

Freud, Sigmund. *Totem and Taboo*. New York: Vintage Books, copyright 1918 and 1946 by Dr. A.A. Brill. This is Freud's exploratory attempt to deal with the individual psyche as it relates to society and culture. Projection is the fundamental phenomenon and totemism and taboo are held to have their roots in the Oedipus complex.

Mills, Theodore M. *The Sociology of Small Groups*. Englewood Cliffs, N.J.: Prentice-Hall, 1967. This volume is probably the best general introduction and overview of the study of small groups. Basic models of groups are examined, with chapters or levels as aspects of group process behavior, emotion, norms, goals, executive functions and culminates in a paradigm for groups and group development.

Newton, Peter M. and Levinson, Daniel J. "The Work Within the Organization: A Socio-Psychological Approach," *Psychiatry*, Vol. 36, May, 1973, pp. 115-142. The theoretical framework for the analysis of the work-group. A critical link between the organization and the individual is developed using the complex interrelated perspectives of task, social structure, culture and social process.

Morris, Desmond. *The Naked Ape*. New York: McGraw-Hill Book Co., 1967. An important reminder of the biological urges of the human animal and an urgent call to recognize and deal with them in ways that tailor our advances to our behavioral requirements.

Muller, Herbert J. *The Children of Frankenstein: A Primer on Modern Technology and Human Values*. Bloomington, Ind.,: Indiana University Press, 1970. These creative and stimulating essays explore the social and cultural consequences of the transformation of our economy by modern technology with an historian eye toward the deeper trends and basic problems.

Perls, F.S. *Ego, Hunger and Aggression*. New York: Vintage, 1947 and 1969. This book expresses the theoretical roots of Gestalt therapy, yet it is an extension of these materials beyond in its group processes in a manner vital to an understanding of human behavior within groups.

Thelen, H. *Dynamics of Groups at Work*. Chicago: University of Chicago Press, 1954. This very readable book strikes a fine balance between attention to process and task problem-solving in group functioning. It offers theory, practical application and contains examples for bringing group dynamics to bear on social action.

Chapter 6

THE USES AND ABUSES OF POWER:
AN ANALYSIS OF PLAYS, GAMES, AND SCENARIOS

Power is the medium through which individuals in groups and organizations pursue their own and the group and organizational goals. Power is seen as an essential to the accomplishment of organization and group purposes. Organizational and group relationships are laden with the impact and consequences of power. An understanding of the context, sources, resources and operations of power in groups and organizations is therefore crucial to the accomplishment of work as well as the rectification of worker alienation and oppression. It is also an important key to achieving in the long run more effective productivity in a humane way. The context, nature and dynamics of power in groups and organizations is the concern and focus of this chapter. Power plays are ever present and ongoing throughout the manifest and private structures of most groups and organizations.

Banal Work Groups: The Context of Power

Power is experienced as in scarce supply. Its absence is felt; to be without it is bad; to be full with it is to be tempted to use it blindly, arbitrarily and willfully. It invites degrees of competition ranging from gentle to ominous. When a person feels he has power and is perceived to have power by others, he may in the exercise of it be said to "throw his weight around." In the negotiations concerned with nuclear weaponry and their missile delivery support systems, one of the measures used between the United States and the U.S.S.R. is comparative throw weight. This is a significant "measure of power" in arms negotiations.

Power can intimidate, manipulate, persuade, or be charismatically seductive. Power which intimidates involves either a direct or implied threat. This may involve threats of bodily harm, loss of status or wealth, harm to loved ones, harmful consequences to one's community or a variety of other consequences concerned with something that the recipient of the intended intimidation values. Using power through manipulation is devious. Such manipulation may be conscious and explicit and experienced as persuasion or it may be unconscious, ulterior and hidden from view. Manipulative uses of power can be directed to and from positions of strength and weakness. It is generally calculated to appeal to the most vulnerable aspect of the receiver. Persuasive power can appear like a simple direct request with overtones that the receiver could please the power user. Or it may involve the most devious and sophisticated appeals available in modern advertising. Finally, charismatic power involves surrender of one's own control of one's actions to someone generally felt to be special, one-up and often is perceived as larger than life.

The fundamental power relationship finds one human being one-up, one-down, or relatively equal in relationship to one other person or to other members of the group. These persons themselves are either one-up or one-down in a relationship to each other and to other groups. Power relationships may embody an actual differentiation of skills, or a division of authority to further task accomplishment. When these relationships are formalized and institutionalized it looks like hierarchy. For example, some power relationships are noble and good and may involve a position in the operating room, a traffic policeman directing traffic on a corner, or a lifeguard saving a drowning victim from the surf, a nurturing parent comforting and caring for a child. So power involves power to make other persons do things or to prevent other persons from doing things.

Power plays are operations used to get one or more persons to do something they would not otherwise do. Power plays may be used to resist doing something one or more persons do not want to do. A power maneuver is a one-down power response to a one-up power play. The exercise of power over another for the purpose of doing harm seems to have two basic origins. The first is in scarcity. Here where something in scarce supply is sought or a need exists, and there is less than necessary to fulfill all the needs of the people in that situation, then people who have more power will use that power against people to take their "fair" share and sometimes more than their "fair" share. At times this is done by physical force as when one steals, robs or kills another.

It can also take the form of psychic force where the powerful person creates a situation in which the powerless person gives up his or her fair share without resistance. Steiner identifies this as "mystified oppression."[1] This is a situation where a person or a group of people allows another person or group of people to oppress them and they internalize the deceptions and rationalize and obscure the oppression, which effectively maintains it. It somehow is made tolerable by this process. It is in this situation that the workers become the staunchest defenders of their own fetters.

The second reason why people use power over other people is as a defense against feelings and accusations of one's own sense of worthlessness. When a person feels worthless or "not O.K." this feeling seemingly may be "passed on" or transferred to another person by somehow trying to make that other person "not O.K." This seems to relieve the "not O.K." feeling of the person who is unwilling to confront those feelings. Thus by finding a defect in another person this somehow makes oneself "O.K."[2] There is yet another reason. Power is sometimes converted into aggression which is spawned not from a desire to control, make conquest or to dominate but from an effort to increase the security and safety of one's own group. William Blanchard identifies this as "inadvertent aggression." Its cardinal characteristic, he suggests, is "the concealment of intent" and the maintenace at all costs of the "appearance of innocence" of the intention behind the aggressive act. Thus an act of aggression may be justified if, in the pursuit of a good cause, the perpetrator is blameless.[3]

Power plays within groups and organizations involve security, competition, authority, obedience, inequality and definite payoffs. The power plays and maneuvers occur amidst the context of a banal work group and between such groups. The payoffs are either winning or losing and the feelings that go with each. The engine of the drama triangle as it operates within a group or organization is guilt and resentment. Resentment and anger when unexpressed, bottled up or unreleased will, when withheld, build up in someone occupying one of the positions on the drama triangle, e.g. the Rescuer, and he or she will eventually switch to the Persecutor position. Likewise, when guilty feelings build up to the extent that they can no longer be contained, the occupant of one position, e.g. Persecutor, will switch to either the Victim or Rescuer position. These switches may direct the focus of their activity toward the same person or persons originally concerned or may orient to different players. Figure 6-A is a graphic of these role switches.

A supervising nurse who is a perennial rescuer may, for example, switch into a persecutor with a particularly petulant licensed vocational nurse or an obstreperous

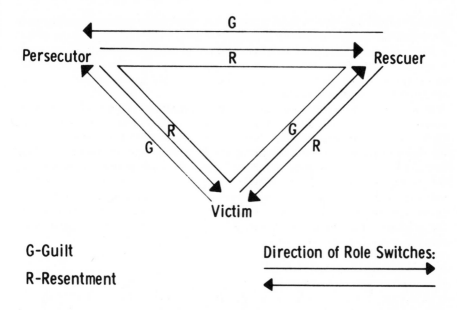

G-Guilt   Direction of Role Switches:

R-Resentment

Figure 6-A: Rescue Triangle Action

patient as a result of a steadily increasing build-up of resentment from having to "tell the LVN what to do all the time," or withholds resentment until it explodes onto the deserving or undeserving patient. In a similar vein, a rigid, persecuting group member engaged in continuous criticism and discounts of his or her co-workers may build up so much guilt about what he or she has done will manage to switch to the victim position to obtain the "punishment" that is felt to be deserved.

Power plays and games involve playing from positions of one-down power, playing from positions of one-up power and among players who perceive themselves as relatively equal in power. In the latter instance, the power play may be designated as a "pitched battle." A collection of power plays operated to achieve a specific objective may be designated a power scenario. Power plays operating from any one of these three positions have important ramifications within the organization and within the work group. Factions and alliances develop and organizational programs with their attendant problems of budget, resources and human energy weigh in the balance.[4]

Group and Organizational Power Plays, Games and Scenarios

Group processes upon which the outcome of task groups and even combat groups depend are laden with the drama of power plays, games and scenarios. The word "game" is reserved for the variety of interpersonal transactions between one or a few persons which involves a series of transactions leading to definite personal pay-offs.[5] The power play is utilized here to identify the transactions, singular or in series, where a person, group or organization tries or actually succeeds in getting someone, a few persons, a group or organization to do something that those involved do not want done. In groups and organizations, power is ultimately sifted through the minds, mouths and hands of their members. A series of power plays linked together within an organizational network and designed to achieve a specific overt or covert end may be designated a power scenario. Such scenarios may be overtly recognized or may be felt but not overtly perceived. Such scenarios may be disguised and hidden from view and not admitted or they may be pushed out of the consciousness of those affected. They may to some degree be recognized (even fully recognized) and struggled against.

Power transactions from authority may be characterized as coming from a one-up position. Such communication is frequently found in the guise of personnel evaluations, controls, routines, organizational management rules and orders which reinforce the alienating nature of the work environment. Work groups themselves are subject to a variety of more or less intense rigid controls which succeed in maintaining the defeat and surrender of personal power, relative to such things as monitoring standards, job performance and evaluation and personnel reviews. Competition continues the oppression, pits co-worker against co-worker, and precludes developing the intimacy, closeness and spontaneity required if people are to feel good about themselves and perform meaningful, effective, productive work.

One-Up Power Plays and Scenarios

One-up power plays may be imposed by official hierarchical authority, forwarded by a distinct person or group of organizational members or involve an admixture of both. One-up power plays may, in the most extreme form, be cruel, overbearing, and tyrannical. These may occur in transactions among the membership as well. The oppression within a typical work situation takes on a generally moderate character and is, nevertheless, maintained and sustained by the lies, deception, and power plays which characterize organizational life.

One-up power plays successively increase in intensity until ultimate victory or defeat. They may begin at a very low intensity and, if unsuccessful, are followed by successive power plays, cascading one after the other, each subsequent one of increasing intensity. The aim is to win—to end up "on top." The one-up power play operates from the position usually of righteousness or logical correctness, "backed" by the authority of virtue, law and reason. It is calculated always to place the one-down player on the defensive rendering the behavior inappropriate, unreasonable, unjustified, against the rules and sometimes unlawful. Appeals of the one-up players are always to legitimacy, tradition, reason, law, virtue, goodness, fear, and sometimes to God. Generally, when scarcity and values are involved, the scenario becomes more crude, more obvious, and may culminate in the use of brute force.

One example of the abusive use of power within organizations is provided by the private sector in a program conducted by Ohio Bell Telephone Company. Management there became concerned over low employee morale and reduced output and management determined to utilize mystified fear as an "antidote." Groups of 15 to 20 employees were ushered into a small conference room. Management turned out the lights and proceeded to let the employees watch a series of simulated television newscasts which projected the complete economic collapse of Ohio Bell Telephone right before the very eyes of the employees. The result of this fear-inducing experiment was that worker productivity jumped nearly 10% for a period of time.[6]

This is exploitative, manipulative and mystified use of a one-up power scenario upon the employees. This cynical use of fear is indicative of a contemptuous and calculating management. A one-up power scenario was utilized to induce employees to produce in a banal work group, where the pervasive atmosphere is apathy and disinterest and boredom. The fear generated by possible company failure produced a seeming, but counterfeit, cohesion which in turn produced significant rises in employee production. Group members or employees up against this kind of cynical exploitation of their behavior without power resources are vulnerable to the abuses of this fashion.

One-Down Power Plays and Scenarios

In contrast to one-up power plays, one-down power plays are not played in an order of increasing intensity. They are basically defensive in character and are sporadic and not sustained in operation. One-down players tend to react and take, on occasion, the appearance of guerrilla warfare. It is most frequently never played to win but it is played with calculation to interfere with the one-up person's privileges and authority. Just as in guerrilla warfare, one-down power plays are utilized by the weaker, more oppressed, of the conflicted parties. A primary element of one-down power plays is surprise and knowledge of the territory. One-down players use their power selectively where it is most useful and then beat a hasty, sometimes strategic, sometimes tactical retreat or withdrawal from the action. The primary goal is to interfere with the goals and drive for power of the one-up person, and there is no immediate expectation of reversing the tide or of winning. One-down players use guilt-arousing maneuvers, measures designed to retaliate and techniques to get even by wasting the time, energy and physical and psychological resources of the oppressor.

In bureaucracy one-down scenarios take on the character of behavior which is akin to guerrilla warfare. James Marshall advocates the use of guerrilla warfare tactics in non-violent ways to obtain access into the positions of power by those interested in making significant social change. He suggests that such a strategy is not a direct transference of guerrilla warfare from its violent illegal context to the non-violent context of administration in the public sector.

Rather, Marshall has effectively articulated the strategies and tactics for organizational guerrilla warfare in a non-violent way to alter the policy choices, resources, behavior and context of organizational life. He advocates this as essential to achieve the kind of change required for overall national survival and the survival of humankind on the planet. He suggests that to try to change this system is difficult. He states modern urban publics have not been educated in the necessities or requirements for making social change. Such publics define the problems, but are unable to develop scenarios, strategies and tactics for their resolution. This lack of ability, he observes, is not coincidental: institutions, by virtue of the fact that they hold systemic power, are anti-change—change threatens their power—and such organizations do not teach people how to change things beyond writing letters and voting in elections.

Societal institutions, Marshall notes, control education, in the formal and informal senses, and they use this control to prevent change. To meet this gap in our education and to equip ourselves for making social changes means, Marshall writes, developing strategies and tactics which will accomplish such needed change. The package of analysis, strategies, and tactics he presents may be identified as "institutional guerrilla warfare" or "new guerrilla warfare" and is aimed primarily at the public administrator.[7]

Marshall's work is an articulate presentation of the application of non-violent guerrilla warfare to the achievement of social change adapted to modern institutional context. The use of guerrilla strategy and tactics within organizations, how-

Table 6-1:   **POWER PLAYS: ONE-UP, ONE-DOWN AND PITCHED BATTLE**

POSITION OF PLAY	IDEOLOGY	CHARACTERISTICS OF THE PLAY
ONE-UP **Aim**: Winning **Style**: Offensive **Power**: Unequal/more	Righteousness Virtue Truth Logic Reason	Cascades in increasing intensity until ultimate victory, defeat or a transition to pitch-battle occurs. These usually range from mild to crude brute force.
ONE-DOWN **Aim**: Wasting oppressors time, energy, resources. **Style**: Defensive **Power**: Unequal/less	Redress grievance Retaliation Vengeance Moral correctness	Uses guilt, manipulative actions designed to hurt, retaliate, delay, postpone, and procrastinate. Careless wasteful "inadvertent" damage to oppressor's physical plants, resources and supplies. Surprise, timing and knowledge of the territory characterize the play.
PITCHED BATTLE **Aim**: Staying or getting "on top." **Style**: Alternately offensive and defensive. **Power**: Equal	Alternate appeals to One-up/One-down ideology.	Escalates and erupts suddenly and unexpectedly. Resentment vented and often seeds long-term "get even" games of power. Each victory is temporary until opponent regroups for eventual inevitable retaliation.

Table 6-1: Power Plays: One-Up, One-Down and Pitched Battle

ever, is usually narrow and does not focus on the achievement of grand social change, but rather takes on a rather unique character distinctive of private structure group processes while, at the same time, fulfilling the script strivings or hidden agendas of the individual players. The use of organizational guerrilla warfare may well invite harsh retaliatory measures by managers who sense threats and betrayal in their use.

Pitched Battle Scenarios

Where power is approximately equal among the players or among the groups involved maneuvers, counter-maneuvers, scenarios, strategies, and alliances are developed. Here agreement is seldom reached. Every discussion escalates and scores are kept over who's winning and the "number of points" and who's losing. Generally, formal and informal forms of mediation, arbitration and imposed settlements occur when this situation becomes dysfunctional to the accomplishment of organizational purposes. It is freqently never quickly settled and may proceed for years until there is a clear victory of one side over the other.

There are some alternate appeals to one-up or one-down ideology. Struggles escalate and erupt suddenly and unexpectedly. The resentments vented often seed long term disputes leading to a pattern of retaliation. Each victory is temporary until the opponent regroups for the inevitable retaliation. Frequently, a loss by one of the equal players in one arena will draw a response by the seeming "loser" after regrouping to transfer the struggle into a different administrative, political or judicial arena in the effort to obtain victory there.

Table 6-1 is a summary of these overall power play conceptualizations. It is important to remember that secrecy is a fundamental component in many power plays. In an open system, group, society or relationship between two people where secrecy is an anathema, power plays, games, and scenarios are diminished in effectiveness for the opportunity for their contravention is enhanced.

Group and Organizational Power Scenarios: Manifestations

Power scenarios are used for a variety of reasons by those within groups and organizations who use them. For example, persons of dubious ambition seeking to gain ascendency in an organization may use them to suit such purposes. The allies of such persons may participate. Those who are the victims of such persons will attempt to retaliate through power plays. Others might attempt to neutralize such persons through the use of power plays. Still others might use them to fend off blame or failure, or in an attempt to survive. Power scenarios and the accompanying power plays will occur across a wide variety of group and organizational processes.

Power plays may occur during a budgetary crisis where the very existence of the group or organization seems at stake; they may take place at preliminary meetings where people are positioning to get the best possible economic advantage for their group within the organization prior to the establishment of the official operating budget. Power plays will develop as measures which are taken to counter the dominance of a clique which appears to be running the organization.

Power plays will be utilized when a person or group is "nursing a grudge" for a real or an alleged wrong. For example, failure to grant salary increases which are felt to be deserved or the publication of two conflicting promotional lists or the failure to get the recognition felt to be deserved. Power plays will develop in response to pressure from a hostile external force such as legislative investigation, a threatened outside audit, or media attack by an angry citizens' group. These struggles may occur in a variety of internal arenas or they may occur in a number of different external arenas where a perceived loss in one arena may be recouped in another. Thus a struggle may transfer from a legislative committee hearing, to an administrative hearing, to the courtroom.

Power scenarios and their accompanying plays and games sometimes proceed for whole lifetimes and beyond, with new generations picking up the unfinished drama. Even where the players change, as within a group or organization, they may simply fit into already existing roles in the power drama. Frequently, they are selected for that very reason and so power plays and games proceed unabated except for the delay necessary to integrate the new players into the game. The consequent stress upon personal health and organizational health ranges from mild to fatal in impact.

The parallel of the organizational drama to the drama of war is clearly revealed in the language used in the everyday vernacular of the organizational member, employee, managers and workers. The language used in a banal work group reveals the "warlike" quality of the power games that occur there. The following series of statements are often stated in the vernacular which public administration practitioners frequently hear in the context of their workday:

1. "Maybe we can torpedo him."
2. "Let's axe him."
3. "You can kill that idea."
4. "He was shot down."
5. "Those two really butted heads."
6. "He got the shaft."
7. "He came out of that meeting shellshocked."
8. "They sent him back to the trenches."
9. "He's been wounded."
10. "He came up through the ranks. He's a mustang."
11. "They buried him so deep it'll take him a month to recover."
12. "He started like a rocket but fizzled out."
13. "He was a dud."
14. "They really blitzed him during the interview."
15. "He couldn't take a frontal attack."
16. "His idea went down in flames."
17. "He got burned."
18. "He met his Waterloo."
19. "He was discharged, booted, sacked, eliminated."
20. "They brought out their big guns."

Each of these are language clues which provide some sense of the psychological processes that occur in the private or covert structure that relate to the intermittent, continuous and continuing power plays and games that occur there.[8]

Group and Organizational Power Scenarios: Abuses and Consequences

Power relationships are the pervasive characteristics of organizational life. Power within organizations has impact and influence over the actions and transactions of the members involved in that organization. There is no equality nor satisfaction in the operations of power which wax and wane over time. The drama of power is a pervasive and significant part of all human relationships within groups and organizations. It is implicit in behavior, dress, language, symbols, gestures. It may be disguised and subtle, covert, overt or direct, but power is a fundamental aspect of groups and organizations.

Power scenarios and their accompanying games and plays are real. Some people win; some people lose; most get hurt. The reward in winning is the seeming appearance of security, control and the accoutrements of material well-being. For the losers there is humiliation, a pervasive sense of powerlessness, the disappearance of meaning in one's life, self-reproach, loss of self-respect. The consequences for the organization are lessened cohesion, effectiveness and productivity, for the conflicts spawned are not abated—only continued. Power plays are not intrinsically satisfying to the human beings involved. The payoffs for the one-up players are generally status, comfort, privilege. The payoffs for the one-down players are seemingly fewer cares, less responsibility and less worry, not having to make hard decisions or tough moral choices.

The traditional goal of management has been to control, manipulate and manage in order to obtain a high performing, steady worker who "cares not" and "wants not." Common uses of power sought by an individual in an organization are to get someone or several persons to do something or to avoid or fend off threats happening to themselves. This is ultimately related to the fantasies and realities of immediate and long run personal survival within the organization.

Power overlays and currencies within an organization are related to sex role scripting, hierarchical and managerial authority, traditional aspects, and real and perceived skills and competencies. These power overlays give control and access to knowledge, information practices, clerical, technical, professional, and personal competencies, organizational positions, resources and funds, organizational procedures, and overt and covert alliances which are the daily fare of organizational life.

Whole books are devoted to telling how to get and use power within this context. Such books merely succeed in continuing the mystification, the alienation and the oppression which are a concomitant of the modern work group.[9] One of these writers unscrupulously and blatantly lays bare the alienated self-destruction characteristics of modern organizational life. The author seems to tout alienation as a virtue and supports the continuance and extension of the conditions which produce it. In speaking of the necessity of letting people go, "firing," he observes:

> Half the trick in firing people efficiently lies in inventing for yourself reasons why they deserve to be fired, the most pervasive reasons being, of course, personal and irrational. People who have to do a great deal of firing steel themselves by careful inventory of the victim's annoying character traits, physical characteristics and clothes, and search for forgotten grievances and slights. The actual reasons may be inefficiency, corruption or stupidity, but such valid causes are seldom sufficient for the person who has to do it. He needs to find something personal.[10]

And again:

> A good rule for those who have the power to promote others is to ensure that they maintain absolute control over the process. Many executives insist on being the bearers of good news, with sound reason, and not a few are addicted to creating false rumors, building people's hopes and generally fogging up the issue, in order to keep everyone in suspense and dramatize the final decision.[11]

Yet another relates to sex-role scripting:

> Accomplished players can easily put down a woman and flatter her at the same time, and the use of sexual signals is a basic tactic in a whole series of complex power games that have nothing to do with sex. Flirtation, flattery, seduction, innuendo, all can be turned into a technique of control.[12]

In office life, such signals have a specific function: They establish a sense of false intimacy which, by its very nature, becomes conspiratorial. Because of these sexual signals in the office, power games often tend to be played from the bottom up, one-down, organizationally speaking, and can be used by women and men. These are but a few examples of the alienated, manipulative, exploitive power relationships that occur within the organization and how one writer has traded off the mystification and alienation and oppression which are the nature of its context. To alter the basic character of the banal work group is a fundamental challenge. It requires attending to the task of demystifying power relationships within organizations. It then requires designing and implementing the changes required to release the full potential of the human beings who work within such organizations.

Group and Organizational Power Scenarios: Analytical Possibilities

Group power scenarios may be analyzed as a series of ongoing events within the manifest/public (overt) and private (covert) structure of groups and organizations. Group power scenarios are a series of power plays which are an integral part of hidden agendas or games of individual players. These link into power nets of groups and organizations. They then become part of the overt and covert contexts of dynamic group processes. The context includes official rules articulated through the official arrangement of the organization and the individual roles which emerge in the private structure. There thus evolves a complex or network of intricate power relationships. These power relationships relate to the articulated or inarticulated agendas of the players. Consequently, all relationships within an organization exist implicitly or explicitly within a context of power. These relationships may be understood, implied, misunderstood, intentional, unintentional and mystified.

At the core of the group power scenario lies the individual group member and his or her implicit, explicit, recognized or unrecognized reasons for participating in the play. One of the drama themes ultimately taking place concerns the participant member and his or her fantasy (idea) about the leader and that member's judgment about what the leader thinks of that member. This is the operative principle identified in Chapter 4. This sets the operative imago into action.

Judgments based on this operative imago define whether the member is going to be loyal or discontented, one-down and humble or a "strong right-arm," a willing worker or a grudging participant. Indeed, an individual participates for his or her own psychological reasons, but the quality of that participation depends upon the judgment the individual member makes as how he is valued by the leader. It is possible to utilize the conceptual tools developed in the previous chapters to advance an analytical construct which would disclose power scenarios within groups and organizations.[13]

An Analytical Construct

Name: Each power scenario can, after its analysis, be identified by a distinctive name which characterizes the play, the key player or the focus of the play. Some observed power scenarios will be identified later.

Focal Position: Each particular power play or power play in response to a power play (which may be appropriately designated maneuver) may be played from the position of one-up, one-down, or pitched battle. This is the position from which the role player, or actor, generally moves. It is the basic role position occupied by the group member or group of members as he or she or they become participants in the power play processes. Even though the words below are written in the singular, it is important to remember these apply to groups and alliances of members as well as individuals within a group. The singular is used here for ease of presentation. Each event in a power play may be initiated by the persons occupying a one-up role, one-down role or be in a position of relative equality.

The response to such an initiation would be a maneuver to fend off the impact and effects of such a power play. If the maneuver is successful, the person engaged in the one-down power maneuver may get one-up to the person previously in the one-up position. The person previously in the one-up position may feel and be one-down to the person or group in the previously one-down position. Thus the "loser" then takes steps to get one-up again. This keeps the power play ongoing and alive.

When the participants perceive one another as equal the power battle is played from a relative position of equality, in which case it is a pitched battle.

It is important to keep in mind here the difference between the primary focal position and the power position as they change from event to event. It is important, too, to distinguish between the manifest structure which may officially cast a relationship in one-up and one-down terms and the covert group role which, within the context of the group itself, may be the reverse. Thus a young naval lieutenant aboard ship may outrank the chief petty officer in the formal hierarchy but the chief petty officer may be in a far more powerful position because of his skill and competence and his position in the covert structure of the ship's crew. In this category it is possible to identify a number of roles by both their official name and their covert role designation, as reviewed in the previous chapter, and the position, the primary focal position, from which these various roles are played: one-up, one-down or pitched battle.

Primary Boundary Involvement: The primary focus of the play may be internal to the group or organization, in which case the focus may be on the major internal boundary which separates authoritative power from the membership or across the minor internal boundaries which separate the membership from one another and involve individual proclivities transacting across those minor boundaries. Boundary involvement may involve the major external boundary, in which case it would be a response to an unexpected, unusual occurrence or to an actual invasion of such a boundary. It may involve defense or preparations to respond to these possibilities. It might involve actual combat across the major external boundaries.

Rescue Triangle Positions: The key positions on the drama triangle may be located and identified for each role and may be used to identify the individual players as well as a collectivity of players involved in alliances which may be overt or hidden from view. Thus the position of the authority figure can be identified and located on the drama triangle. In-groups, factions and alliances can also be identified and located and the focus of the action indicated as well. All power plays move from positions on the drama (rescue) triangle. Table 6-2 summarizes the power distribution as it ranges around the drama triangle.

A characteristic of the drama triangle worth noting is that sometimes these positions become co-extensive with actual professions. Thus the persecution position is not too far from the kind of task a district attorney is fulfilling in his public position. Likewise, nursing is very akin to "professional" rescuing. Finally, there are "professional" life-long victims located in prisons and in mental hospitals across the land. Yet a word of caution must be written here. Even though a particular profession

TABLE 6-2:   **POWER DISTRIBUTION: DRAMA TRIANGLE**

SITUATION	CHARACTERISTICS	PROCESS
A. Victim	One or more group members appear stupid, confused, helpless, handicapped, or "one down." Emotions of the one down members are discounted and they are seen as weak and fearful.	The group identifies one member as less competent and less able to take care of themselves. A Group member or a few group members see themselves as less valuable in relationship to the group than other members.
B. Rescuer	One or more members feel they do more than their "Fair Share" of the work and reflect "do-gooder" insecure behavior. They often display "one up" actions and a rigorous sense of obligation.	One or more group members need to do more than anyone else to feel valued by the group. One or more members feel it necessary to do more than others in the conduct of the group work. Someone in the group takes full responsibility for the conduct of group business.
C. Persecutor	One or more group members become involved in blaming, hostile, retributive behavior. Words and actions of one or more reflect withheld resentments.	One or more group members select a target Victim on whom to vent withheld hostility and rage, or focus on to win a power play.

Table 6-2: Power Distribution: Drama Triangle

may seemingly be "locked into" a specific position in the drama triangle, never-theless, in the daily life of a particular member of that profession may find these persons racing around the drama triangle being a victim one moment, a persecuter the next, and a rescuer the next—depending upon the circumstances in which they find themselves. Of course, power play analysis must be finely tuned to this kind of phenomenon.

Degree of Intensity of the Play: The degree of intensity of the power play and its accompanying maneuvering may be classified according to degrees. First, those with no lasting consequences; second, they may involve lasting consequences but with little significant damage to person or property; third, they may involve lasting consequences (usually with tissue damage) which end in the courtroom, the hospital or the morgue. Thus a first, second or third degree of intensity may be identified in power play analysis.

Scarcity: Each power play involves a competitive struggle for that which is per-ceived to be or is actually in scarce supply. The reality of that scarcity may or may not exist or it may be mystified, i.e. there actually may be enough of something to go around, but people are taught otherwise—tender loving care, for example. Thus Steiner observes:

> *Competitive, hoarding behavior is predicated on unrealistic anxiety based on fears of scarcity. Oppressive as he is to others, the hoarder is in himself oppressed by it. The stroke economy is an example of artificial scarcity in a basic human need—strokes. O.K. feelings are in scarcity and people have difficulty feeling smart, beautiful, healthy, good and right-on, except by proving that others are not—if there was only enough beauty, intelligence, health, and goodness for a few. It is possible to hoard, compete for, and create scarcity of O.K. feelings in the same manner in which food and strokes are hoarded.* [14]

In groups and organizations scarcity is created around power, money, status, pro-motions, space, and a variety of other overt and subtle aspects. The architecture, office design, equipment and supplies all reflect the subtle nuances of power and status inequity. It is around these perceived scarcities that group and organizational power struggles occur.

The goal of a power play may be ultimately to achieve that which is in scarce supply, survival or the fending off of a loss of that which is in scarce supply or to prevent failure. These are a few of the possibilities that might be overtly or covertly sought by the key players and groups of players within a group or organization.

Ideology: This identifies the supporting myths which explain and rationalize the power transactions of the players. It may involve official organizational policy, politics, psychology, religion. It may be cast in ultimate truth or individual self-interest and it usually involves language of virtuousness and righteousness which legitimize the individual act in the transaction which occurs.

Strategy: This involves the overall plan to reach the goal which is sought by the power plays. The objective may be determined in an aware and intentional manner or it may be conceived in the unaware reaches of the mind. Once determined at some level, the design for its achievement is created and developed. This may involve "patterns of striving," about which there is little awareness, or determined plans of action which are intentionally designed to arrive at the objective.

Tactics: Tactics may be divided into techniques and moves. Techniques are the specific overt and covert processes behind the moves, and the moves themselves are the specific transactions which lead toward the ultimate payoff. These techniques and moves relate to the overall strategy and reflect the internal morality of such strategy. These are the links through which the design is carried out. They involve an "arsenal" of "weaponry" which may be utilized. These include such things as threats, promises, payoffs, rewards, punishments and a variety of other economic and psychic "tools." These tactics involve timing, power, routines, available options such as transfer of the action to different arenas. When failure is threatened in one, elaborating new challenges and many others. Each may ostensibly be used to accomplish legitimate ends. Each is designed to move the player closer to achieving the goal of the power play.

Process Clues: These are transactions which reveal tactics or disclose the strategy involved in the power plays. Group role differentiation may be identified and the process of such group role differentiation designated. Where such processes can be identified and more than one person supports overtly a two-person transaction (overtly, covertly or even silently), a group power play may well be underway. Blaming, fault-finding, scapegoating and evasion of the group's understood (or agreed upon) procedures will also reveal power play processes. Support may come from a position of participation, involvement or engagement. These processes will tend to reveal the kind of splitting and projection that goes on within the context of the group process.

Group Process Diagrams: Here structural and transactional diagrams for each event can indicate the group dynamics over a period of time. These are particularly effective tools in visualizing power play processes.

Role Collusion: Within the structural diagrams, a role matrix may be identified or role matrices may be located by utilizing structural diagrams and identifying the roles located therein. In addition, the individual members of a particular alliance or system of alliances can be designated, and finally the specific individual transactions which are keys to the power play process can be identified through the use of transactional diagrams where appropriate.[15]

Transactional Games and Alliance Systems: Each group power play links into the games of the individual members. If one member succeeds in establishing leadership and he or she is functioning within an hamartic (tragic) script, the group is in for serious difficulties—"troubled waters" lie ahead. Each of the men and women around Richard Nixon went on his journey for their own reasons with few able to take personal responsibility for interrupting the process by exercising individual moral choices until the resignation of Attorney General Elliot Richardson and his Deputy William Ruckleshouse. The signals came prior to this, of course, but this initiated the unraveling of the series of one-up plays in which President Nixon was engaged and signaled the success of the efforts to dislodge him which may be characterized as one-down power plays including the use of a secret informer named "Deep Throat."[16] Power plays are linked to the transactional drama of the engaged players when a group power play is underway.

Such hamartic leaders are supported by the silent, participating, involved or engaged support of one, few, many or all of the group membership. Since this is part of the hidden group process such alliances may be designated as collusions. It is observable that as an analytical designation power plays are morally neutral, i.e. they can be used in the pursuit of any virtuous or infamous cause. The drama is behavioral and power plays may become moral or immoral, legal or illegal in their unfolding.

It is useful to identify the individual players and define how each one links into the power play process. This is accomplished, where possible and appropriate, by identifying the name of the player's game, the player, the role, and the specific pay-off that each particular player gets for his or her participation in the group power play. This can be done for the role players who are significant to the power play action. Here it would be most important to rely on the definition of a game articulated by Eric Berne. Games are a series of transactions between individuals which are ulterior in purpose, repetitive in nature, and have a well-defined psychological payoff. The psychological payoffs are the feelings that the actor gets and seeks as a result of playing the game.[17] Alliance systems involve the collectivity of group members who overtly or covertly support power plays and maneuvers through several events.

Group Consequences: The focus of this analytical category is upon the ultimate impact of the power play by and upon the group. Here the concern is the cohesiveness of the group, its ability to fend off external threat, and carry on an orderly internal procedure. The focus here is also upon the immediate impact of the event, on the orderly procedures of the group, and upon present events which are integrative, disintegrative, or whether such an event contributes to long-term cohesion, disintegration or decay. This aspect of the group process will be examined more thoroughly in the next chapter.

Operative Group Mode: A group power play event may initiate Bion's basic assumption groups, i.e. pairing, flight/fight, or dependency. Where the group has developed beyond these responses to stress (and a power play is a stressful imposition in the group process), the orderliness and cohesion of the group can be linked to a concept of development which derives from Berne's imago classifications identified earlier in Chapter 4. These are more thoroughly examined in the following chapter.

Contravention: This is the action which can or has been taken to stop the power scenarios, plays and games which are underway. This is distinctive in that it is designed to stop the power play, game or scenario. Contravention means actually opting out of the power play. It does not mean disengagement, however, but focuses on taking action which brings a halt to the action. It is straightforward, out in the open, and stops the power play "dead in its tracks." It does not respond with a one-up or a one-down maneuver. It will undoubtedly vary from situation to situation. It may involve confrontation, straight talk, and risk. It will certainly not involve secrecy, lies, deceptions, or power maneuvers in response. Contravention must clearly not spawn additional power plays. Some contravention possibilities and opportunities will be identified in the later chapters on intentional change and cooperative work.

Power Scenario Analysis: Power scenarios, games and plays may be analyzed by utilizing the foregoing categories. Prior to application and depending upon the thoroughness with which the group process analyst wishes to assess and observe, it would be necessary to develop a narrative of the critical events and transactions in any particular power play and identify the plot and the persons, or cast, involved in such events.

A Preliminary Thesaurus of Power Scenarios

One theorem involved concerning group power plays may be stated as follows: If one or more group members support a two-person power transaction, a group power play is underway. A two-person transaction may or may not be a power transaction. If it is, it may be the opening gambit in a power play. Power scenarios, plays and games reflect the "hidden agenda" and "script strivings" of the individual players.

Power play analysis thus focuses attention on the actors but does not detract from the characteristics of the group processes and the nature of the transaction of these actors nor from the scenarios and games involved.

Full understanding of power scenarios will enable group participants to more effectively confront their own process and avoid the disintegrative impact of such power plays. More complete understanding may be developed for the implications they hold for the decay of the group wherein cohesion is diminished and the capacity of the group to carry on orderly and productive work is interfered with in a manner as to preclude its possibility or threaten the actual survival of the group or, indeed, lead to the demise of the group. Full investigation, analysis, classification, cataloguing and contravention options yet remain to be realized. Yet it is possible to develop some brief descriptions of a few that have been identified up to the present time. The following is a preliminary thesaurus of power scenarios:

An Eye for An Eye: This is an ancient and venerated one-down group game which sometimes continues over centuries and seeds intense, continuing quarrels in its third degree form. It is often played for keeps. In March 1977, the leader of a small Moslem sect, Hammas Abdul Khallis, led the members of his small Hanafi Muslim sect into an assault that took over 134 hostages in the B'nai B'rith building in Washington, D.C. This was done in generalized, non-specific retaliation for the assassination of his own children, whose death he blamed on the black Muslims and on whom he also laid the murder of Malcom X.[18] Such a game as this even in a smaller, less intensive, degree will tend to shatter the cohesiveness of any group.

In most organizations and groups it is played in a milder form. Professionals, such as engineers, professors, lawyers, etc. who mistreat support persons may find such treatment subtly returned. A secretary can delay a needed typing draft or misroute "important" data; an administrative assistant can leak information, or increase the work load of the ungrateful boss. The players in this game keep score and stay even. It is continuous and ongoing until one of the players is promoted, transferred or dies.

Divide and Conquer (Divide and Rule): Divide and conquer, a one-down game, together with its corollary divide and rule, a one-up game, is frequently characteristic of organizational life. The goal is to create hostile, warring factions and take over control as a result of the dissension, unrest and insecurity which follows. Often the victor rides to power at the front of a discontented faction which "splits the booty" of organizational power, status and privilege following the victory. Here the struggle for the rewards of status, promotion, resources and power within the context of an organization become the scarce commodities around which organizational power struggles occur. In this instance, power which endures overcomes transitory power which may arise from time to time to challenge the established leadership. Oftentimes the lessons of divide and conquer and divide and rule are not lost on the membership. The leaders who gain power that way frequently come to lose their power through similar power play methods.

Holier Than Thou. This is perhaps one of the most ancient and venerable of all one-up power plays. This and the many alternate forms that can be identified within this classification have strewn the pages of history with human misery. God, Right and Tradition are presumably on the side of the one-up players in this drama. They use the ideological roots located in righteousness in a way that has led to persecutions, inquisitions, and war.

In colleges and universities throughout the United States, this game may take place over the lifetime of an academic department or college faculty. It takes its toll in broken careers, reputations, and through stress, disintegration of personal health. The academic variety may be identified as "I am more academic than thou." It relates not only to those professors who have published as against those who have not published, but can become exquisitely complex and relate to the prestige and reputation of the journals wherein a particular professor has published—with one journal being more prestigious than the other and enabling the one to have published in the more prestigious journal to get one-up on the professor who has published in a less prestigious one.

There are infinite elaborations of such a game as this. Another variation of this ancient and venerable power play is found on the streets among policemen. The game there may be identified as "I am colder than thou." Here prestige, power, glory, and righteousness are on the side of the policeman who is cold, cool, calculating and unfeeling as he deals with offenders at the street level. Other variations include "I am tougher than thou," "I am lefter than thou," "I am more loyal than thou," etc.

Kill the Patriarch (Matriarch): This involves a series of power plays usually played from a one-down position and operated against a visible powerful, effective elder member of the group or organization. The position of the patriarch (father-like figure) may be either official or he may simply be seen as an older, yet effective, leader. It may, as well, be played against a powerful woman (mother) figure in the group. In any case, the challenge comes from a member who, for whatever reason, begins to undermine the group position of the patriarch or matriarch. (Patriarch is used for convenience of illustration.) The attack usually focuses upon the perceived status and prestige enjoyed among the group by the target figure.

The initial attacks are suggestive, intermittent and focused upon the affectual ties between the patriarch (matriarch) and the other group members. This is done by attacking the trust bonds and denigrating his personal strengths. At first, the effort is subtle and then, as allies and support develop, the attack is escalated in intensity. These may involve such tactics as "cornering," i.e. putting the patriarch on the defensive; for example, having to "explain an alleged misjudgment," or devising and delivering an attack upon his character and then a quick withdrawal, making accusations, staining his integrity or his competence, making suggestions impugning the sincerity of his motives, or the use of guilt manipulation and peer pressure to obtain allies. When the target person is rendered fully vulnerable and the challenger feels sure of his/her position with the group (having gained enough allies and sufficiently damaged the strength and power of the target person), she/he will put the overt challenge in front of the full membership, usually with a flourish and drama in a manner which renders the patriarch totally ineffective as a valuable and contributing member of the group or organization. If the challenger fails, he/she is isolated and frequently expulsed from the group.

Lord of the Flies: In this situation, the group is leaderless, either from death or demise of a leader, beloved or hated, or the leadership is voluntary and ineffective, or for some other reason the major internal boundary of a group is ill-defined, soft and porous, so that the leadership is, or appears to be, ineffective. In this kind of one-down group power play, the more rational leaders come to the fore and are assassinated early in the play. It begins to take on the characteristics of a Bion dependency group and ultimately the leadership which emerges is the most pathological member with leadership qualities within the group and expresses the basic fears, angers and wishes hidden within the group. He or she becomes one-up to the rest of the members.[19]

Two Tigers Cannot Occupy the Same Mountain: This involves a series of power plays operating from a position of relative equality. Its method of play is that of pitched battle, that is, it alternates between one-up and one-down play. It frequently involves alliances and support which vary through time and proceed until one of the players is a clear winner and the loser is eliminated from the scene or, at least, rendered ineffective. This power play sequence was identified by a professor of Japanese literature who was familiar with it as an old Japanese allegory.[20] In organizations and groups, the struggles take place over control, among other things, of program, resources, budget and territory. It escalates and erupts seemingly very suddenly and unexpectedly. Sometimes the events are disclosed in a planned and calculating manner. Each victory by one of the antagonists is temporary until the eventual and inevitable retaliation occurs. When and if there is a clear winner, the loser suffers ignominy and oblivion. He generally must "leave the territory" and reestablish elsewhere. Sometimes clear territory is identified and each learns to respect the territory of the other and not penetrate or challenge the identified boundary of the other. Such a boundary may be subject matter, special tasks, control over specific programs, etc.

In an engineering organization this might be a struggle over a project design or involve program control between two superintendencies, one headed by a mechanical engineer and the other headed by an electronics engineer. It might occur between a fiscal vice president and a program vice president over the control of a substantive organizational program. These struggles will occur over budget, promotion, employment programs, benefits and a variety of other agency processes. It could occur between a mayor and a police chief over how federal funding should be spent to abate juvenile crime. Where there is no clear victory it could go on for years and involve a great variety of issues.

Queen of Hearts: This is one-up matriarchial rule where the woman who holds power distributes the supplies, the rewards, and determines whose work gets done and whose work does not get done. She bestows the benefits of her supplies and her larder to some and denies it to others. In a word, she decides who shall "eat cake" and who shall be denied the cake. She often decides, almost in a whimsical fashion, whose heads will roll and whose heads will remain—in an arbitrary fashion like the Queen of Hearts in Alice in Wonderland from which the name is derived.

Righteous Ruler(s): The rise of power of this person within an organization is usually through attention to meticulous detail and careful command of organizational procedures. The Righteous Ruler is the self-appointed guardian of organizational truths and standards. He measures all activity according to his own hidden, preconceived judgments and patiently waits to impose these judgments upon the unwary, the powerless and the non-believers in the organization. His position is righteous. He plays from a one-up position. His actions are cruel yet always clothed in "correct" even virtuous reasons. This person lacks compassion, is unyielding and unforgiving. He has a long memory, brooks no opposition, and once in control consolidates his power and judges all. The Righteous Ruler has highly selective hearing—screening and seeking only what confirms his preconceptions. Paper trail power games are frequently a distinctive and tell-tale part of the play. Productive tasks are subordinated to concerns of order, control and correct behavior. Retribution is a key aspect of the hidden agenda. The goal is to impose virtue to the organization and the language he uses frequently encompasses words such as "excellence" and "efficiency." These are the "hangmen" of an organization and they lay devastation in the wake of their actions. Those who oppose them are frequently broken in spirit and body at the end of the struggle. Under this kind of leadership organizational activity shifts into decline, creative and innovative spirit dissipates and control and orderly procedure dominate. It is a one-up game played with fear as the currency of power. Where organizational survival weighs in the balance cohesion disintegrates and if this leadership is maintained group or organizational survival is in doubt.

Yeoman of the Guard: This power play sequence involves the long tenured, experienced, competent, highly skilled, "blue collar," members of the organization. These persons are frequently perceived as the "backbone" of the organization. The reservoir of their power is experience and "know-how." These persons are the chief petty officers or the "master sergeants" of the organization. Woe be unto a young junior professional who offends one of these "old hands," for their fury will be swiftly delivered. If there is a change in top management and someone is appointed who is unacceptable to this group, agitation and pressure will be skillfully brought to bear until a truce is reached or until the new head is replaced. It is a power play which is played from a one-down position if the impact sought is above their official position in the hierarchy. It is played from a one-up position if it is played toward those below in the organizational hierarchy. It is pliant, yet firm, as the player seeks his goals upward. It is unyielding and authoritarian when it is played facing downward.

Power Scenarios: Impacts and Consequences

These are a few of the power scenarios which have been identified. They are described here in abbreviated form. Power scenarios and the accompanying games and plays occur amidst the backdrop of organizational rules, orders and procedures. The drama of organizational power plays utilizes language, jargon (ideology) and procedures specific to the particular organization involved. Formal organizational procedures generally mask these psychological, and sometimes actual, physical abuses and betrayals of the human personality. The cost to organizational productivity and cohesion is immense, let alone the human psyche and special costs. In regard to power plays, Steiner has observed:

> *Power plays do not lead to satisfaction or equality. They always lead to increased or continuing one-up/one-down situations. The reward of winning through power is a sense of security achieved from having control over the situation. But control and power are not intrinsically satisfying; no quantities of power or control can ever fully satisfy the needs of any human being. Satisfaction, from having enough of what we really need—food, shelter, space, strokes, love, and peace of mind. The way to those is not power plays but cooperation.* [21]

Power scenarios are fundamental components in political affairs. Such power scenarios may be experienced in a manner ranging from crude and brutal to subtle and barely perceptible. Power plays are an essential ingredient in such scenarios. The competitive political struggle for scarcity is a more acceptable, non-violent alternative than the tragic wretchedness of war with its deceptive promise of glory and victory in an age where human degradation and nuclear holocaust has been its measure. Power is a prime commodity in politics. Politics is the struggle of power, i.e. control over the use of human energy and resources and the distribution of scarcity.

Power scenarios, games and plays are some of the techniques used by persons and groups to accomplish such objectives. Politics, then, involves continual power struggles and struggles for power and is surely a more appropriate arena for those kinds of struggles than war.

The Usefulness of Understanding Power Scenarios

Once a power scenario is identified, analyzed and classified, a clearer understanding of the impact and consequences of such power scenarios on the persons, groups and organizations involved can become ever more available. Individuals can learn how to take care of themselves in better and more straightforward ways. Groups and organizations can obtain more effective and creative work by altering the conditions which are prone to spawn such behavior. The analysis and understanding of power scenarios have been utilized in several local governments in Southern California to reduce the dysfunctional consequences of their impact where such power plays have seriously affected program design, implementation, coordination, results, and frequently distorted the feedback process as well. Efforts were designed to encourage the cooperative behavior among the antagonists and considerably reduce the animosity among the players. Conflict is a frequent concomitant of such power operations, and conflict resolution procedures may be utilized to reduce their possibility.[22]

In addition, ongoing programs can be established which are designed to reduce the incidence, lower the intensity and moderate the impacts of such power operations. For the individuals caught in power scenarios, understanding power scenarios and taking steps to reduce and eliminate such power operations could lessen the personal costs involved, reduce personal and organizational stress, and encourage more creative, effective performance on the job. Deena Weinstein identifies some constructive uses of the power of opposition within organizations. Bureaucratic opposition, she suggests, can be used for achieving change from below. As helpful as this might be it is, nevertheless, change that is still achieved with the framework of the strategic and tactical operations and maneuvers of individual and group power operations.[23]

These are only a few of the possible advantages which may flow from a full understanding of the context of group and organizational power. This offers a ripe field for further investigation, analysis and rectification. The ability of a group or ogranization to carry on orderly procedures and fulfill its task of mission relates to group cohesion. Effective group cohesion is essential in the successful development of a group itself. This relates, not only to the elimination or at least reduction of the dysfunctional and disintegrative impacts of power operations, but to the development of effective group cohesion as well.

SUMMARY

Groups and organizations are structured relationships directed toward the accomplishment of purposive activity. These groups and organizations have manifest, latent, overt and covert aspects within their processes. Membership in groups is attractive, sometimes financially rewarding, often exciting and frequently ambiguous. Group members always have "hidden agendas," i.e. they bring to the process their own needs and wishes, some of which are consciously or unconsciously withheld from the group. The hidden agendas (script strivings) are derived from personal scripts learned early in life and reinforced throughout childhood combine with group process to produce the drama within the group. The group becomes its own distinctive process. Overt and hidden group processes are laden with the drama of power plays which may be operated from positions of inequality, *viz.* one-up/one-down position or from a position of equality, *viz.*, pitched battle. They involve the public (manifest) structure and the private structure as well.

These power struggles often take on the caricature of war. They are played from alternating positions on the drama triangle and may include elaborate strategies and alliances. They can be analyzed, utilizing an analytical construct which can disclose the myriad complexities which group and organizational power scenarios involve. On the basis of such an analysis, group power scenarios can be identified, classified and presented so as to develop responses which will contravene their dysfunctional impacts upon the persons, groups and organizations concerned. These responses will range from conflict resolution, implementing intentional change and the development of programs designed to moderate the impact and consequences of such power plays.

NOTES

1. Claude Steiner, *Scripts People Live*, N.Y., Grove Press, Inc., 1974, p. 66; cf. R.D. Laing, "The Mystification of Experience," in his *The Politics of Experience*, N.Y., Ballantine Books, a division of Random House, Inc., copyright R.D. Laing, 1967, pp. 57-76, on power within organizations see M.N. Zald, *Power in Organizations*, Nashville, Tenn., Vanderbilt University Press, 1970, *passim*.

2. See generally Thomas A. Harris, *I'm O.K. – You're O.K.*, N.Y., Harper & Row, 1969; Muriel James and Dorothy Jongward, *Born to Win*, Reading, Mass., Addison-Wesley Publishing Co., Inc., 1975; Jean Piaget, *Logic and Psychology*, N.Y., Basic Books, 1957.

3. William H. Blanchard, *Aggression American Style*, Santa Monica, Ca., Goodyear Publishing Co., Inc., 1978, pp. 2-11, for more on the uses of social power see Dorwin Cartwright, *Studies in Social Power*, Ann Arbor, Mich., Michigan Institute for Social Research, 1959.

4. Steiner, *op. cit.*, pp. 212-223. The origin of how power is learned and taught is explored as a phenomenon of childhood experience and through sex-role scripting. This is carried into the work situation and supplied the *raison d'etre* of the interpersonal dynamics therein.

5. The game formulae is a definite process including well defined steps. Specifically it is a series of ongoing complementary ulterior transactions proceeding to a well defined, predictable outcome, see Eric Berne, *Beyond Games and Scripts*, N.Y., Grove Press, 1976, pp. 69-82 from Eric Berne, *Games People Play*, N.Y., Grove Press, 1964, pp. 48-65, and also Eric Berne, *What Do You Say After You Say Hello?*, N.Y., Grove Press, 1972, pp. 11-27.

6. *New Times Magazine*, November 12, 1976, p. 18.

7. See James Marshall, "The New Guerrillas; Public Administration in the New Industrial State," unpublished doctoral dissertation, University of Southern California, available from Xerox University Microfilms, 300 N. Zeed Road, Ann Arbor, Mich. 48106.

8. These are some typical examples of phrases characteristic of war and violence which were collected by the author from the public administration practitioners in his graduate seminars during the years 1975-77 at California State University, Los Angeles.

9. An example of this kind of book is Michael Korda, *Power! How to Get It, How to Use It!*, N.Y., Random House, 1975.

10. *Ibid.*, pp. 147-148.

11. *Ibid.*, p. 161.

12. *Ibid.*, p. 222.

13. This analytical scheme draws its conceptual inspiration from the material developed by Claude Steiner, *Scripts People Live*, N.Y., Grove Press, 1974, pp. 222-223, and integrates much of the material developed by Claude Steiner within its contents, the concept of the degree of intensity of the play is taken from game theory, see Eric Berne, *Games People Play*, N.Y., Grove Press, 1964, p. 64.

14. Steiner, *op. cit.*, p. 159.

15. Steiner, *op. cit.*, pp. 26-48.

16. See Carl Bernstein and Bob Woodward, *All the President's Men*, N.Y., Warner Books (by arrangement with Simon and Schuster), 1975, pp. 73-75, 78-79, 136-141, 179-180, 218-221, 269-274, 336-7, 362-65, see also Leon Jaworski, *The Right and the Power: The Prosecution of Watergate*, N.Y., Readers Digest Press, 1976, *passim*.

17. Information on game sequences including an applicable formula can be obtained in Eric Berne's *What Do You Say After You Say Hello?*, N.Y., Grove Press, Inc., 1972, pp. 21-25. See also his *Games People Play*, N.Y., Grove Press, Inc., 1964, pp. 48-65.

18. *Newsweek Magazine*, March 21, 1977, pp. 16-27.

19. The characteristics of this power play is similar to William Golding, *Lord of the Flies*, N.Y., Coward-McCann, 1955 (fiction).

20. I am indebted to Kazumitsu Kato, Professor of Japanese Language and Literature, California State University, Los Angeles, for identifying this power play sequence.

21. Steiner, *op. cit.*, p. 222.

22. Alan C. Filley, *Interpersonal Conflict Resolution*, Glenview, Ill., Scott, Foreman & Co., 1975, *passim*, see also L. Pondy, "Varieties of Organizational Conflict," *Administrative Science Quarterly*, May 1969, pp. 499-507.

23. Deena Weinstein, *Bureaucratic Opposition: Challenging Abuses at the Work Place*, N.Y., Pergamon Press, 1979, *passim*.

RELATED READING

Blanchard, William H. *Aggression American Style*. Santa Monic, Ca.: Goodyear Publishing Co., Inc., 1978, p. 2-11. This effort examined the unique expression of American aggression as it is expressed in American foreign policy. Specifically, he suggests the danger of aggression lies in our tendency to attribute it to others, while denying in in ourselves.

Hummel, Ralph P. *The Bureaucratic Experience*. New York: St. Martin's Press, 1977. This is a very crative and important effort which examines the varieties of experience which link the human being with the structure and processes of bureaucracy. It presents an innovative conceptual analysis of bureaucracy which is exceptionally relevant to the understanding and rectification of alienation.

Kahn, R.L. and Boulding, Elsie. *Power and Conflict in Organizations*. New York: Basic Books, 1964. These papers were prepared for seminars conducted in 1960-61 by the Foundation for Research in Human Behavior in cooperation with the Center for Research in Conflict Resolution and focus upon the means and modes of power in organizations and studies of responses and coping styles for conflict.

Lasswell, Harold D. *Power and Personality*. New York: W.W. Norton, 1948. A significant effort which explores the uses of power by the humans in their relations due to another and focuses upon the struggle between those who would sustain free society as opposed to those who would re-introduce caste upon the social order.

Russell, Bertrand. *Power*. London: George Allen & Unwin, Ltd. Published in the United States, New York: Barnes and Noble, 1962. Russell views power in the social sciences as energy is viewed in physics. This point of departure leads to an analysis of the uses and impacts of power in social and governmental settings.

Skinner, B.F. *Beyond Freedom and Dignity*. New York: Vintage, 1972. A significant, if mechanistic, psychological orientation toward human beings which centers upon the uses of rewards, negative payoffs as conditioning to adjust the human being to the requirements of the social order.

Sorokin, Pitrim and Luden, Walter. *Power and Morality: Who Shall Guard the Guardians*. Boston, Mass.: Porter Sargent Publ., 1959. A hopeful book calling for new moral leadership and the use of human knowledge, wisdom and love to resolve the forces leading to nuclear holocaust.

Chapter 7

STRESS, COHESION AND DEVELOPMENT WITHIN GROUPS

The drama of power plays pervades every aspect of organizational and group life. Group dynamics center on activities related to the major and minor, internal and external group boundaries, the context and quality of the individual proclivities that occur among the transactions between the members and, finally, the cohesion within a group that provides for the orderly existence of a group, its ability to respond effectively to threats and its ability to do work.

Groups and organizations are the primary social units through which the work of society is accomplished. The capacity and ability of groups and organizations to perform the meaningful and productive work required rests, among other things, upon the ability of the concerned groups and organizations to successfully respond to stress so as to provide for the orderly existence of the group. This is the first priority which commands the group's attention if work is to be done at all. The effective and successful response to stress is achieved through the development of a fully cohesive group. This is an ongoing process and is not static nor assured once attained. The focus of this chapter is precisely upon those aspects of stress, cohesion and development which are so essential to the conduct and achievement of meaningful and productive work.

Group Development: A Perspective

The three facets of group activity which are vital to understanding group development are: 1) **Task**, i.e. the nature of the work the group does which is also its reason for existence; 2) **Process** is the work required of the group in order to promote orderly activity of the group and must be attended before tasks can be accomplished; and finally, 3) **Combat**, which is required when a group is immediately or potentially threatened with immediate destruction of its existence.

Bion suggests that "undeveloped" groups are groups which "hold a basic assumption" that is shared either tacitly, sometimes overtly, by the other members of the group.* This shared basic assumption may derive from resentment, fear, anger, sorrow or concern and leads to group behavior in a manner that precludes the group from girding for combat, performing its task or dealing with its own process. In contrast, a fully developed group is cohesive, i.e. it has an orderly existence and has the ability and the capacity to work. It is, as well, a productive, creative, orderly, safe, nurturing, game-free and task-oriented group. A threatened group which is undeveloped appears disorganized, disorderly, conflicted and alienated.

Group Cohesion and Group Development

A developed group is cooperative, creative and productive. It can, among other things, creatively problem-solve in such a manner as effectively to achieve its task or mission. A fully developed group is able to focus, maintain, cooperate and problem-solve in such a manner as to assure ongoing order and safety for the group. A developed group maximizes the permission that each person in the group feels to become an authentic individual fully realizing his or her own personal power and competence. It is a group able to provide positive and nurturing reinforcement to its individual members. A developed group minimizes individual mindlessness, powerlessness, joylessness and lovelessness. It is supportive of authentic emotional

* These materials are more thoroughly presented in Chapter 3.

expression in safe ways. Individuals are valued for themselves and their contributions to the life of the group.

The performance of group work depends upon the effective resolution of the tensions and problems within a process group.[1] These tensions and problems within the process group directly concern the achievement, nurturing and restoration of human intellectual and emotional capacities. Cooperation is fundamentally related to the resolution of the tensions, stress and problems contained in the process group. Productivity and task performance depends upon the outcomes of the process group. A fully developed group, then, is able to use the skills available within the group and the competencies available within the group collectively and cooperatively in such a way as to accomplish the value-laden mission and objectives of the group. This, in turn, depends upon the effective integration of the group member into the context of group process. Productivity is the activity required to accomplish the group's mission and is achieved through the effective performance of the group task. It is the effective performance of the group task which is necessary to the fulfillment of the value-laden goal of the group or organizational mission. The effective performance of the group task depends upon the development of a cohesive group which, in turn, depends upon the context of group process.

Survival of the group depends upon the group's ability to do organized work (productivity) and to maintain and establish the structure to do that work (process). Productivity is a matter of task competence. Survival as a matter of group process is frequently beyond the view and consciousness of the group members. Both require adequate physical and human resources. Resolution of process group problems and stress precede and underlie productive accomplishment.

Cohesion is the aspect of group dynamics which seems to account for the capacity of the group to fend off real and imagined internal and external threats. Berne suggests it is "an operative force derived from the needs of the members to maintain the orderly existence of a group."[2] He suggests the real test of a group's cohesion is its ability to do a measurable amount of work against opposition, i.e. to overcome external pressure and internal agitation. Further, he suggests, a successful outcome of such a struggle strengthens a group ideologically and failure may result in the termination of the group. An absence of group cohesion or diminished group cohesion would impair a group's capacity to carry out task activity. Cohesion is a condition essential for the conduct of process, task, work and combat. Group cohesion, when absent or severely diminished, would seriously interfere with the group's capacity to survive and carry on work. The total consumption of a group's cohesion on work, combat or process alone would leave little group energy and resources in reserve on which to draw should a shift be required from one group posture to another for survival purposes, i.e. work is required to obtain resources, combat is required to ward off threats, process is required to engender the cooperation needed to conduct work. All require cohesive force.

Berne suggests an effective empirical measure of cohesion could well be attendance. Attendance in any group may derive from compulsion from without, pressure from within, and individual needs and choices. He suggests the easy way to measure this is to examine attendance records. He suggests that where attendance falls below 75%, cohesion of the group is in peril. It matters not whether the attendance is induced primarily by legal compulsion as in public schools, social pressure as in Rotary Clubs, or voluntary commitment as in therapy or growth and awareness groups.[3]

Bion suggests that it is as difficult to define the healthy group as it is to define the healthy individual, but he suggests the qualities associated with group health appear to derive from the following:

A. A common purpose whether that be in overcoming an enemy or defending and fostering an ideal...

B. Common recognition by members of the group of the "boundaries" of the group and their position and function in relation to those of larger units or groups.

C. The capacity to absorb new members, and to lose members without fear of losing group individuality, i.e. "group character" must be flexible.

D. Freedom from internal subgroups having rigid, i.e exclusive boundaries...

E. Each individual member is valued for his contribution to the group and has free movement within it. Personal freedom of locomotion being limited only by the generally accepted conditions devised and imposed by the group.

F. The group must have the capacity to face discontent within the group and must have a means to cope with discontent.

G. The minimum size of a group is three. Two persons have personal relationships; with three or more there is a change of quality (interpersonal relationship).[4]

These qualities, Bion suggests, are associated with "good group spirit." Bion thus locates group spirit, the kind necessary to the ongoing group, as emerging out of these aspects of group life. Certainly, it is not wrenching his meaning to say his focus upon "good group spirit" is the cohesive force within a group which concerns the work required for task accomplishment and survival: 1) to provide for the orderly existence of the group; 2) for the effective conduct of its task; and 3) to respond successfully to threats to its existence. These are rooted in the conditions of "good group health."

Philip Zimbardo notes that an individual within a group which has undergone "individualization" (differentiation), i.e. where each member is valued for his or her own personality, competence and contribution to the group, is less likely to opt for alienating, violent choices and behavior. This is very close to identifying the reasons for the specific behavior which occurs within a basic assumption dependency group where a kind of permission is spawned to hide in anonymity. In such a group anonymous action and easy escape from personal responsibility make it easier to engage in violent, aggressive choices and behavior.[5] Third degree consequences can emerge more easily in these groups where violence seems to lie endemically in the structure and personality is warped to fit the group's oppressive requirements. It is this group as well that casts forward its most pathological leader who seems to express the specific latent and shared fears of the group and offers an easy solution to the group's survival problem.

If attendance is the heartbeat of a group and a certain measure of the quality of its health, stress is certainly an essential aspect of understanding group life as well. It is stress which impacts upon the individual and it is stress within groups and organizations which reflect group tension and impacts upon group cohesion. Stress is any aspect of the environment which poses a threat to the individual or the group.

Stress and Group Development

Prolonged personally experienced stress in groups may be indicated by a variety of symptoms such as absenteeism, high injury rates, high incidence of illness, loss of time on task performance, among others. In addition, stress may be somatocized into the group member's body through a variety of short or long term illnesses. Stress may relate to the problems of an individual's long term survival in an organization. Stress may also affect the worker or group member's behavior and task performance even where the stress is unrelated to the job. Such stress may occur at home around a wife, husband or children, or it could relate to an unresolved problem external to the group itself.[6]

It is in the analysis of stress within the structure and dynamics of groups and organizations that Bion and Berne come together in a unique and distinctive way. It is necessary for every fully developed group (Berne identifies this as "a healthy group") to be durable, to be effective, and to utilize its internal competence collectively for the accomplishment of the group tasks. To achieve this, the group must survive until the task itself is accomplished or completed. It is helpful to observe here that the termination of the group upon completion of its task, or the alteration of that task, in such a manner as to render the continuation of the group irrelevant, is a matter to be considered later.

In Chapter 3 it was observed that survival threats to the existence of an organization can come from two sets of influences: disruptive forces from without and disorganizing forces from within. When a group undergoes stress in such a manner, the problem of dealing with such threats is immediate and takes precedence over everything else in the group to insure survival. The group's capacity to respond to both these forces are determined by the cohesiveness of the group itself. Berne prefers the word anancasm to describe these aspects of group dynamics. He observes:

> ANANKE, the Greek Goddess of Necessity, had precisely the three connotations desirable to emphasize the ineluctibility of the forces involved in group dynamics. Freud was fond of her and in one place even refers to her as "the sublime Ananke"... The external disruptive forces would become the external anancasm, fateful dangers that must be met; the cohesive forces would become the group anancasm, the intimate ties of blood and friendship; and what is here called mildly an individual proclivity would become an individual anancasm, the character which is man's destiny and which drives him inexorably to his fate at the hands of his fellows.[7]

The three forces he found affecting group process were 1) external pressure on the group, 2) internal agitation within the group, and 3) the force within the group which responds to these other two for the purposes of group survival. Cohesion is encompassed within the meaning of "group anancasm" as used by Berne to designate a "force" within the group responsive to survival threats.

The three specific varieties of survival include ideological, where survival is solely in the minds of the members; physical, where it is solely limited to the geography structure, and physical resources, and where little else is available; and effective which includes each of the others but adds the elements of the group's ability to do organized work and to fend off outside attacks and resolve internal threats.[8]

Berne identified three ways in which a group existence may be terminated, decay, destruction and disruption.[9] To this may be added a fourth, intentional termination. A group may be intentionally terminated by withdrawing its legitimacy, authority and resources through appropriate governmental process. This may be accomplished by having legitimacy, authority and resources withdrawn by superior authority.

Threatening transactions across the major external boundary; unexpected, unusual, and unanticipated transactions across the major internal boundary; or intrigue and conflict within the private structure which goes unresolved place the group under stress. Such stress may range anywhere from mild to intense and may be tentative or enduring. In these instances, they pose in some degree a survival threat. A group which has not developed fully its own cohesiveness (group anancasm) will be exceptionally vulnerable and under stress exhibit Bion's basic assumption group modes.

The internal group structure and the processes determine the crucial responses to external threat, internal decay and physical catastrophe. Where the group is effectively organized and fully developed the membership may be mobilized into a response. If the threat is very great, all other work may be suspended so that every ablebodied member is thrown into the survival fight and the group becomes a combat group. A similar phenomenon occurs when the internal threat is grave. Where a group fails to maintain its existence long enough to accomplish its task, it is due to the incomplete development of the internal cohesive forces (group anancasm). In the former instance, the threatening forces are capable of overwhelming even the most intense effort of loyal members or in the latter, when cohesive forces are weak and poorly developed, the group is unable to respond effectively to its own survival needs. All groups and organizations are laden with drama related to this; all reflect events of poignant heroism, tragedy and banality.

Group Activity: Process Group and Task Group

Individual behavior within task and process groups unfolds in a way distinctive to each person, yet within a general pattern which can be identified through analysis. Roles provide a distinctive focus to better understand this aspect of group process.

Process Group Development

In Chapter 5 it was observed that role differentiation within groups occurs on the basis of individual needs, experience, wishes and emotions combining together with the individual member's group imago, which alters through time. The imago evolves from provisional through operative, and role differentiation unfolds as the imago evolves.[10]

New group members and continuing members of a group may be viewed according to their ability to adjust into the group. This involves two different skills: adaptability and flexibility.

Adaptability rests upon accurate judgments made with the best information available. These may be tactful, diplomatic, prudent, calculating, etc. The goal is to obtain as much as one can to meet one's personal needs and wishes (i.e. the needs of one's script). In this instance, the imago is adjusted according to experience and observation. An arbitrary person proceeds blindly on his way into the group process unaware of his or her own transactions and often lays havoc in the path in a most unaware fashion.

Flexibility rests upon the individual member's ability and propensities to modify or resign parts of his or her own personal agenda or needs (script). A rigid person can neither modify or relinquish essential elements of his own or her own script needs. Thus there are four basic positions to an individual's adjustment within a group:

1. **Adaptable-Flexible.** This person will carry out his or her operations within a group smoothly, patiently and will always settle for the possible.
2. **Adaptable-Inflexible.** This person will carry on patiently and with diplo-

macy but will be unyielding in the pursuit of his or her own goals.

3. **Arbitrary-Flexible.** This person will shift from one goal to another with very little insight or sophistication and will settle for what he or she can get without changing the manner of his or her actions.

4. **Arbitrary-Inflexible.** This person is the authoritarian within the group. He or she is the dictator ready to accomplish his or her own purposes without regard for the group or its members and always the words used are couched in righteousness and virtue.[11]

Closed and openmindedness and their relationship to these membership behavioral variables would certainly be important to study, especially as they relate to the role of ideology and violence within the group. An initial study linking flexibility to openness and rigidity to closedness and their relationship to political ideology has been done by Michael S. Cummings. He writes:

> ...past and present empirical data favor the proposition that belief-system closure in citizenry favors conservative and conventional political and social attitudes, while openmindedness is significantly more likely to culminate in idological radicalism.[12]

Cummings suggests in light of the empirical evidence it is reasonable to argue that to the degree major social problems such as poverty, crime and alienation remain unsolvable within the limits of existing institutions that the open mind is a potential threat to the maintenance of the established system.

In the private or covert structure, members move at their own pace, from participation to involvement to engagement, and occasionally (rarely) to belonging. As the private structure develops and the individuals' perceptions of one another begin to alter and the imagos of each person changes, the individuals become involved in group process and role differentiation begins to occur. Further elaboration of the role and further delineation and differentiation of roles find individuals engaging one another in the private or covert structure in order to satisfy their own hidden needs and wishes and oftentimes to articulate in transactional language each person's own particular game or hidden agenda. If the private structure or covert process is confronted at this point, and individual and group processes "worked through," the possibility of moving into authentic acceptance of individual members, so that each one achieves a sense of intimate belonging, may be achieved. But this is infrequent and rare.

The link between the individual personal process and the group process can be identified as defining the group's cohesion as it moves toward optimum group development. In this instance, the group cohesion is defined; (a) through the transactions in the private structure leading to role differentiation; (b) individual participation in transactions designed to further the internal orderly processes of the group; (c) individual participation in transactions which are designed to use those processes in such a way as to satisfy individual wishes and needs. Figure 7-A, entitled Private Structure Role Differentiation: Process Group, actions, is a graphic of the relationship between a group member's personal process within the group and the assimilation of members into the group processes. This figure specifically relates to the patterns of transactions which occur within the private structure of the group and therefore relate specifically to the process group with particular reference to covert role differentiation.

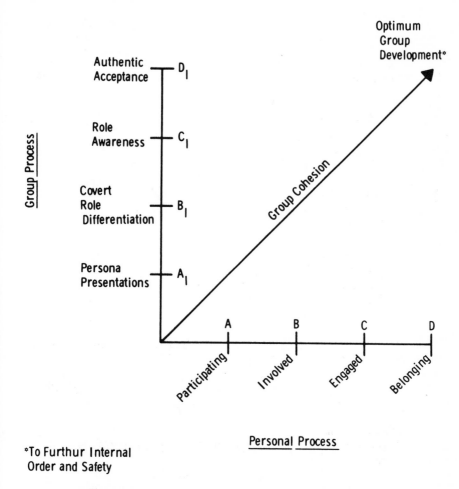

Figure 7-A: Private Structure Role Differentiation: Process Group

Task Group Development

The task group is concerned with fulfilling the organizational or group mission. It is responsible for achieving the value-laden objectives of the group. The task group performs the activity required to accomplish such purposes and is the main reason the group exists. Individual relationship to task includes, (a) orientation of an individual into the group membership, (b) problem-solving discussions as to how personal skills can relate to the collective task of the group, (c) contributing these skills to the task group activity, and (d) receiving feedback on the work performed.

To integrate the individual into the group involves sharing initial information concerning the focus and the task of the group itself and the relationship to the task to the individual. Next, the group must provide procedures integrating individual skills and competence into the collective activity of the group. The ongoing group must then utilize those skills and competence collectively in order to accomplish the value-laden purposes of the group and ultimately contribute the group's work

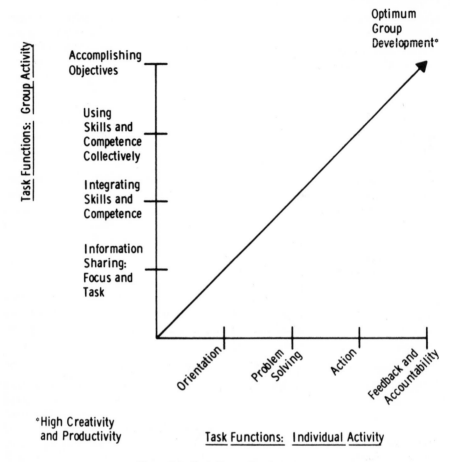

Figure 7-B: Task Group Development

to the overall purposes of the larger organization. The task group is therefore concerned with integrating individual competence into the collective activity of the group in order to achieve effective productivity.

A group utilizing the full human resources available to it in the service of task development would also indicate a high level of cohesion and creativity. The contribution the task group makes to cohesion and optimum group development is to identify the purpose and the reason for the group's existence and, more importantly, to provide an opportunity and vehicles for the creative use of individual competence and skills in a manner which encourages productivity and effective personal development.

Individuals in a task group can be isolated, alienated, separated from one another and procedurally linked through a supervision system in which each person's contribution to the ultimate goal of the group is not recognized by each of the group members or is seriously excluded from view of the group members. In such a system, leadership or management's relationship to group members would involve rigid, closed, authoritarian postures, fostering the utilization of reward and punishment system with a consequent loss of group cohesion and optimum group development. Rewards and punishments are substitutes for inadequate personal motivation and commitment. Elaborate reward and punishment systems diminish the possibility for the full emergence of the human personality.

Ultimately, authentic acceptance of each member by the group is accompanied by a sense of belonging to the group in individual members encourages an open, caring and nurturing intimacy. The development of cooperation and intimacy now become available within the group. This group develops reciprocal and satisfying emotional bonds among the members. It is a group in which the members feel they belong, where they feel safe, to which they feel committed, and from which they derive a sense of nurture and support.

Within an organization, from time to time a sentient group is cohesive, effective and productive, particularly in the short term. If the group is an ongoing one and the membership fails to continuously process the emotional life of the group and the membership, i.e. the emotional aspects of group life, in effective ways, reversion to collusions, persecutions, rescues, power plays and basic assumption behavior emerges to dominate group life and concerns.[14]

Figure 7-B, Task Group Development, indicates the relationship of individual task activity to the collective task of the group itself. It is important to realize that role differentiation in the private structure and the evolution of individual imagos within a private structure can and does proceed underneath and out of view of task group activity which is easily visible and is symbolized by files, typewriters, in-and-out baskets, telephone calls, memos and meetings.

The Process Group: Stress and Development

Earlier, attention was directed to the dynamics within a group related to stress across the major external and major internal boundaries and to the interpersonal transactions related either to task, hidden process or to power plays. The overwhelming amount of individual time structuring is associated with the drama and structure of power plays. Attention centered also upon the necessity for group cohesion is an essential required for optimum group development. Group cohesion, it was suggested, is an operative force within a group derived from the need of the members to maintain an orderly existence of the group. The aspect of group activity concerned with a group's own process centers on the activity required to promote the orderly existence of the group itself. Group process, according to Berne, involves:

> The conflicts of forces resulting from attempts to disrupt, disorganize or modify the structure of a group. The major external group process results from conflicts between external pressure and the group cohesion and takes place at the external boundary. The major internal group process results from conflicts between individual proclivities and the group cohesion as represented by the leadership and takes place at the major internal boundary. The minor group process results from conflicts between the individual proclivities and takes place at minor internal boundaries.[15]

Relating the concepts of stress, group development, and group cohesion, it can be observed that stress involving a major internal or major external boundary in the form of a threat, or an unanticipated or unexpected event will result in significant impact upon the group. When such stress occurs, work immediately stops; specifically, work concerned with the performace of the group task is interrupted. The group immediately turns to its own process in an attempt to deal with the unanticipated, unexpected disruption. Group members in the vicinity of such a disruption physical-

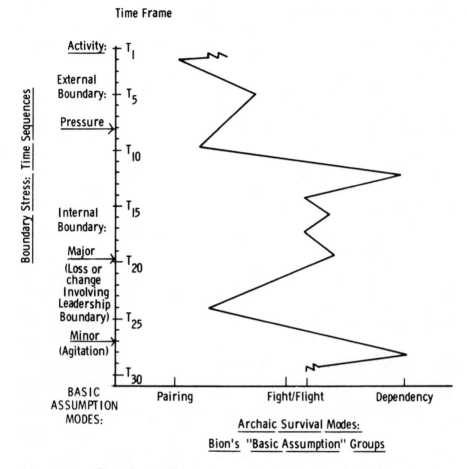

Figure 7-C: An Undeveloped Process Group: Stress Responses

ly stop all work and attend to it. In the outer reaches of an elaborate organization, news travels through the informal communication networks, depending upon the intensity and the seriousness of such a disruption. If a group is cohesive and developed enough, it may respond in a cooperative, integrated and collective way—sometimes moving even into combat in order to reduce or eliminate stress so that it can proceed with the group task.

If a group is and remains undeveloped, a reversion to Bion's Basic Assumption mode will be observed. Figure 7-C, An Undeveloped Process Group: Stress Responses, indicates a way of viewing the concept of boundary stress through time and the relationship to Bion's basic assumption survival modes. Thus it can be seen here that where a group is undeveloped and lacks cohesion, any stress across the major internal or external boundaries will produce, depending upon the nature of the internal process within the group involved, pairing, fight/flight, and dependency reactions. Oneness is not included in this conceptual presentation because the conditions for its emergence have not yet been identified.

Where a group has achieved some modest amount of development and some degree of group cohesion has emerged, focused, cooperative energy is available to respond to internal and external stress. In this instance, the group seems "in charge" and "organized" in its response. When it is in a basic assumption mode, the behavioral contrast is one of panic, being out of control, or "giving power away" to an anticipated future event or to fate.

Thus a group, in order to accomplish its work, which includes not only the task involved in its reason for being but the maintenance of its own existence so that its members may achieve the psychological and social rewards, must attend to its first objective: namely, to maintain its own orderly existence. This is the concern of the process group. Once a group has responded to the threat, eliminated, altered or abated it, a group is then able to turn concerns again to task activity. It is at this point that Berne's observation can be thrown into full perspective: ". . . the effectiveness of the work group depends on the success of the process group." No significant work concerned with group task can proceed as long as the group has experienced serious disruptive stress at its major internal and external boundaries. The power play transactions which occur among group members may reduce cohesion and contribute to internal decay.

Unless the major internal boundaries are seriously threatened by internal agitation or an attempt by leadership to convert internal process to its own purposes the role differentiation, imago development, and power plays occurring within the private structure will tend to continue unabated as the psychological payoffs for the individuals in the ongoing process oftentimes are equally and frequently more important than any economic rewards derived from their own participation in the group or organization. The process group, then, is crucial to the optimum development of a group itself for it is at this level, usually covertly, that the first responses to stress within and without the group occur.

Much remains to be learned concerning the relationship of the process group to the task group and the milieu of power which characterizes a group. Task groups perform a variety of functions, intimately reflecting the resolutions achieved within the process group. Thus some groups may not move to full development, yet involve tradeoffs which allow the group to proceed with its task. Thus a symphony orchestra may respond to a variety of leadership patterns. For example, extremely authoritarian conductors who have been greatly feared by members of the orchestra have, at the same time, been able to elicit magnificent sounds from the orchestral membership. Perhaps this entailed a tradeoff involving the recognition of the expertness of the leader (within the constraints of authority which are limited to the time and task boundaries of rehearsal and performance) and the satisfaction and indentification deriving from membership in and quality of the orchestra, even while the members, at the same time, blanched under the dictatorial baton.

The process group reflects the private structure and in the development of effective group cohesion has a significant contribution to make. The forces within the process group can reduce the cohesion and foster group disintegration or enhance cohesion and encourage group development. Where fear, paralysis, isolation and alienation pervade the nature of the process group and role differentiation becomes negative or destructive, dominated by intensive second and third degree games, the group will not develop and individuals will remain in an isolated position unable to contribute effectively to group cohesion, group process, and group tasks. The process group, then, can contribute to group development by creating an environment of safety within which persons are encouraged to risk and failure per se is minimized. Development in a process group seeks to maximize personal safety, encourage risk-taking, and provide opportunities to members to use their competence, power and intelligence. It also must provide for effective yet safe confrontation of members' hidden agendas, script strivings, power plays, etc., all of which may rip a group apart if not properly attended. This confrontation process is considered in the chapter following concerning intentional change.

The social milieu of a process group is concerned with provisioning the safety that group members feel toward one another. The social milieu may be conflicted, in which instance there is little safety for group members except in collusions and alliances, one with another and one against another. It may be competitive, which precludes intimacy and cooperation in the face of some real or illusioned scarcity involving emotional or physical needs. It may be accommodative for each member or group members give up a little of themselves in return for what the group has to offer. Finally, the social milieu may be cooperative, in which instance it involves great safety and includes acceptance by the group of the members and a sense of belonging on behalf of the members themselves. In this situation, group members feel safe enough to be vulnerable and to risk that vulnerability through intimacy. The social milieu thus sets the parameters of safety for the group members.

Individual transactions into the group process move from ritualistic work and behavior where one is guarded and takes no risks to pastimes which are transactions which deal lightly with the environment and are basically unrelated to group activity and group process, into games which involve a group member's "hidden agenda" (script strivings) or his or her "ulterior transactions," leading to a consequence for the group member that has a "payoff" which is of a psychological nature for the group member. This is the psychological game defined by Berne.[16] When an individual sheds his or her game and works cooperatively, he or she risks the possibility of achieving "game-free intimacy." This includes, among other things, good feelings around one's own competence as it relates to work performance and psychological transactions. The contribution that a process group has to make to optimum group development is to create enough safety and permission within the group so that individual members will be encouraged to take risks and exercise personal initiative. Such safety and permission establishes a mutual trust that no group member will be mistreated or "trashed" by the group and thus each member is supported to perform competent work and maximize his or her own psychological rewards.

The process group can contribute to a cohesive group force by evolving a safe environment within which group members can trust one another, risk their own humanness and achieve their own competence and obtain positive rewards and payoffs. To the extent that this occurs within the process group, the process group is more able to respond when stressed in an effective way. Figure 7-D, Process Group Development: Safety and Risk, presents this relationship between the social milieu of the group process and the evolution of the individual process in that social milieu from a place where safety and risks are absent to a position of cooperation and intimacy which provide great safety and encourage risk-taking, achieving great personal power, and encouraging effective personal competence.

Optimum Group Development

Optimum group development involves an orderly internal existence, a highly cre-

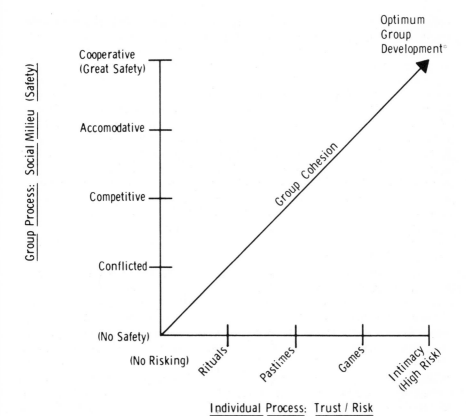

Group Process: Social Milieu (Safety)

Optimum
Group
Development°

Cooperative
(Great Safety)

Accomodative

Group Cohesion

Competitive

Conflicted

(No Safety)

(No Risking)

Rituals

Pastimes

Games

Intimacy
(High Risk)

Individual Process: Trust / Risk

°Maximize Group Permissions,
Personal Power, Positive Strokes

Figure 7-D: Process Group Development: Safety and Risk

ative and productive membership, a humane environment which is safe, supportive and psychologically rewarding. It is cohesive and effectively responsive to external and internal threats, yet open to alteration and change. It looks, appears, and is mindful, powerful, joyful and caring.

The role differentiation that takes place within the private structure is linked into the adjustment of the individual into the group itself. Thus an individual's imago evolves from provisional, then participative through operative and, on occasion, into a secondarily adjusted imago as a group member becomes integrated within the group. These adjustments of the individual to the group are equivalent to the stages in time structuring that characterize group transaction sequences as the individual links into that group process.

Individuals whose imago is provisional generally engage in simple, safe, ritual transactions. Persons whose imagos have undergone some adjustment and adapted to some of the realities of the group will risk engaging in pastimes irrelevant to the group itself and casual in nature. When an individual has gained his or her own place in the group and gauged either consciously or subconsciously what the leader thinks of him or her and this is reinforced from time to time "existentially" from the leader, the individual will engage the group process in ulterior and covert ways to get the psychological payoffs for which he or she remains in the group. These covert or ulterior transactions are part of the games and power plays and are more often than not hidden from the participant's own consciousness. At this level, the group member has a high degree of understanding about who the members are and how they are behaving within the group and can judge accurately the behavior of those with whom he chooses to get involved for his own purposes. This is where the power plays within the private structure, as they relate to role differentiation, take place.

In the evolution of a group, there is some evidence that at this stage in its development that a critical point is reached which involves individual moral choice and organizational survival. This point involves the confrontation of one member (or a number of members) by the group or the group authority and the individual is required to relinquish some individual proclivities or script strivings in favor of "playing" the group's way. This critical point has a direct impact on the cohesive force within the group and may shift from a second to a third degree intensity of activity.

It is at such a point that the senior members of the Committee to Reelect the President (men such as Maurice Stans and John Mitchell) put pressure on other men (younger men such as Jeb McGruder, Herb Porter and Hugh Sloan, III) to commit perjury to protect the President and to protect the survival of the committee to Reelect the President. McGruder and Porter capitulated at that critical point, Hugh Sloan, III did not. At the White House, young John Dean withdrew his commitment to organizational survival on the basis of an individual choice and the decay which had begun much earlier than even the break-in at the Watergate Hotel by the "plumbers" began to unravel and ravage the Committee to Reelect the President and the Nixon Presidency.[17]

Not enough is yet known at this point fully to understand the nature of this critical juncture, yet it seems to occur at a particular point in the evolution of most groups and centers on the nature of the cohesive force within the group. It is a point at which those who are in leader or member positions, who may be driven by hamartic or tragic scripts, dominate the task activity and process group so effectively so as to move the group into hamartic activity.

Much more study and work needs to be done to understand the linkages between role differentiation within the private structure to the dynamics of the process group that impinge on this critical juncture. There is enough evidence to warrant that it is a juncture which occurs within a family group, a work group, or a voluntary group and that the results, once that critical juncture is reached, will be: 1) the group moves to an hamartic or tragic activity; 2) the group becomes "locked in" to banal, everyday garden variety, ho-hum activity with a soap opera context to it; or 3) the group disintegrates because the cohesive force is dissipated at that point. Finally, if the group moves through this critical juncture, some of the members leave and some of the members are confronted and drop their games in favor of playing the way the group wishes. They are accepted by the group and receive assurance that they are indeed members and they respond with warm, full and committed participation. Either an hamartic or banal group may look on the surface to be able to respond effectively when stressed, but when put to the test or in the "clutch" its capacity to cohere and respond effectively to stress may disintegrate in the face of it.

Belonging and Participation

Elliot Jaques observes that "Participation is. . . intimately associated with belong-ingness and alienation."[18] The opportunity to belong requires the opportunity to "have a say" in "what goes on" that affects the individual group member or employee. Jaques suggests such participation is a right and has to do with access to participate in determining change. This can be accomplished, he proposes, by taking part in formulating and agreeing to new policies or modifying existing policy. The lack of such a right, whether exercised or not is intensely paranoiagenic.[19] Effective partici-pation in a group or organization, therefore, involves participation in determining policies affecting the group member, whether or not that policy is determined with-in the group or outside of the group. In some way participation must affirm, modify or deny policy options. When this occurs, the individual participates in a manner which contributes his competence in a way he feels good about and for which he is valued by the group.

The effective, developed group survives and proceeds with its tasks and meets the needs of its membership. Groups can, over a period of time, arrest in any particular stage in their development or can move on to growth or termination. Groups revert to previous outmoded or archaic behavior if stress or change cannot be assimilated within the private structure. It is also important to realize the task with which the group is concerned, the activity of the group, role differentiation within the private structure of the group, and the power games that go on within group process may be carried out regardless of the state of any particular member's imago. Thus role differentiation, games and power plays may well continue within a group while the group is also performing its work task.

What occurs within a process group occurs generally below the level of conscious-ness of its members and involves covert and overt role collusions as role differentia-tion takes place within the private structure. This relates as well to the nature of the power plays that occur within the private structure as they affect (enhance or dimin-ish) the capacity of a process group to respond effectively to threats when stressed. Thus a group may well limp along at some level until it is stressed, at which point it becomes a test of its own survival and of its cohesive force which links the task, process and the combat group together purposively.

Figure 7-E, entitled Process Group Development: Imago and Transaction Se-quences, is a graphic representation of the imago development of individual members and the corresponding time-structuring transaction sequences which occur within the group process. It indicates, as well, the evolution of cohesion toward optimum development through ritual, pastime and game transactions and identifies the place of the critical point which might well occur should a group move to that point in its process. It may well be observed from this matrix that individual adjustment to the group, as indicated through the imago sequences, matches an increasing level of in-tensity in the group time-structuring transactions as well.

Group Process and Personal Moral Choice: The Critical Point

The evidence is emerging that where groups contain members whose patterns and strivings, script, or hidden agenda include hamartic or tragic components and the group power plays and role differentiation range around that player or those players and there is no confrontation of the operations of those members, the group may well move from a banal to an hamartic one. Such a transition involves relinquishing

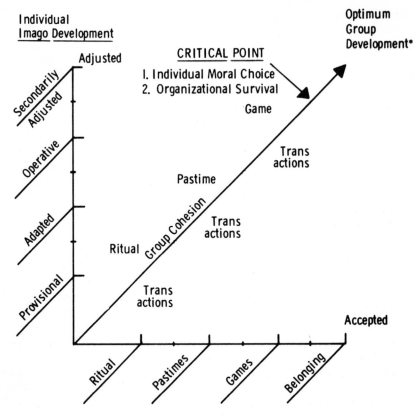

Time-Structuring Transaction Sequences

*Game Free Intimacy

Figure 7-E: Process Group Development: Imago and Transaction Sequences

individual moral choice, the continuation of individual and group powerlessness together with the empowering of the hamartic player or players. When this occurs the group process moves from banal to hamartic and personal and organizational survival often hang in the balance. This point is indicated in Figure 7-E as the critical point. At this critical transition point, progression of the group into cooperative, game-free, rewarding, supportive and involved task and process activities may occur whether the crisis is spawned internally or externally. If the hamartic option dominates group choices, the tragedy will most likely play itself out. The group will either move to termination, return to its banal ongoing nature or make a transition into a fully developed group.

Most work groups do not become either hamartic or fully developed. Rather, they remain banal work groups, concerned with tasks involved from time to time with process, laden with power plays, exhibiting role differentiation and being, to some degree, stressed. Such is the case in public organizations during times when their budget is being considered or their mission and funding is under attack.

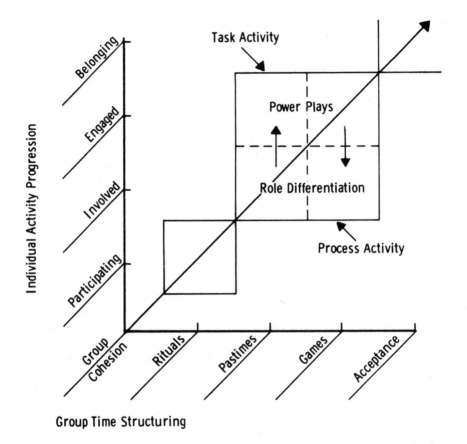

Figure 7-F: The Banal Work Group: Time Structuring and Member Activity

Group time is structured to include mostly transactions that are pastimes and games. Rarely does a work group move into a position where it is a fully developed, supportive, game-free group. Member transactions relate to the nature of the power game which impinges upon them, their psychological makeup and whether their needs are being met, how secure they feel in their employment and a variety of other personal and employment related aspects. Figure 7-F, The Banal Work Group: Time Structuring and Member Activity, identifies the kind of time structuring and activities which characterize most work groups.

Cohesion in this group is not a strong force and the problem of organizational survival and overall organizational purpose in the long run in the public sector is left to the strategic aspects of management. It is this level of public management activity which is concerned with development of effective legislative support for the organization which assures an adequate budget for survival. Management, at this level, is directly concerned with reinforcing such support by developing links with the clientele with which it is involved or which it serves. Any alteration of outside support or public attack may sufficiently stress an administrative organization so that effective fulfillment of the mission is impaired. A good example is the public schools, colleges and universities and libraries which have experienced a drastic decline in public and legislative support since the middle of the 1960's. Failure of bond issues put to public vote, hostile public attacks through tax limitation initiatives, inadequate and elimination of funding by the legislature in those program areas which are liberating to the human spirit such as music, drama and art and even physical education have all been at one time or another in this period curtailed in significant ways. As the public schools in some areas become less able to perform their mission, drop-outs, reduction in attendance, vandalism, gang conflicts and a variety of interpersonal stresses which result from scrambling for the scarcity that remains inhibits and sometimes precludes the public schools, colleges and universities from performing their educational mission. This in turn increases their vulnerability and thereby increases as well greater probability of further attack.

The Process Group: Stress, Cohesion and Power

Stress and Power. Organizations in the public sector may be stressed from without by direct physical threats to their existence (a) through the actual or threats of withdrawal or elimination of the physical and budgetary supports required for their ongoing existence, (b) by the failure or loss of legislative, public or clientele support for their ongoing mission or attacks on the integrity of the agency itself. These threats may range in intensity from moderate effects to severe threats wherein the latter may involve the survival of the agency itself. This will be met with activity responses of varying effectiveness depending upon the nature of the internal cohesion of the organization itself. The effectiveness of that cohesion is enhanced or diminished according to the nature and quality of the linkages with support environment.

Internally, a group can be put under stress a variety of ways, e.g. by an attempt of leadership to convert or alter the nature of the mission, or an attempt at a takeover of the operation itself by agitation and rebellion that ultimately threatens and perhaps overcomes internal leadership. Struggles for power within the leadership or struggles for power within the membership which become pitched battles involving great numbers of agency, group or organizational personnel. Where the group is undeveloped and cohesion relatively weak and insignificant, the group response to any initial threat would tend to reflect one of Bion's basic assumption positions. Cohesion in this instance is an insignificant group force and even may be non-existent. Where the group is partially developed or developed to a great extent, the group may respond effectively in a variety of ways and degrees to these stressful threats.

The imposition and occurrence of stress across the major group boundaries involving individual transactions and group transactions among the members of the group are separate, observable and definable phenomena. This concept is separate and distinct from its consequences for individual persons who are members of groups and organizations. Personal stress is a concomitant of membership in an organization and such stress may be a concomitant as well in family membership or personal situations unrelated to the concerned group or organization. This may have an unanticipated or continuing impact and consequence for that specific member of a work group.

Stress within a task or process group has consequences for the individual which are distinctive and can be observed and measured. There is an abundant literature supported by respectable empirical data relating to the impact of stress upon workers.[20] It is beyond our purposes here to review these materials. It is, however, important to take cognizance of them and point up the possibility that continuous, unresolved stress within a group may spawn and exacerbate personal stress and be accompanied by great personal costs.[21]

Stress and Cohesion. The development or impairment of cohesion is reflected in group development and depends a great deal upon what occurs within a major external boundary and in the transactions across the major internal and the minor internal boundaries. These transactions are the media through which stress is transmitted.

Many students of organizational stress have concluded that conflict and ambiguities spawn organizational stress. Conflict, of course, involves struggles for scarcity of real resources and status where the participants in a conflict win and lose and involves the power plays examined earlier. Ambiguity relates to unclearness around status, expectations, competence and task performance.

Robert Kahn and his associates identify stress as arising in the contradiction between the ceaseless, continuing and often accelerating conditions and change within the group or an organization and the requirements of flexibility of response and the demand from leadership or supervision for conformity within such ceaseless change.[22] Stress may also be rooted in three basic endemic conditions in the work situation: 1) the dependence upon the organization within which they work and its concomitant fear of potential layoff; 2) the continuing demand and need to remain defined as individuals in the face of this dependence on the organization; 3) the demands from the organization for the constant adjustment and readjustment of the member and employee to the organization itself.[23] Thus the contradiction between the demand of the worker on the job and psychological needs of the worker as an individual provide a constant source of continuing discontent which, as noted earlier, is a constant source of oppression and alienation which is reinforced daily.

Stress and Accountability. In situations where survival is assured or if at least the fear of termination is somewhat abated, internal stress in its long run consequences and its immediate effects may be seen as inhibiting development of the group anancasm: i.e., the cohesion the group needs to perform its tasks and resolve the stresses and pressures characteristic of the process group is inhibited in development when stress disrupts task and process activity. Process group activity requires that stress be "worked through." It cannot be controlled or managed out of existence. A consequent loss of cohesion will be followed by an attendant drop in productivity and an increase in group and individual vulnerability. In addition, the group becomes particularly vulnerable as a result of the drop in productivity. Apathy frequently sets in and the ability successfully or effectively to fulfill organizational missions is impaired. The group can become particularly vulnerable to "head hunting" or in the public sector "witch hunting," wherein the political sector or the media (TV or news) will hunt for some one who is the "cause" of the low productivity, the "bungled" job or made the disastrous administrative decision.

Thus punishment is easily substituted for problem-solving and once the "head rolls" or the "witch" is found, TV, newspaper, legislative investigators or county supervisors lean back "knowing" that the causes of disorder, low productivity, slothfulness, and inefficiency have been effectively dealt with and the organizational problems have been effectively solved. Unfortunately, this is not only untrue, but also it contributes to increased stress by inducing unspecified and generalized fear, encourages retrenchment and prompts behavior primarily concerned with "covering your ass" (known among public administration practitioners as the "CYA factor") which encourages uncreative, defensive, protective withdrawal and non-participation by the employee in the kinds of activities that are needed if the hard problems and demands of the public service and the agency mission are to be examined, defined and met. This is accompanied with increases in the symptomatic behavior that is related to stress, such as absenteeism, injury, sickness, listlessness, unmotivated workers, apathy, and the like. Alienation and oppression are continued and once again powerlessness, joylessness, lovelessness and mindlessness is taught as a way of life.

This is not to say the corrupt, the laggard, or the inefficient worker or administrator are not to be identified and held accountable for their actions. It is to say that substituting fault-finding for dealing with the hard task of problem-solving around the problems which face the organization in the delivery of its mission will inhibit or preclude group development in such a manner that the group cannot effectively fulfill its mission.

Accountability through witch hunting is no substitute for effective accountability through the performance of agency tasks which requires effective cohesion, motivated, integrated task-group operations. The kind of punishment or threats of blame or punishment which engenders CYA behavior where it exists over a long period of time promotes apathy, disintegrates cohesion and inhibits and oftentimes precludes adequate performance of the task and consequently impairs the ultimate fulfillment of the agency mission. It may well contribute to the immense costs involved in the expression of inadvertent aggression identified by William Blanchard. Here, elaborate denials are manufactured to hide hostile aggressive acts designed to make it safe for the concerned group or organization to survive.[24] It encourages the development of an elaborate hierarchy of administrative positions across a broad range of functions wherein the managers possess little authority to perform their tasks. It leads to a debilitated civil service which encourages promotion based on effective "political" skill within the administrative structure rather than competency in one's job.

The requirements to "protect yourself" encourages strict adherence to rules and regulations (in the face of contradictory "organizational wisdom") even when such rules and regulations are ineffective, outmoded and dysfunctional. An individual under these pressures will choose frequently to protect himself (herself) rather than risk trying to achieve creative and effective change. Job security and job benefits are available to those who choose to remain and these persons learn success is achieved by risking little and performing little. Those who are creative, ambitious and motivated either move on to other public sector employment or move into the private sector of the economy. Those who remain are, among other things, frequently manipulative in regard to persons with whom they work and protective of themselves by a variety of avoidance behaviors. No one becomes a friend of another. Fear and suspicion are endemic. Emotions are controlled and buried with important consequences for the private structure.

Members of the bureaucracy become emotionless, regulation-oriented, defensive, unsympathetic, and apathetic. Activity and initiative are stultified. New approaches are discouraged and safety in behavior is sought. The bureaucracy becomes responsive and vulnerable to those outside interests able to stress its external boundaries and its attention is directed to that concern.

Stress and Hierarchy. Organizing and integrating human effort where there is one person at the top and many at the bottom in a structure that can be described as pyramidal and where power, prestige, authority, wealth and reward are distributed in ever-diminishing amounts downward through a pyramidal structure is characteristic of the great bureaucratic civilizations throughout history. It is Max Weber who forwards the idea that pyramidal bureaucracy is an ideal type or a model which is the highest manifestation of rationality and efficiency, containing a system of integrated, coordinated, and specialized roles in which little deviation or alteration can be tolerated. Weber observes that bureaucratic organization is technically the most highly developed means of power in the hands of the man who controls it. Weber was not American and much of his work did not refer to the American experience. Yet he has had a significant influence on administrative theory within the United States.[25] Weber's concept of ideal bureaucracy, together with the strivings for efficiency initiated by Frederick W. Taylor's *Principles of Scientific Management*, dominated the transition in the United States from a rural agrarian nation into an industrial urban nation.[26]

Positing this as an ideal sets the worker and manager up against a system in which both lose, for the reality of the human personality and the nature of the group life creates a contradiction between what "is" and "what ought to be." Bureaucracy imposes this "artificial reality" as correct, yet "what ought to be" is neither desirable nor obtainable in light of present understanding of group and individual behavior. For example, within bureaucracy today efficiency sits as a ghost demanding its measure from the present and in the backwash it contributes significantly to organizational stress in a variety of ways. Implicit in the concept of efficiency is the tacit psychological assumption derived from a comparison of a worker with an ox and discloses a naive and negative orientation toward workers.[27] The anger and guilt which subtly impacts on the capacity of the worker to perform aside from its significant role in drama triangles and power plays, motivation to work through guilt is also a tax on the human personality and development of effective group cohesion.

The ideal type of bureaucracy posited by Weber up against the reality of individual and group behavior fails to deliver its promise.[28] This is so because there is no accounting in his theory for the behavior of role differentiation, group dynamics, and group process as they relate to individual and group behavior. Thus a bureaucracy cast in the shadow of Max Weber and measured by his ideal in our society becomes more often internally stressed, frequently apathetic and defensive in its posture in relation to its public. The workers become isolated and fearful, fearing criticism, punishment and non-promotion. Creativity is stultified and initiative squashed. Its public mission delivered ineffectively, and its capacity to perform cohesively and effectively is defective. Table 7-I summarizes what bureaucracy is said to be and the way it is actually experienced by employees as it relates to a governmental county jurisdiction in California.

To alter the pathology of this situation is a formidable challenge. To alter this situation which is probably characteristic of many bureaucracies in the public sector at all levels of government requires effective and persistent change efforts. Such change efforts will require the full creative and cooperative talent of the public, the legislature and the administrative units involved. It requires a steady and effective revision of how we in this society get our public work done.

The uncritical acceptance of hierarchy prevents us from creatively designing, applying and utilizing the vast amount of information and understanding which is

Weber's Ideal Bureaucracy	A Southern California County: Bureaucratic Reality.
Hierarchy of authority: Pyramidal in structure.	County bureaucratic hierarchy has the semblance of authority but not the substance.
Employment and promotion based on competence, merit and job performance.	Civil Service rules, regulations and practices encourages promotion through manipulative interpersonal activity.
Regular, dependable rules, orders and regulations.	Witch-hunting and head-hunting combined with outmoded rules and orders discourage initiative and creativity and encourage apathy and defensive behavior.
Development of a career service to encourage commitment and competence.	Continuous debilitating stress discourages effective utilization of available employee competence.
Impersonality in human relationships.	Bureaucrats emotionless, rule-oriented, unable to feel or act decisively. Mistrust, betrayal, suspicion and secrecy poison the wellsprings of personal feelings with disastrous consequences for the cohesion necessary for productive effort and personal reward.
Specialization of function.	Rigid job specifications isolate and discourage individual growth and development and contribute to the isolated, alienated feelings of the worker.
Authority is legitimate and accountable.	Fear of exposure paralyzes taking effective risks to produce, make decisions and take responsibility.

Table 7-1: Bureaucracy: Ideal and Real

emerging today about individuals and group behavior for the accomplishment of human purpose.[29]

Cohesion, Process and Productivity

Group cohesion is a fundamental and essential component to effective productivity, effective group process, and cooperative and humane interpersonal relationships. Pervasive, continuous stress which becomes an ongoing concomitant of group life inhibits and debilitates the development of effective group cohesion. Group cohesion, i.e., "the effective survival of a group is measured by its ability to do organized work," together with Berne's Law, *viz.*, "the effectiveness of the work group depends on the success of the process group," are important contributions to understanding group behavior.[30] If these observations of Berne are accurate, the process group becomes the key to getting the work done. It becomes the key to task group performance. It is the process group which deals with and works through stresses which must be resolved for work to be done effectively, productively and humanely.

Essential to the process group is its contribution to the development of group cohesion. Thus the effectiveness and, again, the success of the process group depends upon its effective response to stress, its contribution to the development of cohesion, and its provisioning of the basis for effective development. Cohesion, it will be remembered, is the internal force of a group which derives from the need of the members of the group to maintain the orderly existence of the group. Berne observes:

> The real test of a group's cohesion is its ability to do a measurable amount of work against opposition, i.e., to overcome external pressure and internal agitation. A successful outcome strengthens the group ideologically; a failure may terminate the life of the group.[31]

Too often the work of the process group and its contribution to cohesion has been overlooked, misunderstood, manipulated, exploited or ignored. Productive effort conducted in a humane way must emerge out of the process group activity. It is the process group which deals with and "works through," among other things, stress—organizational and interpersonal. Failure to address these needs may spawn consequences leading to the disintegration and termination of the group or the maintenance of the group in an ongoing fashion in a way which remains unproductive, unrewarding and full of stress, strain and pain.

Cohesion, Groupthink and Consensus

Cohesion is not "team work" in the sense of a blind, rigorous impulse to success and conformity. It seems to contain a contradiction and a paradox. Effective group work and productivity means giving up some individual proclivities on the part of the membership in favor of doing things the group way. When this occurs an individual may be accepted in the group because the other members recognize that he or she has given up some individual propensities and thus support group cohesion.[32] The indication of belonging is the assurance and reinforcement the group gives the member. The indication of acceptance is that the member gives the responses required by the group rules and orders and informal understandings. Belonging, then, and its concomitants of acceptance and adjustment may be the critical factors in group cohesion. It does not mean, however, abject surrender or conformity in which a member abdicates his own moral judgment. Irving Janis identified this urge as "groupthink" and defined it as a mode of thinking people use when ogranizational pressures and strivings for unanimity override personal motivation to realistically appraise alternative courses of action. Groupthink refers to an obscuring of mental efficiency, reality testing, and moral judgment flowing from in-group pressures such as amiability and *esprit de corps.*[33]

Consensus is distinguished from groupthink in that the latter is derived from in-group pressures and consensus is derived by each group member working through his or her own personal process in an autonomous and unpressured manner and coming to support an evolved group decision which emerges out of discussion reflecting that process. Each member participates genuinely in the discussion and dialogue within the group through which is evolved the group decision. Consensus is the most accurate and reliable form of group decision-making. It is rooted in a group which is valued by the group members and in which the group members value one another. Barry E. Collins and Harold Guetzkow examined a number of conditions under which both substantive and affective conflict lead to consensus. They found that the expression of many self-oriented or personal needs were detrimental to the reaching of consensus, yet when the personal and self-oriented needs are "...satisfied through rewarding and personal interrelations...." among those involved in the group or the broader organization concerned that "...there is a significant tendency for the group to achieve consensus." In addition, they found that when these conditions exist there is "...a significant tendency for the group to achieve consensus, especially when intense conflict prevails."[34]

Belonging, then, involves personal commitment which requires adjustment to the group and acceptance by the group and carries with a special psychological and social membership rewards. Yet, because it has an aspect of relinquishing some of one's own games or proclivities, it requires the continued awareness of one's moral responsibility and powers of personal choice. This, in turn, requires maintenance of personal autonomy and the willingness to contribute to the group in responsive and cooperative ways. Thus as each group member engages the group process, he or she has a set of options which, when taken, have significant consequences for one's self, for the group and for the organization.

An Alternative to Groupthink: Pathway Y

Figure 7-G identifies two pathways which are possible for an individual to travel within the process group. On the one hand, the group member may participate in ritual, become involved in pastimes, and engage in games which have profound social impact, maintain alienation and oppression and may reach, on occasion, as suggested before, third degree consequences with tissue damage and end up in the courtroom, the morgue or the hospital. This is Path X.

On the other hand, group members may gain insight and awareness by being confronted or confronting his or her own games and those of others. Then by receiving support from the group, together with authentic contact, one may work through significant and attendant problems. It could well occur that in return for adjusting one's own needs to the interests of the group one will receive the support of the group to make significant personal change. Thus one confronted with his own hidden agenda and supported by the group to make effective changes may become aware of a variety of choices and actions not previously realized. The group member, under these circumstances, could well be encouraged to pursue the moral implications of those choices and pursue individual action which is informed rather than blind. This is Path Y. Again, a member may choose to "give up" the struggle and withdraw. This is Path Z.

These three alternative pathways are portrayed graphically in Figure 7-G, entitled Process Group: Member Alternatives. Where members are blind to their own behavior in a group, lack of understanding of group process to deal with the process, will in the long run preclude the development of an effective task group which is primarily concerned with productivity. Rather, alienation and oppression are maintained. This process of achieving effective individual, group and organizational change is explored in the following chapter. Not only is productivity impaired but the maintenance of

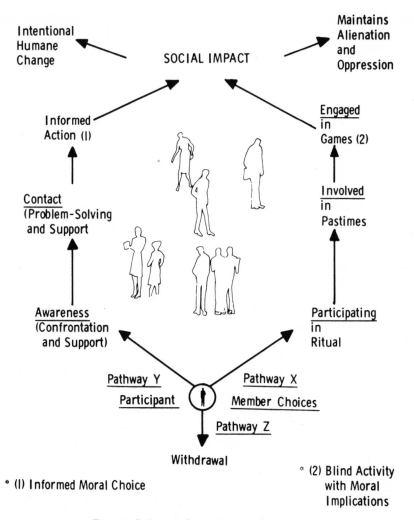

Figure 7-G: Process Group: Member Alternatives

alienation is continued and oppression, along with the accompanying strain and losses in human dimensions, are significant consequences in many organizations. Thus organizations must face the problem of dealing with the pathology of continuous stress and its attendant consequences for the organization, the manager and the members of such an organization.

Significant group time must be spent, if not continuously, certainly intermittently, on working through the critical aspects of the process group. Time must be spent on it if the process group is not to be superfluous, subversive or detract from the mission of the organization itself. This is essential if the organization is to obtain productive results and humane results. Covert role differentiation, power plays, threats and disturbances across the major internal and external boundaries when ignored, misunderstood, manipulated by management have costly consequences for the human beings, for the productivity, for the mission of the group or the organization. A humane and productive group depends upon a cohesive group performing its task competently.

The revisioning of our groups and our organizations must proceed from a new understanding of the individual and the group and the relation of one to another. The individual must experience his or her own value in the group and this is done by his or her being task-competent, i.e. competent in performing one's own intelligence. One's capacity to nurture one's colleagues in an authentic way needs sensitive encouragement and group members need to be supported to share their personal joy genuinely and encouraged to develop a sense of individuality and autonomy. A person experiencing one's own values and once accepted by the group experiences a sense of belonging to the group.

Commitment to the group is essential and contributes to cohesion when it is not born of guilt or of fear. The group, too, must be seen as a whole, a functioning unit, and appreciated realistically as it does function. It must be viewed in all its dimensions, dominated by the urgency of its own survival, with a unique life and existence of its own including transactions which are a consequence of the fantasies and the projections of its members. Groups and organizations are admixtures of dynamics and processes. Awareness and understanding about the admixture can be gained. When that occurs individuals within the group can make previously unavailable choices as to how to behave, what their identity is, and how they may choose to be seen. In this context a group's relationship to survival, mission and primary task can be more realistically assessed and understood.

Care must be taken to avoid the use of power and manipulation in the service of group development. In the process group a transaction which is not a genuine expression of individual member autonomous initiative betrays the human personality and is done at one's peril. It is usually indicative, among other things, of undisguised fear, withheld anger, or a hidden personal agenda or game. It is possible now to raise into view, conscious view, the conceptual and analytical categories by which we can better understand our groups and how we behave in them so we may more ably and more effectively understand how we mutually aid one another, are valued by one another and organized into groups and then into systems of interdependence. If we are thus to avoid pervasive decay in our bureaucracies, and the tempting destruction that such decay would encourage, we must revise and reconstruct our system of getting our public work done or succumb to an everlasting apathy and disorder which encourages conflict, decline, and challenges our survival. This must be done while reaffirming our own aspirations, our own goals, and our own values for ourselves.

SUMMARY

A developed group is cooperative, creative and productive. A developed organization provisions this possibility. A developed group can, among other things, creatively solve problems in a manner so as to effectively fulfill its task. A fully developed group is able to focus, maintain, cooperate and solve problems in a manner as to assure the ongoing order and safety of the group. Group cohesion (group anancasm) must be available for the conduct of group work, process and combat. An absence or lessening of group cohesion would seriously impair the group's ability and capacity to carry on effective work and survive. The resolution of stress and process group problems is a condition precedent to the development of effective cohesion. Personal stress is reflected in activity involving the dynamics of the process group and is frequently expressed in symptomatic behavior such as absenteeism, high injury rates, high incidence of illness, lost time, etc.

Optimum group development involves an orderly internal existence, a highly creative and productive membership values for each person's unique competence and personhood in the contributions he or she makes to the group. It provides a safe, supportive, humane and rewarding environment. Group cohesion is a fundamental and essential component to effective productivity, effective group process and co-operative and humane interpersonal relationships within the organization and with the clientele and publics with which it is linked. Group development must be authentically achieved and not derived through power plays and manipulation, otherwise it is a betrayal of the human personality and fraught with inhumane and dysfunctional consequences for the group, the members and the organization and the social system.

NOTES

1.　F. E. Kast and J. E. Rosenzweig, *Organization and Management: A Systems Approach*, N.Y., McGraw-Hill Book Co., Inc., 1970, p. 116.

2.　Eric Berne, *Structure and Dynamics of Groups and Organizations*, N.Y., Grove Press, 1966, copyright J. B. Lippincott, 1963, Evergreen Edition, pp. 72-73, p. 76.

3.　*Ibid.*, pp. 82-91.

4.　Wilfred R. Bion, *Experiences in Groups*, N.Y., Ballantine Books, Inc. (Tavistock Publications, 1959), by arrangements with Basic Books, pp. 16-17.

5.　Philip G. Zimbardo, "The Human Choice," in W. J. Arnold and D. Levine (eds.), *Nebraska Symposium on Motivation*, Vol. 17, Lincoln, University of Nebraska Press, 1969; see also Johan Galtung, "Violence, Peace and Peace Research," *Journal of Peace Research*, No. 3 (1969), pp. 167-172, and Johan Galtung and Tord Hoivik, "Structural and Direct Violence," *Journal of Peace Research*, No. 1 (1971), pp. 73-77.

6.　See generally R. L. Kahn, et al., *Organizational Stress*, John Wiley & Sons, Inc., 1964, see also Warren G. Bennis and H. A. Shepard, "A Theory of Group Development," *Human Relations*, Vol. 4, 1956, pp. 415-437, reprinted in Warren G. Bennis, K. Benne and R. Chin (eds.), *The Planning of Change*, (1st ed.), N.Y., Holt, Rinehart & Winston, 1961, pp. 321-340.

7.　Berne, *Structure and Dynamics of Groups and Organizations, op. cit.*, p. 79.

8.　*Ibid.*, pp. 68-72, see also Chapter 3.

9.　*Ibid.*

10.　*Ibid.*, pp. 165-166.

11.　*Ibid.*, pp. 162-163.

12.　Michael S. Cummings, unpublished M. S., "Dogmatism and Radicalism: A Reassessment," Political Science Department, University of Colorado, Denver, presented to the McKenzie River Conference on Political Science, sponsored by the University of Oregon, May 1977, p. 25. This is an important initial step to relate empirical evidence to this kind of qualitative categories.

13.　*Ibid., et. seq.*

14.　David L. Singer, Boris M. Astrachan, Laurence J. Gould, Edward B. Klein, "Boundary Management in Psychological Work with Groups," in *Journal of Applied Behavioral Science*, Vol. 11, No. 2, 1975, p. 131.

15.　Berne, *Structure and Dynamics of Groups and Organizations, op. cit.*, p. 244.

16.　Eric Berne, *Games People Play*, N.Y., Grove Press, 1964, *passim*, and his *What Do You Say After You Say Hello?*, N.Y., Grove Press, 1972, pp. 11-27.

17.　Leon Jaworski, *The Right and the Power: The Prosecution of Watergate*, N.Y., Readers

Digest Press, 1976, *passim, The Senate Watergate Report*, N.Y., Dell, 1974, *passim*, Carl Bernstein and Bob Woodward, *All The President's Men*, N.Y., Warner Books Edition (by arrangement with Simon and Schuster), 1975, *passim*, John Dean, *Blind Ambition*, N.Y., Pocket Books, 1976, *passim*, John J. Sirica, *To Set the Record Straight: the Break-in, the Tapes, the Conspirators, the Pardon*, N.Y., Norton, 1979, *passim*.

18. Elliot Jaques, *A General Theory of Bureaucracy*, N.Y., John Wiley & Sons, Inc., 1976, pp. 190-191.

19. *Ibid.*

20. Hans Selye, *The Stress of Life*, N.Y., McGraw-Hill Book Co., 1956, p. 3-36, Matthew J. Culligan and Keith Sedlacek, *How To Kill Stress Before It Kills You*, N.Y., Grosset & Dunlap, 1976, p. 28.

21. Robert Caplan, Sidney Cobb, John French, Jr., R. Van Harrison, and S. R. Pinneau, *Job Demands and Worker Health: Main Effects of Occupational Differences*. National Institute of Safety and Health, Government Printing Office, 1975, p. 3; Selye, *op. cit.*, p. 56, see also his *Stress Without Distress*, N.Y., J.P. Lippincott, 1974, pp. 27-32.

22. Robert L. Kahn, Donald M. Wolfe, Robert P. Quinn, J. Diedrick Snock, and R. A. Rosenthal, *Organizational Stress in Role Conflict and Ambiguity*, N.Y., John Wiley & Sons, Inc., pp. 6-12.

23. Charlton R. Price and Harry Levinson, "Work and Mental Health," in *Blue Collar World: Studies of the American Worker*, Arthur B. Shostak and William Gomberg, (eds.), Englewood Cliffs, N.J., Prentice-Hall, Inc., 1965, p. 399.

24. William H. Blanchard, *Aggression American Style*, Santa Monica, Ca., Goodyear Publishing Co., Inc., 1978, pp. 13-36 and especially pp. 287-303.

25. H.H. Gerth and C. Wright Mills, (eds.), *From Max Weber: Essays in Sociology*, N.Y., Oxford University Press, 1949, pp. 196-266, and Reinhard Bendix, *Max Weber: An Intellectual Portrait*, N.Y., Anchor Books, Doubleday & Co., Inc., 1962, generally.

26. Frederick Winslow Taylor, *The Principles of Scientific Management*, N.Y., W.W. Norton, the Norton Library, 1967. First published by Harper & Row under copyright by Frederick W. Taylor.

27. *Ibid.*, pp. 38-68, especially p. 59.

28. Alfred Diamont, "The Bureaucratic Model: Max Weber Rejected, Rediscovered, Reformed," in *Papers in Comparative Administration*, Ferrel Heady and Sybil L. Stokes, (eds.), Ann Arbor, Mich., Institute of Public Administration, University of Michigan, 1962, see generally.

29. cf. Frederick C. Thayer, *An End to Hierarchy! An End to Competition!*, N.Y., Franklin Watts, New Viewpoints, 1973, *passim*.

30. Berne, *Structure and Dynamics of Groups and Organizations, op. cit.*, pp. 68 and 76.

31. *Ibid.*, p. 72.

32. *Ibid.*, p. 166.

33. Irving L. Janis, *Victims of Groupthink*, Boston, Houghton Mifflin Co., 1972, p. 9. See also Irving L. Janis and Leon Mann, *Decision Making*, N.Y., The Free Press, 1977, pp. 219-308.

34. Barry E. Collins and Harold Guetzkow, *A Social Psychology of Group Processes for Decision-Making*, N.Y., John Wiley & Sons, Inc., 1964, p. 109, see also pp. 88-118 and pp. 120-138 for an informative and important analysis on interpersonal power and influence within a group.

RELATED READING

Ardrey, Robert. *The Territorial Imperative*. New York: Atheneum, 1966. This effort emphasizes in creative and distinctive ways the importance of boundaries and territory to the maintenance and survival of human groups. Indeed, Ardrey suggests human behavior cannot be understood apart from this.

Boulding, Kenneth E. *Conflict and Defense*. New York: Harper & Row, 1962. This effort uses a number of formal analytical models (well presented and easily understood) as a means to analyze and resolve major conflicts involving individuals, groups, organizations and nations. This is a landmark book, well written, carefully developed, and offering a clear message of hope.

Gamson, William A. *Power and Discontent*. Homewood, Ill.: Dorsey Press, 1968. A very helpful study of the power relations between authority and its partisan challenges. Gamson's effort is particularly helpful in examining group uses of power as it relates to influence, political trust and social control.

Williams, Leonard. *Challenge to Survival*. London: Andre Deutsch, Ltd., 1971. A remarkable book by a leading primatologist with very distinctive perspectives presenting through fact and historical synthesis an entirely new conception of human nature in prehistory and its implication for human survival today.

Thayer, Frederick C. *An End to Hierarchy! An End to Competition!* New York: Franklin Watts, New Viewpoints, 1973. An examination of a variety of available alternatives to contravene the alienating nature of competition and hierarchy. Thayer calls for the elimination of competition and hierarchy and their replacement with more humanistic organizational forms. A refreshing and innovative approach to organizing human affairs.

Janis, Irving L. and Mann, Leon. *Decision Making: A Psychological Analysis of Conflict, Choice, and Commitment*. New York: The Free Press, 1977. This is a landmark effort providing a comprehensive theory of how people cope with the dilemmas and conflicts of decision making.

PART III
ACHIEVING HUMANE, COOPERATIVE AND PRODUCTIVE GROUPS AND ORGANIZATIONS

Chapter 8

ACHIEVING INTENTIONAL CHANGE

Significant change in organizational behavior rests upon significant change in human behavior.[1] This requires a shift in human consciousness. Human beings within and without organizations need to represent, interpret and participate in creating and changing their world.[2] There is a need to enhance our understanding of human behavior, individually and in groups, and within groups. Enhancing our consciousness in this manner can enable us more effectively to explore conflict and interdependence and through this add to our capacity to make intended change. This has been the concern of the preceding chapters. Heraclitus was the Greek philosopher who discovered change.[3] Heraclitus observed that change is continuous. Gordon Lippitt suggest that change is "any planned or unplanned alteration of the status quo in an organism, situation, or process."[4] What needs examining is its directions and how to manage and use it in a constructive way.

Achieving Creative Change: The Challenge

Organizational management and membership most frequently react to change impinging upon them. Within the context of these events individuals or organizations are constantly reacting and responding to series of events which are generally outside their capacity to influence or to manage, except in specific dimensions of a particular unfolding event, such as might occur between the exchange of teacher with the pupil, the policeman and the thief, the welfare worker and the recipient. Yet it is possible to conceive a person or an organization anticipating change, creating change designs and proceeding to forward such change designs into action, i.e. intervene in the process of development so as to alter the consequences in the future.

Elliot Jaques observes that where organization is concerned imposed changes are best understood and analyzed as a response to coercive force.[5] To avoid the dysfunctional consequences which flow from such imposition requires the participation of those affected by the change to be involved and to participate in the change design and in the policies developed for implementing such change. Policy provides the criteria for executive action and the design sets the context for such executive action. This contrasts with executive decisions *per se* which are action and involve target completion times. Change design and policy therefore must involve those affected.[6]

Jaques further suggests, "... firm, strong and effective management of bureaucratic systems demands equally strong and effective employee participation in the control of change. Such participation gives the essential sanction to managerial authority which it requires to make it workable."[7] He firmly asserts that "... citizens of a democratic nation have a right to be taken account of in matters which affect their livelihood, their careers, their self-esteem, and their socio-economic status in society.[8] Change accomplished in this fashion may be designated intentional change.

The achievement of intentional change is within the possibilities of individual and organizational action. Change can be planned and designed. Lippitt suggests planned change is an intended, designed or proposive attempt by an individual, group, organization or larger social system to influence directly the status quo of itself, another organization or situation.[9]

If creative intentional change is to be a part of modern organizational processes and modern social systems there needs to develop among the participants, especially those involved in strategic planning and decision making, a high value consciousness. This is a prior requisite to knowledgeable participation in change. Warren Bennis states:

> ... *adaptability to change becomes increasingly the most important single determinant of survival. The profit, the saving, the efficiency, and the morale of the moment becomes secondary to keeping the door open for rapid readjustment to changing conditions.*[10]

He further suggests that we are undergoing a profound change away from the autocratic and arbitrary systems of the past toward more democratic and participatory systems:

> *This change has been coming about because of the palpable inadequacy of the military-bureaucratic model, particularly its response to rapid change, and also because the institution of science is now emerging as a more suitable model... democracy in industry is not an idealistic conception but a hard necessity in those areas in which change is ever present and in which creative scientific enterprise must be nourished. For democracy is the only system of organization which is compatible with perpetual change.*[11]

By democracy Bennis means not a set of permissive parameters available to all citizens or a *laissez faire* economics but rather a system of values, or as he identifies them, "a climate of beliefs," governing behavior where people are internally compelled by their behavior as well as by their words to live such social value. Five primary values form the imperatives of Bennis' understanding of organizational democracy. They are:

1. Full and free communications, regardless of rank and power.
2. A reliance on consensus, rather than the more customary forms of coercion or compromise, to manage conflict.
3. The idea that influence is based on technical competence and knowledge, rather than on... personal whim or prerogatives of power.
4. An atmosphere that permits and even encourages emotional expression as well as task-oriented acts.
5. A basically human bias, one which accepts the inevitability of conflict between the organization and the individual but which is willing to cope with and mediate this conflict on rational grounds.[12]

Robert Tannenbaum and Sheldon Davis, writing of the changing values and their relationship to change, suggest organizational core values are not absolute but are giving way. They observe "we are now in a period of transition, sometimes slow and sometimes rapid, involving a movement away from older, less personally meaningful and organizationally relevant values, for these newer values.[13]

Concern with changing values is a significant aspect of that dynamic tension between stability and change. Values are reflected in behavior so the nature of human behavior and particularly the nature of human behavior in organizations as an expression of values is a matter of concern for those involved in understanding and designing change.

Responsibility of the Present Generation

The burdens of this generation are particularly difficult. Communication technology (television, movies, billboards, newspapers, news magazines and the like) tend to render yesterday past history with no continuity nor impact on the present. Tomorrow is something that will happen like an event to be reported. It is the present moment, the now, to which all consciousness in the developed world is tuned and focused by these expansive media. Human existence seems a series of events isolated from any past, uninvolved with any future. It is important to learn from history that we may alter the future and avoid the pitfalls of the past. Changes and ongoing process have roots in the past which impact on the status quo and have significance for future events. The processes of human life, its direction and its future and the life-sustaining processes of the planet are dependent totally upon the nature of choice and change which occurs in the now, in the status quo. Sir Geoffrey Vickers observes, "The present does indeed belong to the living but only as a trust property belongs to trustees, even where the trustees are tenants for life."[14]

The technological world of today requires a fully educated population. No other human generation on the planet has faced the requirements of training its younger generation to deal with the tremendous challenges, possibilities, and impacts of science and technology on the planet. Investment in the young is an essential requirement. Citizens in the United States are willing to support the research, development and manufacture of the instruments of war and the means for their use, yet evermore frequently these same citizens fail to invest adequate sums in the educational programs, libraries, cultural resources, etc. which will provide the young with requisite cultural values, conceptual and technical skills required to solve the problems which they will ultimately face.

To fail to invest in the young, to fail to give them the tools with which to broaden their understanding and to elaborate the choices available to them is sheer folly. An example of this folly is the growing and continued tendency of the present generation to diminish their investment in the education of their young.[15] When this occurs, educational institutions at the elementary, secondary and tertiary levels become simply custodial institutions, or at the most, training schools. They are less and less able to provide the depths of experience and education required for a generation facing the awesome problems of survival that require revisioning the future in imaginative ways.

To involve organizations and individual persons in intentional change, i.e. change which anticipates intervention in the trends and processes presently operating, or to intervene intentionally at some future date, it is helpful to develop an intentional change sequence. There are many models for change. Developmental models focus on a growth process centering attention on the development of a process from inception to conclusions. Systems models focus on the dynamics and links within a particular system. Intersystem models elaborate the systems model orientations. These separately or in combination with others may be used to conceive, design or carry through an intentional change sequence.

An Intentional Change Sequence

Intentional individual, organizational and social change are distinctive and unique, yet the phases to achieve such change for each are quite similar. Intentional change, be it individual, small group, organizational, bureaucratic, or social, requires: 1) awareness; 2) problem-solving; 3) decision network; 4) implementation and action; 5) results; 6) feedback and accountability. The intentional change sequence offered here has been successfully applied in its simpler form by individuals effecting personal change. It has, as well, been applied in its more elaborate form to effect successful organizational change with particular reference to those persons affected into the design and implementation of desired change. In the presence of unintended change, the individual, organization or social unit affected is reactive, often defensive and subject to events which impinge upon each and over which they exert little influence or control. Even though intended change is implemented there may result from such change, not only crisis and other anticipated events and consequences, but unanticipated consequences as well. It is difficult to anticipate every event or contingency nor is it probably desirable, yet there is some utility in perusing the options which might be available given a set of expectations and contingencies. The goal of intentional change is not to seek total control but to pursue intelligent action concerning the goals sought.

Organizational, individual and social change is responsive to individual and collective efforts. These are affected by intentional change as well as random change introduced or impinging from sources outside their own boundaries. Intelligent responses by concerned administrators must be readied and action taken where necessary to assure that sought after social values which the administrator is charged to implement may be achieved. Yet in the achievement of such change one's own essential humanity must not be lost or abandoned for either personal exigencies or higher purposes, for it is at this point where civilized action can go awry. Concern here attends individual and organizational change. An intentional change sequence involves first developing an awareness concerning the nature of the problems, their causes and that change is required. This includes gaining awareness of changing needs, the context of the psychological transactions, the value nets, power configurations and relevant knowledge and information. Once awareness is gained and desired change identified, the next step is to problem solve. This is the phase where choices and alternatives are developed. Once these are determined, a decision may be made designating a course of action, i.e. program to be implemented. Change programs center on individual, group and organizational action sequences to achieve the change(s) sought.[16] The action is then taken and change results which may then be subject to some mix of accountability procedures. Thus the intentional change sequence includes: 1) awareness; 2) problem-solving, 3) decision networks; 4) action; 5) results; and 6) accountability. Figure 8-A is a summary of these sequences involved in an intentional change. It is now possible to proceed to a more detailed discussion.

Phase I: An Intentional Change Sequence-Awareness

Awareness: Changing Needs. It is important as a prelude to intentional change to gain some awareness of the altering needs—societal, political, organizational and personal—prior to designing an intentional intervention sequence. Bennis observes that if an organization is to continue to be effective the crucial determinate is its response to the changing nature of its environment. Bennis identifies nine needs which face public organizations within the American situation. They are summarized as follows:

1. The need for fundamental reform in the purpose and organization of our institutions to enable them to adapt responsively to rapidly changing social, cultural, political and economic environments.

2. The need to develop such institutions which permit a person to retain his

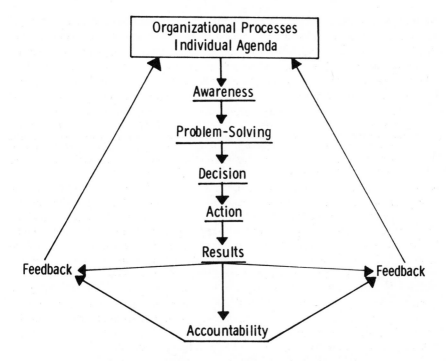

Figure 8-A: Overview of the Intentional Change Sequence

or her identity and integrity in a society increasingly characterized by massive, urban, highly centralized governmental, business educational, multimedia and mass institutions.

3. The needs of young persons who are posing basic challenges to existing values and institutions and who are attempting to create radical new lifestyles in an attempt to preserve individual identity or opt out of society.

4. The increasing demands placed upon all institutions to participate more actively in social, cultural and political programs designed to improve the quality of American life.

5. The accelerating technical changes require the development of a scientific humanism.

6. The necessity of a world movement to bring human beings into better harmony with their physical environment.

7. The need for change toward a sensitive and flexible planning capability on the part of the management of major institutions.

8. The rising demand for social and political justice from deprived sectors of society.

9. The compelling need for world order which gives greater attention to the maintenance of peace without violence between nations, groups or individuals.[17]

Consciousness of changing personal needs, the fluctuating political setting, and altering societal needs cannot be belabored. It is sufficient to note meaningful, significant, effective, intentional change must account for these in the design. Understanding of these needs can be gained through increased knowledge and information.

Awareness: Knowledge and Information. Knowledge and information are certainly essential to make informed judgments about the nature of the changes sought. Knowledge and information, however, are not synonymous. Fromm notes:

> The pathetic superstition prevails that by knowing more and more facts one arrives at knowledge of reality. Hundreds of scattered and unrelated facts that are dumped into the heads of students; their time and energy are taken up by learning more and more facts so that there is little left for thinking. To be sure, thinking without a knowledge of facts remains empty and fictitious; but "information" alone can be just as much of an obstacle to thinking as the lack of it.[18]

Knowledge and information are essential, but the quest for truth is rooted in the interests and needs of individuals and social groups. Without such interest the stimulus for seeking truth, knowledge and information would not exist. Some groups have interests that are furthered by the truth. Other groups have interests that are furthered by lies, deception and power plays. So it is essential to know the interests involved as information and knowledge are generated. What kind of information, what kind of knowledge is needed, the nature of knowledge. How we know what we know are perhaps imponderables, but nevertheless it is important and essential that some awareness develop within the individual and the organization concerning the kinds of knowledge and information needed to accomplish any intentional changes sought. Essential to effective use of knowledge and information is to understand their value laden content. Values, too, underlie and inform human behavior.

Awareness: Value Networks. Values are an important aspect of how individuals or organizations adapt and contribute to their own survival or their own disintegration. Values are a central component in individual and organizational behavior. Values influence the way reality is perceived by individuals and by management within organizations. A person's values influence the goals one seeks and the action chosen to achieve those goals. The same applies to management within an organization. The goals of a person within the organization and the goals of the organization are fundamentally distinct. Both include compatible and divergent values which coalesce from time to time to satisfy the needs for each. For this reason it is essential that individual values and organizational values be made explicit so as to enable awareness to develop concerning the nature of the values which control individual and organizational choices.

Charles Hampden-Turner calls for "value full" investigation—not a "value free" investigation. He suggests:

> Where men choose between aspects of their past experience to create their preferred combinations, then moral choice is at the very heart of existence and cannot be exorcised from the investigator or his subjects. To detach oneself and treat others like so many objects is not to be value free but to choose to de-value others.
>
> The moment we conceive of creativity and communication as mediated by codes and values, then we must ask which values facilitate successful and creative communication which impede this process. The thousands of values which we urge others to adopt can only be fashioned and exchanged if those core values supportive of creativity and communication themselves are constantly affirmed.[19]

The general theory of value is known as axiology. It comprehends all facets of the value problem, *viz.*, economic, aesthetic, moral and ethical. Values attend all stages of problem solving. Moshe Rubinstein suggests three stages to problem solving: 1)

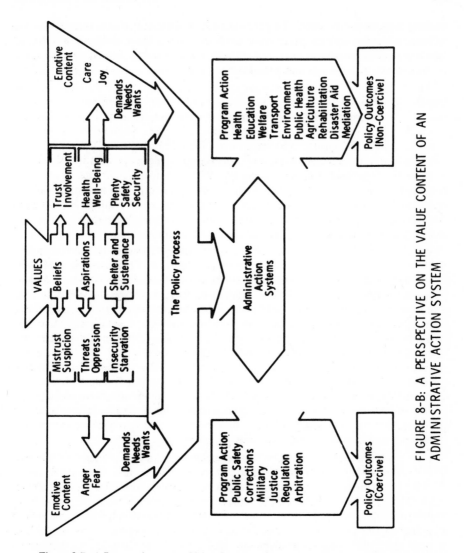

Figure 8-B: A Perspective on the Value Content of an Administrative Action System

describe what is; 2) describe what is desirable; 3) analyze and describe how you go from what you perceive is to what is desired, i.e., what to do and how to do it.

Values apply to the ends sought or the means used to achieve these ends. They may be competitive, conflictive, accommodative, cooperative or compatible. A value judgment is a decision matching that which is important (valued) to a variety of alternative possibilities and selecting a course of action.

Values and knowledge are interrelated. Values are symbols and are therefore an aspect of knowledge. It is knowledge which helps realize values. It is knowledge which may give the clue to intrinsic or unspoken values which are compatible or incompatible with human beliefs, aspirations and needs. Rubinstein suggests a good working hypothesis is to consider survival a supreme value in the sense that it serves to predict human behavior in a very general way. Using this hypothesis, a model of behavior may be suggested, *viz.*, human beings will generally behave so as to maximize survival.[20] This is also confirmed in the work of Eric Berne and Wilfred Bion.

Where survival is the dominant mode, the traditional values of honesty, dignity, charity, loyalty, discipline, responsibility, accountability sometimes yield to its urgency. These are means values. Values alter, rather importantly, with the age and psychological maturity of an individual. Values will change when economic scarcity is replaced with affluence or vice versa, when broader perceptions and greater horizons through knowledge are enhanced and when new developments in science and technology or politics shift in emphasis and importance. Values can be directed toward the achievement of benefits as they relate to energy, time and money or the undertaking of a risk. Values can be deceptive and false or they can be accurate and true. Generally, individual values are integrated into group values which are reflected in an organizational context and in organizational communication.

Value nets provide a guide for administrative action through which organizations seek to fulfill articulated social needs, wants and demands. These are often stated as beliefs, aspirations and requirements to satisfy physical needs and sustenance. Values reflect a trusting, healthy well-being orientation towards the needs, wants and demands. These generate activity within the policy process which lead to noncoercive policy outcomes. Needs and wants and demands expressed through anger and fear generally reflect mistrust, a felt sense of injustice and suspicion. Program action rooted in these reflect demands to reduce, alleviate or eliminate such fear, anger, injustice, suspicion and unfair treatment. These are achieved frequently through coercive policy and programs. The freedom to create, to build, and to do must be accompanied by sufficient controls to provide order, safety and avoid disaster and starvation. Values are the guideposts, the reference points, which are used to strike this delicate balance. Gaining awareness of these value nets applicable to the specific situation is an essential precedent to intentional change.

Figure 8-B is a representation of this perspective of the value content of administrative action systems in the public sector. It will be noticed that values are linked to the vehicles of their expression, *viz.*, beliefs, aspirations and shelter and sustenance needs. These are then articulated through postures of trust, mistrust, fear and threats, health and well-being, security and insecurity, etc. – each of which convey and reflect a distinctive emotive content. These values then become expressed and articulated through the policy process as demands, needs, wants and these are sometimes related to specific ideological or philosophical orientations. These policies once determined by the policy process, which occur generally within a political setting or arena, are achieved through coercive and noncoercive programs effected through administrative action.[21]

Awareness: Organizational Concerns and Responsibilities. These programs of administrative action are expressed and delivered by specific organizations primarily within the public sector. They are more and more frequently being delivered through private sector activity as well by utilizing the contract device. Within these organizations human beings use their collective skills, competence, knowledge, and energy in a coordinated manner to accomplish program related tasks. These tasks are conducted by persons utilizing the resources provided and within the restraints and requirements of the social-political-economic system in which it is rooted and which it serves. The responsibility for the conduct of these efforts rests with organizational management. A primary focus of management concern is the organizational membership through which these efforts are accomplished. Such concern requires an awareness by management of the changing values which relate the individual to the work place.

The new values at the work place relate to a different perspective and orientation toward the individual. By the time most persons are tied into continuing and ongoing groups and organizations for career, professional or work purposes they are fairly well developed as individuals. The problem is to treat them in a manner which is reinforcing, unthreatening, and yet encourages the full development of their human potential. This must be achieved in a way which enhances the organizational mission as well. Old values relating to individualism are insufficient. Employment which provides a "decent living," work incentives, personal identity linked to the work role, and the male as breadwinner for the "little woman at home" is altering rapidly.

Organizational Concerns. Work opportunities must now provision leisure time, account and provide for the symbolic significance of the job, which now is of relative importance, and jobs must provide opportunities for affective human contact. They must become less depersonalized.[22] The concept of role must be fully understood within the group and organizational context. Role is used to identify the kind of assignments given to group members as a result of the collusions, splits and projections which fulfill the stroking and time structuring and psychological (scripts) needs of the individual member which characterize group process in the private structure of groups and organizations. Role is also used to identify an essential element of the manifest (formal) organizational structure, i.e., task assignments are organized on the basis of the functional skill and then related activities required to perform the work of the organization. Role behavior is compelling, even awesome, when individuals fully succumb to its requirements.[23]

Role Orientation: The Inward Focus. Individuals occupying officially assigned roles in the manifest organizational structure fill specific positions and are expected to behave in particular ways. These expectations are derived from the experience, education and training persons have received prior to obtaining the present position, from those who interact with them in a variety of relationships including those in super-ordinate, subordinate, and coordinate (equal) positions. Thus a person who occupies a specific role will have some subordinates generally reporting to him. Second, a person will have peers or colleagues at the same horizontal level as is he or she and a person will have a few superiors to whom he or she reports and relates. In each one of these relationships a variety of expectations occur.

Robert Kahn and his associates have suggested that this nexus of expectations is the focus for achieving change within an organization.[24] These expectations may be identified as role expectations. People who communicate expectations to one who occupies a role may be identified as role communicators. These role communicators may send to the focal person a clear or ambiguous message of their expectations. In addition, a set of expectations by a number of persons delivering messages to the focal person may be conflicted, inconsistent and ambiguous. To the extent they are unified, they may encourage harmonious interaction and unambiguous behavior. To the extent that they are diverse and inconsistent, they introduce conflicted feelings and ambiguous behavior into the total pattern of expectations communicated to a particular person. The totality of the number of role communicators sending role expectations to a role player may be called, for analytical purposes, the role set.

Once role conflict occurs the stress level felt by the individual is increased and the focal person feels caught in the middle between two conflicting persons or factions. The emotional cost of role conflict for the focal person includes low job satisfaction, low morale, low confidence in the organization and a very high degree of job-related tension.

A person within an organization and little outside contact is vulnerable to the dubious rewards and coercions of power plays and is more amenable to the kind of influence processes that occur within the organization. Kahn and his associates indicate that the most harmful effects of role conflict are the greatest where the network of the individual's organizational ties bind that person very closely to the members of his role set. In this case, a person develops involved patterns of dependencies with those who have power over him or her and those over whom he or she has power. The role situation is ripe for the power plays.

Role Orientation: Client Centered. Where organizational ties are less effective, the role expectations impinging upon the focal person from, e.g. the clientele sector, introduces conflict where those expectations differ substantially from the expectations received from role communicators inside the organization in conflict with the goals of the clientele. It is at this point co-optation in either direction may occur. The individual representing the organization may begin to identify and merge his concerns and interests of the clientele group. This individual may become the "client's representative" within the organization.[25] Although in the public sector it is rarely the other way around, it is possible that co-optation here could work the other way, i.e. the client could represent organizational interests to his own organization.

This is a crucial point of tension for the individual and the organization. Kahn and his associates also discovered that persons of greater emotional sensitivity are able to more effectively mediate the relationship between objective conflict and tension and are able to withstand a greater degree of conflict. For the individual who is achievement-oriented with a great deal of ego and personal involvement at stake in the job, a sense of possible loss is greater, a higher risk seems to exist and thus there are greater adverse effects when role conflict occurs.[26] The role set may be used by management as the key unit to achieve change. Its appropriate use in the change process will increase the probability of making effective changes.

One goal of organizational change is to provide a setting where organizational members would be more able to handle the psychological frustration and anger that is apt to occur at these points of tension. If there is an awareness of the psychological transactions apt to occur at such points and the eligible worker is encouraged and permitted to respond in a flexible and understanding manner to the client, the institutional environment could be altered to allow for the safe venting of rage or anger when disappointment or frustration occurs. This could be accompanied by some effective listening and some modest problem-solving surrounding the immediate event.

Organizational Responsibilities. Important alterations in organizational structure and process are required if organizations are to move effectively into the future. The responsibilities of management are to be responsive to altering needs, constantly changing environmental conditions and demands, and the requirements to convert the possibility of human dignity into organizational reality. If role is the focus, power is the medium through which such changes may be achieved.

Two aspects of power within an organization provide the basis for such change. First, those dimensions of power found within interpersonal relationships, and second, the organizational power resources upon which management may draw to accomplish organizational tasks. Both are important in achieving effective intentional change. Elliot Jaques observed from his studies that a group member cannot simply announce a new position of power with himself as the occupant.[27] Power, if it is to be possessed, must be sanctioned or at least "suffered" by others, as both Mary Parker Follet and Chester I. Barnard discovered in their separate studies.[28] Even the exercise of revolutionary power requires sanctioning and suffering by the members in a process, not altogether dissimilar to establishing Barnard's zone of indifference.[29] Acquiescence and indifference substantially support power because they do not interfere or inhibit its exercise. Effective change within the organization and group must, among other things, rest upon an understanding and awareness of the relationship of power to alienation. Organizational leadership must understand, comprehend and rectify the sources of alienation and oppression within the person and within the context of the organization and group concerned. Management must understand how such alienation and oppression are sustained and maintained within group and organizational networks so effective responses may be developed. Organizational leadership must center upon the nature of group and organizational stress, cohesion and development so as to provide opportunities for the emergence and integration of the whole person into the dynamics of the organizational milieu.

To accomplish this result there needs to be a fundamental change in the basic philosophy which underlies managerial behavior. Warren Bennis suggests these:

1. A new concept of man, based on increased knowledge and shifting needs...
2. A new concept of power, based on collaboration and reason, which replaces a model of power, coercion and fear,
3. A new concept of organizational values, based on humanistic-democratic ideals, which replaces the depersonalized mechanistic value system of bureaucracy.[30]

These conceptual modifications are urgently required by management if organizations in our time are to move into the future, meet the turbulence which is prevalent and face up to the uncertain, ever changing demands of our technological society.

Awareness: Individual Concerns and Responsibilities. Individuals wishing to and concerned about change must gain awareness of value networks and the nature of the psychological transactions which are such an integral part of group and organizational living. Understanding these is a necessary precedent to making effective and intentional change. This includes knowing the values and psychological aspects of one's own transactions as well as others within the group and organization.

Gordon Lippitt has suggested significant individual change is a prior condition for organizational change, and it is achieved through the process of what Lippitt calls interfacing. This involves dialogue, confrontation and searching for alternatives and coping with the results. He suggests that when confrontation is combined with search and coping that recrimination and unpleasantry tend to be eliminated. Awareness, as the first premise necessary to change, may not occur without effective confrontation. Confrontation means facing up to the tangled web of relationships, issues, problems, challenges, values, and potentialities which invariably obscure human relationships.[31]

The process of this confrontation within the individual is through growth and awareness experiences. Organizational development is the rubric under which organizational processes may be confronted. Through these processes the inhibitions and restraints on the awareness which individuals have concerning the actions needed to change are reduced or even eliminated.

Confrontation may be with oneself, another, or group of others in the organization. The searching is the problem solving phase and the coping is a resolution of the lessened tensions. The results may not always be entirely satisfactory to all participants but the goal is to arrive at constructive change which is acceptable to the participants. Out of this process, change, individual and organizational, occurs.

Individual Concerns. Much has already been suggested about the nature of psychological transactions within an organization. Each concerned person needs to understand how he or she conducts his or her own "psychological business" within the group and organization. Understanding of how one is perceived by others and an understanding of others' behavior is essential.

In the organization individual identity and needs are generally subordinated to organizational pressure to be different from what you "are." Frequently, organizational requirements are placed upon members to behave and perform as "expected." Thus the real human drama within organizations is removed to the private structure of the group and organization where this contradiction is expressed behaviorially. Behavior my be quite inconsistent and perceived and experienced as such, as one goal and one set of means dominate behavior and alternate with another goal and the related set of behaviors. The contradictions between words and behavior often emerge under these circumstances. Such contradictions may not be in the consciousness of the person concerned.

The response to this is a growing concern to make task assignments, requirements and personal fulfillment within the organization more attentive to the needs of the whole person and available within a more humane setting. Humane values involve experiences expressing among other things tenderness, compassion, and empathy as contrasted with the inhumane, e.g. exploitive, detached and hostile projective behavior. This contradiction finds expression within the organizational context and is reflected in the tensions placed on individuals within the organization. One of these tensions involves the subtle distinction between duty and responsibility.

Eric Fromm develops an important distinction between duty and responsibility. He suggests that responsibility is an important concept in the realm of freedom whereas duty is a concept applicable to a realm where freedom is absent. He states:

> *This difference between duty and responsibility corresponds to the distinction between the authoritarian and humanistic conscience. The authoritarian conscience is essentially the readiness to follow the orders of the authorities to which one submits; it is glorified obedience. The humanistic conscience is the readiness to listen to the voice of one's own humanity and is independent of orders given by anyone else.*[32]

To the humane experience, then, Fromm would add a sense of identity, a sense of integrity or authenticity, and a sense of vulnerability. He identifies these as the essential values of the humanistic society. Fromm suggests any significant hope for the building of a "humanist industrial society" rests upon the condition that the values and the traditions which brought to life love and integrity be revitalized within the emerging organizational society.[33] Individual responsibility must be assumed for such revitalization by those persons most concerned.

Individual Responsibility. Individual identity within an organization and frequently in a group is role dependent. An individual's own wishes and goals are sub-merged while the organization commands the person's energy, the person's attention and the person's loyalty. To the extent that a person's identity is submerged into the official organizational assignment and role dependency established, it approaches what Fromm suggested when he wrote of the distinction between responsibility and duty: duty grows out of role dependency. Responsibility tends to be generated from task freely and voluntarily assumed. Social anthropologist, H.G. Barnett, has ob-served a positive correlation between individualism and the innovative potential. Thus the requirements within an organization for greater role dependence which may result from more clearly communicated role expectations may actually inhibit the innovative potential. Barnett observes:

> The greater the freedom of the individual to explore his world of experience and to organize its elements in accordance with his private interpretation of his sense impres-sions, the greater the likelihood of new ideas coming into being. Contrariwise, the more the reliance upon authoritative dictates, the less the frequency of new conceptualizations. When individuals are taught to revere and fear authority as the ultimate source of the good, the true, and the proper they cannot be expected to have variant notions. When they are indoctrinated with the virtue of dependency, the ideals of curiosity, personal inquiry, and evaluation are denigrated; whole blocks of societies and individuals become nucleated to single ranges of possibilities. [34]

Ronald Samson, focusing on the *Psychology of Power*, indicates the psychic cost of role dependency totally swamps a person's individual identity. Samson observes:

> Each (person) has an inner self which exists, however weakly, and tries to be heard and to influence conduct. Failure occurs because of the external pressures which make it impossible for the individual to act up to the demands of the ideal self without arousing acute fears of putting beyond reach keenly desired pleasures. In the grip of the ensuing conflict, the individual is subjected to powerful temptation to deceive himself as to his real situation and his duties in that situation... And the individual becomes increasingly aware of the joylessness, loneliness, and lovelessness of a life doomed to incommunica-bility with others. Ultimately the individual pays a very high price indeed for his tempo-rarizing and his fear and his need to dominate or to be liked. [35]

An employee within an organization or group member often feels trapped and de-spairing as he or she attempts to transcend the manipulation and the messages of expectation which generate from the other group members surrounding him or her. An awareness of this double-bind is essential if constructive change within the in-dividual and the organization is to occur.

The essential point is whether men and women within groups and organizations can be free and responsible to choose important personal options or whether through some kind of behavioral science or management device human behavior ought to be controlled and imposed to achieve approved organizational goals. In the well-known dialogue between Carl Rogers and B.F. Skinner the issue was joined. Carl Rogers supported the point of view that it is possible for human beings to choose self-actualizing values and then proceed through the methods of science to discover the conditions precedent and necessary for the implementation of those values and through continuing experimentation find even better ways of achieving those values. He suggests it is possible for groups or individuals to establish these conditions uti-lizing only a minimum of power and control.

The only authorities necessary are those related to exercising responsible relation-ships in interpersonal transactions. He suggests exposure to a set of conditions where choice is nurtured, controls minimized, and responsible behavior encouraged, that individuals become more self-responsible, more self-actualizing, more flexible, and more creatively adaptive. He suggests the present state of psychological knowledge supports this.[36] Thus he urges the initial inauguration of a social system in which these values, knowledge and adaptive skill will be continuing, changing and self-transcending so that men and women in this process will be a continual process of becoming. Skinner, on the other hand, joins the issue with the following conclusion to the Rogers-Skinner exchange:

> If we are worthy of our democratic heritage we shall, of course, be ready to resist any tyrannical use of science for immediate or selfish purposes. But if we value the achievement and goals of democracy we must not refuse to apply science to the design and construction of cultural patterns, even though we may then find ourselves in some sense in the position of controllers. Fear of control, generalized beyond any warrant, has led to a misinterpretation of valid practices and the blind rejection of intelligent planning for a better way of life.[37]

This struggle between freedom and control is a riddle to which the individual and organization alike must be concerned. Individual responsibility is to confront the dilemmas and contradictions suggested here and proceed to their resolution.

Awareness: Summary.

Commanding change requires an awareness of the constant shift in societal, political and personal needs. Life in modern society requires understanding the unique and distinctive functions of groups and organizations in the design and implementation of significant intentional change. Managing and using change to advantage requires informed judgment about such changes. Such judgment must be sustained by competent knowledge and accurate information. Values and value networks must be fully understood for values are the essential guides to administrative action. It is through such administrative action that organizations seek to fulfill the articulated requirements of societal needs, wants and demands and change.

Individual change is a prior condition to organizational change. Individual change means gaining awareness of the value networks and psychological transactions which underlie organizational life. This involves dialogue, confrontation, and searching. The tangled web of relationships, issues, problems, challenges, values, power-plays, covert roles, manifest roles, responsibilities, duties, mission and potentialities which obscure relationships, inhibits management and hinders effective change must be confronted and resolved. There is a growing urgency to revitalize organizational life with the values and traditions of love and integrity.

Management responsibility is to understand the complex aspects of organizational life and center upon, among other things, the nature and operation of stress, cohesion and development within groups and organizations. Opportunities must be provided for the emergence and integration of the whole person into the life of the group and organization. Organizational management must, within the requirements of production and accomplishment, translate this new awareness into opportunities for converting the possibility of human dignity into organizational reality. Full awareness and understanding of the context and ambience out of which change issues and into which change impacts is required as a first step to making intentional change.

Phase II: An Intentional Change Sequence—Problem Solving

Problem solving within an organization when an intentional change is contemplated involves (1) needed individual changes (2) changes needed inside groups and organizations concerned and (3) changes in the organization interface with its clientele and resource and support systems.[38]

Individual Problem Solving. A person may creatively engage in effective problem solving when one feels he or she is an autonomous, whole, powerful and creative in one's own right. One can then relate conscious value choices to the alternatives available and take action which alters the situation and the aspects of the social system concerned.

Change requires an immense amount of courage, responsibility and risk on the part of the individual to confront his or her own fears and "own" his or her own transactions. J.F.T. Bugental states:

> This responsibility is not one that can be delegated or displaced. One is certain to find that at times it involves feelings of guilt, of great emotional pain, and of course, remorse. It can also lead to an awareness of one's own potency, dignity, and meaningfulness.[39]

Where an organization fails to account for, consider and engage each person involved in the change, the reception of such change by those not included in the design phase will be hostile, often to the intensity of endangering the success of the intervention. Such engagement must be genuine – not "window-dressing." Persons ignored in this manner feel betrayed and the impact on cohesion may be considerable. When a person's own perceptions are confused, where there is no feedback or awareness into one's capacities and situation, there is no available insight, no knowledge and no information to explore choices. Thus, personal problem solving is paralyzed and the one becomes subject to outside events. One indeed is powerless and "fate" does rule.

Figure 8-C is a graphic of this powerless situation where intended change and problem solving are absent. A person who has little or no awareness, no information from which to measure his choices and no psychological support for the choices he or she does or does not make will frequently seem to be run by rituals, routines and the whims and commands of others with little regard for one's self or the substantive content of what these might be. Under such conditions a person seems unable to make effective and useful personal choices and seems to exist for the convenience of others to command. Any action taken is at the behest of others or is not taken until another person supplies information about what "should be done." This person reacts, drifts aimlessly, and is seen as ruled and feels ruled by fate.

Individual change requires risk taking, confrontation and a search for alternatives. The problem solving process then relates to the individual's preparation, i.e. recognition there is a problem and developing an awareness of the variety forces reviewed earlier which affects the concerned person. Obtaining feedback relevant to one's own behavior, reflecting over these problems and the nature of the causal forces of which one has now become aware through some combination of confrontation, inspiration, reflection and reason is essential. Finally, choices and alternatives may be perused which become available for action. On occasion, conflict may be a concomitant of such a process.

Elliot Jaques, in his studies of group conflict, felt that individual behavior and the influences affecting behavior and spawning conflict could be approached and resolved by "working-through" the conflict situations and feelings involved. By this Jaques meant:

> When we speak of a group working through a problem we mean considerably more than is ordinarily meant by saying that a full discussion of a problem has taken place. We mean that a serious attempt has been made to voice the unrecognized difficulties, often socially taboo, which have been preventing it from going ahead with whatever task it may have had.[40]

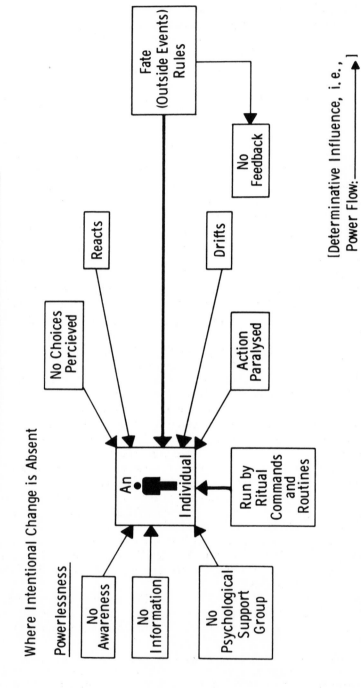

Figure 8-C: An Unintended Individual Change Situation

"Working-through" for Jaques and his colleagues involved three steps. The first was to recognize existence of a felt difficulty, i.e. the group itself or one of its members articulates for one's self and the others an uncomfortable or even a painful problem. Second, a sense of solidarity and cohesiveness evolves, i.e. a trust sharing group grows from such a personal sharing and is an essential component in the "working-through" process. Finally, third, the participants have a shared commitment to the group and to the objectives of the group. Commitment and motivation to the group and to each other make it safe to participate in a problem solving process either for the group itself or for individuals within the group.

A Support Group: A Requisite for Intentional Personal Change. A support group is probably an essential requirement to make it safe enough to confront the feelings and interpersonal transactions elsewhere which would otherwise be repressed and denied, and if they were to surface in a difficult situation, risk exposure and pain. When such feelings are expressed inside an ongoing trust group they can be expressed with safety, i.e. a person can be vulnerable and exposed but still feel safe and caring support from the group members. In this situation personal change can occur and be implemented. Within the context of the group and the organization as well, change can then be safely implemented because the energy and the power for that implementation are released and encouraged and risk of change is "safe" because the fear of change is reduced. Then one takes the risk and acts. Long term effective organizational change cannot be effective without (1) those being affected by the change participating in that change and (2) personal problem-solving involving continuing and ongoing support for such change.

Figure 8-D is a graphic representation of an individual intentional change sequence. A person who chooses to take charge of his or her own choices and actions cannot be seen as ruled by fate and will tend to achieve enhanced personal power when effective psychological support is available. This is particularly true if the psychological support is from a group of persons where trust, respect and safety are concomitants of the group's process. In this case the member will seek and the group will provide a place where dialogue, confrontation and problem solving can occur in safe and helpful ways. These would include, among other things, straight, but caring, feedback about one's games, script strivings, hidden agenda and the like which are operating to one's personal effectiveness. Such a group could well provide feedback and support to risk taking action or not on alternatives developed through the problem-solving process. In this case, "Rule by Fate" is diminished and power over one's life is enhanced.

Organizational Problem Solving. Primary responsibility for organizational problem solving generally occurs at the strategic levels of the organization. Design and initiation of intentional change is sited here and identifies the purpose, goals, policies, programs and changes needed. Such a design specifies, among other things, a number of possible options to effect such change. These options are subjected to critical analysis for suitability, feasibility and acceptability. Finally, the appropriate options are articulated into program development. Organization problem solving occurs at all levels and focuses upon generating choices and alternatives which will effect the particular change intended, once the needed change is identified and defined.[41]

Bennis suggests that organizational change programs will occur in greater frequency through more participative, open systems structures which are adaptive and

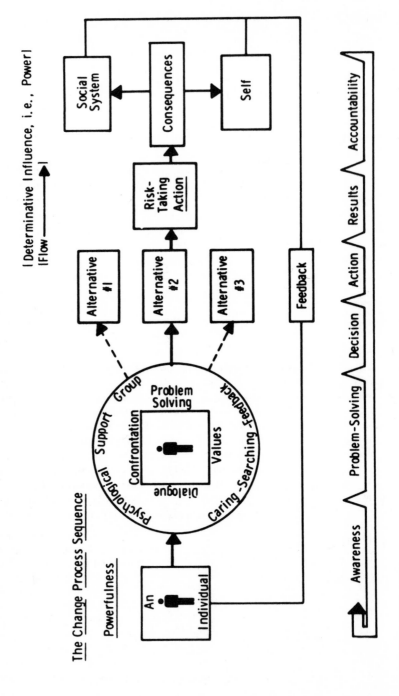

Figure 8-D: An Individual Intentional Change Sequence Model

responsive rather than the more tight, rigid, authority-centered bureaucracies. The goals of change are to render the individual more effective, the organizational infrastructure more effective, and to enhance the delivery of the organizational mission and activity within its environment in a more effective way. Bennis has identified three models of organizational change:[42]

1. the equilibrium model;
2. the organic model;
3. the developmental model.

The equilibrium model achieves change through releasing tension and reducing anxiety by focusing upon the nature of the social structure itself and lowering the defensiveness against intervention into that social system. It is achieved through programs involving data collection and feedback, group discussions, situational confrontations and reviewing conceptually role orientations. Such programs are implemented by management and are introduced through change agents who may be consultants, researchers, trainers or counselors. The leverage for the change is to focus on the nature of the manifest and covert roles, accompanying role expectations, collusions, role identifications and modify and alter these roles to re-establish a more effective personal equilibrium.

The organic model focuses upon redistributing power within the organization and upon conflict resolution. The focus of the change is to achieve more effective problem solving activity and enhance team management. The change process is implemented through problem solving exercises, awareness experiences, such as T-groups and sensitivity training, and utilization of more open system orientations within the organization. The leverage for change is to focus on creating and innovating new conceptual arrangements for interorganizational and interpersonal transactions.

The developmental model focuses on transforming individual and organizational value constructs. The target or focus of the change is the interpersonal confidence of the actors within the system. The goal is to reduce defensiveness and create more authentic, human interpersonal relationships. The implementation of the change program is through T-groups and problem-solving activity and the leverage for change is to help communications become less deceptive, more straightforward, in the interpersonal transactions and to encourage the development of new symbolic devices. Change agent roles, as in the two preceding models, may be through utilizing researchers, trainers inside and outside consultants and counselors.

An organization may have responsible and sound financial management, impeccable and correct administrative management and yet still support a human environment which is corrupt in the conduct of interpersonal psychological business. By this is meant the emotional content of the transactions are repressed, denied, rationalization of behavior is pervasive, and one-up defensiveness characterizes official communication. Anger is hidden behind a smile, fear is disguised by arrogance, compassion is seen as weakness and joy condemned as frivolous and childish. The result is a harvest of bitterness, distress, hostility, mistrust, suspiciousness, secrecy and power plays resulting in incalculable losses of creative talent, energy and cohesion, all of which are required to maintain excellence in the conduct of individual and group tasks and the organizational mission. Inevitably, this will seed decay for the preoccupation with the interpersonal events reflecting these charcteristics generally precludes adequate attention to critical survival needs.

To alter such a situation is a difficult task. The first step would be to develop awareness among the involved participants of their own psychological transactions as well as others, i.e. confront them in ways where their transactions can be safely demonstrated and "owned" by those for whom such dissembling is part of the currency of power within the organizational setting. In the final analysis power plays are interrupted by straight talk, i.e. no lies, deception or dissembling, owning one's own feelings, and no engagement in power plays, i.e. no persecutions or rescues or playing victim. Problem solving in an organizational setting must encompass this most difficult of tasks.

An organization change model generally encompasses seven requisites. (1) The first requires goal seeking behavior by the individuals involved that is as open as possible, where intellect and feelings are integrated and reflected in creative and purposeful behavior. (2) The second requisite requires goals be established within the system so that the individual, group and organizational goals are linked effectively together without loss of personal psychological and moral integrity. (3) The third requisite is that organizational goals which relate to overall system goals be integrated into the organizational process. (4) Fourth, a careful analysis and understanding of the hindrances and blocks to goal accomplishment within the projected change situation must occur. (5) Fifth, the available forces which are external and internal to the organization or group which can be utilized to direct the organization or group towards its goals must be identified. Then strategies and tactics developed to take advantage of those forces in a creative and positive way. (6) Sixth, there must be a constructive, reciprocal, positive relationship among the members and groups within the concerned system. (7) The resources must be available to accomplish the change and the goals sought.

Phase III: An Intentional Change Sequence – The Decision Networks.

Group and organizational decisions determine the plans, the specific alternatives to be used, the programs to be developed, the activity to be set in motion, and relate also to the strategies and the tactics to be utilized to implement the change programs. Such decisions, either organizational or individual, may derive simply from random chance, may be rooted in a rational, logical system; they may be computational, inspirational or intuitive. Decisions may rest upon expert judgments such as advice and judgments of a lawyer or an engineer. Decisions may involve majority rule, consensus or authoritarian command.

Decision strategy relates the particular alternatives designed and the choices made generally at the strategic level through the middle-range and operational levels of the organization.

The organizational decision network must be fully understood and explicated. Individual and small group participation within this decisional network must be provided. Strategiees for implementing decisions must account for the processes within both the manifest and private structure of the concerned groups and organizations. It must also take cognizance of the decision maker as a person under stress, with an internal agenda, doubts and inner conflicts. Decision analysis must provide for assessment of the conditions and circumstances required to arrive at stable and effective choices.[43]

When intentional change is contemplated, it requires also that group members or employees participate in the decision process, not only in its initial phases but in carrying out such decisions and sustaining them through time. Individual choice involving intentional change is more effectively obtained by working the problem through in a problem solving group or situation where support and trust create the atmosphere of safety required for such personal processes to function.

Once a critical organizational or individual decision is made concerning the program or action to be taken, it must then be implemented. Tannenbaum and Davis aver such an effort will not be an easy one. They suggest it will be necessary to continually deal with resistance to change, including the resistance within one's self. They wryly observe that people are "not standing in line outside doors asking to be freed up, liberated and up-ended." Commitment to implement effective, desired and needed change is not commitment to an easy or safe journey.[44]

Phase IV: An Intentional Change Sequence—Implementation and Action.

The role of the person introducing change as well as the changing person is tough, difficult and sometimes lonely. For the organization it is stressful and fraught with difficulty as well. Persons involved in change are better able to process such changes where support and permission to make change exist and are available in a nurturing and caring way. Psychological support groups are essential aids to the change agent and the changing persons. Change requires constant re-evaluation and through the use of positive support and a continuous, heightened consciousness concerning the introduction and maintenance of the changes.

Bennis suggests the implementation of change decisions in an organization involves four basic elements. Summarized, they are as follows:[45]

1. **The client system** is the persons who will receive the change and its consequences. To assure effective acceptance of the intended change, the members of the client system need to participate fully and influence the development and directions of the change. Trust and confidence in oneself, each other, and in the change initiator is essential.

2. **The change effort** needs to be authentic and self-motivated. Thus change must be open, legitimate, reinforced and sustained by management participation as well as through participation of the client system affected.

3. **The change program** must include a focus and concern for the emotional characteristics of the transactions and the value network as well as the cognitive aspects, i.e. information and knowledge levels and problem solving processes, in order for successful implementation to proceed.

4. **The action phase** involves finally a change agent who can, regardless of the role played (whether as a consultant, researcher or counselor) by encouraging effective psychological supports and skilled intervention reduce resistance and lessen actual risks as well as risk perceptions.

Change, Stress and Crisis. Crisis internal to the organization, crisis impinging upon the organization as the result of external events or crisis deriving from the active introduction of an organizational change activity may occur. Where change implementation activity is poorly planned and incautiously introduced, conflict may well generate among the persons involved in the organization. Organizational crisis may derive from the following six situations:[46]

1. Varying, contradictory and ambiguous role expectations.
2. Competition resulting from a scarcity of resources.

3. Policy differences unresolved prior to implementation of the change program.

4. Other sources of stress, tension and hostility stemming from the ongoing power drama involving organizational participants as their needs conflict with organizational tasks.

5. A perception or expectation that conflict will occur as a result of certain events that either are happening or are expected to happen.

6. The impact of an internal or external trauma such as changes in personnel and management intervention which has threatened established power centers.

These are tension points where crisis and conflict may occur. Conflict behavior which is underway is like a whirlpool and brings participants at the fringe into the conflicted arena. These conflict situations generally are not separate and distinct but may be related one to the other at different phases of an evolving conflict episode.

Conflict and Crisis. L.R. Pondy identifies five stages to a conflict episode. They are as follows:[47]

(a) latent conflict (conditions);

(b) perceived conflict (cognition);

(c) felt conflict (affect);

(d) manifest conflict (behavior); and

(e) conflict aftermath (conditions).

He suggests the sources of latent conflict are from competition for scare resources, the search and thrust for autonomy and the divergence of goals among the persons and sub-units involved. Perceived conflict may not actually exist except in the suspicious fantasies of the beholder. Felt conflict carries either overtly expressed or latent threats and when it threatens the core of an individual's identity it must be acknowledged, for it usually has behavioral concomitants which involve consequences. Generally, persons tend to repress awareness of conflicts where there tends to be no serious threats. Since a carefree, anxiety-free, trouble-free world is comfortable it is always sought, even when it is illusory. This is consistent with the behavioral masks people wear within a group or organizational context.

Manifest conflict may be of the variety of power plays previously identified, e.g. drama triangle action, "one-up" game playing, "one-down" game playing, and "pitched battle." It may range from nonverbal, covert behavioral involvement to verbal abuse and physical violence against person or property. Where manifest conflict coalesces and a subgroup emerges, a schism occurs. In this instance, one group uses orthodoxy, appeals to loyalty, dependency on the established or perceived legitimate leader, appeals to appropriate traditional law which may be, in an organization, its ritualized, routinized printed rules of procedure or handbook. This subgroup adheres to traditional identity and uses tend to occupy what could be the orthodox symbols. They identify themselves as the "in-group," the legitimate group.

The out-group coalesces around discontent, articulates the need for change, alteration and revision. This reciprocal subgroup supports what is called "new ideas," often utilizing organizational guerrilla warfare. These groups cannot exist without each other. They have a reciprocal dependency which involves continuous power plays and power maneuvers. The ends of each group are the same—namely, to take power. The game to achieve it is different. In such a situation, the language symbols used in each group may be totally divergent, but the behavior very synonymous, so even the holders of power may change and the winners become losers and the losers winners. The new rule is similar to the old rule, except for a "changing of the guard," no fundamental change in organizational behavior occurs.

In felt conflict, conflict itself is personalized and internalized within the persons concerned. Anxieties may increase which result in or spawn an identity crisis for the individuals involved, separate from the organizational pressures. Generally, in a work situation which is not highly alienated the face-to-face relations tend to be authentic and may involve caring messages and activity as well as open expressions of hostility among the participants. Generally, in closed organizations such as the military, residential colleges, families, or monasteries, institutionalized procedures for the release of tension and withheld hostilities usually develop and function as a safety valve. Where they are absent, latent conflict which moves into felt and even manifest conflict is frequently dysfunctional to both the individuals concerned and the ongoing processes of the organization. Another characteristic of felt conflict is that it may "ride" on hostility directed toward a different objective than actually the generated hostility. Manifest conflict is accompanied by behavior which is intended to deliberately frustrate, rile and interfere with another person or another group.[48]

In the absence of effective problem solving, covert and overt conflict is a pervasive and dominant aspect of group and organizational life. Conflict generally concludes with the parties involved experiencing feelings of loss and actual losses. Problem solving moves toward ends where the needs of the individual and groups involved are achieved. Problem solving generally results in more effective decisions and the reduction of social and psychological costs in "losing" are reduced or avoided. People who feel fairly treated and feel good about a satisfactory resolution of a conflict in which they have been involved generally will have more energy, creative attention, awareness than those who have to cope with the feelings of loss and failure.

Conflict Resolution. Conflict reflects unresolved private structure process which peaks to the surface. It is thus indicative of a problem which needs attention if task activity is to be improved or restored. Such a conflict may reflect solely an interpersonal problem or it may derive from and be related to a task function. There have been several innovative approaches to the creative use and resolution of anger.[49]

Allen Filley has identified three basic conflict resolution strategies: 1) win-lose; 2) lose-lose; and 3) win-win.[50] Win-lose strategies involve the following: a) The exercise of legitimate organizational authority and superior position to impose a decision on an unwilling subordinate. This is the open use of power and no doubt is a sequence in or will spawn a power play response resentful retaliatory in the future. b) The use of overt or covert threats by a superior to obtain the compliance from the subordinate which results in the same effects as the preceding method. c) Simply failing to provide a response to a request or suggestion. This will again invite the same results as the two previous strategies. d) Majority rule is another win-lose strategy which may be acceptable, yet it involves seeding hostility and retaliation because it spawns resentment in the losers. e) This involves dominance of many by a few, i.e. minority rule as exists within a corporation or typical American neighborhood school. In all of these cases, further conflict is generally the harvest and the drama triangle is either begun or maintained.

Lose-lose methods involve no winners for all parties involved in the conflict only get some of what they want, and generally come feeling to some degree "ripped off," losers or unfairly treated. Partial victory is accepted and conflict seemingly avoided. Compromise where all parties give up some of what they want is the typical lose-lose strategy and is sustained with the rejoinder, "Well, at least we didn't lose everything!" A second lose-lose strategy involves a bribe of some kind, i.e. psychological, monetary, or something else of value. In this case, the "winner" buys the decision of the "loser" to be the loser and the costs to all parties in this transaction involves a loss of integrity and a set-up for continued games on the drama triangle. A third lose-lose strategy is the use of arbitration, i.e. submitting the issue to a third party, the decision of which all parties to the dispute or conflict agree to abide by. A decision of this sort generally satisfies no one so the seeding for future conflict occurs. Finally, the appeal to rules as the final settlement of a conflict of issues is clear use of lose-lose strategy. For example, the use of a flip of a coin, or the use of a specific organizational rule to avoid facing an uncomfortable situation are examples. Here the conflict is avoided but the loser carries away angry and hurt feelings, thus seeding future drama triangle activity and the one who appears the winner is set-up for later attack.

Win-win strategies involve consensus and what Filley calls integrative decision methods. Consensus involves a judgment where the solution is reached which is not unacceptable to anyone. It contrasts to compromise in that there is no polarized feelings or conflict and the parties are genuinely interested in arriving at a solution which accounts for the feelings and needs of all. It ends in a development of an acceptable solution to the problem. Integrative decision making sequences a decision through a series of steps which accounts for the goals, wishes and needs of all the parties to the dispute. It involves a high concern for quality and acceptance, rests upon responsible, open, full and honest sharing of all feelings, facts, and opinions with no lies, deceptions, or power plays involved. All parties agree to follow the prescribed group process for the arrival at such a decision.

A conflict may be resolved satisfactorily to all the participants in the conflict episode if it is confronted and the feelings emptied and constructive resolutions result. Thus a more ordered, safe and more direct and clear understanding can flow from the aftermath of a conflict. Where conflict is suppressed, unresolved, and continuing, it may aggravate and explode to the surface from time to time until either resolved or conflict episodes are manifested and become a series of related crises. Pondy observes:

> ... Conflict is frequently, but not always, negatively valued by organizational members. To the extent that conflict is valued negatively, minor conflicts generate pressures toward resolution without altering the relationship; and major conflicts generate pressures to alter the form of the relationship or to dissolve it altogether. If inducements for participation are sufficiently high, there is the possibility of chronic conflict in the context of a stable relationship.[51]

Generally, pressures generate to reduce and eliminate the conflict either through resolution, repression or avoidance. It is generally functional for individuals and groups involved. Where repression of the conflict symptoms occurs or they are avoided or ignored, conflict is generally dysfunctional. It will persist and endure so long as the payoffs for the participants are great enough for its continuation.

Strategies and related tactics must be designed to meet the specific situation encountered. The careful and thoughtful introduction of planned intentional change has the potential to considerably reduce random and unexpected conflict events. This is because otherwise frustrated personal needs are identified and creative responses designed. Failure to respond effectively to organizational conflict or to deep and needed change could spawn organizational crises of varying intensity.

Every organization, whether change is being implemented or tasks are simply proceeding, may confront bad behavior, evil behavior, violence, jealousy, greed, exploitation, laziness, malice, falsehood, cruelty, psychopathic, sociopathic, criminal behavior, i.e. a whole panorama of essentially "crazy" behavior. These must be confronted and personal and organizational processes for their effective modification, reduction, and elimination where possible developed. This is particularly important in an intentional change sequence.

The action phase is a critical aspect of intentional intervention. Well-planned change encourages effective implementation where crisis, conflict and duplicity can be minimized and organizational purposes enhanced. This is the phase where individual behavior does change and organizational processes are actually altered.

Phase V: An Intentional Change Sequence – Achieving Results

The implementation of intentionally designed change alters the conditions in the organization and in the interfacing network of groups and individuals involved. This results in change within the organization which impacts upon the external environment as well. Planned intentional change alters the values which are applied within the organization and can result in more effective implementation of the organizational mission. It enhances the capacity of the organization to satisfy the social values (generally stated as needs, wants and demands) required of it. Planned change helps the organization more effectively deal with the problems it faces through reducing or even eliminating the causes leading to those problems because the awareness in determining what those causes are is considerably enhanced.

Traditional organizational values lead to a decrease in individual production and a decrease in organizational effectiveness in achieving the goals sought through organizational change. Non-traditional organizational values which emphasize the humane enhance individual production and enhance organizational effectiveness in achieving the goals sought through organizational change.

Values, Ambience and Results: Traditional and Non-Traditional Organizations Compared. Comparing a traditional, closed organizational value system with the values of the non-traditional, open systems approach toward organizational change is very useful at this point. The underlying values of the traditional and non-traditional approaches to organizational change can be identified and compared. The personal responses which flow from these differing sets of values can be distinguished, and the distinctive interpersonal process engendered by each can be discerned.

The Traditional Organization. Traditional organizational values encompass the following: (1) The only important human relationships are those contributing to the goals and objectives of the organization. All others are to be discouraged and on occasion penalized. (2) Rational, logical and controlled communication increase human worker effectiveness. (3) Personal feelings and individual identity interfere with work and decrease personal effectiveness. (4) Orders, commands, controls and coercion are needed to accomplish the organizational mission. (5) Rewards and penalties which reinforce "rational" and acceptable behavior are essential to the performance of organizational work.

Personal responses within the organization are inauthentic and masked. The traditional organizational values encourage negative and evaluative feedback which is primarily judgmental and power oriented. Projection, denying, introjection, splitting, self-righteousness, defensiveness, etc., are maintained and reinforced. Manipulation, collusion, power games, competitiveness, secrecy and avoidance characterize interpersonal transactions. Rigidity, fearfulness, and withheld contained anger characterize the average worker who is closed to new ideas, suggestions and changes.

The results of these values and their concomitant personal responses is a decreased personal competence and deskilled interpersonal competence. This forwards and maintains defensive, secret, dependent, rigid and competitive organizational and group processes which are laden with suspiciousness and mistrust. Intentional change within this structure and process is frequently inhibited, frustrated, and prevented.

The Non-Traditional Organization. Non-traditional organizational values encompass authentic, cooperative, and supportive human relationships as requirements essential to organizational outcomes. Open organizational values are seated in reciprocal confidence and mutual trust which are invested in open group and organizational process. Effective decisions and actions are based upon reason, logic, problem-solving and effective communication which can only be achieved by "working through" the emotional dynamics characteristic of the process group within the private structure. Competent, creative and effective membership is derived through a process which allows for emotional vulnerability and provides a safe place for the expression of personal emotions engendered by organizational, and group process. Compassion, empathy, anger, conflict, joy, caring and the like are encouraged as functional to organizational goals.

These values provide an ambience which supports the development of full human potential. Helpful constructive feedback is sought and provided. Owning one's own feelings values and attitudes, providing non-judgmental feedback and contributing to the safety of others to do the same is a characteristic of the open organization and group. These values support openness to new attitudes, values and ideas. Under these conditions, the membership is supported to become responsible, powerful, creative and spontaneous. This encourages individual members to become self-contained, open, yet questioning and experimental concerning new feelings, new ideas, new attitudes, new values, new knowledge and new techniques.

The results of these values and their concomitant personal responses is increased personal competence and an enhanced interpersonal competence. This encourages a searching, open and problem-solving orientation toward work. In concert they forward and maintain a cooperative, trusting, supportive, and flexible group and organizational process. Personal and organizational effectiveness is increased and enhanced. Intentional change within this kind of structure and process is encouraged, sought and often achieved with enthusiasm and grace.[52]

Phase VI: An Intentional Change Sequence – Accountability

Measurement and analysis of the results and impact of intentional change is essential to realize an effective conclusion to the change process. It must be determined if the values, policies and goals have been achieved and whether the operating programs have been effective. These understandings are derived through accountability processes. Such accountability is essential to the integrity of the change process. The narrow auditing approach must yield to a broader perspective which follows the process from the articulation of policy through to fulfillment. Achieving such accountability for change is the final phase of the total intentional change effort.

Accountability in the Public Sector. Accountability for public sector organizations within democratic processes is achieved through the individual conscience, judicial review of administrative actions, and administrative and legislative audits. Legislative charters and statutes establishing an organization and defining its purpose and activity are reviewed and altered through the legislative process. An agency budget moves through the legislative process and is subjected to review and audit. These are each aspects of review and accountability.

Within the organization itself, accountability is sought through program review, budget analysis, financial and administrative audits designed to enhance organizational effectiveness and achieve organizational integrity. An organization's strategic executive may be elected either singly or as an independent elected official or may be part of a politically appointed body. In this instance, the election process becomes, in effect, an accountability process. Both within an organization and externally within the political context, vindictiveness, scapegoating, blaming, etc., i.e., persecution which are all too frequently substituted for effective accountability which could more appropriately center, among other things, upon goal-value achievement, change and its consequences, problem causes and resolutions as they relate to program activities and a myriad of other structural and process related aspects of organizational efforts.

Other accountability mechanisms may be developed and utilized, e.g. the Office of Ombudsman patterned after the very successful Swedish office.[53] Still another development that might well contribute to obtaining more effective accountability of public organizations is public interest administration: a new idea which encompasses the development of a distinct administrative entity charged with monitoring other agencies as to their effectiveness in achieving their mission and satisfying the needs, demands, wants and value net they are charged with satisfying.

Accountability in the Private Sector. Private corporate behavior is not sufficiently accountable to the public through the market place, the traditional political processes, regulation by independent commission, legislative investigation or media muck-raking. These are inadequate in and of themselves to accomplish the task.[54] The establishment of either independent boards with status equal to a board such as the Federal Reserve or separate standing committees of both Houses of the Legislature which are continuous and have established and secure administrative staffs which focus, among other things, on the corporate administrative process and traces their activity and processes through to outcomes is one device which might be used. Such agencies could function like the Select Committee on Nationalized Industry in Parliament in Great Britain has in the past.[55] The Committee in the past has contributed significantly to the level, quality and usefulness of parliamentary debate as they pondered the problems of production and accountability in nationalized industries. More recently, suggestions have emerged which would formatize broadranging, wide-gauging reviews of nationalized industry and other autonomous and semi-autonomous agencies.[56]

Managerial Responsibility and Accountability. Elliot Jaques has done quite significant work in relation to accountability particularly concerning the accountability of the manager for the work of his subordinate. He deems as essential to that relationship that the manager be able to de-select a subordinate in relation to the task for which he/she, the manager, is to be held responsible for accomplishing.[57] Yet he surrounds this with a number of significant safeguards which he identifies as basic employee rights not in the least of which is the right to abundant employment.[58] Further, he recognizes the stress, personal malaise, and anxiety that may be a concomitant of such a relationship and anchors much of the prescriptions for the repair of organizations upon the effective design of the accountability process.[59] An essential core to this redesign is the elimination of secrecy. Jaques suggests that, "Secrecy arouses all the deeper-lying feelings of alienation, of inferiority, of being left out...From secrecy, which shades all that is profound and significant, grows the typical error according to which everything mysterious is important and essential."[60] He asserts that secret reporting must be actively discouraged for such secrecy is simply not acceptable within a democracy. Further, he states any sign of tacit acceptance of secrecy "contributes to a sense that unfair judgment and victimization are always in the cards."[61] Secret tale-bearing spawns deep-seated paranoia. Thus Jaques holds inviolate that "Every criticized individual is entitled to receive the criticism personally and to his face in the first instance and to have the opportunity to rebut it or modify his behavior."[62]

Accountability through Public Adminstration. Organizations charged with identifying the diverse value nets applicable to a program area and concerned with public interest dimensions which are applicable might possibly make a significant contribution to solving the public interest riddle in public administration. The satisfaction of the public interest through program action systems promises a relevant and useful method and could constitute an important addition to provisioning public accountability of organizational and personal responsibility for the administrative effort, in addition to those which already exist.[63] Private corporations which receive a significant segment of their "profits" (i.e. revenues) from the public sector through contracts or grants, etc., could well be subject to this kind of public interest review as well.

Accountability is essential to ensure programs achieve the objectives established for them by legislation, regulations, and guidelines. Accountability must ensure effective use of assigned funds and resources. In addition, the prevention of waste, misdirection or diversion from the purposes for which funds were allocated is a requirement.

Auditing is a requirement where wrong-doing is or may be involved. Yet the auditor's mentality which seeks to identify and affix blame and fault needs to be diminished and refocused. If it could to some degree center on task and mission of the group or organization and encompass within their review and their guidelines, the values and practices of humane administration, a significant contribution could well be made towards alleviating the oppressive aspects of group and organizational life.

The public, too, must be effectively integrated into this process. George Williams has observed:

> The accountability systems of the future, if they are to exist at all, must be instruments of city halls. Citizen participation, as a part of that system, must be involvement, not control. But that involvement must be genuine, and public hearings will not be enough.[64]

The challenge is great and as yet unmet.

The intergovernmental network is non-systematic and is rife with conflicting values. Not in the least is this struggle for control of expenditures in the local jurisdictions between the locals and the federal officials. The policy environment is, as a result, quite conflicted. The problem of whom to hold accountable for what is confused, vague and ill-defined. Essential accountability problems reflect the conflictive society. Accountability procedures have yet to be devised which encourage creative and essential change without stultifying controls.

SUMMARY

The intentional change sequence within the organization or as it applies to the individual must confront consequences and utilize feedback. Their meaning within the change process for both the individuals and groups involved must be understood and assessed. Thus the process of the intentional change sequence involves unblocking and developing choices and alternatives. One or more of these are then implemented through strategies and tactics which intervene and effect change within the persons, groups and organizations concerned. Such changes have consequences which result in altered personal behavior and achieve significant impact upon and within the organization as well as the environment within which it exists. Each sequence of the intentional change model then corresponds to a specific process which relates to fulfilling functional objectives of the sequence phase.

Figure 8-E is a summary of the Intentional Change Sequence and the related processes presented here. These conceptual arrangements identify an available process to enable individuals or organizations to plan, initiate, implement, and evaluate intentional change. This embraces an intentional change sequence encompassing the following phases: raising awareness, engaging in problem solving, making decisions, implementing action, evaluating results, using feedback and achieving accountability. This Figure (8-E) displays the sequences and the processes involved in achieving intentional change. Each sequential phase involves processes which are essential steps in achieving the goals of the intended change. In groups and organizations, the specifics of these processes will vary as it will with individuals. This Figure identifies a number of options and characteristics which might be utilized within an intentional change program. The first step in achieving intentional change involves obtaining a greater awareness of what that change needs to be and how it will impact upon the persons involved and upon the various aspects of groups and organizational culture. Participation of those who will be involved in the change is of crucial importance in this phase and throughout the change program.

Intentional individual change is a prior condition to effecting intentional organizational change. Organizational change is a helpful prior condition to effecting intentional social change. Each involves change programs assisted by persons and groups with skills and competence in aiding the change process.

Public bureaucracy, in particular, is concerned with the delivery of important value components into the everchanging social process. It must exercise this power in a civilized manner, interpreting its own well-being as being dependent upon an overriding sensitivity for human beings. Lacking this basic commitment to humane values, no external check or combination of obstacles is capable of channeling bureaucratic power in the modern state toward humane ends.

Today human beings and their organizations are faced with a crisis of limited perspective. Individuals are concerned with the narrowness of their own role, their own function and their own specialization. There is no point of responsibility for the ultimate social outcome of organizational actions. No one in any position of authority can say definitely, "I am responsible for this action." This spawns power without accountability, since responsibility cannot be located. To alter this oppression and its results is partially contained in developing the opportunity and possibility for cooperative work. The conditions and processes which will encourage and

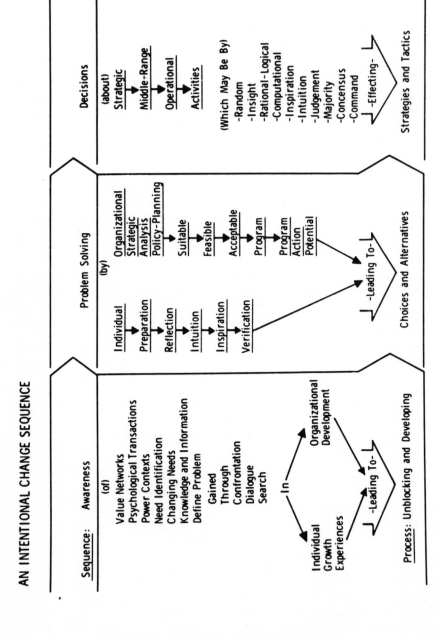

Figure 8-E: An Intentional Change Sequence (part 1)

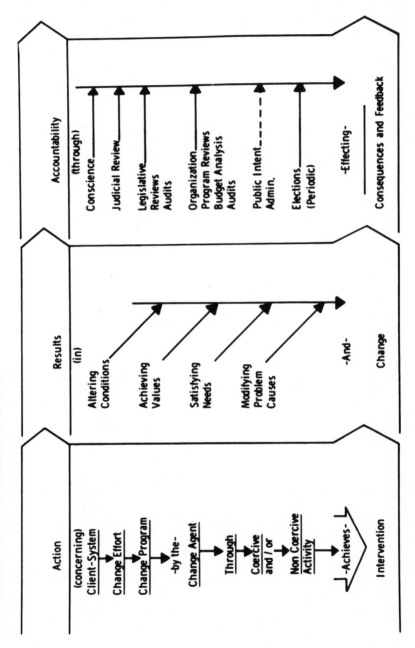

Figure 8-E: An Intentional Change Sequence (part 2)

create the opportunity for cooperative work will, of necessity, be derived through intentional change. It is important that such intentional change focus upon creating the conditions which will diminish or even eliminate the alienating and oppressive aspects of group and organizational life while, at the same time, encouraging, nurturing and creating opportunities for participating in meaningful, fulfilling and cooperative work.

NOTES

1. H.G. Barnett, *Innovation: The Basis of Cultural Change*. McGraw-Hill Book Co., N.Y., 1953, p. 71, *et. seq.* For another perspective on this theme, see Lawrence K. Frank, "The Need for a New Political Theory," *Daedalus*, Summer, 1967, p. 184, Journal of the American Academy of Arts and Sciences.

2. Sir Geoffrey Vickers, *Value Systems and Social Process*, Basic Books, N.Y., 1968, p. 181.

3. Karl R. Popper, *The Open Society and Its Enemies*, Vol. 1, Harper & Row Publishers, N.Y., 1962, pp. 11-17, 204-208.

4. Gordon Lippett, *Organizational Renewal*, N.Y., Appleton-Century-Crofts (a division of the Meredith Corp.), 1969, p. 2.

5. Elliot Jaques, *A General Theory of Bureaucracy*, N.Y., John Wiley & Sons, 1976, p. 162.

6. Jaques, *op. cit.*, pp. 197-199.

7. *Ibid.*, p. 199.

8. *Ibid.*

9. Lippitt, *loc. cit.*

10. Warren G. Bennis, *Changing Organizations*, used with permission of McGraw-Hill Book Co., Inc. 1966, p. 19.

11. *Ibid.*, pp. 20-21.

12. Bennis, *op. cit.*, p. 19.

13. Robert Tannenbaum and Sheldon Davis, "Values, Man and Organizations" *Industrial Management Review*, Vol. 10, pp. 67-83.

14. Vickers, *op cit.*, p. 110.

15. "Brown Vetoes Riles' Education Reform Measure," by Robert Fairbanks, pp. 1-3, *L. A. Times*, September 10, 1976; Bruno Bettleheim, *Love is Not Enough*, N.Y., Free Press, 1960, and his *Children of the Dream*, N.Y., Macmillan, 1969, James C. Coleman, *Power and the Structure of Society*, N.Y., W.W. Norton and Co., 1974; Ronald G. Corwin, *Education in Crisis*, N.Y., John Wiley & Sons, 1974; Emile Durkheim, *The Division of Labor in Society*, 1933, reprint, N.Y., Free Press, 1964, and his *Moral Education*, N.Y., Free Press, 1961; William Ryan, *Blaming the Victim*, N.Y., Pantheon Books, 1971; Seymour Sarason, *The Culture of the School and the Problem of Change*, Boston, Allyn and Bacon, 1971; Charles E. Silverman, *Crisis in the Classroom*, N.Y., Random House, 1970.

16. George A. Shipman, *Designing Program, Action – Against Urban Poverty*, University, University of Alabama Press, 1971, *passim*.

17. W.G. Bennis, "A Funny Thing Happened on the Way to the Future," *American Psychologist*, 1970, Vol. 25, No. 7, pp. 595-608, reprinted in J.M. Thomas and W.G. Bennis, (eds.), *Management of Change and Conflict*, Penguin Books, Baltimore, 1972, p. 113.

18. Eric Fromm, *Escape from Freedom*, Holt, Rinehart and Winston, N.Y., 1941, p. 248.

19. Charles Hampden-Turner, *Radical Man*, Anchor Books, Doubleday & Co., Inc., N.Y., 1971 (by arrangement with Schenkman Publ. Co. who first published this book in 1970), p. 34. See also Maury Smith, *A Practical Guide to Value Clarification*, La Jolla, Ca., University Associates, 1977, *passim*.

20. Moshe F. Rubinstein, *Patterns of Problem Solving*, Englewood Cliffs, N.J., Prentice-Hall, 1975, pp. 513-515.

21. Shipman, *op. cit.*, pp. 81-119. See also generally David Easton, *A Systems Analysis of Political Life*, N.Y., John Wiley & Sons, Inc., 1965; Fremont Lyden, George A. Shipman,

Morton Kroll, *Policies, Decisions, and Organization*, N.Y., Appleton-Century-Crofts, 1969; Herbert A. Simon, *Administrative Behavior*, 3rd Edition, N.Y., The Free Press, 1976; David B. Truman, *The Governmental Process*, N.Y., Alfred A. Knopf, 1951; William C. Mitchell, *The American Polity*, N.Y., The Free Press, 1962; Karl W. Deutsch, *The Nerves of Government*, N.Y., The Free Press, 1963.

22. See e.g., Daniel Yankelovich, "The New Psychological Contracts at Work," in *Psychology Today*, May 1978, p. 46; and Irving Janis and Dan Wheeler, "Thinking Clearly about Career Choices," in *Psychology Today*, May 1968, p. 66.

23. Stanley Milgram, *Obedience and Authority*, N.Y., Harper & Row, 1974, *passim*.

24. R.D. Kahn, D. Wolfe, R. Quinn, J.D. Shoek and R. Rosenthal, *Organizational Stress*, John Wiley & Sons, Inc., N.Y., 1964, Chapter 19, pp. 375-98.

25. For support of the contention that co-optation of the public sector's clients is a possibility see Selznick, Philip, *TVA and the Grass Roots*, Berkeley, University of California Press, 1949. Selznick said that co-optation of groups which might have views divergent from the organization averts the threat which the "outside" group might pose to the organization.

26. Kahn, *et. al, op. cit.*, pp. 375-398.

27. See generally E. Jaques, *The Changing Culture of a Factory*, Tavistock Institute, London, 1951.

28. Chester I. Barnard, *The Functions of the Executive*, Cambridge, Mass., Harvard University Press, 1938, pp. 161-184; Mary Parker Follet, "The Process of Control," in Luther Gulick and L.Urwick, (eds.), *Papers on the Science of Administration*, N.Y., Institute of Public Administration, 1937, pp. 161-169.

29. Barnard, *op. cit.*, pp. 168-169.

30. W.G. Bennis, "Changing Organizations," *Journal of Applied Behavioral Science*, 1966, Vol. 2, No. 3, pp. 247-263.

31. Lippitt, *Organizational Renewal, op. cit.*, p. 125.

32. Eric Fromm, "What Does It Mean to be Human?" *The Revolution of Hope: Toward a Humanized Technology*, Harper-Row, 1968, reprinted in J.F. Glass and J.R. Staude, *Humanistic Society: Today's Challenge to Sociology*, Goodyear Publ. Co., Pacific Palisades, Ca., 1972, p. 47.

33. *Ibid.*, p. 52. cf. Kenneth Boulding, "The Role of the Social Sciences in the Control of Technology," in Albert H. Teich (ed.), *Technology and Man's Future*, St. Martin's Press, N.Y., 1972, pp. 273-274, copyright 1972 by Kenneth Boulding. Paper presented at the 1969 meeting of the American Association for the Advancement of Science.

34. Barnett, *op. cit.*, (Note 1) p. 65.

35. Ronald V. Sampson, *The Psychology of Power*, Vintage Books Edition, A.A. Knopf, Inc., and Random House, Inc., 1965, pp. 138-139.

36. cf. Abraham H. Maslow, *Toward a Psychology of Being*, 2nd Edition, P. Van Nostrand Co., Inc., Princeton, N.J., 1962, p. 155.

37. Carl R. Rogers and B.F. Skinner, "Some Issues Concerning the Control of Human Behavior, a Symposium," *Science*, Vol. 124, Nov. 30, 1956, pp. 1057-1066.

38. D. Katz and R.L. Kahn, "Organizational Change," in *The Social Psychology of Organizations*, John Wiley & Sons, N.Y., 1964, see generally Chapter 13, pp. 390-451.

39. J.F.T. Bugental, "The Humanistic Ethic – The Individual in Psychotherapy as a Societal Change Agent," *Journal of Humanistic Psychology*, Spring, 1971, p. 12.

40. Jaques, *The Changing Culture of a Factory, op. cit.*, p. 307.

41. For additional materials centering upon organizational problem-solving and "working through," see Alex Osborn, *Applied Imagination*, N.Y., C. Scribner's Sons, 1957; C.H. Clark, *Brainstorming*, N.Y., Doubleday & Co., 1958; Tudor Rickards, *Problem Solving Through Creative Analysis*, N.Y., John Wiley & Sons, Inc., 1974; Andre L. Delbecq, Andrew H. Van de Ven, and David H. Gustafson, *Group Techniques for Program Planning: A Guide to Nominal Group and Delphi Processes*, Glenview, Ill., Scott, Foresman and Co., 1975, esp. Chapters 2, 3 and 5; Amitai Etzioni, *The Active Society: A Theory of*

Societal and Political Processes, N.Y., The Free Press, 1968, esp. Ch. 12; Gerald Nadler, *Work Design: A Systems Concept*, rev. ed., Homewood, Ill., Richard D. Irwin, Inc., 1970, esp. Chapters 18 and 19; Norman R. F. Maier, *Problem Solving Discussions and Conferences: Leadership Methods and Skills*, N.Y., McGraw-Hill Book Co., 1963; see also his *Problem Solving and Creativity in Individuals and Groups*, Belmont, Ca., Brooks/Cole Publ. Co., 1970; see Newton Margulies and Anthony P. Raia, *Conceptual Foundations of Organizational Development*, N.Y., McGraw-Hill Book Co., Inc., 1978, for an excellent presentation of change materials as they apply to modern organizations; Wendell L. French and Cecil H. Bell, Jr., *Organizational Development*, 2nd ed., Englewood Cliffs, N.J., Prentice-Hall, Inc., 1978.

42. Bennis, *Changing Organizations, op. cit.*, generally, and Gordon L. Lippitt, *Visualizing Change*, Fairfax, Virginia, N.T.L. Learning Resources Corp, Inc., 1973, p. 286 and pp. 215-332.

43. Irving Janis and Leon Mann, *Decision Making: A Psychological Analysis of Conflict, Choice and Commitment*, N.Y., The Free Press, 1977, *passim*, see also Charles H. Kepner and Benjamin B. Tregoe, *The Rational Manager: A Systematic Approach to Problem Solving and Decision Making*, N.Y., McGraw-Hill Book Co., 1965, *passim*, David Bragbrooke and Charles E. Lindblom, *A Strategy of Decision: Policy Evaluation as a Social Process*, N.Y., The Free Press, 1963.

44. Robert Tannenbaum and Sheldon Davis, "Values, Man, and Organizations," *Industrial Management Review*, Winter 1969, p. 83; for more on decision strategy see Robert H. Simmons and Eugene P. Dvorin, *Public Administration*, Port Washington, N.Y., Alfred Publ. Co., 1977, pp. 559-572 and accompanying bibliography.

45. Bennis, *Changing Organizations, op. cit.*, p. 176.

46. cf. L.R. Pondy, "Organizational Conflict: Concepts and Models," *Administrative Science Quarterly*, Sept. 1976, Vol. 12, No. 2, pp. 296-320.

47. *Ibid.*, p. 300.

48. W.R. Bion, *Experiences in Groups*, Tavistock Publ., London, 1959 (Ballantine Books, N.Y., by arrangement with Logic Books, Inc., 1974), pp. 114-115.

49. See for example Rensis Likert and Jane Gibson Likert, *New Ways of Managing Conflict*, N.Y., McGraw-Hill Book Co., Inc., 1976; Thomas W. Scheidel and Laura Crowell, *Discussing and Deciding: A Desk Book for Group Leaders and Members*, N.Y., Macmillan Publishing Co., Inc., 1979; and George R. Bach and Herb Goldberg, *Creative Aggression*, N.Y., Doubleday & Co., 1974.

50. Alan C. Filley, *Interpersonal Conflict Resolution*, Glenview, Ill., Scott, Foresman & Co., 1975, pp. 21-34; see also Richard E. Walton, *Interpersonal Peacemaking: Confrontations and Third Party Consultations*, Reading, Mass., Addison-Wesley Publ. Co., 1969.

51. Pondy, *op. cit.*, p. 312.

52. cf. Rensis Likert, *New Patterns of Management*, N.Y., McGraw-Hill Book Co., Inc., 1961 and his *Human Organization*, N.Y., McGraw-Hill Book Co., Inc., 1967; Douglas McGregor, *The Human Side of Enterprise*, N.Y., McGraw-Hill Book Co., Inc., 1960 and Abraham Maslow, *Eupsychian Management*, Homewood, Ill., Richard D. Irwin, 1965.

53. See generally Roy V. Peel, (ed.), "The Ombudsman or Citizens Defender: A Modern Institution," *The Annals of the American Academy of Political and Social Science*, Vol. 337, May 1968, particularly, Ake Sandler, "An Ombudsman for the United States," Jesse M. Unruh, "The Ombudsman in the States," and Frank P. Ziedler, "An Ombudsman for Cities," pp. 104-127.

54. See e.g., Tovis Kohlmeier, Jr., *The Regulators, Watchdog Agencies and the Public Interest*, N.Y., Harper & Row, 1969, Emmette S. Redford, *The Regulation Process*, Austin, University of Texas Press, 1969; John Winslow, *Conglomerates Unlimited: The Failure of Regulation*, Bloomington, Ind., Indiana University Press, 1973; York Wilbern, "Administrative Control of Petroleum Production in Texas," in Emmette S. Redford (ed.), *Public Administration and Policy Formation*, Austin, University of Texas Press, 1956, pp. 3-50; James W. Fisher, *The Independence of State Regulatory Agencies*, Chicago, Public Administration Service, 1942; Emmette S. Redford "Administrative Regulation: Protection of the Public Interest," *American Political Science Review*, Vol. XLVIII, No. 4, Dec.

1954, pp. 1103-1113; Robert H. Simmons and Eugene P. Dvorin, "Fragmentation, Responsibility and Accountability," in their *Public Administration: Values, Policy and Change*, N.Y., Alfred Publishing Co., Inc., 1977, pp. 41-74.

55. Robert H. Simmons, "The Role of the Select Committee on Nationalized Industry in Parliament," *Western Political Quarterly*, Sept. 1961, pp. 741-745.

56. E. Leslie Normanton, "Public Accountability and Audit: A Reconnaissance," in Bruce L.R. Smith and D.C. Hague, *The Dilemma of Accountability in Modern Government: Independence vs. Control*, Macmillan, London, 1971, pp. 312-313.

57. Jaques, *A General Theory of Bureaucracy, op. cit.*, pp. 64-86 generally but specifically pp. 71-78.

58. *Ibid.*, pp. 181-242.

59. *Ibid.*, see e.g. pp. 78-86, 260-301 and especially pp. 69-71.

60. *Ibid.*, p. 79.

61. *Ibid.*, p. 80.

62. *Ibid.*, p. 81.

63. Sidney L. Gardner, "The Intergovernmental Debate: Straw Men Stumbling Toward Middle Ground," in Joseph D. Sneed and Steven A. Waldhorn, (eds.), *Restructuring the Federal System: Approaches to Accountability in Postcategorical Programs*, Crane, Russak & Co., N.Y., p. 61; Marshall Kaplan, "Model Cities and the New Inventory," in Sneed and Waldhorn, *op. cit.*, p. 81; Roslyn D. Kane and B. Ann Kleindienst, "Department of Health, Education and Welfare and Accountability," in Sneed and Waldhorn, *op. cit.*, p. 96.

64. George Williams, "Federal Objectives and Local Accountability," in Sneed and Waldhorn, *op. cit.*, p. 139. See also Orville Poland, "Program Evaluation and Administrative Theory," *Public Administration Review*, July/August, 1974, pp. 333-338.

RELATED READING

Bennis, Warren. *Beyond Bureaucracy*. New York: McGraw-Hill Book Co., Inc., 1966. This is a landmark effort in identifying the "decline of bureaucracy" and the essential necessity of planned change to design and introduce its replacement. It focuses, among other things, upon change agents, change programs, change strategies and tactics. A remarkable and important book.

Benveniste, Guy. *The Politics of Expertise*. 2nd edition. San Francisco: Boyd & Frasher Publ. Co., 1977. This book examines the uses, function and role of planning and planners in achieving what the society deems useful and important to achieve. Accountability and evolution are not neglected nor are the tactics and strategies required to achieve change; indeed, they are examined quite skillfully.

Burns, T. and Stalker, G.W. *The Management of Innovation*. Chicago: Quadrangle, 1961 (2nd edition 1966). This book is based upon the Tavistock approach to group process and explores the covert political and status structure which underlie and shape the internal or private structure of groups and organizations.

Caiden, Gerald. *Administrative Reform*. Chicago: Aldine Publ. Co., 1969. A systematic and thorough presentation of the diverse interdisciplinary literature on administrative reform and notes the essential link between such reform and the achievement of effective social change.

Likert, Rensis. *Human Organization*. New York: McGraw-Hill, 1967. A thorough presentation of organizations and management styles ranging from rigid and authoritarian and closed to flexible and participative and open.

Lippitt, Gordon. *Organization Renewal*. New York: Appleton-Century-Crofts, 1969. A response to the need for organizations to reexamine their objectives, review their structure, improve their relationships and rediscover their responsibility to members, clients, employees and the broader social system.

Lippitt, Gordon. *Visualizing Change*. Fairfax, Virginia: NTL Learning Resources Corp., 1973. An eclectic approach to change which emphasizes the use of models and model building as a significant aid in designing and achieving change.

McGregor, Douglas. *The Human Side of Enterprise*. New York: McGraw-Hill, 1960. A presentation emphasizing underlying and implicit assumptions concerning the nature and ambience of an organization and positing two distinctive perspectives concerning the underlying assumption guiding management behavior.

Schein, E.H. and Bennis, W.G., editors. *Personal and Organizational Change Through Group Methods*. New York: John Wiley & Sons, Inc. 1965. Laboratory training, i.e. self-analytic and sensitivity training groups is described as an experience with regard to its uses, research strategies; and it presents a conceptual scheme of learning and attitude change which seem to govern the processes and outcomes of laboratory training.

Chapter 9

COOPERATIVE WORK: UNCHARTED TERRITORY

The challenge to achieve the humane in work situations in the face of an increasingly bureaucratic, urban and technological world is a monumental task. The avenues and the tools for such achievement are available. This route is clearly delineated by Erik Erikson:

> It will be the task of the next generation everywhere to begin to integrate new and old methods of self-awareness with the minute particulars of universal technical proficiency.[1]

The requirement is to utilize the scientific knowledge and technological proficiency which have brought us to this evolutionary moment of time to our continued advantage and shed that paraphernalia of the past which retards, inhibits, and precludes access to humane and cooperative work.

Establishing Requisite Institutions for Humane Work

Organization and control of bureaucracy must be modified and redesigned in a manner which establishes structure and process so as to assure that the resultant impacts on human behavior support, re-enforce and are consistent with open democratic society. Elliot Jaques supports that the alienating, paranoiagenic organizations which dominate life and times today spawn mistrust, envy, hostile rivalry and anxiety. These become pathological aspects of humane behavior and split individuals off from society and community. Jaques suggests that social institutions can be designed to facilitate awareness, trust, confidence, competence, and cooperation which achieve social cohesion and personal well being. He identifies these institutions as requisite institutions.[2] Such institutions are anti-entropic where "...work can be done and energy created and stored in the form of physical and cultural objects and knowledge and information.... By contrast anti-requisite institutions are entropic: suspicion and mistrust undermine collaborative interaction and work: man's relation to his physical and social environment becomes increasingly closed. Xenophobia is the social paradigm and social life runs down."[3] Anti-requisite institutions are, thus, alienating, paranoiagenic and entropic.

Jaques conceptualizes a context of organization and bureaucracy which establishes, undergirds and sustains requisite social institutions wherein a sense of community can be achieved. He designates two major components of such requisiteness; viz., (1) structural soundness which matches authority and accountability and (2) trust and confidence in working relationships where individuals have the opportunities to work to their full work-capacities. Jaques accomplishes this by forwarding a theory based upon empirical evidence which links the "stratified depth-structure" of an organization to the differing developmental patterns and plateaux of individual work-capacity supported by felt-fair pay differentials, social justice in employment and effective, responsible and accountable management.[4] This framework of Jaques is a truly creative alternative to the dysfunctional aspects of authority and hierarchy pointed out by James D. Carroll, viz., including among other things rigid pay schedules, restrictive and secret personnel procedures, inflexible time, attendance and program requirements which bear little relation to individual capacity and productive work.[5]

The concern of this chapter is focus upon the work group and define a requisite structure which will spawn an ambience wherein the full unfolding of the human potential may have an opportunity to emerge. This involves, among other things, a work setting responsive to people working within ongoing, intermittant committees and groups or even project teams or groups constituted for short term assignments. Each of us would like to be a part of groups where cooperation and intimacy can occur. Yet very few of us know what the structure and process of such a group might be. Most of us know what they "feel" like, because we have memories of times when we have occasionally participated intimately, cooperatively, effectively, and with great personal rewards in groups which felt good. Thus it is possible to identify and define some of the characteristics of cooperative work.

Characteristics of an Ideal Cooperative Work Group

Everyone has experienced, if only in an ephemeral and almost illusory way, being a part of a group which worked cooperatively. When the work ends and the group concludes, people who have belonged and participated feel it was productive. The members feel they made an important contribution; it was fun working together, even exhilarating perhaps; it was a fine accomplishment. These are supported by the verbal expressions and expressed feelings which tend to follow the conclusion of successful cooperative work. Such a process is often spontaneous and therefore not easily available to analytical review.

It is possible to identify some of the characteristics of a cooperative work group. There is an open acceptance by the members of each other. This may be identified clearly as relationships of trust. There is generally compatible sharing of the work, accompanied by an almost intuitive understanding about what that sharing is. This is true even if diverse authority, skill and function are involved. Those involved in the work feel valued by the others involved in the same work. Members are considerate and caring for one another. Individual members are quick to own their responsibility when the job could have been done more effectively.

In the final analysis, such a group feels good to members. There is a great deal of satisfaction at the conclusion of such a process and it may be said that the atmosphere of such a cooperative group is enjoyable, wherein members care for one another and are interested in one another's well-being. It is an effort where the autonomy of each member is enhanced. There is an existing mutal respect. Each member is valued for him or herself and the competence and energy each provides to the group. Such groups are possible. Such groups are attainable. Cooperative work groups are trusting, safe and vital groups in which to be a member and in which to participate. Yet the cooperative work process, for the most part, is not well understood. It all happens, it happens well, it feels good, but no one quite understands why it all comes together.

Cooperative work may be further defined by identifying what a cooperative work group is not. There is an absence of scarcity and competition. Status, power and authority are not sought after competitively by the group and where supplies and resources are scarce, there is an agreed sharing of such supplies and resources. Blaming, retaliation and vindictiveness are absent. Conflict is "worked through" and resolved. Each person's personal boundaries and rights are respected by every other person within the group. Each individual person is recognized and is recognized as having the same access to respect and rights as the others. Each takes responsibility for his or her own process within the group and takes his or her ownership for his or her share of that process. There are no power plays. There are no secrets. There are no rescues, withholding of resentments, discounts and no "trashing."

There are no first, second and third degree games. In cooperative work groups, game-free intimacy is available as are straightforward, nurturing, affirmation. This is an ideal work situation yet it is possible to attain.

Characteristics of the Banal Work Group

Oppressive work groups may appear to work cooperatively when viewed from the outside yet when the measures that apply to a cooperative work group are used, such groups fail the test. Trust is replaced by fear and exploitation of human personality. Sharing is calculated and laden with secret expectations. Nurturing and care are absent and are replaced by power plays which are frequently related to sexual exploitation. Blaming and fault-finding are frequent concomitants of the process. Secrets and intimidation are pervasive, as is competitiveness, collusions and alliances directed to obtaining a greater part of that which is in scarce supply. Group process is dominated by struggles for power, prestige and wealth which spawn moral irresponsibility. The drama triangle operates and there is frequent "trashing" of individual members. Blaming and discounting of individual intelligence and competence also occurs with frequency. Guilt and resentment easily predominate a large portion of the interpersonal transactions of the group.

Members of a banal work group generally have a low level of trust for one another and feel unsafe. Fear rather than care is reflected in the elan of the work group. Retaliation rather than support is a concomitant as well. There is within the group a "pecking order," identifying in subtle ways the psychological and social rank of each member. The winners and losers are known and there is frequently a pervasive sense of powerlessness and dependency with power given away to "leaders" within the covert structure who exploit the group. On occasion, an outside force is seen as more threatening and perhaps more powerful and this spawns seeming group cohesion so long as that outside threat exists.

Alienation within such groups is sometimes reflected through acts of random violence against person and property, frequently involving innocent persons, and derives from blind anger and rage which reflect a desperate human condition. Continuous and prolonged alienation at the workplace is frequently reflected in behavior which reflects resignation, boredom and a pervasive ennui. These are symptomatically expressed through delay, time-wasting, inattentiveness, petty theft, and the like. Increasingly, somatic expressions of such alienation begin to appear, e.g., high blood pressure, heart problems, bad backs, personal injuries and a variety of physical responses which link into "workman's compensation," so as to find a way of escape from the oppression and still maintain a personal income.

The traditional organizational responses involve superficial symptom management with no effective attempts to correct or redress the causes of such symptoms. This is simply because their causes are endemic to organization and bureaucracy as it currently exists. The outcomes of activity related to legitimate group or organizational activity is not to be confused with tragic group process. For example, collecting taxes due through the use of court process, performing needed or emergency surgery in the hospital, using as much force as is necessary to subdue a person threatening bodily harm to another, are each tragic outcomes of hamartic processes begun outside the organization or group concerned and to which it is the mission of the group or organization to respond. It does not define the group performing these activities as hamartic. It would be only that when such a group or organization process goes awry and translates into hamartic process that such a group becomes tragic.

If a group engages in basically first or second degree activities and ranges around the tasks assigned the group in a work situation, it is simply a banal group and the members are blind to and ignore the oppression which is an everyday characteristic of such a group. The fundamental components of such oppression are. 1) the Protestant ethic which is seated in its motivational concomitant of guilt and atonement; 2) the implementation of unequal power through the application of hierarchical authority or arrangement where power, prestige, and wealth are distributed in ever diminishing amounts downward through a pyramidal structure in the bureaucratic setting, and 3) the demands for production which utilizes measures of efficiency which encompass very narrow standards and are maintained by judgments, discounts, negative personnel evaluations, and a variety of penalties varying in consequence.

Cooperative and Banal Work Groups Compared

Participation in a cooperative work group must be from a position of competence and autonomy by human beings who do not "split" parts of themselves away and "pour" them into other parts of the group or other persons in the group in the covert manner that has been suggested in the earlier chapters. Production which results from the activities of a cooperative work group is humane in its impact and contributes to a creative and life-sustaining process in the culture and society of which the group is a part.

The production within a cooperative work group is performed by sensitive and aware people, secure in their own competence and confident in respect to their own personalities. These persons are fully autonomous individuals. A few such persons may also be high-energy, self-fulfilling people. Where the purposes of these persons and the needs of others of the group diverge and are conflicted, mediation procedures can be used to resolve the issue. The derivative results of such group process, aside from effective production and satisfaction of the group's mission and such production, is that it nurtures and supports community life and encourages a satisfying future for those involved.

Productive effort within banal work groups is generally unrewarding. Interpersonal alienation continues and promises a harvest of continued social, economic and environmental disasters which, among other things, involves competitive depletion of the earth's resources, the interference and perhaps destruction of the planet's life support system, because the competition to gain and maintain access to those scarcities frequently moves to the option of violence in seeking resolution to such stress. In oppressive banal work groups, persuasion, manipulation and threats usually accompanied by the seductive promise of rewards often pervade power-laden management, employee (member) or management-employee (member) relationships. The goal is always "high production" and "high efficiency," and in the private sector, profit as well. Personal and social costs remain unassessed and unimportant. Personal responsibility for activity outcomes are virtually non-existent.

Persons within cooperative work groups have increasing awareness of their own interpersonal transactions and seek to be straightforward in their interpersonal exchanges. In oppressive banal work groups, alienation permeates the atmosphere of the work group. Transactions are frequently crooked, contaminated and honest feelings denied, repressed and avoided. Within a cooperative work group the process nurtures protection of its members, gives group members support and permission to be creative. Such a group fosters and nurtures individual members to be powerful and competent. Each member in a cooperative work group assumes his or her own responsibility. Individual energy and individual choice as to how participation in the group will be is initiated by each individual who seeks to negotiate his or her contribution in a manner which feels equal and good. In some instances, groups and organizations are both oppressive and nurturing, altering according to differing time and circumstance. The models of the banal work group and the cooperative work group presented here are in the manner of ideal types with clear distinctions being drawn concerning their differences.

The Transition from Banal to Cooperative Work

How is it possible to move from the typical and traditional oppressive banal work group to the cooperative, intimate and rewarding task group? Such a change requires the modification and alteration of hierarchy, a revisioning of the authority process, a redefinition of the concept of efficiency, and the introduction of processes and procedures which create the framework, promise and possibility of a transition to the cooperative work group setting. This may well be a threat to the established manner and conduct of work. It will be bitterly fought unless the payoffs for all concerned enhance individual, work group, and client well-being. Effective change must take cognizance of this and other areas of possible trouble as well. An intentional change sequence might well be used to achieve the transition to cooperative work.

An Intentional Change Sequence Applied – Phase I: Gaining Awareness

Organizational development may be used as a primary tool for managing such change. Organizational development is rooted in change theory, action research, effective consultation and problem solving orientations. It is a value conscious process which utilizes planned change, strategies, tactics, knowledge, technology, feedback, and accountability to achieve its purposes and enhance organizational effectiveness.[6] It offers a most useful and attractive avenue to confront the covert aspects of traditional organizational life. Such a step is crucial in achieving a humane organization.

The first focus of the change sequence is to gain careful and complete understanding of the ambience of the specific groups and organization(s) involved. This includes identification and analysis, among other things, of the value networks, transactional dynamics, power contexts, resources and task and production requirements.

The return of meaning to work rests to a great extent upon the individual feeling outcomes of joy, accomplishment and appreciation. Where the emotional life of the worker is devalued, meaningful work is unavailable because its essence rests upon access to the emotional dimensions of human life. Competence, credibility and co-operation come from mindfulness, joyfulness, use of one's authentic power and caring about what one is and does. If the ambience and management of the workplace discourages or penalizes these, the investment of meaning into human activity and work cannot occur. Meaning, satisfaction, pride of workmanship derive from emotional roots. These are some of the important aspects of work life which contravene alienation and banality. Anger, too, when expressed in healthy and constructive ways, validates the human presence and provides avenues to meaning, well-being and rewarding work. Competence comes with skills, training and education supported by a sense of self-worth which is fully intact. Credibility comes with straight talk, no rescues, no power plays and reliable trust-laden transactions. Cooperation rests upon effective work with others which encompasses the absence of discounts, injunctions and attributions and the restoration of positive affirmation and appreciation of one's fellow workers.

The introduction of cooperative procedures and the establishment of a framework which will support cooperative work must be open, straightforward and honest. Hidden management agendas for the purpose of escalating production betray the worker and subvert the process and simply become another power play within the context of a traditional oppressive banal work group. The focus for the introduction and application of cooperative work procedures must involve the participation of all persons and groups affected. Such a focus needs to be directed toward the processes of the specific organization concerned and focused upon the specific work groups involved.

Cooperative work and cooperative work groups will provide and reflect within the membership a variety of task related activities, (1) participation in decision making, (2) independence of thought and movement, (3) autonomy of choice and discretion, and (4) independence of judgment. These will be reflected in the aspects of group and organizational activity which concern time, space, competence, resources, and coordination and control.

Phase II: Problem Solving

Problem solving is concerned with defining the goals, policies and programs needed to achieve the change. It is concerned with the plan and design of the change process. It focuses upon the intervention strategies and tactics required to activate the change process. This requires varying yet meaningful participation of those at all levels of the organization who will be affected by the changes sought. A primary concern is the role and function of the traditional work group. These groups must be assessed, and the functions and processes well understood.

The effectiveness of a work group or task group depends wholly upon the success of the process group. The outcome of the process group depends upon the nature of the private structure. Thus the interpersonal processes within the group provide the clue and key to achieving a humane, cooperative, intimate and productive work group. Group process in the interpersonal world of the group is concerned with establishing the equilibrium and boundaries of the group. The private structure relates to the satisfaction of the needs of group members and the experience, wishes and emotions of each group member and as they transact their individual psycological business within the group. As observed in previous chapters, the individual members may be involved, participating or engaged in their own personal games within the private structure of the group with significant dysfunctional consequences for the outcome of that group.

What will move the individual group member to a position and sense of belonging where each member gives up his own individual proclivities in favor of playing the cooperative group way? The relinquishment of individual proclivities must leave the integrity and the wholeness of the human personality intact. The private proclivities of group members cannot be relinquished until they are established. They must be relinquished before individual members of the group are valued by the group and thus given permission and support to participate cooperatively within the group. There is very little understanding and personl awareness concerning this process. When it occurs, it occurs below the level of conscious awareness of the members of the group and is generally intuited.

The private proclivities to be relinquished relate to the individual script or agenda that each person carries into the group. Such proclivities relate to the games a person plays in the group so as to receive the strokes sought by the operation of the game. Part of these script propensities must be relinquished if one is to belong to and be productive in any group of which one is a member. The parts to be relinquished are those relating to the personal script games played by the member concerned. The payoff for this relinquishment must become the restoration of personal autonomy, increased enhancement of personal choice, the restoration of personal power and an emerging sense of a fuller control over one's own personal life. Individuality is not the maintenance of script-strivings, personal games and hidden agendas. Individuality, on the contrary, is permitted, encouraged and enhanced by this process. Of equal importance is the payoff which comes from the joy of working cooperatively with others. The point at which these personal proclivities are relinquished and the group members feel a sense of intimacy and belongingness is the critical point. If it is worked through successfully, cooperative group work becomes possible and the results are exhilarating. If the group fails to negotiate this point successfully, the group will experience frustration, stagnation and eventually either disintegrates or reverts to a stultified, boring and banal existence.

The Individual and Cooperative Work. Before exploring the process and procedures for obtaining humane organization, it is essential to observe that the two fundamental rights that provided the threshold and access into dignity in the agrarian age are not available within the structure of public or private organizations, *viz.*, the right to free speech and the right to free assembly. Within a democractic agrarian society, these have been powerful tools and they were utilized to change, alleviate and redress wrongs. They are the essential basis underlying the identification and redress of oppression and injustice. Most human beings within organizations are rendered powerless and without these traditional tools to redress or alleviate the oppression and alienation at that workplace. When such alleviation is sought, it is through either covert and underground collective response or through joining an organization which will respond to power with equal power. Both of these alternatives are frequently as oppressive as the oppression from which alleviation is sought.

Complex organizations, *viz.*, bureaucracy fundamentally alter interpersonal social relationships where two individuals relate to one another in relative equality and reciprocity. Within organizations "superiors" are empowered and personal power is relinquished to them. This teaches persons in their midst to always look to superiors for answers of how we must look, what we must do, what is the correct and appropriate thing to say, what is good and what is bad. Insitutional norms are substituted for the diverse personal norms of its members. Complex organizations tend to destroy the integrity of the human personality and contribute to the creation of dependent, fragmented beings.[7]

The individual within bureaucracy is subject to direct manipulation from outside one's own person and survival and promotion are dependent upon, at the least, mute acquiescence in such manipulation and frequently outright syncophancy is rewarded. The individual stands mute, fawning and intimidated before superiors. Rendered powerless, they neither talk back nor seriously question their activities or orders. At the same time, members of the bureaucracy become accepting and responsive to the orders and directions flowing down through the chain of command directing ever more completely the behavior of each.

Bureaucracy, i.e., complex organization, has significantly contributed to the fragmented, dehumanized worker who, within its operations and structure, as Ralph

Hummel observes, is, "socially crippled, culturally normless, and psychologically dependent, linguistically mute, politically manipulable and economically vulnerable."[8] Such degradation and fragmentation of the human personality within bureaucracy seems somehow disguised when one happens upon the hustle and bustle and happy faces appearing on the surface.

This stands in marked contrast to the personality required to sustain and maintain democratic government where these very persons play a fundamental part. Democracy depends upon a politically literate, informed and responsible public. The member of bureaucracy is both the servant and the citizen. He or she can only be smart, intelligent, autonomous and powerful before and after his working hours, i.e., before 8 A.M. and after 5 P.M. The absurdity of this is obvious. The implications for democratic government are dismaying perhaps even ominous.

To reclaim the integrity of the human personality within organizational process poses an immense and awesome task. If the human being is to be reclaimed and the integrity of the personality restored, skills and competence must be linked to feelings before the creative spirit can unfold. This must be achieved within an atmosphere inside the bureaucracy and within the face-to-face task groups which are emotionally safe, which nurture the permission for the creative spirit to unfold, and gives permission and support to individual human beings to be individually and collectively powerful.

Phase III: The Decision Network

The decision network must be fully understood in all its ramifications if full and effective intentional change is to be achieved and maintained. Once these networks are defined and understood integrated and meaningful decisions about implementing change can be made. Such understanding may enhance the change design. Some decision patterns must be altered themselves in light of the values designated and the goals sought. Attention must be paid also to the reception of the decisions by those affected by them.

Before decisions concerning task activities can affect cooperative effort, i.e., production, the covert group processes derived by mindlessness (spawned by discounts of emotions and intelligence), lovelessness (spawned by the stroke economy), joylessness (spawned by injunctions, attributions and demands), and powerlessness (spawned by the drama triangle) must be elevated into conscious awareness among group members and continuously confronted in safe, yet straight, ways. The collusions, splitting, projections, and one-up and one-down power plays and alliances, together with the covert role differentiation which characterize the expression of these group processes, requires that the group front-up to them as well.

In the traditional organization, taking care of such interpersonal process has been mystified, frowned upon, frequently penalized, criticized, discouraged, and generally prohibited. The essential process work which must get taken care of prior to effective task performance occurs in a mystified and covert way in, around, beyond, and through the traditional formal organizational process.

Coffee breaks, time wasting, secret rendezvous, conversations about work that are really conversations about interpersonal affairs, and a whole variety of other communication devices are required and developed by persons in every organization which give the cues and messages relating to individual success and survival within the organization. These processes are generally mystified and the participants blind to their own behavior. In this situation organizational rituals, pastimes, games, power plays, secrecy, persecutions and rescues continue. Within the traditional organization, oppression is thus maintained. Under these conditions intentional change is difficult to implement.

The structure and process for achieving cooperative work is available. The concepts of hierarchical authority, work assignments, job descriptions, work measurements, and the paraphernalia of traditional organizational work groups must be confronted and modified. The process, function and structure of the work group must be altered. Paradoxically this is a part of the change process and a prior condition to the achievement of substantive and lasting changes in task and production. Understanding and modification of the decision networks is essential to such a task.

Phase IV: The Action Program

Implementation of the action program for achieving the humane group or organization must encompass the values, structure and processes of cooperative work within the implementation activity, i.e., humane means need to be utilized to achieve humane ends. Claude Steiner and those associated with him have evolved a group structure and process which involves safety, nurturing, support and problem solving. In addition, out of their efforts have come important processes in support of cooperative work. Much of the material which follows is evolved from their exceptionally creative work. The groups are generally ongoing and no more than seven or eight persons. Their primary focus may be personal problem solving, support, task performance or cooperative work. No matter which of these functions is the group focus, the structure for a cooperative meeting remains the same.[9]

A Structure and Process to Achieve Cooperative Work. A possible structure to achieve cooperative work is as follows:

1. **Facilitation.** Chose a facilitator and timekeeper from among the members. Where the group is ongoing, facilitation and timekeeping of the group needs to be rotated among the members.

2. **Shared Feelings.** This is followed by sharing "personal space." Personal space is an authentic sharing, usually swiftly accomplished, about the predominant feelings each one brings to the group process. This encourages each person to come out of "hiding" and share a part of him or herself with the others. This helps the group to know the quality of the energy and attention that each person has available for work. If it is an ongoing group sometimes past feelings among two or more members may have to be "cleared" before group work can proceed. The procedure to accomplish this is similar to the closing process identified below. Where there are unfinished feelings, a present or future time must be set aside to clear those feelings and may involve mediation at some appropriate future time.

3. **Setting the Agenda.** An agenda is then developed for the group whether the focus is problem solving, support or task cooperative work.

4. **Doing the Work.** After the agenda is made negotiations may be required depending on the kind of work to be done and the time for that work to be accomplished. The work then proceeds until the end of the time established. At that point the group immediately moves into closure.

5. **Closure.** Closure involves the following process:
   a. clearing unclear feelings;

  b. sharing self-criticism and criticism;
  c. clearing held resentments;
  d. checking out paranoid fantasies;
  e. the group concludes with sharing "strokes," i.e., positive feelings felt toward other group members.

Each person in this process has a right to equal satsifaction and an equal share of the process and shares equally in the responsibility to carry it through. Now it is possible to take each of these step-by-step and elaborate on their meaning and define more clearly the processes which relate to such a structure.

A Process of Cooperative Work. The coming together for work assumes there will be no rescues, no power plays, no secrets. It is assumed that each participant will share authentically in the work and be equally vulnerable. No one will do anything that he or she personally chooses not to do, there will be no covert or hidden agendas or secrets among the workers or particpants. Members participate openly and share any information relevant to the work, concealing nothing that is relevant and specific to the task at hand. This basis for cooperation underlies a meeting, whether it is for problem solving, support, task performance or cooperative work.

A word of caution concerning these tools needs to be suggested. Training and experience in their use is helpful even required if the pain of trial and error are to be avoided and they are to be used most effectively, constructively and intelligently.

1. **Facilitation.** Any meeting for problem solving, support or task performance needs to begin by choosing a facilitator. When the group is on-going such facilitation needs to be rotated among the membership, i.e., a new facilitator for each meeting chosen in an agreed upon manner. To maintain a sense of shared responsibility, an awareness needs to develop around each participant's variety of skills. Some have skills as a facilitator in a problem solving meeting, while others may have skills in facilitating a task, support or cooperative work meeting so that, in the long run, such facilitation is shared equally. Once the facilitator is chosen, personal "space" is assessed and then the amount of time available for the meeting is determined and the facilitator asks for the designation of an agenda. As suggested before, sometimes a timekeeper is needed. The process of selection is the same, i.e., voluntary rotation in sharing responsibility. The same requirement applies to any "scut" work or "dirty" work that needs to be done as well. An equal sharing of all work is essential. All participants participate in the creation of the agenda. Each member needs to ask for what he or she needs and wants in relation to the work and of the timeframe required to accomplish the work required.

2. **Shared Feelings.** Prior to determining the agenda, it is important to take a brief moment and let each person share their "psychological space." A lot happens in any one day or one week. Everyone comes to a meeting with a feeling which will affect and impact on the quality of the work in the group and the quality of the individual participant's work in the group. Thus it demystifies the rest of the group for each person to tell where he or she is "coming from" emotionally. A person who is coming from high energy with lots of zest may be perceived accurately and not threaten other group members by the energy and enthusiasm expressed. A person from a position of low energy perhaps experienced sickness, sorrow, accident or a death of a loved person can put such feelings forward so the group may be made aware of the quality of that person's energy which is available to the group. A person who has had a fight at home or has just received a traffic ticket on the way

to work can share his frustration or her anger in ways that define the quality of energy available to the group and demystify one another in that work situation. No response is necessary. Just a quick, but straight, communication as to where each person in the group is emotionally.

3. **Setting the Agenda.** Work may then begin by defining the agenda and determining the time for each agenda item or the time for the accomplishment of the particular tasks required. Once the agenda is set, the facilitator puts the question to the group something like this: "Is there anything that will keep anyone from working effectively today?" This is for the purpose of cleaning the slate and taking care of any leftover business which may interfere in obtaining good cooperative work. It is here that residual resentments or paranoias (suspicions) among the members which interfere with cooperative work may be resolved. If there is anger, suspicions and resentments to the extent that they may interfere with the performance of the group, then an effort at clearance needs to be made before process and work proceed. Where work is to be effective, process work must precede task work. Truly efficient and effective task work is preceeded by careful, full and frank attention to process. Indeed, it is quite safe to assert that the overwhelming portion of all "daily work" is taking care of the interpersonal process work which is required if work is to be done at all in other than compulsory or slave conditions—even then minimal process is required! The rule is: Process must occur before task work can be done. Process will be taken care of one way or another, either overtly or covertly, in a group or organization.

4. **Doing the Work.** Cooperative group procedures will vary to meet the task at hand. It may be things such as problem solving, support of a specific task. Thus a group of clerks assessing filing, mail collection and delivery functions, typing needs, errands, supply requests, etc. would need to assess what needs to be done, the time required, how the functions and tasks are to be shared, and then finally proceed to the tasks, opening and closing the process as suggested here and concluding the workday with a group meeting with the same format as well, to clear any interpersonal business which might be left over from the day. This is a fully different manner of organizing work and has important implications for work management. It restores power and responsibility to the worker for the conduct of his or her tasks and gives mutual responsibility for the conduct of group work and supplies a process for its accomplishment in a humane and caring manner.

Application of a Cooperative Work Process. One manager, a Regional Librarian in the Library of the City of Los Angeles, utilizes a task problem solving process to make difficult choices. Those concerned with book selection from a number of branch libraries come together to decide how to expand limited funds among ten branches for a given expenditure period. It is a six-step process designed to focus on identifying and solving problems in areas of shared concern. It is based on participation of a small group, with one person serving as a facilitator, one as a recorder, and one as timekeeper. The facilitator guides the discusssion and keeps it to the agenda decided; the recorder writes down what is said on paper large enough for everyone to have what has been said in view at all times. Moving from one step to the next is achieved through group consensus as follows:

—Step I: **Definition of Terminology** (15 min.)

This sets the scope of the concern, e.g. what is meant by "book selection?" Take all given definitions and edit them down to one which incorporates all elements to the mutual agreement of group members. This gives everyone a chance to "warm up" to the technique.

—Step II: **Stating the Problem** (30 min.)

The problem is presented as "how to," e.g., "how to strengthen or improve the process of book selection," e.g. for young adults. Again record all "how to's" and refine them to two or three, then choose a few to work on. They need to be tangible and of reasonable proportion, with a probably successful resolution, not intangible (like solving the problems of all the young adults of the world), with clearly defined timeframes established and consideration given to the tools required for implementation.

—Step III: **Reasons Why This is a Problem** (30 min.)

This provides an opportunity to "blow off steam" in a safe, controlled forum. Group members relate personal experiences to illustrate why this is a problem they would like to solve. Facilitator makes sure no persons are attacked or trashed and that statements are non-judgmental.

—Step IV: **Solutions** (45 min.)

Any and all suggestions for solutions are to be recorded—from the ridiculous to the sublime. These will then be grouped in categories according to sameness, using the same editing techniques as described above. These need to include times, dates, and tools for doing, evaluating, and also who is responsible for doing what. All this needs to be clearly understood.

At this point, if smaller groups have been used, each group reports to the larger group how they have defined terminology, what problems they chose to solve, and suggested solutions. The total time utilized up to this point is approximately two hours.

—Step V: **Implementation** (time required varies)

This may or may not happen on the same day, but might if, for example, the group wants to draft a letter. Other things take longer.

—Step VI: **Evaluation**

The tool(s) for evaluation need to be provided within the solution part of the process. This procedure has been utilized very effectively to perform cooperative work.[10] It is not an exclusive way and is presented here to indicate the flexibility of the cooperative work structure which may encompass a procedure such as this. More importantly, this procedure is an example of the manner in which certain tasks may evolve from the traditional milieu to the humane and cooperative milieu in groups and organizations. This procedure has been utilized and applied effectively and successfully within the traditional work group as a separate and distinct process from the framework for cooperative work presented here. It may thus be viewed as pointing the way to similar useful and helpful interim measures which may be taken in achieving the transition to the cooperative work group.

There is much to be learned concerning the conduct of cooperative task groups, yet the application of the structure and processes for cooperative work suggested here have been and can be helpful where utilized. It must be remembered that each person must share their competence and be authentically valued by the other members. Where the perceptions and expectations are not shared and understood, there is room for resentments and rescues to develop. Thus it is important to air these in the open either in the work group process or in a personal problem solving meeting set for that purpose. Different work tasks and needs require different competencies, internal structure and process, yet the parameters, structure and process of cooperative work suggested here are relatively constant.

5. **Closure**. If process must be attended to covertly in the organization the consequences suggested will be at least minimally dysfunctional to the individual members and to the group as a whole. Certainly, the dramas described in the earlier chapters will not be abated, but they will rather flourish under such circumstances. Most organizations and groups will not be open and receptive to this information. Some will even be hostile, for these processes are not seen as legitimate components of work. Yet they get done, one way or another, or the work does not get done. It seems therefore, rather sensible to take care of such business in safe and supportive ways rather than abandon such activity to the chaos of the covert processes.

A. **Clearing Unclear Feelings**. Sometimes group members are troubled, confused or vaguely uncomfortable concerning someone, an event, a transaction or some other aspect of group work or process. It is helpful to take time and try to clear these feelings. They may be first stated in a vague way and then, as they are articulated, given shape and specific content. Once this occurs, they may move from a vague discomfort to specific in form. Once identified as a paranoid fantasy, held resentment, self-criticism/criticism, they may then be handled accordingly. Sometimes just articulating the unclear feeling and obtaining a response is suffcient.

B. **Sharing Self-Criticism/Criticism**. Owning your own part of any event or transaction is a powerful stimulus for others to do the same. In addition, it helps create and maintain a situation wherein a felt criticism or the group or a group member can easily hear such criticism and the information relevant to it in an open and safe way. It avoids placing "all the blame" on another. Indeed, it alleviates the overt and covert blaming transactions which can be so hurtful to the group and to themselves. It confronts a difficult event, transaction or an aspect of the group in a straightforward way. If someone specific is involved, it is important to seek that person's permission prior to delivering the criticism or even the self-criticism. This respects the person to whom it is intended and maintains group safety. In delivering self-criticism and criticism, it is important to be specific, concrete, to deal with real feelings, and refrain from "yes, but" and other defensive responses. As in held resentments, no response is given, but it may be discussed outside the group at another time.

C. **Clearing Held Resentments**. Anger deserves special attention. To bury anger simply pushes it out of the sight of the bearer and the recipient(s). All involved can be surprised by its aggressive expression when effective interpersonal work around anger is not accomplished. The goal is to become aware of anger in one's self and others and then learn to express it in ways which take care of the bearer and recipient better, heal any wounds (or at least avoid new wounds and set the conditions for the healing of old ones) and free up such energy for cooperative work by removing the anger blocks to the process.

To keep the group safe for all work, it is important that the psychological, i.e. personal boundaries of each individual, be respected and the integrity and safety of the group maintained. Therefore, when anger or resentment is held toward one person by another, an appropriate procedure which maintains the safety and the integrity of the group and the persons involved require that the individual holding the resentment and anger ask permission to deliver it. The same is true of unclear feelings, self-criticism and criticism and any paranoias. Giving two resentments in a row to the same person from other group members borders on trashing and is to be avoided.

The form for the delivery of anger or resentment is cast in language which refrains from empowering the participants and focuses on the act itself. Thus the appropriate way of presenting a held resentment is as follows: "When you did so-and-so (action, I felt (feeling)." Discounts, analysis, accusations are not appropriate and the statement needs to be delivered as cleanly and as precisely as possible. Caution must be taken as well to make the "I" message a clear message, *viz.*, "When you criticize me, I felt you were really out of line," is a double-you message with an analysis disguised in the word criticism and a feeling disguised as a resentment.[11] More properly, it would be delivered as follows: "When you interrupted my sentence, I felt angry and discounted." It is important that the person to whom the resentment is delivered simply acknowledge and try to hear. It does not mean necessarily that he or she agrees with such resentment. It is only important that the feeling and the cause of the feeling be truly heard. The person to whom the resentment is delivered gives no response. That is, there is an honest attempt by the person receiving the resentment to perceive what he or she was doing and the emotional reaction to that event. That is all that is needed. No argument need be implied; just an authentic communication. If further discussion is required between the two, arrangements can be made to talk about it outside the present meeting. Where such resentments are too stressful to one or more of the members, mediation will be required.

D. **Checking Out Paranoid Fantasies**. A paranoia is a feeling of suspicion or fear about another person. The delivery of a paranoia, like unclear feeling, self-criticism/criticism, or held resentment is the same format. Permission first needs to be obtained. The one's own feelings and suspicions associated with these feelings are stated within the paranoia. For example: "I have the suspicion that the reason you didn't come last week is that you were afraid to deal with the anger stemming from not getting your work done on time." It is important that the recipient of a paranoia validate at some level a piece or part of it. That is, find the "grain of truth" in the paranoia. No paranoia is without some germ of truth—some justification, even if when stated it seems very distorted and "crazy." The goal is to validate a piece of it so that the board can be cleared and work proceed. An appropriate if authentic response to the paranoid fantasy stated might be: "Yes, I was afraid that I might have to face some anger for my not completing the work that I said I would do for the last meeting and the illness of my little boy made it that much easier not to face that discomforture. Yet had my little boy not been ill, I am sure I would have been there."

E. **Strokes**. The meeting itself should close on a nurturing tone with shared good feelings. These are "strokes." Such strokes must issue from authentic feelings, not manipulative maneuvers with ulterior designs. In using this structure and process, authentic feelings and their expression in safe ways are sought. This is a very powerful, nurturing, energizing, healing part of the group process.

The Function of Closure. The goal purpose of the closure procedure is to clear up relationships and remove the blocks to cooperative work. Jargon and ritualization of this structure and process are to be discouraged and the tendency to slip into this mode must be avoided. These are tools to be used to take care of oneself more effectively in group and work situations and to free up the energy to do cooperative and creative work as well.

If people are not in a frame of mind to deal with held resentments, self-criticism/ criticism, paranoias or unclear feelings, then the facilitator must ascertain whether the meeting can effectively continue without clearing such feelings. If the meeting cannot effectively continue, then the person carrying those feelings may have to absent himself or herself from the meeting and clear the feelings with the individual concerned prior to the next meeting of the group. Such clearance may be obtained separately by conversing with the person after the meeting is over or through a mediation, if that is required.

The offering of held resentments, self-criticism/criticism, unclear feelings and paranoias can proceed continuously throughout the work process. The same applies to good feelings, called strokes, as they arise authentically and become relevant to the process. The material developed in the group by each of the members must be held in confidence by the members. Such information may not be related outside the group in the form of reports, gossip, news and the like. Such confidentiality is essential to maintain the safety within the group for the individual members to do their process work, clear their feelings and free up the attention and energy for task and cooperative work.

Confidentiality is not to be confused with secrecy. The difference between confidentiality and secrecy is essential to keep in mind. Confidentiality is essential to the maintenance of trust and safety in interpersonal and group process. A violation of confidence is a betrayal of trust. Secrecy is rather a fundamental part of power plays and maneuvers. It is used to gain a one-up or one-down advantage and is used thereby in manipulative and exploitive ways to gain hidden advantages. Likewise, organizational controls and audits must respect the integrity of the processes as well. Otherwise, members will be betrayed and process work proceed covertly as in the past. Confidentiality does not apply to illegal actions. Such activity cannot be protected by process work. This needs to be made clear as it is the rule that participation in group work requires the absence of drugs and alcohol. Persons under such influence cannot remain in the group in such a condition.

Frequently, the ideal situation of clearing authentic feelings at the moment they arise in someone is not desirable or obtainable. Therefore, the beginning and the end of the meetings are frequently and appropriately reserved for these purposes. Once the structural and process preliminaries are accomplished, the meeting proceeds according to the agenda which has been determined, with the facilitator making sure that individuals stick to the topic and the timekeeper reminds people of the progress of time in relation to the task.

Resentments, unclear feelings, paranoias, criticism and self-criticism, and strokes may proceed throughout the meeting whenever possible. Even when that occurs and certainly when it is not available, then a period should be reserved at the end of the meeting in which those activities can proceed. This diminishes the build-up of poweful emotions and minimizes the splitting and projections so characteristic of the covert process in banal work groups.

In summary then, fear, anger, sorrow and love are the emotional concomitants of the interpersonal operations which characterize the private, i.e., the hidden aspects of group life. These translate into activity and drama and are expressed in a myriad of ways through the dynamics of group life. When group members are blind to their own processes and transactions within the group they become "tricksters" sowing the seeds of mistrust, faction, conflict and hurt within the group and the harvest is irreparable harm to the group and to the involved members. The closure process diminishes, repairs, and may even avoid such consequences by bringing such aspects of the hidden group process into the consciousness of the group membership and then clearing them so as to reduce or eliminate their impact upon future group process. The operations of Berne's Law is thus addressed in an orderly fashion and closure provides the safety and the procedures for such an accomplishment. Anger is thus cleared through the use of held-resentments, mediations and criticism/self-criticism. Hurt and sorrow can be partially cleared by criticism/self-criticism. Fear and suspicion may be cleared through the use of sharing and validating paranoid fantasies. Life affirming care can be provided through the authentic sharing of strokes. The stage is thus set for the accomplishment of effective, productive and cooperative task work.

Application: Clues to Emerging Power Plays, Factions and Alliances. Power struggles within traditional hierarchical organizations are an ongoing concomitant of those organizations. Such struggles, depending upon the nature of the internal organization and the scarcities at stake and the payoffs and rewards sought, may be played in first, second or third degree game forms. These games and their concomitant interpersonal transactions involve splitting, projections, agitation, contradiction, moves and counter-moves, counter-accusations, back-biting, gossiping, lying, secrecy, righteousness, self-effacing humility, taking sides and making alliances, betrayals— all the things that go to make up one-up and one-down and pitched battle warfare. The intensity of this activity waxes and wanes throughout the life of the group and the organization until there is an ultimate winner or until the organization peters out into monotonous survival or disintegrates through failure in its funding and resource base. There are certain clues or symptoms which provide warnings of an oncoming on continuing power struggle.[12] These are as follows:

1. **Gossip and rumor mongering.** As the intensity and viciousness of gossip increases, fault-finding, blame and recrimination are split away and placed upon other members of the group.

2. **Secret meetings and covert agreements.** These may be informal, accidental, or planned intentional meetings. At first they are random, and as the situation moves forward in intensity, planned and secret meetings occur in which the tactics and strategies for future battles are mapped out.

3. **Name calling and labeling.** These are emotionally loaded words often bearing ideological orientation which are used in a derogatory, scornful or sarcastic manner. These epithets, political and personal, are hurled back and forth or used in private conversation as a way of discounting and rendering the enemy or the new enemy less than human so that they may be set up for battle, exclusion and harm.

4. **Blaming, fault-finding and scapegoating.** Failing to own one's own piece of any particular problem situation and blaming exclusively and completely upon another person or the other side. The tendency to locate the fault or cause of a difficulty in one person and avoid "guilt" for the results of a problem. The absence of self-criticism in owning one's own part in the problem.

5. **Choosing sides and making alliances.** Demands for loyalty, accusations of betrayal, the use of righteousness and self-righteousness political correct-

ness, rules and orders confirm commitment, deny access of group members to their own individual conscious choice. The development of two "sides" around the dominant players in the struggle for power.

6. **Manipulation and intimidation.** Implied overt and covert threats of intimidation and retaliation begin to permeate and poison the waters of personal and group relationships.

7. **Acting out on paranoid fantasies and suspicions.** Paranoid fantasies move from a germ or speck of truth to elaborate distortions which feed the flames of discontent and stimulate a growing labyrinth of suspicion.

8. **Productivity recedes and malingering rises.** Intimacy, cooperation and productivity recede and preparation to fight "the enemy," which may seem like productivity, cooperation and intimacy yet is counterfeit in nature, unrewarding in its ultimate application, and self-defeating, merges to dominate the attention, the activity, and the energy of the group.

9. **Authentic communication disintegrates.** There is a growing unwillingness to mediate struggles, to work through difficult interpersonal relationships and to problem solve around production and performance. These activities are replaced by fearful, often frightened, sometimes angry exchanges and discussions. Body movements, choice of seating and struggle for control of the agenda begins to dominate meeting arrangements.

These symptoms may range from mild in form to great intensity. Hierarchical organization, in order to contravene these developments, responds usually in an authoritarian manner, and creates a situation in which the worker is required to be obedient, punished if he is not, and rewarded if he is compliant. In the absence of authority, the chaotic anarchy discovered by Wilfred Bion tends to be the dominant mode of the group so long as it is in existence.[13]

Cooperative work provides the possibility for the avoidance of these debilitating encounters involving splits, factionalism, alliances and collusions. It is possible to move through the heat and splits of these dramas, heal and work successfully together. Where healing does not occur, not only is there a toll on production, but the ultimate long-run viability of the group is threatened as well. The toll on the health of the individuals involved in such a struggle is immense. The tools for the avoidance of these social and personal traumas are available.

Application: Conflict Resolution. When a group is stressed such as, for example, a major invasion of the major external boundary, the major internal boundary, when a group is faced with individual anancastic behavior (agitation and rebellion) or leadership conversion (takeover), the cooperative work structure suggested here focuses on the symptomatic behavior preceding such events. Thus the members and the group can front-up to these processes directly and in a straightforward manner. In addition, the mystified behavior within the group itself generated out of the covert, but not well understood, and shared fantasies identified by Wilfred Bion can likewise be confronted and raised into the awareness of the group membership.[14]

Games and power plays, rescues and the like can be confronted. This can be done by disclosing paranoid fantasies, unclear feelings, self-criticism/criticism, held resentments which are delivered in such a way as to expose in a safe and caring way such mystified transactions on the part of the individual members. A group sinking into pairing, fight/flight or dependent behavior can be internally confronted by its own members and these covert processes raised into view, identified and explored at an aware and conscious level. For example, the pairing phenomenon can be confronted through the delivery of a paranoid fantasy as may be fight/flight and dependency also. Criticism and self-criticism, unclear feelings, and held resentments also provide avenues for the exposure of the unconscious shared fantasies.[15]

Positive affirmations or "strokes" nurture good feelings, support healthy self-images and re-energize the individual members of the group so they are able to proceed with meaningful, productive, rewarding work. The structure and the procedure suggested here provide a set of tools which are adaptable to productive task activities, personal problem-solving activity, and support group activity. Each of which is an essential in cooperative work. Likewise, they are essential ingredients in managing effectively the aggressive impulse, healing and repairing relationships and nurturing creative fulfillment which each human being on the planet deserves.

Sigmund Freud observed in his final essay in *Civilization and Its Discontents*, "The fateful question for humankind seems to be whether aggression and self-destruction can be mastered through human cultural development to the extent that human life and community life can be obtained on the planet.[16]

Aggressive behavior can shatter the safety required in a group necessary to create the atmosphere of safety which encourages group participants to risk the kind of activity and vulnerability essential to cooperative work, human growth and effective production. Trust and safety is the foundation of the cooperative work group. Without these cooperation cannot proceed. With it the individual participants in a cooperative work group can risk in a way that restores joy and returns meaning to work, creates a place where mutual caring can occur, where group members can explore their competence by risking failure and members of such a group can receive the nurturing and support necessary to pursue their own competence and strive to achieve their own personal power.

Thus aggression which comes out covertly or crookedly through the use of snide remarks, put-downs and discounts, threats, and power plays must be abated. The structure for such abatement is provided through the cooperative work procedures described earlier. The goal is not to repress, deny, or push aggression and anger out of conscious view, but rather raise its occurrence into conscious view. Everyone in a cooperative work group has, and will, feel angry and discounted from time to time and the authenticity of this feeling needs to be recognized and then a place for its expression and care provided within the cooperative work group. Acting-out on the aggressive impulse or delivery of it in a way that invades the individual safety and boundary of another, whether that boundary be psychological, physical or social, cannot be tolerated.

Aggression willfully, arbitrarily, sarcastically or whimsically expressed interferes with the group's safety and is a threat to each member. Its elimination by threat, penalty or punishment simply maintains the cycle of aggression and seeds possible conflict in the future. The pathway to moderating and eliminating aggression as a problem and converting it into a resource lies in the pathway of mediation and interpersonal conflict resolution. Where these fail the group will have to be protected from the ongoing ravages of irresponsible aggression and protected from the possible violence that such aggression may spawn. To the extent that this option is utilized cooperative work is thereby diminished.

Within a work group abuse, corruption, banality, waste, violence, theft, power plays, discounts, and rescues cannot be tolerated. In addition, high standards of personal participation, personal responsibility, and competence must be encouraged and maintained. Debilitating events and their associated symptoms occur and frequently have been long in developing. The group therefore needs to move swiftly to confront their possibility and respond to the symptoms when they surface. A safe group with plenty of support will allow and even encourage the confrontation required for individuals to be powerful in making moral choices and developing the moral standards required within the group to interrupt the occurrence of these events and conditions.[17]

Aggression and its concomitant conflict must be resolved within the group in a responsible manner and in a way that puts such energy to creative and constructive use within the group. Aggression must be seen as a fundamental resource for the group to utilize in the accomplishment of its task. How to harness this energy is the problem that has to be solved. Failure to confront it, to contain it, and to utilize it effectively will threaten not only the production of the group but the ongoing possibility of the group's existence in the long run. Therefore, it is important to focus on procedures for handling the expression and exchange of aggression and anger within a cooperative work group in safe ways. Such procedures are available. There is a growing literature concerned with interpersonal peacemaking, mediation and conflict resolution.[18]

Conflict Resolution through Mediation. Mediations are specialized problem solving activities and sessions which may involve two or more persons or groups who are having particular difficulty in handling problems arising among them which prevent effective ongoing relationships, productivity, nurturing, and, in particular, spawn aggressive and destructive behavior. Where continuing relationships are involved, mediation may take one or more mediating sessions. Mediations do not necessarily solve problems, but rather define the ongoing work that needs to be done if the problem is to be solved and cooperative work to proceed.

The main function of a mediator is to help those involved feel safe so as to be honest and direct with one another about their feelings. This requires an atmosphere of safety and protection. This can be provided in a manner not unlike the cooperative work process described earlier. Mediation is only available through voluntary, willing participation. It may not be imposed or forced upon unwilling participants. The mediator must be selected and trusted by the participants involved in the mediation. Each participant in the mediation must ask for 100% of what each one feels and thinks he or she needs and negotiate from that point to a point which is acceptable within the range of possibilities available. To ask for more than 100% is crooked and part of a game.

Once a mediator is selected his or her main function is to listen compassionately and fairly to the participant's problem. To help define and work through what is happening in the relationship. This is done by helping to clarify the communication that occurs and then proceeding to help those concerned work cooperatively to decide on how each and all will proceed to work on the problem in the future.

Frequently, more than one mediator is helpful in a mediation where a number of persons are involved. Where several persons or groups are involved, a series of mediations might be required. Where it involves struggles between groups and among groups, the negotiations need to proceed in a manner that keeps communication open and clear and provides an opportunity to resolve the aggression in a manner in which each person involved is fully accounted for in the process.

The role of a mediator requires impartiality. The function of a mediator is to help persons or groups experiencing difficulties in their relationship work those difficulties through to re-establish a cooperative, supportive relationship or at least reduce the misunderstanding and animosity to a level where cooperative work may proceed. It focuses upon interpersonal work and is concerned with helping people discover who is doing what to whom, how one person or group contributes to the feelings of another person or group and how each person or group contributes to that process.[19]

Anita Friedman suggests a series of steps are involved in a specific mediation process once the agreement to mediate and the mediator or mediators are agreed upon. These are:

1. Developing understanding about what those involved want from the mediation.

2. Unloading held resentments, demystifying unclear feelings and sharing paranoid fantasies.

3. Discussing, feeding back and clarifying the varying perceptions of the problem and difficulty.

4. Self-critical and critical discussion concerning the problems in the relationship.

5. Encouraging each participant to ask for what he or she wants and supporting each to say no if he or she is not able to give what is asked.

6. Making contracts which is a clear understanding about what those involved are going to do about their behavior in the future so that the relationship is different.

7. Closure.[20]

At the conclusion of the work, an understanding is developed about the work to be done by all parties concerned and this is called the contract. The contract is an understanding among the participants about future work that specific persons agree to do. It differs from a legal contract in that it is not binding in law and the offer, the acceptance and the consideration are absent. The contract is an agreement, founded in trust, between two or more people that personal work will be done in a particular way and that an extra effort will be made to proceed along those lines.

In a mediation, the contract is specifically designed to focus on the problem which needs to be solved. This enables the facilitator to bring into clear focus the nature of the problem which persons involved in the mediation work through. When resolution is developed, contracts are negotiated and plans made for actualizing such contracts. The meeting then concludes the same as the others, clearing unclear feelings, paranoid fantasies, held resentments, criticism/self-criticism and, finally, sharing strokes and good feelings about the process that has occurred.

Achieving Cooperation. The key to cooperation is creating a new environment in which there is a great safety for people to risk the possibility of failure and thereby seek to achieve their ultimate competence through their own creative capacities. A group must therefore provide protection and safety so that risks may be taken and the restoration of individual competence and personal power be nurtured through permission and encouragement. Thus a safe group is not one in which ridicule, put-downs, competitive one-up banter and discounts occur. Exploration, mutual help and encouragement are a concomitant part of cooperative groups.

The use of one's own power and creative potential in a group is the result of nurturing, encouragement and safety. There is a distorted belief abroad that what we accomplish we accomplish "on our own" and without help of others and when we fail it is our own distinctive and unique fault. When failure does occur this is not to deny that each person in the failure has a piece and needs to "own" his or her own piece of that process, and take responsibility for it. Blaming, however, does little to repair the loss and when learning becomes an available option to such an experience, together with nurturing, forgiveness and problem solving, there can begin a repair and restoration of an individual's power to participate creatively, productively and wholly in the human experience.

Individualism which is rooted in win-lose and lose-lose relationships results in the isolation of human beings, one from the other, so they are unable to obtain the support and nurturing needed to grow. Such individualism is a fundamental concomitant of the more destructive forms of competition. Competitiveness is spawned in scarcity, inequality, and fear and when contained in a game such as occurs on the athletic field where the enemy is defined and aggression contained in safe ways, scarcity and inequality do not have particular long-lasting or harmful results. In a finite organization with limited resources receding in availability, the temptation to compete to the point of ultimate destruction becomes a tempting option. Cooperative work can take place amidst persons of varying skills, differing competence and work capacity and across generational boundaries.

Cooperation requires equality of access, authentic sharing and the absence of power plays, rescues, lies and secrets. Relationships based on power plays sink people into unhappy, unrewarding, unsatisfying patterns of skirmishes, battles and wars, accompanied with frequently changing sides, alliances and friends in which the overwhelming number of players lose.

Action Guidelines. Cooperative work is readily sustained by observing the following guidelines:

1. **Scarce resources are shared cooperatively.** If a scarcity exists that cannot be remedied, it is very likely that a cooperative compromise can be negotiated so that all persons involved can feel satisfied, given the absence of power plays and secrets and the existence of full information and problem solving help is available.

2. **Equality of access to cooperative work.** In cooperative relationships all persons involved have equal rights to participate in and seek satisfaction from the group.

3. **Equal responsibility for the cooperative structure and process.** All group members have equal responsibility to participate authentically in cooperative work. Each member has a responsibility to "own" his or her part in the cooperative process.

4. **Refraining from all power plays.** Power plays are based on scarcity, competitiveness, envy, greed and fear. Power plays may never be a part of a cooperative relationship.

5. **Asking for what you need.** In the absence of power plays, persons in a cooperative relationship need to learn to ask for 100% and no more of what they want and be willing to negotiate downward from that to a point where

each involved can abide by the results. Any less is a rescue; any more is a lie and a part of a power play.

6. **Abstention from all rescues.** Persecutions and rescues which stem from resentment and guilt from doing more than a felt fair share of the work or doing for someone what they can do for themselves is a set-up for the disintegration of a cooperative work situation.

Where these guidelines are not followed, mystification, oppression, manipulation and exploitation of participants will occur.[21] Access to one's own potential, the nurturing of the potential of others, and the essential strokes which sustain our work, i.e. good feelings become unavailable. In the absence of these rules, situations develop which are oppressive and feel bad, and participants feel exploited and miserable.

Phase V: Results

The accomplishment of the change achieves the results desired and designed in the change plan. The ambience within the concerned groups and organizations is altered. The new values implemented in ongoing action programs. Personal, group and organizational needs are more effectively fulfilled. Problem causes are rectified.

The ambience of cooperation and intimacy stand in marked contrast to alienation and isolation. The latter characterizes the competitive struggle and manipulated work within an hierarchical organization. People are generally without access to cooperative and intimate work situations and when achieved such cooperation and intimacy is generally felt to be a limited, momentary, ephemeral, fleeting experience.

Intimacy involves sharing, both in love and in work, not necessarily together, and it does not solely or exclusively have to do with sex or sexual relationships. A sexual encounter may or may not be intimate. A non-sexual encounter may or may not be intimate. It is not the sexual encounter which is of concern here. Rather the intention is to achieve personal and social intimacy in the work setting. Most persons in their lives have had access to a non-sexual intimate experience. As momentary and fleeting as it might have been, it felt good, was rewarding and nurturing, and centered around shared work.

To love one's neighbor as one's self means one must be capable of loving one's self. To care for one's self in the workplace, one must be able to nurture one's self, understand one's needs and ask for them where one can get them. This must be done in a place and manner where discounts, ridicule, injunctions, put-downs, competitive one-up banter, sarcasm and attributions are absent. The safety, permission and protection required for the presence of cooperative work must exist, be sustained, nurtured and encouraged.[22]

Cooperative work requires an accompanying experience of intimacy. One needs to feel close to the people with whom one works and lives. Everyone needs positive affirmations, i.e., strokes, to survive. Everyone needs intimacy in order to grow, to learn, to be validated as human beings, to repair and to be renewed, as well as to have a good, joyful, even rewarding time. In the absence of intimacy, people are static, predictable, non-dynamic, non-spontaneous, easily manipulated, and easily exploited.

Strokes alone do not constitute intimacy, even though they are a fundamental and functional part of intimacy. Intimacy involves an open, trusting, safe, mutual reciprocal, sharing, cooperative relationship. Intimacy involves sharing anger, bad feelings, paranoias, unclear feelings, self-criticism/criticism and positive strokes in safe, loving ways. It is the process of caring about oneself, caring about others with whom one is working and caring about what is accomplished within the work situation.

Intimate relationships feel powerful, feel good, feel rewarding. They validate the human personality and reinforce personal competence and good feelings. Most humans have the capacity for intimacy, yet most persons have been deceived, oppressed and misled around the possibility of its attainment. Where it has been reached or obtained in view of others, it tends to raise the sceptre of envy—a most powerful human emotion which invites the aggressive or subtle destruction of the envied object.

The absence of intimacy is a fundamental concomitant of alienation. The reclamation of intimacy is essential to the restoration of the person to powerfulness and wholeness, the restoration of meaning to work and the accomplishment of rewarding, productive effort. Its renewed occurrence may become available within a humane group or organization.

Phase VI: Accountability

Cooperative work needs to occur in a context where individual, group and organizational action can be confronted, reviewed and where necessary changed. Accountability in a cooperative work process is best achieved within the framework of a problem solving and support groups where the individual is concerned. Individual behavior needs to be rooted in ethical behavior which comprehends imperatives of human dignity. Individual action must be open to review and challenge in honest, straightforward yet safe ways which provide the opportunity for effective and autonomous personal change.

The organization and group must be held accountable through the application of ethical guidelines which include considerations of humanness and productivity. This whole problem of accountability cries out for revision which avoids the narrow orientation of the auditor and the considerable abuses of blaming and scapegoating. The narrow parameters that confine work solely to production must be revised to include activities which take place within the private structure of a group. Precisely, this means taking care of the emotional business of the group which is necessary process work. Therefore, work must include process, i.e., taking care of emotional business. Efficiency as an ideal must be redefined completely so as to include within its measurement humane treatment.[23]

Organizational Accountability. Hierarchical authority must give way to learning, understanding and participating cooperatively together. The artificial scarcities of status, prestige and wealth must yield to equality, dignity and sharing. When the aggressive impulse can be confined, managed and resolved, the energy and safety required to risk creative, meaningful and productive involvement in cooperative work groups will become available. *Human dignity is the only acceptable and morally justified end to which the uses of organizational power may be put.* It must become part of the interstitial tissues of organizational and bureaucratic processes as well.[24]

There may be many roads to working cooperatively. The structure and process presented here is not suggested as an exclusive pathway. It is one which has been utilized and is more readily understood when related to the analytical framework developed in the previous chapters. In a banal work group time structuring moves from rituals through pastimes to games. It is characterized by power plays, discounts, the stroke economy, injunctions, the drama triangle, and covert role differentiation.

Individual member activity proceeds from participation and involvement through, when the operational principle occurs, to engagement in hidden agenda operations and covert games within the group process. This relates to the individual imago development of each member. Participation comes from a provisional imago. Involvement comes when that imago is adapted and behavior moves and links into the group through pastimes activities. Once one knows where one stands in the imago of the leader one becomes engaged in one's own games and power plays within the group. Group cohesion develops through these stages and when the critical point is reached it involves an individual in a moral choice about what one will give up in order to belong to the group. At this point group survival weighs in the balance. On occasion, such a group may develop optimally if the members resign some of their individual wants and needs, i.e. proclivities, and adjust their imago accordingly (this Berne calls the secondarily adjusted imago) and is thereby accepted into the group and a sense of belonging occurs.[25] The group accepts the person into membership and the person feels he or she is now a member. Identification with the group occurs.

In traditional banal organizations the pathway to optimum group development is covert and blind with the processes necessary for its achievement subject to prescription, penalty, discouragement, exclusion and preclusion. Thus the processes required to achieve optimum group development which focus on "taking care of emotional business" have to occur outside traditionally understood, officially acceptable and recognized group procedures. In addition, frequently these processes occur within the covert processes of the group itself. Is it any wonder under such conditions work remains oppressive and depressing? Organizational accountability procedures must take cognizance of these processes and become concerned with assessing the measures for their rectification.

Organizational structure, process and routine are essential. Planning, organizing, staffing, directing, coordinating, reporting and budgeting are essential functions and are amenable to the structure and processes for cooperative work suggested here. POSDCORB are certainly functions which cannot be excised; indeed they are still required.

What the structure and process for cooperative work provides is a way of elevating covert group processes within traditional processes into view. It provides a method and a set of tools to confront, in relative safety, individual transactions and behavior that characterize the covert spheres of interaction within a group. These tools also when used in a genuine and authentic way will diminish the buildup of the destructive energy associated with the dynamics of the covert process. The safety provided by this structure and process establishes a superb setting to confront power plays and role differentiation and the other aspects of the covert processes. It provides the possibility of successfully moving through that critical point where the development so essential for working cooperatively occurs.

The processes suggested here must be supported by experiential learning informed by personal intellectual and reflective process. The controls applied, sought and frequently required in traditional groups and organizations are not generally compatible with these processes since they are conceived in a basic mistrust of human behavior.

POSDCORB Revised

Stephen Blumberg suggests an additional set of guidelines based on this venerable acronym within public administration POSDCORB, *viz.*, EVPOSDCORB. These are a set of humanistic guidelines which are important to follow in the conduct of bureaucratic activity. Blumberg suggests the letters additionally stand for: Ethics, Values, Patience, Openness, Sensitivity, Dignity, Cooperation, Responsiveness, Beneficence. The worker in the vineyards of bureaucratic organizations will go a long distance in the creation of humane organization when the guidelines are implemented throughout the organizational process.[26] The cooperative work group offers a superb starting point for their realization. These processes have been utilized in varying degrees with excellent results in a variety of public agencies by practitioners who have become acquainted with their operations.

In public bureaucracy structure, process, progam action, public policy development and implementation can adapt the material suggested here for the achievement and fulfillment of their organizational mission rather than through the traditional means which include, among other things, manipulation, threatened and applied applications of force and the use of elaborate controls. The anit-intellectual posture traditional to public and private bureaucracy and the manipulative use of knowledge and information to achieve narrowly conceived organizational goals of survival, production and efficiency must give way to comprehensive organizational goals and processes which, among other things, subsume within their context structures and processes which encourage emotional growth, intellectual advancement, personal competence and human fulfillment.

, **Individual Accountability.** The immense challenges of our emergent technological society requires a renewed moral awareness. A guideline for responsible behavior in the groups and organizations which comprise this technological society is *that line of action alone is justified which does no harm to any person*.[27] The word harm would include any combination of economic disadvantage, physical suffering, social indignity, loss of self-esteem and latent vengeance. One example of how this rule might apply is illustrated by an incident which occurred in the Environmental Protective Agency. Early in 1975, the Agency approved a plan to have a hospital in Mexico feed known cancer-causing fungicides to Mexican patients in massive dosages to see what effects would occur on the thyroid. This plan was blocked at the last minute by an agency attorney, Jeffry Howard, who felt it was antiethical, shocking and completely against the principles of the Agency itself. In this instance, personal moral choice was not abandoned, yet in the absence of Attorney Howard, the Agency program could have culminated in an ethically indefensible humanly degrading result.[28] To stand might and powerful against the continuing pressures for profit, secrecy and organizational self-interest, an individual must be strong indeed.

A first step is to restore to the human being high self-esteem, which will help a person confront moral dilemmas. The first requirement, therefore, for participation in a cooperative work group is that the members of such a group consider themselves whole, competent individuals. Members of cooperative work groups need, as minimum, to be involved in processes which enable them to rediscover their own autonomy and give them the strength and support to utilize it effectively and competently with a work group.

Additional steps need to be taken as well. Membership in on-going stable problem solving and support groups is profoundly helpful to contravene alienation and isolation and obtain important renewal of one's own power, competence and strength. These are small groups, no more than eight in number, which meet for about two hours weekly on a regular basis. In this group people may work on their own problems and seek psychological support in safe and nurturing ways. Support in this situation means not only deriving important psychological support but the opportunity to confront one's own inner situation and learning by such a confrontation to better take care of one's self in more effective, healthy, and ethical ways.

Such a group meets only for problem solving and support. The cooperative work process detailed earlier is generally but not always used. Family members and immediate work group members are not included in such a group. Neither are these groups substitute families or social groups. They meet solely for the purposes of personal problem solving and support. It is a place to do personal work, learn about one's self and give and receive straight feedback and healthy nurturing. Yet it is a place where one can be safely confronted as to one's own games, hidden agendas, patterns, etc.

These groups are distinct from therapy groups, "T" groups, sensitivity groups and the like. They may be facilitated by professionally trained persons or they may be self-help groups designed to meet the situation required. This is a place and situation where personal problem solving and caring feedback occur. The goal of such effort is to enhance personal competence and enable the member to return to the work and family situation and among other things be more responsible and effective. This is a place where one can be "called in to account" for one's behavior and choices and effective change encouraged.

The implementation of a network of problem-solving, task and support groups is encouraged. Training and involvement for such participation is also encouraged. The tools, structure, processes, information and knowledge are available to accomplish this task.[29] Training in this process is certainly essential to its initiation, maintenance and success.

The reclamation of the individual autonomy, including the power to make moral choices, is not the only reason for achieving humane groups and organizations. The more significant reason is that in our society it is worthwhile *per se*. It is important to achieve for the value inherent in its attainment and the promise it holds for contributing to a joyful, dignified, productive, creative and caring human person.

SUMMARY

To introduce, implement, apply and develop cooperative humane work groups is an essential task. Task and production must be reorganized in a way which designs and incorporates the structure and processes of cooperative work, whatever these might be. Using the cooperative work design provided here is but an initial step. Changes can begin on a small scale within the groups and organizations concerned. Personal transactions with one's supervisor, workers, work group, secretary, etc., can be altered and invested with more humane dimensions. An emerging network of problem-solving and support groups can be developed to help achieve these results.

More extensive and organic changes may then be encouraged utilizing the intentional change sequence. Organizational development is an important avenue to use in planning and implementing such change. Organizations must provide a context which nurtures the possibility of obtaining human dignity within their context while at the same time maintaining and improving production. Achieving these changes deserves the full attention, energy, and devotion of those persons interested in nurturing the necessary conditions for achieving optimum human development. In our time the power and responsibility resides within complex organizations to establish and provide the conditions to obtain meaningful work, and support the opportunity to achieve creative personal and social fulfillment.

NOTES

1. Erik H. Erikson, *Insight and Responsibility*, N.Y., W.W. Norton & Co., Inc., 1964, p. 243.
2. Elliot Jaques, *A General Theory of Bureaucracy*, N.Y., John Wiley & Sons, 1976, pp. 1-9.
3. *Ibid.*, p. 7.
4. *Ibid.*, p. 373 and pp. 180-329.
5. James D. Carroll, "Noetic Authority," *Public Administration Review*, September/October, 1969, p. 499.
6. See e.g., Newton Margulies and Anthony P. Raia, *Conceptual Foundations of Organizational Development*, N.Y., McGraw-Hill Book Co., Inc., 1978, pp. 3-26; see also generally on the subject of organizational development C. Argyris, *Management and Organizational Development*, N.Y., McGraw-Hill Book Co., Inc., 1970; F. Friedlander and L.D. Brown, "Organizational Development," *Annual Review of Psychology*, Vol. 25, 1974; E.F. Huse, *Organizational Development and Change*, St. Paul, Minn., West Publishing Co., 1975; N. Margulies and A.P. Raia, *Organizational Development: Value, Process and Technology*, N.Y., McGraw-Hill Book Co., Inc., 1972; Jong S. Jun and William B. Storm (eds.), *Tomorrow's Organizations: Challenges and Strategies*, Glenview, Ill., Scott, Foresman and Co., 1973.
7. See generally Chris Argyris, *Integrating the Individual and the Organization*, N.Y., John Wiley & Sons, 1964, and his *Interpersonal Competence and Organizational Effectiveness*, Homewood, Ill., Dorsey Press, Richard D. Irwin, Inc., 1962.
8. Ralph P. Hummel, *The Bureaucratic Experience*, N.Y., St. Martin's Press, 1977, pp. 220-221.
9. This presentation draws heavily on the work of Claude Steiner, particularly "Cooperative Meetings," *Issues in Radical Therapy*, (Winter 1977), p. 11. *Scripts People Live*, N.Y., Grove Press, 1974, pp. 295-302. "Cooperation" in Hogie Wyckoff (ed.), *Love, Therapy and Politics*, N.Y., Grove Press, Inc., 1976. See also generally Wyckoff, "Equalizing Power in Groups," pp. 83-90; Anita Friedman, "Mediation," pp. 91-106; Joy Marcus, "Intimacy," pp. 213-220, in Wyckoff, *op. cit.*
10. This procedure has been used with excellent results by the City of Los Angeles Regional Librarian Virginia Walter, I am indebted to her for supplying this example.
11. See Thomas Gordon, *Parent Effectiveness Training*, N.Y., Peter H. Wyden, Inc., 1970, pp. 115-139.
12. See Claude Steiner, "Working Cooperatively," *IRT*, Vol. 3, No. 4, Fall 1976, pp. 22-25.
13. Wilfred Bion, *Experiences in Groups*, N.Y., Basic Books, Inc., 1961, see also Chapter 3.
14. Wilfred Bion, *Experiences in Groups, op. cit., passim*; see also Chapter 3.
15. See C.G. Jung, "The Concept of the Collective Unconscious," pp. 59-69, and "On Synchronicity," pp. 505-515, in *The Portable Jung*, N.Y. Penguin Books, copyright Viking Press, 1971, from the *Collected Works of C.G. Jung*, translated by R.F.C. Hull, Princeton University Press as Bollingen Series XX, Collected Works, Vol. 9, i, pars. 87-110, Vol. 8, pars. 969-997.
16. Sigmund Freud, *Civilization and Its Discontents*, N.Y., W.W. Norton & Co., Inc., 1961. First English edition, London, Hogarth Press, and Institute of Psycho-Analysis, N.Y., Cape and Smith. Translator: Joan Riviere.
17. D.E. Zand, "Trust and Managerial Problem Solving," *Administrative Science Quarterly*, Vol. 17, 1972, pp. 229-239.
18. e.g., Richard E. Walton, *Interpersonal Peacemaking: Confrontations and Third-Party Consultation*, 1969. Addison-Wesley Publishing Co., Inc., Reading, Mass.; Alan C. Filley, *Interpersonal Conflict Resolution*, Glenview, Ill., Scott, Foresman & Co., 1975; George R. Bach and Herb Goldberg, *Creative Aggression*, N.Y., Doubleday & Co., 1974; see also Chapter 8.

19. Anita Friedman, "Mediations," in Wyckoff, *op. cit.*, p. 94.

20. Friedman, *op. cit.*, pp. 95-104.

21. For more complete information on the roots, development, structure and process of these important developments, see generally, Claude Steiner, (ed.), *Readings in Radical Psychiatry*, N.Y., Grove Press, Inc., 1975; Hogie Wyckoff, (ed.), *Love Therapy and Politics*, N.Y., Grove Press, Inc., 1977; Claude Steiner, "Revised Principles of Radical Psychiatry," *IRT (Issues in Radical Therapy)*, Spring 1977, pp. 12-14. See also generally R. D. Laing, *The Politics of Experience*, Ballantine Books, 1967.

22. cf. Joy Marcus, "Intimacy," in Wyckoff, *op. cit.*, p. 217.

23. cf. Frederic W. Taylor, *The Principles of Scientific Management*, N.Y., W.W. Norton Co., by arrangement with Harper & Row, 1947, (first copyright by Taylor in 1911), *passim.*

24. Eugene P. Dvorin and Robert H. Simmons, *From Amoral to Humane Bureaucracy*, San Francisco, Canfield Press, (Harper & Row), 1972, *passim.*

25. Eric Berne, *Structure and Dynamics of Organizations and Groups*, N.Y., J. B. Lippincott Co., 1963; Grove-Evergreen Press, 1966, pp. 163-166; for an excellent selection of materials and a complete annotated bibliography of Eric Berne's work, see his *Beyond Games and Scripts*, edited by Claude M. Steiner with the help of Carmen Kerr, N.Y., Grove Press, 1976, pp. 329-335.

26. Stephen K. Blumberg, "The Manager's New Role: Add a Little EVPOSDCORB," *Public Management*, Vol. 59, No. 10, October 1977; "Notes on the Art of Administration," *Midwest Review of Public Administration*, December, 1980; and his *POSDCORB Revisited: Humanistic Guidelines for the Executive*, unpublished manuscript shared with the author, 1977; see also Luther Gulick and L. Urwick, *Papers on the Science of Administration*, N.Y., Institute of Public Administration, 1939; and Robert H. Simmons and Eugene P. Dvorin, *Public Administration: Values, Policy and Change*, Port Washington, N.Y., Alfred Publishing Co., 1977, pp. 477-516.

27. Erik H. Erikson, *Insight and Responsibility*, N.Y., W.W. Norton, Inc., pp. 219-243.

28. *L. A. Times*, October 19, 1977; see also e.g. material on Occidental Chemical Co. in Chapter 1 and Note 67.

29. See for example Howard Kirschenbaum and Barbara Bloser, *Developing Support Groups: A Manual for Facilitators and Participants*, La Jolla, Ca., University Associates, 1978; Morton A. Lieberman and Leonard D. Borman, (eds.), "Self Help Groups," the *Journal of Applied Behavioral Science*, Vol. 12, No. 3, July/August/September 1976; Thomas M. Scheidel and Laura Crowell, *Discussing and Deciding: A Desk Book for Group Leaders and Members*, N.Y., Macmillan, 1979.

RELATED READING

Argyris, Chris. *Integrating the Individual and the Organization*. New York: Wiley, 1964. This volume represents Argyris' early thinking and theorizing about how organizations might be redesigned to take into account the energies and competencies that human beings have to offer.

Coser, Lewis. *The Functions of Social Conflict*. London: Routledge & Kegan Paul, Ltd., 1956. This very significant effort is concerned with functions of social conflict. Not only with its negative and dysfunctional consequences but it is an essential mediator, among other things, in determining such things as boundaries, membership and policy. He identifies a significant number of basic propositions and relates these to psychoanalytic and empirical research.

Filley, Alan C. *Interpersonal Conflict Resolution*. Glenview, Ill., Scott, Foresman & Co., 1975. A truly remarkable and practical little book which is readily usable in identifying the types and sources of conflict and then identifying helpful methods of problem solving and conflict resolution.

Freud, Sigmund. *Civilization and Its Discontents*. New York: W.W. Norton, 1961 (First English edition, London: Hogarth Press, 1930). This is one of the last of Freud's books and centers upon the problem of the destructive aspects of aggression and the tensions between the individual and his need for freedom and the demands of society for constraint.

Gendron, Bernard. *Technology and the Human Condition*. New York: St. Martin's Press, 1977. This book addresses two fundamental questions concerning the role of technology in society. First, what is the impact of technology on individual lives and social institutions? Second, to what extent is the impact beneficial or harmful? This is an excellent presentation of the ills technology has wrought and the prospects for emancipation from such ills.

Maslow, Abraham. *Eupsychian Management*. Homewood, Ill.: Richard D. Irwin, 1965. A journal which stresses the need for enlightened non-authoritarian management as a requirement to dealing more effectively with the changing requirements and conditions of people who aspire or seek more effective personal development, dignity and self-respect.

Newton, Peter M. and Levinson, Daniel J. "The Work Group Within the Organization: A Sociopsychological Approach," *Psychiatry*, Vol. 36, May 1973, pp. 115-142. Four conceptual perspectives: task, social structure, culture and social process are used to analyze the effects of task conflict (ambiguity) resulting in low task effectiveness, poor staff morale and a dehumanizing environment. The work group is found to reflect similar patterns and suggestions for change are offered.

Steiner, Claude, editor. *Readings in Radical Psychiatry*. New York: Grove Press, 1975. An important collection of readings centering upon alternatives to traditional approaches to mental and community health. These materials are experientially developed and are useful and intriguing. It is an effort to identify, create and use a new basic social unit which is responsive to the alienation and oppression which is the fallout of the present social-technological order.

Thompson, Victor A. *Without Sympathy or Enthusiasm*. University, Ala.: University of Alabama Press, 1977. A dispassionate and reasoned defense of traditional organizations.

Walton, Richard E. *Interpersonal Peacemaking and Third-Party Consultations*. Reading, Mass.: Addison-Welsey, 1969. This book is concerned with the "peacemaker," i.e. the third person in a two-party dispute or conflict in a group or organization and presents a model for diagnosis, confrontation and resolution of such conflict. It is pointed particularly to conflict within organizations.

Chapter 10

ACHIEVING HUMANE, PRODUCTIVE AND
RESPONSIBLE GROUPS AND ORGANIZATIONS

The first essential step in provisioning humane organization is to confront the full meaning of groups, organizations and bureaucracies in the context and fabric of our political, social and personal lives. Effective production is dependent upon this step. Too frequently, large organizations, whether in the public or private sector, are the source of personal, social and economic oppression. The accomplishments of such organizations, for good or ill, are immense and effective responsibility and accountability is nil. Bureaucracies, with their matrix of groups and organizations, have been used to create and maintain degrading human circumstances. Bureaucracy has become, as well, the vehicle to achieve some of the most sublime accomplishments of humankind. The attainment of humane bureaucratic organizations is crucial for the full achievement of human dignity in industrial urban society. The social "payoff" is creative and producing human beings fulfilling their own capabilities, contributing to stable social institutions, and challenging the unknown horizons of human existence and understanding.

The Challenge: To Achieve Full Human
Capability in Modern Complex Organization

It is the challenge of the present generation to utilize the context of bureaucracy and its component groups and organizations for the maintenance and the creation of the conditions necessary to achieve the maximum human potential and accomplishment, while at the same time diminishing, even eliminating, the oppressive dimensions.[1] The processes of democracy, which shaped and molded bureaucracy in its modern form, as a primary instrument for the restoration and maintenance of human dignity and economic well-being, is threatened by the very institutions it created. Today the bureaucratic phenomenon is a considerable threat to the guarantees of human dignity. In the United States the political freedom sustained through the political and civil rights in the constitutional process are not generally available within the context of bureaucracy. Most human beings within bureaucracy do not have available to them within that organizational framework the most rudimentary and fundamental rights required to sustain effective democratic institutions.

Most persons in technological urban civilization are involved in work related to some form of large organization, public or private, and certainly all persons, for the most part, are subject to the activity or the consequences of the activity of bureaucracy. For the worker in the vineyard of bureaucracy he or she is unable to exercise the fullness of his or her humanness during the better part of his or her waking life. The income that the individual worker needs of necessity requires that he or she set aside "voluntarily" basic responsibility and control of his or her mind, his or her body, and his or her labor while serving the organization. The organization, thus, subtly erodes the substantive meaning of human and civil rights, assigning them to a time when they may be exercised only before eight in the morning and after five in the evening, i.e. before or after the working day (or night).

The better part of the waking day for those involved is controlled by the urgent needs of the bureaucratic organization. People succumb to organizational power because of the necessity to earn income with which to purchase the necessities of life and the supplies of leisure. Specifically, this relates to learning skills and competence and then "playing the game" to "get ahead" and "succeed." This urgency for personal survival and personal success within the organization spawns a moral blindness which has, from time to time, led individual members, sometimes whole organizations, and occasionally whole civilizations, to blind themselves to the morally reprehensible activities of their bureaucracies. Angry citizens, feeling mistreated by amoral bureaucracy, strike out in blind rage to destroy it by attacking its funding sources.[2]

Within bureaucracy individuals who do take a moral stand and confront corrupt and immoral or potentially immoral actions frequently do so at a high personal cost. If they are young they are often "cut out of the herd." If they are in their middle or later years they frequently are "promoted" into meaningless activity or transferred to some organizational "Siberia." Such wastelands exist in most organizations and the message of that assignment is quite clear.

In bureaucracy, inevitably, things will go wrong and individual participants in the bureaucratic process who are "responsible" for things gone wrong will be sought out, blamed, scapegoated, and penalized. Personal survival under these circumstances becomes more important than competence and, under such conditions, a pervasive fear and continual anxieties are daily concomitants of existence. Witch hunts within organizations may range from gentle to righteous in intensity. All persons in such a system seek to defend themselves by keeping a close log of their contacts and their work, making sure that all paperwork is appropriate and carefully done and that everything essential to the accomplishment of the task is fully documented. Much activity is expended making sure one can adequately defend oneself against potential charges which might be leveled at him or her. In the public sector CYA (cover your ass) is a dominant personal mode of behavior. This response is calculated to maintain personal survival and is rooted in the fear of persecution and loss of one's employment. This behavior reflects institutionalized paranoia and is deeply rooted in anxiety which characterizes dehumanized bureaucracies.[3]

The equivalent in private sector organizations is "do it to him before he does it to you," i.e. betrayal. In this instance, the aggressive, competitive betrayal of a fellow worker is essential to one's survival where frequently employee mortality is high and whole departments and divisions are severed, depending upon who wins and who loses the internecine struggles. Under these conditions individuals succumb to organizational demands and their capacity to make the moral choices required is diminished or lost and the organization more easily goes awry.

Requisite Action to Achieve Organizational Transformation

Bureaucratic power can be harnessed, focused and required to work in humanizing ways. If and when this is accomplished the adverse effects of complex organization upon life, family and society can be rectified. Elliot Jaques observes:

> *Bureaucracies are complex institutions, and a thorough-going change both inside and out will be required if their transformation is to be achieved. There will be required, for example, abundance of employment with opportunity for all to exercise their natural abilities to the full; a framework for the equitable distribution of economic rewards; safeguards for individual justice; linkages of public bodies with local community through consumer representatives; elimination of inappropriate bureaucratization of universities and religious institutions; provision of requisite organization for the full employment of professional skills and talents.[4]*

To contravene the nature of bureaucratic oppression and set the conditions for the attainment of humane bureaucracy, both within its processes and in the delivery of its mission, its internal arrangements must be substantially reordered. Work, efficiency and authority must be fully redefined so as to include the most recent understandings concerning them. A way must be found to encourage, support and provide the conditions for a worker to achieve his or her own work capacity and derive meaning and self-fulfillment in such work. Equally important, and a condition precedent to this, is the necessity to redefine work to include not only the specific activity necessary to accomplish the task; this concept of work must also include doing the personal emotional and interpersonal emotional work necessary to minimize the covert drama that is a part of the traditional organization.

Human beings must be valued as human beings, *per se.* Work assignments must relate to capability and potential. The bureaucratic malaise which encourages low self-esteem must be altered fundamentally. Production and service must be disciplined by the humane. Efficiency and accountability must include humane qualitative measures, for it is *prima facie* inhumane to abandon the evaluation of human effort to quantitative measures alone, as these are often inadequate, sometimes harmful and not infrequently wrong.

Authority must be limited to a defined tenure more carefully accountable and more fully related to competence.[5] Power and power plays must give way to equality of opportunity in regard to access to status and resources. Responsibility must match accountability for the accomplishment of process and task. Task performance must be linked into networks of cooperative task groups. Problem solving groups and support groups must be established. Time must be set aside, as well, within the work day and work week and work month to do the essential process work which relates to the successful accomplishment of the task and thereby diminish or even avoid the impact of the covert processes within the group and organization. The organizations must relinquish the control and manipulation of human beings for the purpose of obtaining production and production alone. It is the persons within the organization and the persons served by the organization whose dignity must be essentially maintained, supported and enhanced.

Trust is the glue of effective, humane and efficient organizations and groups. Negative controls born of an implicit mistrust of the human being may be "well meaning" but they encourage distrust even by their existence. Control for the accomplishment of the organizational mission and accountability for the organizational process must be seated in mutuality and participation of a kind which nurtures and supports mutual trust.[6]

Transformation of the structure and processes of group, organization and bureaucracy will be exceptionally difficult because tradition, statute, established processes, and a variety of settled understandings must necessarily yield to the development of those structures and procedures which will more readily support the needs of humane organization and bureaucracy. The coordinative and specialized functions within organization with their roots in competence, skill, efficiency and production must be retained with a higher valuation placed upon competence and skill. Efficiency and production must be disciplined by new gauges which integrate humane factors into the measure. The power plays and games so characteristic of bureaucracy must be relinquished and replaced with cooperative work which is sustained by trust and respect. The power arrangements within bureaucracy and organization will therefore have to be significantly altered.

Groups and organizations must become a place where trust can exist and be encouraged. Controls seated in mistrust are an anathema and a betrayal of the human personality. Most workers at one time or another have felt their trust and confidence betrayed by a fellow worker or supervisor. The conditions obviating this must be developed within organizations if truly effective, humane and cooperative work is to be done. The causes of these conditions and their reduction and elimination must be attended. Venal, corrupt, crooked, abusive, exploitive, manipulative behavior within bureaucracy must be confronted and stopped. The occurrence of these behaviors needs to be discouraged and prevented with the utmost vigilance for these are the expressions of the darker side of the organization and they poison the wellsprings of trust required for cooperative work.

Requisite Action: Confront the Status Quo

The situation is complex and difficult. There is no easy or quick way to make the alterations required of our organizations and bureaucracies. Gordon Tullock observes that the "general good" is never readily discernable. He writes it is always difficult to distinguish "what is good for me" and "what is good." Most individuals within an organization he suggests, when confronted with a project that will advance their interest find such a project difficult to resist. Tullock observes that persons who are highly perceptive with well-defined moral perspectives generally avoid employment and participation in hierarchical systems which require the abandonment of personal moral choice. Such persons are unable to remain sufficiently dull as to be blind to the moral dilemmas posed. Therefore, such organizations so blunted that they simply close their eyes or look the other way when confronted with moral or corrupt behavior as insipient as it may be.

Tullock suggests that few people expect career civil servants to behave contrary to their own interests. This cynical orientation toward the civil servant is too broad a generalization. The overwhelming majority of public servants make every effort to carry out their work conscientiously, with dedication and with commitment. They are, on occasion, overwhelmed by the conflicts and double-binds which society and their own needs place upon them. Tullock's solution for this moral dilemma is to suggest that the appropriate rule is to never trust subordinates. Thus, he suggests, action flowing from this orientation will effectively minimize the advantage that a dishonest person has over an honest person within the organization. The underlying assumption is, of course, that some men and women within the organization are untrustworthy.

This is a proposition with which few will quarrel. The best way to counteract this, he posits, is to implement a program which spawns mistrust and suspicion of subordinates by superiors. Proceeding further, he suggests, this climate of mistrust will be allayed by a feeling of mutual confidence which will develop from the feeling that the unscrupulous cannot advance. Thus he proposes to establish a continuous monitoring system which makes it very risky and psychologically expensive to pursue success through cutting corners, lying, distorting the truth, backstabbing, and sycophancy. His goal is not to establish an authoritarian organization, but one that simply takes people as they are, or at least as he believes they are.[7]

If Tullock's organization would not be authoritarian it would certainly be a grim, joyless, loveless and suspicion-filled existence for most persons and it would be fully lacking opportunity for meaningful work, intimacy or self-fulfillment. His assumption is that each person operates wholly for his own private ends and ambitions. Such a person will do only the assigned tasks if this proves to be the most effective way of obtaining individual ends. This obscures and denies the complex nature of the human being in the work situation. Individual necessity brings people to work and is an important motivator in keeping them at work. Within the work situation, however, the message was delivered long ago by the Hawthorne Experiments which discovered once at work, psychological factors and social factors within the work setting are significant motivators and a significant aspect of the work process.[8]

Jaques in a remarkable contrast suggests that such organizations are "...paranoiagenic institutions in the sense that in place of confidence and trust they breed mistrust and weaken social bonds."[9] As such, he observes, they threaten the very fabric and survival of one's own society and more profoundly the human race.[10]

Frederick W. Taylor, in propounding the principles of scientific management, which fostered the "gospel of efficiency," had a rather narrow and restricted view of the human being who was to be used primarily for productive purposes. Each person is seen to fit into a predetermined slot for which he or she is fitted mentally and physically. No mention in his material of psychological components. He observes that the pig iron handler is "not an extraordinary man... he is merely a man more or less of the type of the ox, heavy both mentally and physically."[11] How can efficiency be humane if this was the orientation of the man who propounded the concept?

In the traditional organization production is imposed and the goals achieved through the manipulation of a variety of rewards and punishments, reinforced by promises and threats. Production within an organization which derives from creativity and variety of meanings that the individual brings to it is unknown. High self-esteem is more frequently penalized and punished than rewarded and nurtured. The dilemma of the humane organization, then derives in part because individuals give the organization power over their choices and actions. Pay, promotion and other benefits are determined by relating and conforming to organizational goals, processes and structure. The traditional organization does not effectively respond to people as human beings.

It is time to expand our horizons concerning the emergent and socially dominant role of our organizations and bureaucracies. It is important to admit they are playing an evermore distinctive and significant part in our lives. It is imperative to take more effective charge of the organization and design it so that it will more adequately and appropriately relate to human beings. The growing and emerging interdependence of bureaucratic organizations, public and private, competing for limited resources on a finite planet require the planned integration of all persons into the work force, plenty of leisure, appropriate sabbaticals, and adequate provisions for sufficient recreation and leisure for all those persons involved. In addition, skills and competence and the creative energies of the concerned individuals need to be effectively integrated into the work force. Organizations must be changed and seen not as permanent and immortal, but as temporary and ephemeral. Each must, from time to time, be dismantled without creating chaos in the employment market, society, economy or in the work force. This would diminish the pathological drive toward survival which is a concomitant implicit in all organizational processes.

Careful examination and analysis of the organizational process and mission is necessary to assure fulfillment of the humane requirement for the future. It is equally important to examine seriously and question the mission, function and process of every organization and how organizational policy and activity collude in creating the justification for its own existence. For example, education, welfare, public safety could each serve better if they understood their own part in the creation of their clients, mission, purpose and function. For to the extent that survival becomes the dominant principle, those involved in fulfilling their mission confuse the demands for organizational survival as being synonymous with mission fulfillment. Military requirements economically link nearly every large city in the United States to the military bureaucracy in the Pentagon through the military needs for manufactured supplies and technical equipment. This creates the compelling necessity to continue a high level of support for the military economy which is, in turn, seated in the maintenance of fear. Here is an example of the urge for institutional, i.e. organizational survival linked into community economic survival through maintenance of an eternally prepared vigilant military establishment which abates the continuing community fear and their activity thus becomes synonymous with mission accomplishment. These seemingly inevitable self-justifying links must be fully explored. The organizational imperative of survival blinds those ensnared by its urgency to the social consequences involved in the pursuit of such survival.[12]

The impending menaces are ecological, biological, economic and environmental. The following are only a few examples; the depletion and disappearnace of the forests of the earth, the depletion of the supply of the earth's petroleum, the disappearing supply of fish, the terrible and impending variety of threats to the human life support system on the planet, encroaching deserts, runaway human population, mounting pressures and increasingly depleted resource and energy supplies, among other things. It is important to assess the role organizations play in contributing to the emerging environmental chaos and how their internal processes preclude responsible and effective restraints upon the organizational activity contributing to such impending catastrophe. These scarcities and their emergent stresses will translate into social unrest, economic chaos and political disorder. The solutions required are global and not amenable to a military solution. The ultimate response for the solutions to these problems must come at least in part from the expertise and competence which is available within large complex organizations and bureaucracy.[13]

Great transformations are required in all levels of our global, national, social, economic and organizational life. Private and public organizations need study and analysis of their emergence to dominate the existence of all human beings on the planet today. There is an urgent need to understand their social role and function. There is a pressing need to contain the technological tyranny which is a concomitant of their existence. Political procedures and institutions must be developed to hold these organizations accountable for their role, function and impact on the ecological, biological, economic and social systems. An important first step is to confront the internal facets of bureaucractic and organizational structure, process and behavior which contribute to these impending consequences.[14]

Requisite Action: Transmute Organizational Power, Authority and Responsibility

The abuses of power which characterize the organization in modern life must be confronted. There must be no failure of nerve by those human beings willing to confront those abuses, for they will be deemed the heroes of the future. Intentional organizational change must be strategically introduced encompassing a range of possible objectives which includes the humane.[15] In more limited and modest ways, individuals who work within the middle and operational ranges of organizations must be permitted and encouraged to introduce relaxed and appropriate change where possible and in a manner where such change may be safely and humanely accomplished. The operational levels of organization requires restructuring so that punishment is minimized, even ended, and participation is encouraged so each member may take full responsibility for his or her behavior within concerned work groups and organizations.

Power, authority, responsibility and duty must be redefined and re-examined in relation to the psychological and sociological realities of hierarchy and organizational life. The power context of groups and organizations spawns conflict, competition, dependence, collusions, alliances and encourages an everchanging matrix of these activities.

The emphasis in a humane organization must be on responsibility rather than duty. Responsibility relates to a conscious, authentically experienced individual choice about one's present and future actions. Duty implies role dependency and subordination to another's control and influence. It is not a desirable condition within humane organization. Responsibility flows from and implies individual personal choice. Duty implies an obligation imposed and expected from the outside. A duty imposed in such a manner may easily fog, eliminate from view, and provide a convenient structure for escaping personal responsibility for individual action and moral choice within one's own organization. Duty implies unquestioning role dependency, i.e. obedience.

The abandonment of moral choice becomes easy when one is "one-down," dependent and has low self-esteem. One of the essential components in the humane organization is to provide circumstances where individual energy and activity flow from an inner decision as an authentic, committed activity—not derived from manipulation, control or threats. This is the essence of responsible personal choice.

Our groups and organizations, for the most part, are co-terminus with the greater part of our waking life. What is required is the introduction, maintenance and the nurturing of the humane good life within its context. Structure and process must be designed, developed, introduced, used, tested, modified, adapted, changed and altered in responsible ways so as to effectively meet the challenge and avoid the more alienating dimensions.

Requisite Action: Redesign Organizational Structure

The design or redesign of an organization must be responsive to a perceived need. To be valid, the need must exist and the structural design must be suitable to serve that need.[16] The conception of the organization must be responsive to the need. The emotional needs to be met must be recognized and referenced to tasks required. If the organizational structure is inappropriate or the need does not exist, the organization will in all likelihood fail. For example, organizations that are conceived to meet growth cannot effectively survive or succeed in a contracting, non-growth environment without effective structural and process alterations. Organizations are vulnerable to improper design, ineffective management and environmental changes. Such organizations contribute to and may succumb as well to an ailing or pathological social situation.[17] Some of the more obvious symptoms of an ailing organization may be identified as follows:

1. The inability to respond to a changing environment with effective organi-

zational change.

2. Defensive, secretive behavior designed to hide management and employee failures and weaknesses.

3. Excessive power plays and games among the managers and employees.

4. Distorted communication and defensive inter-personal transactions.

5. The loss of a sense of mission and purpose within the organization accompanied by over concern with personal survival.

6. A rigid and unresponsive stance in relationship to the clients served.

7. The dominance of the organizational decision processes and resource allocations by one of its segments.

8. Impenetrable internal boundaries accompanied by a failure of the process groups to "manage" the social and psychological aspects within key groups followed by the consequent emergence of basic assumption behavior.

9. The existence of pressure which encourage management and workers to participate in secret, dishonest and morally reprehensible behavior.

10. The absence of effective long range planning.

These symptoms point to basic underlying causes which must be diagnosed. Their recognition requires effectively designed responses. Intelligent, intentional and humane change may be designed which is ongoing in nature and which mediates the causes of these phenomena.[18]

Requisite Action: Use Creative Organizational Leadership

Organizational leadership has the power, the responsibility, the awareness and access to the knowledge required to design and provide effective organizational change. It is incumbent upon organizational leaders to recognize their responsiblity and provide the opportunities and policy leadership needed to design and implement the necessary changes. This, of course, is not an easy task. It will take courageous and enlightened leadership to create the opportunities needed to make the changes required. Thus leadership must confront the aspects of structure and process which will block and inhibit the required changes. A first step is to examine their own organizational leadership patterns.

Leadership within groups, organizations and bureaucracy seem to reflect formal hierarchy. Organizational leadership is generally responsive to and reinforcing of traditional organizational patterns. Yet leadership in organization reflects the complexity indicated in earlier chapters. Closer examination will tend to reveal that leadership is obtained or derived in our groups and organizations much as in political states. Leadership and ultimate authority under these circumstances may be obtained by selection, by accession, by preemption, or by assumption. Where leadership is by selection, it may be through an election process or through a system of committee designation, or through some pre-established process within the group or organization which is formally established and generally understood (tradition) to be a guiding system for the determination of who will exercise the leadership and authority within a group. Leadership by accession occurs in tribes, monarchies, private organizations and an occasional public agency, where the order is predetermined by a relational bond which predetermines the person designated. In an organization leadership by accession frequently occurs where long tenure in the upper echelons gives control of the process to those nearest the apex of power. Thus a vice president or executive officer, long in tenure, who has had responsibility for a large segment of the operating program may be in a position to effectively dominate accession. Leadership by preemption occurs where it is imposed, as in the case of a revolution or *coup d'etat*. Leadership by assumption is usually related to a perception of the competence or seniority where a certain person is assumed by most of the members of the organization to be the best qualified individual present.

Where there is a formal process indicating the assumption of leadership such as in a school or college classroom or laboratory, it is generally clear, assumed, understood and accepted by those involved in such a group who the leader is. Presence, age and dress are frequent, yet not always, indicators.

Within the covert levels of these groups frequently new leadership arises which challenges the formally designated leader. Where there is no clear designation of leadership process by selection, accession, preemption or by assumption, emergence and designation of a leader is fraught with danger for both the group and the person forwarding himself or herself for that position, as was noted in earlier chapters.

When power, authority and responsibility are located in a person within an hierarchical organization, a formal position is occupied and a functional task is assumed. When this is reinforced intentionally or accidentally with compatible roles within the covert structure, the person occupying this role becomes a distinctive, significant individual within the group or organizational structure. When such a convergence occurs the person occupying such a position generally has broad discretion and has accumulated great respect, even awe, within the group and organization. This is, in part, because of a history of cascading successes within the organization. Such a person has a profound impact on the organization's structure, functions and process and the related alterations and changes, and upon information assessment, personnel decisions, judgments on resource allocations and program commitments as well.[19]

Decisions in which this person is involved may enhance or threaten the spheres of actions and postitions of those close by and thus enhance or maintain continued competitive relationships within the organization. When the organization is sufficiently complex, interdependence, alliances and cohesions are also introduced into the play. Competition, interdependence, alliances are thus general characteristics of middle managers and managers occupying strategic levels of an organization as presently constituted.

These kinds of organizational phenomena must be addressed, assessed and altered if effective and humane change is to occur. Effective leadership must be put in the service of achieving humane change. Psychological leadership must be recognized, dealt with and utilized in the service of achieving healthy, humane groups and organizations. Ways of achieving these things need to be found and implemented. This is, indeed, an important and urgent task of responsible leadership and membership in modern groups and organizations.

Requisite Action: Undertaking Intentional Change

To challenge traditional group and organizational processes and alter the nature of such groups and organizations is a difficult and complex task. It requires conscious, intentional and broad ranging changes. Those affected by the change need to have the opportunity to participate in the change design.[20] Intentional individual and organizational change, as well as social change, are required. When these change processes are not operating the individual, organization, or social unit involved are reactive, defensive, and subject to the vagaries and unpredictability of events which impinge upon them and over which they have little or no influence or control. Thus the group, the organization, the individual, the social system seems buffeted by events beyond their control because there is no willingness, imagination, resources, intelligence or energy to face the changes required to sustain the survival of the organization and achieve the values and goals sought. The goal of intended change is not to seek total control, but to pursue responsible and intelligent action concerning the goals sought, that is, to achieve rather than to defend, to take charge rather than to react.

Organizational and social change are responsive to individual and collective effort. They are affected by intentional as well as random change which is introduced or impinges from sources outside the organizational or group boundaries. Intelligent responses by concerned organizational members must be readied and action taken where necessary to assure that sought-after social values which deliver the organizational change be implemented, maintained and achieved. Yet in the achievement of such change one's own essential humanity must not be lost or abandoned for either personal exigencies or higher purposes, for it is at this point that civilized action goes awry.

Requisite Action: Utilize Change Agents

Intentional change is generally accomplished through a change agent. Such a change agent could be an organizational developer, a therapist, facilitator, consultant, researcher, trainer, counselor, educator, revolutionary, agitator, manager, an angry person or a concerned person, to identify just a few. Such an individual intervenes into the processes of the status quo to alter the nature of the individual or group behavior and directs such behavior toward objectives that differ from those toward which behavior is presently directed.

Frequently, agents involved in planned social and organizational change discover a paradox in their efforts, *viz.*, these persons are interested in value-oriented change but are frequently servicing and serving organizations whose goals and values are not only not compatible with the values of the change agent, but frequently downright hostile to such values. For example, the management of an organization may simply want problems solved which will increase efficiency and raise output. Organization developers are vulnerable to this paradox.

Organizational developers questioned by Noel Tichy thought they should be striving for such goals as increased democratic participation by members involved in a system, increased individual freedom, aiding society in solving social problems and power equalization within society.[21] Organizational developers who held these values, Tichy discovered, actually were working to improve productivity within the system and thus were involved in frequently betraying the human personality because they became essentially manipulative and exploitative in their relationships to their clients. Thus organizational developers used the new "jazzy" tools of organizational development in the interest of management and at the expense of the worker's personality, trust and commitment.

If organizational development gets trapped into this by ambitious and cynical management, its future will be dismal, as will be the future of all intentional change designed to alleviate the oppressive aspects of organizational life. Tichy, in a flair of cynicism, also questioned the effectiveness of change agents who sought change through community action, systems analysis consultants, and consultants who specialized in "people change," such as those who conducted Tavistock group relations events, behavior modification consultants and job enrichment consultants.[22] There is, however, considerable in each of these approaches that is outstanding and commendable. They have frequently produced excellent results. There is much to be learned and discovered in this emerging field.[23] Change agentry is by no means a fully developed profession but derives from many sources, utilizing many different skills, involving persons of vastly different education, training and experience.

The change agent relationship established in a direct and conscious way within an organization involves a series of progressive steps ranging from diagnosis to resolution of the problem The change agent first diagnoses the problem or problems. Second, the change agent assesses the motivation and capacity for the achievement of change. Third, the change agent needs to be aware of his or her own motivation and the resources available for the accomplishment of the change design. Fourth, a program designating progressive change objectives needs to be selected and negotiated with those involved with the change. Fifth, the appropriate effective role for the change agent needs to be clarified. Sixth, the change, once it has been implemented, needs to be maintained. Seventh, feedback and accountability need to be continuous throughout the change process to determine whether the goal sought is being achieved. Finally, effective termination of the helping relationships needs to be designed and achieved.[24]

Personal and organizational problem solving and change processes must be designed and implemented with full participation of those who will be involved and affected. The nature of power, authority, responsibility, duty, and influence within the system, as well as the variety of communication channels need to be identified and described. Problem solving processes which involve the individual and groups within the organization need to assess the aggressive and defensive behavior against personal social and psychic injury which have occurred in the history of the old power plays and their residues within the organization. Old conflicts and their aftermaths need to be charted, confronted and resolved or abated, for any intentional change can be undermined by failure to assess the impact and operation of old wounds. In addition, group boundary maintenance needs require identification and analysis if intentional change is to be effectively introduced.

Once this is accomplished the change agent can design strategies and tactics related to the overall plan of implementing the specific intentional change sought. The change agent must consider what role to perform or what combination of roles would be effective. He or she also needs, or the team involved needs, to assess how effective recruitment and involvement of those on whom the change is going to impact can be achieved. These may be attained through direct consultation or through non-directed consultation, or through the establishment of an intentionally designed network of problem solving groups which are facilitated by trained, prepared and skilled persons and effective change generated from within these groups.

The initiation of group problem solving skills, support group development, and maintenance and cooperative work procedures must proceed initially with the first introduction of change. This includes, minimally, the participation of those involved in the change early in the planning procedure for the design and achievement of such change. The utilization of problem solving and support groups avoids the onerous characteristics and manipulation, "one-up" power plays and secret maneuvers which occasionally betray the introduction of change in organizations and groups.

The change agent is a facilitator, a trainer, who develops and encourages the training or learning experience as an aid to client change. A change agent role in a group or organization may move from a continuum where the change agent may be an advocate persuading a client to accomplish a specific or a particular kind of objective to that of an expert consultant giving advice to a client. Ethically, a change agent may not impose change upon those who are not amenable or accepting of it. Therefore, he or she needs to address the problem carefully and thoroughly. The barriers to change and how these relate to the integrity of the human personality need to be carefully thought through. A change agent may enter the organization as a person who collaborates, identifies alternatives and joins in the problem solving and support processes themselves. A change agent may be as well, a consultant who is a specialist in the introduction of the problem solving processes into the organizational procedures.

The change agent needs effective interpersonal skills requiring a sense of personal integrity, security and sensitivity to the overt and covert processes which operate in any situation involving numbers of people. The change agent needs an independence and autonomy in judgment and the ability to abstract, even a facility, in developing models which may articulate both the nature of the present process and the change process which is sought.

The change agent needs to be adaptable and flexible as well as responsive and responsible. He or she must be able to absorb a high degree of ambiguity and have a capacity to analyze and synthesize the situations about where there is concern. The change agent must be ready to aid in resolving and responding to organizational crisis which may have been spawned by introduction of such change and to help guide such crisis to satisfactory resolution.

The change agent must be ready to respond to each phase of a crisis process. Traditional relationships under such crisis may be shattered and fragmented. Problem solving and support processes must be effectively related and responsive to this. Established patterns of group relationships may become disjointed and disconnected. Communication may be random and old leadership ineffective, even paralyzed. Problem solving in the traditional way may be non-existent and the organizational structure chaotic. Effective responses to these situations through the introduction of new problem solving and support networks will need attention. Goal orientation may be non-existent. Personal disorientation may result. Organizational roles which undermine change need modification. Many persons frequently prefer the "fetters of their chains" rather than deal with anxieties attending to the unknown future which comes with the first burst of freedom and change. Safe and effective responses to these possibilities are required.

In the initial disorientations and reactions which occur in interpersonal relations, healing and protective cohesions will emerge. The drama of covert group process will unfold and effective responses must be readied. These responses must emerge to be effective from within the organization itself, for when they are imposed from without they will simply sow the seeds for future discontent and nurture the undermining of the change process. An awareness of personal alienation may well emerge and effective support group responses can alleviate disoriented behavior on those occasions.

Effective and authentic communication must be maintained. Routine and ritualized communication identified and exposed as ineffective. Management under these stresses must be careful, for the temptation to recede into authoritarian, autocratic behavior and old problem solving and control rituals is immense. Occasionally, participants hang on most tenaciously to the traditional structure.[25]

Careful forethought, intelligent planning, effective group process analysis, and effective guidance and consultation can lead to new alliances, supportive communications, new searches and the emergence of effective personal problem and support networks. All those involved in the change process need to participate in some useful way in the planning, implementation and assessment of such processes. Mutual exploration of the problems which emerge need to be encouraged and the new problem solving processes, support processes, task and cooperative work processes designed, utilized and encouraged. All those involved need to participate in synthesizing and designing the diverse strategies and tactics necessary to achieve the goals sought in the change. Finally, new interdependence, new procedures of coordination and cooperation among groups need to be developed and applied.[26]

The change agent is a guide along the way, yet the change agent can stumble anywhere along the pathway for a whole variety of reasons. Particular parts of the change situation and people within the change situation may get locked into any one of a number of particular reactions and stay on that plateau unless challenged and confronted. There is a tendency to stay in what feels to be the safest place, although in the long run it is dysfunctional to organizational survival and without contribution to the task or goal of the organization.

Schism, revolution, organizational "guerrilla" warfare and power plays are continually present and effective responses must be readied, not from the standpoint of controlling the process, but letting the process unfold and responding in ways in which responsibility for the action is accepted by those persons involved in that process *per se*. Imposed controlled change, in contrast with planned participative change betrays the human personality, sows the seed for future discontent, and undermines the goals for which the change is sought. The ultimate purpose of the change process here suggested is to seek and establish cooperative, open, task-oriented, caring and joyful work groups.

Requisite Action: Establish an Ethic of Intentional Change

Intentional intervention is a direct attempt to alter thinking, behavior and attitude. Its purpose is to confront and thereby encourage the reexamination of previously controlling value nets as well as the roots of their justifaction and validation. Planned intentional change has important ethical implications which need to be thoroughly considered. Moral and ethical standards are involved as is the problem of individual and social responsibility, all of which must be forged into a constructive process for future accomplishment.

The responsibility of establishing and maintaining an environment suitable for honesty in relationships and the opportunity to make and sustain moral and ethical choices rests heavily on the participants in the process itself, as well as the institutional structure which overlays the particular situation concerned. The new values sought need to serve both individuals and organizational effectiveness. Efficiency is a requirement, yet it must be moderated and leavened by humane values. Such a process is fraught with risks.

Each society to survive must alter and change and within each society are forces which resist such change. Alteration and change and resistance to alteration and change are always present. James Bugental suggests that when a society is affluent the forces which resist change, i.e. the conservative forces, tend to be disproportionately strong and when this occurs there is a danger that the society cannot be responsive to changes essential to its alteration and survival and that needed changes will be stifled. When this situation occurs the conditions of random social violence which fuse into revolution become more likely.

Under these conditions of oppression which precede social chaos, Bugental suggests that the matters of professional discretion, professional judgment and confidentiality become points of conflict, challenge and hurt. He calls for an involved humanistic ethic as required to make a contribution to the evolutionary scheme of human development. Such a contribution requires the courage, the dedication, and the persistence of those who have an awareness of this pitfall.[27] The essence of this ethic is precisely that individual skills must be wed to human feelings before the creative energy and spirit of a person can unfold.

Modern technological bureaucracy can no longer cut away, manipulate and dominate a part of the energy of the whole human being and assign the rest to limbo. We must be whole, powerful human beings, all of the time. Complex organizations and bureaucratic institutions must not be allowed to transcend and dominate humanity. The subservient human being, devoid of feelings, cowed in the face of survival needs, obsequious in relationship to superiors for purposes of promotion and reward must be seen as a violation of the human personality and provisions within the bureaucracy developed where these conditions can be confronted and abated.[28] The organizational environment must be reconditioned and revisioned wherein human spirit and capability can emerge.[29] This can be done by alleviating the necessity for sustained and continuing, even permanent, organizations and linking the essence of what is needed in society to the policy, program and tasks required to accomplish such purposes. Thus the logic of institutional survival could well be reduced, even eliminated, as the focus of cooperative work and coordinated effort is accomplished, *viz.*, the satisfaction of the mission or task which is sought by the implementation of the program efforts impacting into the environment where the change or service is sought and occurs.

Requisite Action: Create Conditons for the Emergence of the Full Capability of Each Person in the Organization

The propensity to empower organizations making them larger than life, superior to human beings and somehow immortal "persons" must be confronted and the implications and consequences seriously examined. The focus of human energy needs to be on the accomplishment of the tasks, the achievement of the goals and values sought through the policy process and program implementation. Each person needs to be linked into the labor force in a way that seeks to utilize and encourage the development of his or her competence and his or her whole personality.[30] Each person must take full responsibility for his or her own personal process.

When the reason for the existence of a program no longer exists a person, rather than suffering loss of income, needs to have available other tasks and opportunities which will utilize his competence. Where the tasks required are ongoing, timeframes need to be established so that no person gets a lifetime tenure on a particular administrative position. In places such as universities where the integrity of the process requires the underpinning of that process with the tenure system, rank and position dealing with substantive competence can be and must be tenured.

The performance of an administrative or institutional task needs to have a timeframe designed which has a time certain ending in the future where the occupant of that position will return to his or her substantive professional craft or occupational task. This maintains the focus of such an organization on its primary mission and diffuses the accumulation of power, the struggles for power and the urge to autocracy which so characterizes the traditional organization and bureaucracy.

Safe places must be developed and sustained where small, ongoing, face-to-face groups can exist and provide an environment in which individuals can be vulnerable and where individual problem solving can be done. For it is in these places where the restoration of individual power and the resources are nurtured to confront the abusive power plays characteristic of groups, organizations and bureaucracy. This is the place where individual competence can be nurtured, supported, permitted and encouraged. It isparadoxical, but accurate, to observe that to be an autonomous and effective person there must be safe places to explore one's own fears, one's own vulnerability, one's own weaknesses so that they do not remain hidden from view but are rather confronted and explored in safe ways. Effective problem solving and personal renewal may be encouraged in such groups.

Groups and organizations must be seen to be and must be a place where the full possession and access to the characteristics of human wholeness and full individual capability can be available for each person within it. Punishment must give way to problem solving and effective behavioral change. Rewards must give way to genuine authentic care and affirmation of the human personality. Promotion, retention and tenure procedures must be responsive to the whole human including personal competence. Institutional evaluations more often than not have little to do with competence and may even interfere with effective performance.

The symptoms of organizational pathology require effective responses but without attention to causality, such response is inadequate. It is essential to go to the root causes which, in part, stem from a betrayal of the human personality so characteristic of large organizations and bureaucracy. Equality of opportunity must exist and the inequality of competence must be recognized and pathologies inherent in status differences, financial differences and authority differentiation must be moderated.

Requisite Action: Avoid Human Betrayal

The introduction of change which does not attend to the private structure will not succeed. Likewise, the effort to dominate and control the totality of the private structure will ultimately debilitate and betray their human membership. The key problem, then, is that management seeks to control and to dominate human beings for purposes of production and efficiency. Yet such control and such dominance frequently become a manipulative betrayal of the human personality and is fraught with difficult consequences. Who controls and who is in control becomes an essential problem. It is this central focus around which much of the power, activity and energy is expended within the organization.

A humane organizational environment will provide the elements for each person to become responsible, whole, in-charge human beings in their task environment. Where there is no premium placed on this, the ambience moves toward the inhumane, mindless, power-oriented, fragmented and alienated condition. Duty is substituted for responsibility. Controls, rewards and punishments are implemented to secure the human energy and human effort required. The ultimate prognosis for this latter is chaos, stultification, paralysis, and ultimate disintegration and collapse. Certainly, the social costs are high whether the organization drags on or dies in a spectacular collapse.

The imposition of controls, rewards and punishments moves in the direction of stultifying, authoritarian organization. Relinquishing such controls, on the other hand, may invite the basic assumption behavior identified by Wilfred Bion explored in earlier chapters. Both of these may be avoided by the implementation of cooperative work groups supported by problem solving and support groups.

In the traditional organization, productivity is obtained by: 1) authoritarian imposition, demands and controls with punishment, i.e. force and threats as the primary motivating factor, 2) productivity can be obtained through the manipulation and persuasion of the participants in the work force. This frequently is seen as "democratic" management, 3) productivity is often sought through a system of alliances and competitive struggles. This is sometimes identified as *laissez faire* management. The fallout in interpersonal relations from this manner of obtaining production generally is a continuation of the oppressive retaliatory process which is characteristic of the operation of the drama triangle. Finally, 4) productivity can be achieved through cooperative work effort derived and designed consensually. Such an effort is sustained by a network of problem solving groups related a) to personal work and b) to cooperative task work explored in the previous chapter.[31]

The psychological dimensions of the work environment supporting each of these avenues to productivity are as follows: 1) Where productivity is a result of authoritarian imposition, fear is the concomitant, penalty is the motivator, and dependency characterized by supervisional dominance and worker submission is the outfall. 2) Where productivity is obtained through democratic management, the psychological environment involves pure approbation and disapprobation, maintained by rejection and manipulative stroking. The outfall from this is competition, conflict and power struggles. 3) Where productivity is *laissez faire* and competitive, spawning systems of alliances, the psychological dimension is the personal urges to success and the fears of personal failure. The sanctions imposed involve the loss of status and reduced financial reward. The outfall is conflict, power struggles and isolation. 4) Where productivity is sought through cooperative consensual arrangement, the psychological dimension is generally one of caring and nurturing with a clearing of hard feelings where each person takes ownership for his or her own processes and provides warm support and straight talk in the environment. The outfall from this generally is a productive, cooperative self-sustaining, cohesive work group.

In the Meanwhile, What is There to Do?

The changes suggested here require a significant metamorphosis within groups and organizations. There are useful and important measures which can be taken immediately in any work situation.

Rosabeth Moss Kanter offers well-developed and thoughtful approaches to achieving a more humane work setting. Her suggestions are modest and promise a harvest of well being for worker and organization far beyond their cost to implement. She suggests job redesigning, increasing and enhancing job opportunities and job mobility, development of new jobs, job rotation, temporary projects, empowering strategies, organizational decentralization and development of more autonomous work units, increasing work discretion, task force and team development and broad use of role models, sponsors and allies.

Personal Measures to be Taken

What are some important personal measures which may be take in the interim?

This is a serious and important question for the worker and for the supervisor. Effectiveness and survival for each is achieved through production and control respectively. This may be best answered as follows:

1. Use the information presented here to take care of yourselves better and more competently within your work situation.

2. Adapt what you can to your work situation and experiment utilizing what works for you by modifying it to suit your needs within the limitations imposed.

3. Become a member of an on-going problem solving and support group so as to aid yourself in making effective and successful changes.

4. Be alert to games, power plays, covert roles and other covert processes which may undermine your effectiveness and betray your integrity.

5. Change incrementally as such change is successful and accepted.

6. Modify your own situation and behavior as you increase your own awareness, understanding, and competence but do it in a way which maintains and increases your personal effectiveness, i.e. use what works for you.

These actions have been tried and tested through personal experience. The actions require courage and risk which sometimes will involve some losses yet will yield positive results far more frequently. Yet they are essential steps to even begin to alter the ominous course of the organizational society in these times.

Counter Your Own Alienation

Still another step is to avoid getting caught in the alienating net of the ogranizational process. Perhaps the best set of rules for staying clear of the power games and interrupting them as they apply to oneself could be the application of the following guidelines:

1. **Refuse to "rise to the bait."** It is at this point of provocation, subtle or direct, a person for his or own reasons gets "hooked" into a power game because of each one's own distinctive vulnerability, blindness to one's own anger or they are functioning from a place of low self-esteem. A person tends, therefore, to be defensive or angry and the drama gets underway.

2. **Stop playing counterfeit roles.** When encounters and transactions are authentic and come from a position where each values the competence and personality of the other, the urge to be one-up or one-down for "safety sake" no longer need be a safe haven.

3. **Stop discounting oneself and others.** Frequently, in the conversations and transactions that occur among persons who are part of every group are the sarcastic bantering, cynical and discounting exchanges often used in the guise of humor, sometimes with deliberate anger, and frequently delivered under the guise of advice, suggestion or a personnel evaluation. This simply lowers self-esteem and invites abuse and retaliation.

4. **Give authentic positive strokes.** Give authentic and positive strokes when they are genuinely felt. Reject those strokes which are given in an effort to manipulate your energy and are therefore deceitful and unauthentic. To do otherwise betrays the human personality and is a setup for backbiting and retaliation.

5. **Invest your time and energy in cooperative work**. Invest your energy and your time in tasks which are meaningful to you and in transactions which are cooperative and intimate. When this is done your energy and personal efforts move in constructive and positive channels. Time-structuring thus becomes positive rather than negative in result within the group.

6. **No power plays. No secrets**. This means being aware of when the rescue or drama triangle is functioning, how you got on it, and to stop at once and get off of it. It means, too, to be aware of when you are using secrecy and one-up and one-down strategies and tactics and immediately stop and get off this organizational carousel.

7. **Straight talk**. Straight talk must be given from a non-manipulative, authentic and emotionally honest place. But it must be given with respect to the personality involved in the transaction. This can be done if it is a matter of delivering anger or feedback by asking permission of the person to whom it is given and thus respecting the integrity of the personality with whom you are speaking. This encourages authentic straightforward relationships which are a valuable and significant component of a cooperative work group.

8. **Join a support group**. Establish or join a support and problem solving group. Personal, group and organizational change is more easily facilitated and achieved when those involved are able to work through the stresses and problems in a shared manner which reinforces and supports those involved.

There must emerge within our groups and organizations the values and payoffs related to these values that encourage strength, restraint, and courage, together with hope, will, purpose, and competence. These, combining with care and a love of knowledge and wisdom, must be a central focus within our group and organizational processes. Relationships within our groups and organizations must be rooted in economic fairness. Social dignity must be available; self-esteem must be nurtured, and the cycle of psychological vengeance abated. All too frequently vast economic inequality, social indignity, low self-esteem, and recurring cycles of psychological vengeance characterize group and organizational transactions. The concern with production and efficiency must be leavened by humane values.[32]

Enhance Your Own Effectiveness. The individual occupying a position in the strategic, middle range or operational level of an organization has the distinctive problem not only of surviving but of also being effective. If one is interested, as well, in forging conditions for the achievement of things humane within these areas of organization, that he or she can effect, the formula is as follows: competence + intuition + resourcefulness = personal effectiveness. This formula, when put into action, requires the confrontation, encouragement and support tempered by the quality of contact and feedback available in a problem solving group.

Competence. Competence is (1) the accumulation and use of skills, knowledge and understanding necessary to effectively complete a task, and (2) the knowledge and understanding of one's own emotional life so as to be fully in charge of one's own transactions. Thus an individual can be fully competent in terms of skills, knowledge and self-understanding. Competence in both of these areas is an essential to becoming an effective person. It is gained through meaningful education which attends to both the intellectual accumulation of information and the physical application of the skills required, together with effective experience and appropriate personal psychological work. This may be individual therapy, participation in a variety of growth and awareness experiences, participation in organization and development activities, membership in an ongoing individual problem solving group, and effective participation in an ongoing cooperative work group focused on performing tasks essential to the oranizational mission.

+ **Intuition.** Personal effectiveness within a group or organization may be enhanced by developing the skill to listen to and trust one's own intuition. This will foster increased awareness concerning the transactions which engage the group. The covert forces within groups can be confronted and handled in creative and constructive ways by linking intuition in a cooperative work process to the demystification of group structure and process. The procedure for accomplishing this rests partially on reclaiming one's emotional processes through appropriate personal psychological work. This will differ from individual to individual, yet it cannot be accomplished alone nor is it once accomplished always maintained. It requires continuous effort.

+ **Resourcefulness.** Resourcefulness is using personal competence and intuition in a way that utilizes personal power and enhances access to the resources available to you in the organization. Resourcefulness is utilizing the full range of your own personal power and tapping the organizational resources open to you to accomplish that which you choose to do. This is accomplished and gained through, (1) raising the levels of your own intellectual and conceptual horizons, (2) increasing your analytical ability, both as a participant in a face-to-face work group and in the broader, complex organization, and finally (3) understanding your own feelings enough that you take care of yourself well within the organization. This means you "talk straight," and be honest in your interpersonal transactions. It means you understand and take responsibility for how you deliver your emotions within the group and organizational process. You do not always need to call what you see, you do not always have to act out on a feeling, you do not always have to respond at once to a situation. Rather you assess each situation that you face, utilize your competence and skills and avail yourself of your knowledge and understanding that in your judgment takes care of you best.

Equals (=) Personal Effectiveness. Being competent, using one's own intuition, and being resourceful enables one to enhance one's own personal effectiveness both inside and outside the organization. Organizations themselves are ongoing dramas of human interaction. Traditional organization linkages are the stuff of banal and hamartic group processes. Alienating and paranoiagenic processes will continue in the absence of a metamorphosis to a more cooperative work environment. Confrontation may bring organizational crisis. Such crisis may have to precede effective change if the alienating, paranoiagenic group processes are to be interrupted. If this is done carefully and authentically, a productive, efficient, cooperative and responsible organizational and group effort becomes possible. Awareness with contact and support can lead to important personal change. Managers as well as workers are more effective and alert to desirable alternatives when they have available broader philosophical and conceptual perspectives. This effectiveness is considerably enhanced if it is accomplished by an increasingly developed awareness of psychological processes within groups and organizations which are both functional and dysfunctional to the accomplishment of personal and organizational goals. Personal effectiveness of worker or manager is enhanced where each knows his or her own vulnerabilities and then associating someone with him or her to fill in and be supportive of those areas wherein the vulnerability and the deficiencies lie.

The mystification concerning personal participation in groups needs to be fully explored and understood. Some individuals pretend that their own personal needs do not exist and they live to serve the group or the organization, so they "just co-operate" with what is required and seek to please those most immediately in control. This works very poorly in practice and exacts a high personal cost to those who practice such denial.

Some workers establish their own personal, private interests and seldom relinquish them. When this occurs, the individual cannot work effectively in a cooperative group, for one must give up some of one's own personal proclivities to establish a sense of belonging to the group. The difficulty is determining the point at which personal integrity fades away and dependency begins. This is probably a point that is distinct and unique for each individual. The group needs to be informed and to understand the process each person goes through as he or she struggles to become a part of the group.

Within a banal work group some members operate from positions of powerlessness, i.e., surrender or abdication. Other members operate to aggrandize personal power, i.e. control. The goal in a cooperative work situation is to relinquish enough of one's own personal proclivities so as to cooperate and achieve a sense of belonging to the group. Essentially this means to contribute one's own competence to the processes of the group, maintain one's own personal integrity, and be accepted as a full participating member within the group.

It is at this critical point of personal choice when an individual can act out of a sense of his or her own integrity or surrender personal power and become dependent upon the group. When this latter occurs, the group may take on the characteristics of a "cult." This critical point is distinct from Berne's operative principle where a personal decision is made about the judgment that the leader has of the individual member.[33] When such a judgment is made either consciously or unconsciously the concerned member engages in the "play" of his or her "games." This latter involves and sustains the drama of a banal group. The former is the critical point in the development of and transition to a cooperative group.

It is at the critical point where the concerned member is confronted in some manner and both the member and the group must deal with the situation as it unfolds. The group member must make a decision at some level and in that decision flow the payoffs involved in either staying or leaving must be assessed. The group decision concerning itself and the member concerned parallels the personal decision. It is a critical point for the member in that he or she decides at some level to remain or to leave and to "pay the price" of either choice. It is critical to the group because the survival of the group is always threatened by such an event and such an event, therefore, must be successfully processed if the group is to remain viable. This point is always overlaid with an equation of power which is explicitly or tacitly understood. This is fundamentally a moral choice.

It becomes useful in a problem solving or cooperative task group occasionally to go around the group and have each one identify what it is that he or she is giving up and what it is that he or she sees as gaining as an advantage or "payoff" from the group. This process tends to identify what is being given up to become a member of the group and enhances the sense of group commitment, one with another. If this is negotiated successfully the group can move ultimately to a cohesive, cooperative work group in which there is a profound sense of belonging, reward, and involved participation for all the members.

Interim Steps to Take in the Transitional Organization

The ideas, concepts and methods presented here are not intended to be an exclusive pathway to achieving humane groups, organizations and bureaucracies—it only charts some of the topography which must be more fully explored and developed. There are emerging indications that the ideas and concepts presented here are desirable, attainable and amenable to implementation within groups and organizations. These changes proceed along three pathways: 1) structural changes within the organization including the links to the external environment; 2) behavioral changes involving the members of the organization; 3) charter and canon changes derived from the political sector which relate to, among other things, policy design, program implementation and accountability.

Structural Changes. This involves experimentation with organizational design and the development of new program foci. Among these would be included such things as the use of alternate organizational structures, problem-solving and support groups, expansion and integration of organizational development with its immense power to contribute to the full release of human capability within group and organizations into an ethical context of humane bureaucracy so it may be utilized in the service of the human being as a primary goal.[34]

Not only within organizations must attention be given to establishment of alternate structures designed to achieve the humane, but in the delivery of service, that nexus between the public served and those delivering such service must reflect the humane as well. Modern organization frequently fails to link successfully with portions of its clientele because of divergent values, norms and expectations concerning the mission. Here, too, participation can be an opening wedge. The effective humane linkage of clients served with organizational processes is essential. Such linkages may include participatory involvement of the human being affected in the design and operation of those organizational impacts which affect them. This is the thrust of the study by Theodore Thomas who examined participatory innovations in organizational process.[35]

Process Changes. These would involve special orientations, training programs, special events and workshops focused upon achieving the changes desired. These would include, among other things, ulilizing the present advances in participatory involvement of employees in the work process to broaden and include the emerging developments in cooperative work, the development of workshops, short course, special programs, media' presentations, trainers and consultants who will develop the knowledge and skills necessary to introduce and forward these efforts in the interested groups, organizations and bureaucracies and enhanced, effective and broad research into organizational and bureaucratic oppression, power systems and power plays, group and organizational private structure and process, intentional change and cooperative work.

Charter and Canon Changes. Statutory changes are frequently required to create the possibility for the above to be achieved. For example, the practice of workers assuming evermore significant roles in planning and decision making on their jobs is increasing rapidly throughout the industrial world. This is being accomplished through legislation, voluntary conversions, negotiated agreements and through bargaining contracts. In several European countries far reaching legislation has been already enacted which provides significant amount of authority to workers over their jobs and conditions of work.[36]

Change the Relation between Work and Income. It is important to emphasize that bureaucracy and complex organizations are not necessarily synonymous with inhumane structures even though that is more frequently the case than not.[37] Rather, it is important to recognize that organizations and bureaucracies can be and sometimes are inhumane, and sometimes they are not. Adam Tom Kohler is one among a few pioneers who are concerned with introducing humane structures and processes into currently ongoing organizations and bureaucracy. He suggests that humane means essentially that the work which one does in an organization must be emotionally satisfying, and not exploitive of the human personality. To this may be added Rosabeth Kanter's notion that it must also provide enhancing opportunities for each employee.[38] Kohler suggests that the organizational structure must be appropriate to the task and the emotional needs to be met must be referenced to the task. Specifically, there must be a recognition of the emotional and competence needs of the worker and these must be incorporated into the organizational and task design. Kohler is attempting to introduce concepts such as these into the design and operations of the organization and develop effective empirical methods for their evaluation as well.[39]

Allyn Morrow and Fredrick Thayer suggest in cogent and direct terms that nothing of significance can be obtained, i.e. the development of a productive and humane work setting cannot occur until "work" however defined is totally separate from "income." They suggest this separation cannot be delayed much longer and it must be global in scope. They note that the separation of work from income would remove any justification for differnatials in income based upon the quality and quantity of work performed and also that this would remove the distinctions between superiors (those who earn more) and subordinates (those who earn less).[40] Elliot Jaques suggests there is a right to equitable differential rewards and these need to be established within a system of abundant employment if social unrest is to be avoided.[41]

The problem of developing a humane work setting within the organization is receiving important current attention. Such a change cannot be brought except through the hard work of altering what is by experimenting with new structures and processes in bold and risk-taking ways. The fear of something new and the fear of failure need not and must not paralyze urgently needed action.

Stephen Blumberg suggests that within an organization there is an inverse relationship between organizational responsiveness and perceived threat, i.e., the more members within organizations perceive or experience threat the less participation will be encouraged. The more members within an organization sense they are secure, the more responsive the organization will be to participation. Individuals and organizations, Blumberg suggests, will be open, cooperative, responsive, trustful, so long as it is perceived that doing so will not be harmful to the person or organization concerned or that the person or organization will not fail in some way. This fear of failure spawns a hesitance to take needed and appropriate action when needed. It is a most difficult hurdle in the pathway to humane organization.[42]

The measures put forth here are proposals for those managers and members of the modern organization who wish to pursue some application and implementation of humane bureaucracy. There is a pressing need to advance efforts such as these if the harvest of paranoia, alienation, enmity, and the social outflows from these and other bureaucratic pathologies are to be leavened, even avoided, within the next several decades.

These are only a few of the changes which have been and can be introduced as interim measures. They contribute immensely to an emerging humane work environment. If fundamental change cannot be wrought at once, organizational reform offers a viable prospect immediately for millions of workers to fundamentally alter their working situation in a manner which has important positive advantages for both worker and organization. These changes must be rooted in full understanding of the nature of cooperative group work or the results will be fruitless. They are addressed to the maintenance of hope, which is so essential to spur creative human efforts.

People "stuck" in dead-end jobs, without opportunity, find their aspirations depressed, their commitment waning, their sense of powerlessness and frustrations growing and despair emerging, all at considerable cost to themselves and to the organization. The costs to the organization in effectiveness and productivity is considerable, let alone the added costs in loss of talent, creativity and a harvest of bitterness. Work needs to be fulfilling, energizing and enlivening. It need not be and ought not to be a source of restraint, dependency and despair. Many of these proposals can be implemented with relative ease and speed in most organizations. Yet they are interim measures and alone insufficient to fully rectify the human condition within organizations.

The Quintessential Requisite: Develop Constitutional Responsibility and Accountability for Complex Organizations, Public and Private

The historic human problem in relation to power is how to avoid its abuse while gaining advantage from its use. Powerful organizations, vast and complex, public and private, invade and dominate human existence. These organizations are in various states of oppression, disarray, disorganization, and entropy. Elliot Jaques suggests that conditions within these organizations too frequently breed suspicion and mistrust which undermines collaborative work. When this occurs, he suggests, primitive irrational and pathological anxiety and dread enter into and distort the judgments men make. This enormously increases the difficulty of achieving that degree of mutual confidence necessary to make effective and accurate assessments and decisions.[43]

He suggests that a constitutional change is required which both sanctions and legitimates authority and harnesses bureaucratic power, *viz.*, through, among other things, participation in very distinctive ways.[44] Jaques identifies the conditions necessary for the achievement of constitutional bureaucracy and suggests such constitutional bureaucracy requires the opportunity for participation in policy development and change efforts by those affected through a very specific and empirically validated process. Constitutional bureaucracy can thus be achieved through establishing requisite institutions which locate responsiblity, accountability and authority within "sound structures" and through the "induction of confidence in working relationships."[45]

Constitutional bureaucracy establishes a framework of responsibility and accountability through which policy can be developed through an orderly decision process responsive to effective participation by all those affected by the organizational policy process. Constitutional bureaucracy must provide a structure (1) within which productive work may be performed effectively and (2) wherein confidence and trust within organizational processes enhance access to personal capability and growth.[46]

Managers must be effectively accountable for their decisions and for the accomplishment of results. This can be achieved, among other things, by providing the manager with the authority to de-select subordinates on whom he or she is dependent for the accomplishment of his/her responsibilities.[47] This manager-subordinate relationship must be sustained in openness and without secrets and is an essential to requisite organizations. Jaques supports this by developing four basic employee rights in an industrialized democracy:[48]

1. *The right to abundant employment and individual opportunity;*
2. *The right to participation in the control of changes in policy in the employing organization;*
3. *The right to equitable reward;*
4. *The right to individual appeal against decisions which are felt to be unfair or unjust.*[49]

Abundant employment must be sustained, Jaques observes, among other things, because community bonds will not somehow strengthen if human dignity and self-esteem are destroyed due to the constant risk involved in the economic underpinning of the community and socio-economic livelihood cannot be assured.[50] The right to participation in control of change rests in the development of requisite structures which assure the effective participation of the employee in the development and control of policy making. Policy may be contained within explicitly defined frameworks which can readily be the subject of negotiation between a manager and an employing association and elected representatives acting on behalf of the employees and to which the representatives are responsible. The decisions in such an organization are to be reached consensually. This leaves executive decisions, which have target completion times within their context the exclusive jurisdiction of management. Such decisions are precluded from negotiation. Thus managerial accountability remains intact.[51]

The right to equitable reward is currently settled by collective bargaining procedures which are coercive, generate anger, discontent and are as such anachronistic. They lead generally to dissensual conflict within the system. There is a need for an institution whereby employee representatives can accept or modify normative adjustments between felt-fair pay and time-span measurement defining the nature of specific work functions. The prime issue is the development of constitutionally requisite methods for achieving social justice in regards to wage payments rather than the varieties of social coercion and duplicity currently utilized.[52]

The right to individual appeal against decisions felt to be unfair or unjust are essential. Effective managerial power is sanctioned power. It must be authorized and must be exercised within requisite limits. Power exercised without the opportunity for appeal against its use is *prima facie* unjust, autocratic and coercive.[53] A humanitarian society is created and sustained through humane social institutions.[54] It is thus imperative to attend to the development of constitutional structures and processes to achieve requisitely humane institutions.

James D. Carroll suggests that authority and hierarchy together with the willingness and capacity of individuals to function in cooperative systems needs to be addressed and reconstructed through open political processes of inquiry and search.[55] Guy Benveniste, in order to achieve such goals, suggests the establishment of a "New System," which would create institutions charged with: 1) the protection of individual careers including evaluation; 2) the protection of organizations; and 3) the protection of clients and the general public. Each of these would be accomplished by creating separate new institutions charged with fulfilling such responsibilities. Jaques' options are more fully developed and empirically seated. Benveniste recognizes the utopian nature of his suggestions and puts them forward as only heuristic.[56]

These broad yet essential changes would have to be designed and achieved within the political system. These suggestions could well be a starting point for considering constitutional redesign. Such a redesign would have to consider organizational role and function in determining public policy and develop accountability procedures within organizations as well as regarding the interface of the organization with its political setting.

Creating a constitutional setting for organizations recognizes their importance and role within the power and policy processes of the political system. Responsibility and accountability could be achieved through appropriate procedural and institutional innovation. The open society so threatened by the modern ogranization can thereby be sustained while organizations are metamorphosed into humane constructive components of the modern industrial world. This is the ultimate challenge if human dignity and community are to be achieved and sustained.

SUMMARY

The challenge to the modern technological society is to create effective, efficient, productive, humane organizations. Such organizations must be effective in the sense that they must survive and accomplish their mission utilizing the values that the social system sustaining them requires. They must be productive in that the output task be accomplished swiftly and efficiently. Such efficiency and production must be disciplined by humane considerations. Humane considerations mean simply accounting for human feelings, creativity and competence within the organization and at the nexus between the organization and its client sector. Thus in setting the conditions for achieving humane organization, it is important that the change program and organizational policy be responsive primarily to the causes while not at the same time ignoring the symptoms of alienation.

Attention must be given to providing a new birth of dignity within groups and organizations and their bureaucratic setting. The metamorphosed organizational environment must nurture human autonomy, human creativity and human expression and provide the safety for all involved when dealing with feelings to be both vulnerable and authentically powerful within the organizational setting. The conditions to achieve cooperative work and authentic human contact must be created. A most promising avenue seems to be the evolution of small face-to-face work groups supported by a network of problem-solving groups. Competition, scarcity and power plays must be contained, diminished and even eliminated. Venality, penury, corruption and degradation must be appropriately abated for these cannot be tolerated in the humane organization. Constitutional responsibility for modern organization is an urgent need.

What is suggested here is simply an agenda for achieving humane organization. Nothing less than such an achievement is worthy of humankind, for the alternative is the continued alienation, degradation, manipulation, and betrayal of the human spirit. Indeed, this is the only avenue through which the awesomeness and alienation spawned by technology can be disciplined, used and subordinated to the service of humanity. This road is uncertain. Constitutional responsibility for modern organization is required. It now remains to be comprehended and detailed by social and political policy, program design, and administrative implementation. No miracles may be expected. The luxury of violent revolution cannot be indulged in the absence of immense tragedy. Rather, the hard, arduous work required to contravene the oppressions within groups and organizations and bureaucracies must be urgently attended. Tenderness, vulnerability, care and competent, productive accomplishment have not yet fully vanished from things humane. The power, skills and creativity available to humans must focus the energy required for human survival. Yet survival alone is not sufficient. Survival with dignity is an imperative of the continuing and everchanging human condition. Up against the possibilities of a nuclear holocaust and environmental catastrophe which could well result from the pathological dynamics of traditional organizations there is precious little time remaining. We must proceed at once with the task at hand.

NOTES

1. See the seminal work of Elliot Jaques, *A General Theory of Bureaucracy*, N.Y., John Wiley & Sons, Inc., 1972, p. 2, *et. seq.*
2. This was particularly apparent with the passage of "proposition 13" by the California electorate in June of 1978. This proposition severely limits property tax revenues which support vast local services and primary and secondary education. Those public organizations affected have experienced serious incapacity in the delivery of their programs and services, see e.g., *Los Angeles Times*, December 17, 1978, January 1, 1979, January 4, 1979, February 1, 1979, February 14, 1979.
3. Jaques, *op. cit.*, pp. 7-9, and 181-189.
4. Jaques, *op. cit.*, p. 3.
5. Jaques, *op. cit.*, pp. 258-329.
6. Alan Fox, *Beyond Contract: Work, Power and Trust Relations*, London, Faber & Faber, 1974, *passim.*
7. Gordon Tullock, *The Politics of Bureaucracy*, Washington, D.C., Public Affairs Press, pp. 24-32, cf. Elliot Jaques, *op. cit.*, pp. 3-8.
8. Chester I. Barnard, *The Functions of the Executive*, Cambridge, Mass., Harvard University Press, 1938, *passim*; see also Note 34, Chapter 1.
9. Jaques, *op. cit.*, p. 6.
10. Jaques, *op. cit.*, p. 7, *et. seq.*
11. Frederick W. Taylor, *The Principles of Scientific Management*, copyright 1911 by Frederick W. Taylor, published by the Norton Library, 1968, by arrangement with Harper & Row, N.Y., W.W. Norton & Co., Inc., p. 137.
12. Jaques, *op. cit.*, p. 5, *et seq.*
13. Robert L. Heilbroner, *An Inquiry into the Human Prospect*, N.Y., W.W. Norton, 1974, *passim*; Lester Brown, "Suddenly, National Security is a Whole New Animal," *Los Angeles Times*, December 4, 1977, Part IV, p. 3.
14. Jaques, *op. cit.*, pp. 60-86.
15. Jaques, *op. cit.*, pp. 62-86, 190-205, 288-301.
16. Jaques, *op. cit.*, pp. 1-9; see also Jeffrey Pfeffer, *Organizational Design*, Arlington Heights, Ill., AHM Publishing Corp., 1978.
17. Jaques, *op. cit.*, pp. 3-22.
18. Jaques, *op. cit.*, pp. 334-360.
19. Jaques, *op. cit.*, pp. 288-301.
20. Jaques, *op. cit.*, pp. 190-220.
21. Noel M. Tichy, "Agents of Planned Social Change: Congruence of Values, Cognition and Actions," *Administrative Science Quarterly*, June 1974, p. 179.

22. *Ibid.*

23. Edgar H. Schein, *Process Consultation: Its Role in Organizational Development*, Reading Mass., Addison-Wesley, 1969; Elliot Jaques, in "Social Therapy: Technocracy or Collaboration," *Journal of Social Issues*, Spring 1947, pp. 59-66; S.A. Davis, "An Organic Problem-Solving Method of Organizational Change," *Journal of Applied Behavioral Science*, Vol. 3(1), pp. 3-25, 1967 and Newton Margulies and Anthony P. Raia, *Conceptual Foundations of Organizational Development*, N.Y. McGraw-Hill Book Co., 1978.

24. cf. Gordon L. Lippitt, *Visualizing Change*, Fairfax, Virginia, NTL Learning Resources Corp., 1973, *passim.*

25. Marilyn Gittell, *Participants and Participation*, N.Y., Center for Urban Education, 1967, *passim*; Peter Marris and Martin Rein, *Dilemmas of Social Reform*, N.Y., Atherton Press, 1967, *passim*; and Robert Morris and Robert H. Binstock, *Feasible Planning for Social Change*, N.Y., Columbia University Press, 1966, *passim.* I am indebted to Stephen K. Blumberg for these references.

26. See Stephen L. Fink, Joel Beak, Kenneth Taddeo, "Organizational Crisis and Change," *Journal of Applied Behavioral Science*, Vol. 7, No. 1, 1971, pp. 15-37.

27. J.F.T. Bugental, "The Humanistic Ethic – The Individual in Psychotherapy as a Societal Change Agent," *Journal of Humanistic Psychology*, Vol. 11, No. 1, Spring, 1971, *op. cit.*, pp. 24-25.

28. cf. H. Roy Kaplan and Curt Tousky, "Humanism in Organizations: A Critical Appraisal," *Public Administration Review*, March/April, 1977, pp. 171-180. These two sociologists in a perplexing attempt to explain or justify the characteristics of the oppressive organization attack as "highly tenuous" the assumptions of "organizational humanists." They oppose the hypothesis that intrinsically satisfying work is a benefit to the worker, the organization and society. They confound the objective conditions of organizational oppression with its concomitant expression in worker alienation. Their narrow orientation is curiously absent of a theoretical foundation and bounded by circular reasoning, viz., workers involved in uninteresting work are not interested in their work and therefore seek other benefits. The empirical evidence they generate impeccably proves this premise, unfortunately it only substantiates the alienating conditions at the traditional workplace.

29. Jaques, *op. cit.*, pp. 333-347.

30. Frederick Herzberg, *Work and the Nature of Man*, Cleveland, World Publ. Co., Inc., 1966, pp. 92-129; cf., R.J. House and L.A. Wigdor, "Herzberg's Dual-Factor Theory of Job Satisfaction and Motivation," *Personnel Psychology*, Winter 1967, pp. 369-389.

31. On motivation, see for example, F. Herzberg, B. Mausher, and B. Snyderman, *The Motivation to Work*, N.Y., John Wiley & Sons, 1959; John P. Campbell, M.D. Dunnette, E. E. Lawler and K.E. Weick, *Managerial Behavior, Performance and Effectiveness*, N.Y., McGraw-Hill Book Co., Inc., 1970; B. Weiner, *Theories of Motivation: From Mechanism to Cognition*, Chicago, Markham Press, 1972.

32. Erik Erikson, *Insight and Responsibility*, N.Y., W.W. Norton & Co., Inc., 1964, pp. 112-113, 115, 119, 196 and 232-239.

33. Eric Berne, *Structure and Dynamics of Organizations and Groups*, N.Y., Grove Press, Inc., Evergreen Edition, 1966, pp. 163-166.

34. Jaques, *op. cit.*, pp. 181-329.

35. Theodore Hubert Thomas, *Innovation in Organizational Structure: Normative Implications of Participatory Styles*, unpublished manuscript (doctoral dissertation submitted to the University of California, Los Angeles Political Science faculty) copyright by Theodore H. Thomas, 1977.

36. *L.A. Times*, December 27, 1977, Part I, p. 1 ff.

37. Jaques, *op. cit.*, p. 2.

38. Rosabeth Moss Kanter, *Men and Women of the Corporation*, N.Y., Basic Books, Inc., 1977, pp. 245-287.

39. The essential concepts in this paragraph have been developed by Adam Tom Kohler and I am indebted to him for this substantial contribution. See especially his "A Social Systems Approach to Program Evaluation," *Journal of Personality and Social Systems*,

Vol. 1, No. 1., April 1977, pp. 65-77; and also his *Brentwood Veterans Administration Grant Proposal on Institutional Change* (1 RO1 OHMH 00812-01), submitted to the National Institute of Health, 1978; see also Arthur D. Colman, "Environmental Design: Realities and Delusions," in Arthur D. Colman and W. Harold Bexton, *Group Relations Reader*, Sausalito, California, GREX, 1975, pp. 329-341; and also see Tom Lupton, " 'Best Fit' in the Design of Organizations," *Task and Organization*, E.I. Miller (ed.), N.Y., John Wiley & Sons, Inc., 1976, pp. 121-141, and see also Einar Thorsrud, "Democracy at Work: Norwegian Experiences of Applied Behavioral Sciences, Vol. 13, No. 3, 1977, pp. 410-421; see also Abraham K. Korman, *Organizational Behavior*, Englewood Cliffs, N.J., Prentice-Hall, 1977; and see also Isabel E.P. Menzies, "A Case Study in the Functioning of Social Systems as a Defense Against Anxiety," *Human Relations*, 1960, Vol. 13, pp. 95-121.

40. Allyn A. Morrow and Fredrick C. Thayer, "Collaborative Work Settings: New Titles, Old Contradictions," *The Journal of Applied Behavioral Sciences*, Vol. 13, No. 3, 1977, pp. 448-457; see also C.B. Macpherson, *Democratic Theory Essays in Retrieval*, Oxford, Clarendon Press, 1973, *passim*; see also Fredrick C. Thayer, *An End to Hierarchy! An End to Competition!*, N.Y., New Viewpoints, a division of Franklin Watts, 1973, *passim*.

41. Jaques, *op. cit.*, pp. 221-234.

42. Stephen K. Blumberg, "Benign Beneficience: The Theory of Doing Good if It Won't Hurt You," unpublished ms., shared with the author, 1977.

43. Jaques, *op. cit.*, p. 7 and pp. 13-21.

44. *Ibid.*, p. 2 and pp. 62-86, p. 21 and pp. 334-360.

45. *Ibid.*, pp. 333-377, see also pp. 190-205.

46. *Ibid.*, pp. 333-347.

47. Among other things, de-selected employees could be reassigned, relocated or dismissed. Special cases are academic and research functions where tenure is essential to the protection of the integrity of research and academic freedom in the classroom; yet, de-selection could apply to the administrative side of academic institutions with professional retrieval rights maintained.

48. Jaques means by constitutional right a right made explicit and established within a constitutional framework with known and agreed procedures, *op. cit.*, p. 199.

49. Jaques, *op. cit.*, p. 181 and see generally, pp. 182-242.

50. *Ibid.*, p. 189.

51. *Ibid.*, p. 207.

52. *Ibid.*, pp. 221-234.

53. *Ibid.*, p. 238.

54. *Ibid.*, p. 376.

55. James D. Carroll, "Noetic Authority," *Public Administration Review*, September/October, 1969, p. 499.

56. Guy Benveniste, *Bureaucracy*, San Francisco, California, Boyd and Fraser Publ. Co., 1977, pp. 205-266.

RELATED READING

Barnett, H.G. *Innovation: The Basis of Cultural Change*. New York: McGraw-Hill Book Co., 1953. Intentional change (innovation) must take into account both physical and cultural approaches to change. It must be a melange of ideas which express the innate aspects of being and culture. Barnett's work is essential to effective planning of intentional social change.

Glass, John F. and Staude, John R., (eds.), *Humanistic Society: Today's Challenge to Sociology*. Pacific Palisades, California: Goodyear Publ. Co., Inc., 1972. A very helpful collection of essays centering upon furthering the humanistic approach to the study of humans and their society.

Benveniste, Guy. *Bureaucracy*. San Francisco: Boyd and Fraser Publ. Co., 1977. A diagnosis of some key pathologies in bureaucracy and the presentation of some helpful innovations and changes which will counteract and diminish such oppression.

Boguslaw, Robert. *The New Utopians*. Englewood Cliffs, N.J.: Prentice-Hall, Inc., 1965. This effort focuses upon the efforts of man to master nature and the advantage that the computer offers to achieve that, yet its greatest danger lies in the opportunity it offers for the control of man over man. This book explores that essential difficulty.

Dvorin, Eugene P. and Simmons, Robert F. *From Amoral to Humane Bureaucracy*. San Francisco: Canfield Press, (a department of Harper & Row), 1972. This offers a critical analysis of the uses of bureaucratic power and stresses the need to alter our institutions so as to reflect humane values rather than just efficiency and productivity alone.

Erikson, Erik. *Insight and Responsibility*. New York: W.W. Norton & Co., Inc., 1964. This superb collection of Erikson's lectures on the occasion of Freud's 100th birthday emphasizes the significant connections between "psychological realities" and personal responsibility for one's own behavior and his own society.

Etzioni, Amitai. *The Active Society*. New York: The Free Press, 1968. An exciting book presenting a theory of societal and political processes which centers upon the reduction of alienation and the transformation to the non-violent moral community which provides the normative foundation for peace and a humane existence.

Fuller, R. Buckminster. *Utopia or Oblivion: The Prospects for Humanity*. New York: Bantam Books, 1969. If we are sufficiently wise to survive, men and women will be able to solve all the physical problems of human existence because the real wealth of the world is information and energy.

Jaques, Elliot. *A General Theory of Bureaucracy*. New York: John Wiley & Sons, Inc., Halsted Press, 1976. A singularly distinctive contribution to the understanding of modern complex organizations. This is a unique and innovative theoretical advance soundly rooted in experience. It is dramatic in its call for fundamental reformation of traditional orientations toward bureaucracy, particularly with reference to task organization, work capability, stratification, social justice, management authority and accountability, constitutional bureaucracy, alienation and community.

Jun, Jong S. and Storm, William B., (eds.). *Tomorrow's Organizations*. Glenview, Ill.: Scott Foresman & Co., 1973. A truly significant collection of material focusing upon the aspects, characteristics, challenges, strategies and requirements of the organizations of the future.

Toffler, Alvin. *Future Shock*. New York: Bantam Books, 1970. A startling and important analysis of the social costs of rapid technological change and calls for a restoration of the balance among the rates of change, the pace of change and the necessary human responses to such change.

GLOSSARY

Alienation. Human beings are unable to experience themselves as the active bearers of their own power and their own human potential. Humans feel impoverished and dependent upon powers outside themselves.

Alliance Systems. Collectivities of group members who overtly or covertly support power plays and maneuvers through several events.

Anancasm. A group's capacity to respond to survival threats (see Cohesion).

Anti-requisite Social Institutions. Those social institutions which are alienating, paranoiagenic and entropic (see Requisite Institutions).

Authority Matrix. The leadership and canon of an organization which provide for its legitimacy and its orderly procedure.

Banal Work Groups. A work group reflecting mindlessness, joylessness, lovelessness and power-lessness and characterized by inequality, competitiveness, and power plays.

Basic Assumption Group. A group pervaded by a shared tacit emotion which dominates the behavior of the group.

Berne's Law. The effectiveness of the work group depends upon the success of the process group.

Boundary. A constitutional, psychological, spatial, or temporal distinction among different classes of organizational and group membership.

Boundary, Closed. A boundary which is difficult, if not impossible, to cross inwardly once the group is activated.

Boundary, Major External. A constitutional, psychological, spatial, or temporal distinction between members and non-members.

Boundary, Major Internal. The constitutional, psychological, spatial, or temporal distinction among leadership and membership.

Boundary, Minor Internal. The constitutional, psychological, spatial or temporal distinction among the different classes or individuals among the membership or leadership.

Boundary, Open. A boundary which can be crossed easily and freely in either direction by members and non-members of a group or organization.

Boundary, Sealed. A boundary which is almost, if not impossible, to cross outwardly once the group has been activated.

Bureaucracy. An organization or collectivity of organizations characterized by ordered, hierarchical arrangements; an established system of authority, rights and duties; maintenance of ordered communication; systematic record-keeping; general rules and orders; and established personnel.

Canon. The organizational provisions which provide for the legitimacy and orderly existence of the group. This includes the basic charter, the definitive laws, and the history and culture of the organization.

Cohesion. An operative force derived from the need of the members to maintain the orderly existence of the group (see Anancasm).

Collusion. (1) A person accepts the projections of other group members regarding his covert role out of his own personal need for stroking and time-structuring. (2) A group member silently concurs with a feeling being expressed in a group and declines to take responsibility for its expression but supports its delivery.

Combat Group. A group responding to perceived or immediate threats from the external environment when sufficient cohesion is present.

Consensus. Unanimity within a group concerning a decision the group makes where the individual members contribute to the decision process in an autonomous unpressured way.

Cooperative Groups. A group which is fully developed, cooperative, rewarding, intimate, productive, cohesive and satisfying. The group and its members are valued and the members have permission, safety and support to be intelligent, joyful, caring and powerful.

Covert Group Process. See Hidden Group Process.

Covert Role Differentiation. The elaboration of specific emotionally laden roles in the private group structure to satisfy the needs of the membership for stroking and time-structure.

Cult. A group or organization characterized by devoted attachment to or extravagent admiration of a person or principle which involves the surrender of personal choice and responsibility to such a leader or idealized principle.

Culture. The ideas, customs, rituals, beliefs and social influences which regulate group and organizational behavior and work.

Dependency Group. A basic assumption group which seeks to attain security and protection from one individual. Group behavior is akin to being stupid, incompetent, or "crazy" in the hope that it will be rescued from its impotency by a powerful god-like leader.

Drama Triangle. See Rescue Triangle.

Duty. This is a task or burden imposed from without on human beings of which the payoff for non-performance is social disapproval, fines, punishment, or death.

Effective Leader. The group member who has the competence and the technical expertise whose decisions are most likely to take effect within the group or organization.

Entropy. A measure of the degree of disorder in a system and a condition where energy always decreases.

Euhermerization. A process whereby a member of an organization assumes after death mythical attributes becoming larger-than-life, frequently being imbued with perfection and god-like attributes.

Fight/Flight Group. A basic assumption group which perceives its survival as resting upon either fighting or fleeing and it frequently fluctuates rapidly between these two extremes.

Forces. External pressure: unanticipated expectations and threats which impact upon and across the major external boundary.

Group cohesion: see Cohesion.

Internal agitation: unanticipated expectations and threats which impact upon the major internal boundary.

Group. An aggregate collection of people aware of their common relationships and sharing significant boundaries.

Group Process. Centers upon the variety, meaning, patterns and consequences of the transactions and interaction linkages and networks which characterize the ongoing processes of human behavior in organizations and groups.

External Group Process. Focuses on events taking place at the major external boundary.

Major Internal Group Process. Focuses on critical events taking place at the major internal boundaries of the organization.

Minor Group Process. Focuses on transaction and interaction patterns involving individual members of the organization.

Groupthink. A strong concurrence seeking tendency in a group where effective consensus is precluded, dissent is discouraged and autonomous critical thinking dissipates. Membership striving for unanimity overrides motivation to realistically appraise alternative course of action. (This is distinct from consensus which encompasses realistic appraisal of and significant alternative options of choice selections.)

Hamartic Groups. An hamartic group is a destructive group. The activities of an hamartic group follow a progression from prologue to climax through to catastrophe which for one, a few, or many ends in the hospital, the courtroom and/or the morgue.

Held Resentments. Angry and resentful feelings which are repressed, suppressed, which are secret and are carried by the bearer which, if they remain undisclosed, betray the bearer in a variety of ways.

Hidden Group Process. The underlying, emotionally laden interpersonal processes within a group. (Also may be identified as covert process.) These involve splits, projections, drama (rescue) triangle activity, basic assumption behavior, etc.

Hierarchy. An administrative arrangement where power, prestige and remuneration are distributed in ever-diminishing amounts downward through a pyramidal structure.

Ideology. The supporting myths rationalizing the power transactions of the players.

Imago, Group. Any mental picture of what a group is thought to be like. This may be preconscious, unconscious or conscious. It evolves through a series of phases:

Provisional: The initial "picture" of the group.

Adapted: An early superficial appraisal of other group members.

Operative: A Fully developed picture of the group combined with a judgment made concerning the perception the group leader has of oneself.

Secondarily Adjusted: The group member gives up some personal proclivities in order to fully belong to the group and is accepted by the group.

Individual Member-Group Transactions. Membership transactions within group process. There are four levels of intensity:

1) **Participation:** Any words or gestures which react to or futher the process of the group.

2) **Involvement:** A group member who remains passive in relation to the activity of another member.

3) **Engagement:** A group member initiates his own activity or game within the group process.

4) **Belonging:** A person who is eligible, adjusted and accepted into a group.

Intensity of Transaction: Group Stages.

Rituals. Predictable patterned interaction.

Pastimes. Complimentary interaction based upon past history or dealing with the environment.

Games. A series of covert, ulterior transactions leading progressively to a well-defined climax in which there is a hidden advantage to the players.

Intimacy. A direct expression of authentic, meaninful emotion among group members.

Intentional Change Sequence. Unblocking and developing choices and alternatives one or more of which are then implemented through strategies and tactics which intervene and effect change within the context of persons, groups and/or organizations which result in altered behavior and significant impacts upon the individuals, groups and organizations concerned. An intentional change sequence involves: raising awareness, engaging in problem solving, making decisions, implementation and action, evaluating results, using feedback and achieving accountability.

Intimacy. Sharing one's emotions with others including anger, sorrow and joy in safe, caring and nurturing ways.

Introjection. The incorporation unconsciously into one's personality attitudes and ideas derived from observations and feelings directed toward another person or object.

Joylessness. An aspect of a group or a person's life script which defeats natural curiosity and feelings of happiness through injunctions and attributions.

Leader. A leader is a group member who is granted or assumes the initiative to propose and take action and impose solutions. This may be a formal role or an emergent role, temporary in nature, within the process of the group.

Leadership. Organizational leadership is reflected in the personal influence within and without the organization by the responsible leader, the effective leader and the psychological leader.

Leadership Hunger. The aspect of group life wherein the group selects a member for leadership who seemingly promises to meet the implicit unarticulated needs of the group at any specific time.

Lovelessness. An aspect of a group or a person's life script learned through the stroke economy which defeats an individual's ability to express warm, nurturing and caring involvement to another human being.

Manifest Structure. Parts of the organization which are in public view and are easily ascertainable from both public and organizational record sources. It includes the formal strategic, tactical, operational and performance levels on processes of the organization.

Mediation. Specialized problem-solving activities and sessions which may involve two or more persons or groups having particular difficulties in interpersonal and intergroup relations.

Mindlessness. An aspect of a group or a person's life script which is achieved by discounting a person's reasoning ability and a person's intelligence is attacked and defeated.

Mystification. Deliberate misrepresentation where humans are manipulated and deceived into colluding with their oppression.

One-Down Power Plays. Power plays are generally defensive in nature, but may assume the character of guerrilla "war." It involves surprise, special knowledge of organizations and individual vulnerabilities with no immediate expectation of winning. It may be played from any position on the rescue triangle. This is played to win or break even.

Oneness Group. A basic assumption group where the membership seeks survival through uniting with a "higher force" through surrender to a methodology to achieve a "higher awareness."

One-Up Power Plays. Power plays begun from a position seemingly based on virtue, law, reason and righteousness. It is generally aggressive or offensive in pressure successively until victory or defeat is determined. It may be played from any position on the rescue triangle. This is played to win.

Operational Structure. Front-line supervision separating management from worker. The primary task at this level is to link management to the worker or organizational member. It includes the technical, administrative, and operations functions of the formal organizational activity.

Operative Principle. A group member does not initiate action or become actively involved in the group until he or she decides how he or she stands in the imago of the leader.

Oppression. The manipulation and/or coercion of human behavior by pressure, force or threats of force.

Organization. An organization is a system of consciously coordinated activities, forces, and behavior involving more than one person, involving one or more groups, designed and created to achieve specific and determined purposes. It may also be perceived as a fully differentiated collection of persons and groups located within defined and understood boundaries.

Organizational and Group Dynamics. The influences and forces affecting the boundaries of the organizational and group structure. These involve pressure, agitation and cohesion.

Organizational Guerrilla Warfare. A non-violent way to alter the policy choices, resources, behavior and context of organizational life.

Pairing Group. A basic assumption group phenomenon where pairing occurs between two individuals who express warmth and affection leading to intimacy and closeness. Other members become inactive and the basic assumption it that in some magic way a savior will be born or come to save the group and help it complete its task.

Paranoiagenic. A condition in a group or organization which engenders behavior rooted in fear and suspicion.

Paranoid Fantasies (paranoias). A feeling of suspicion that something is going on or has occurred which has some basis in reality, regardless of how distorted it may seem.

Performance Structure. The collectivity of persons and groups who accomplish the work of the organization which is specifically related to performing the organizational mission.

Persona. The way a person presents himself or herself to the group. The particular way a person chooses to be seen.

Personal Space. Refers here to the particular personal feelings which a person experiences at any given time.

Pistogenic. A condition in a group or organization which engenders behavior rooted in trust and confidence.

Pitched Battle. A Condition in power plays where the power is approximately equal among the players. This involves maneuver, counter-maneuver, and alliances.

Planned Change. An intended, designed or purposive attempt by an individual, group or organization to influence the course of events in the status quo to alter and interrupt operating tendencies.

Power. The capacity to cause people to do something or not to do something, i.e. perform an action or refrain from action or more subtly to avoid, restrain or fend off some action on the part of others.

Powerlessness. An aspect of a group or a person's life script which involves feeling and sense that a person is ready to abandon or has abandoned self by withdrawal, submission to some form of authority or through blind even compulsive conformance to accepted patterns and expectations.

Power Play. A transaction whereby a person, group or organization gains from another person, group or organization something which is wanted against the opposition and desires of the concerned person, group or organization.

Power Scenario. Collectivities of power plays and games within organizational power nets intended to achieve intentional purposes through a melange of overt and covert power operations.

Primal Leader. A group member and leader who establishes or radically changes the structure and/or canon of the group, always in the face of powerful opposition.

Private Structure. What is going on in the minds of the members with regard to their relationships with each other, the leadership, and the various activities and processes of the group related to these.

Problem Solving Group. A group focusing on confrontation, dialogue and searching involving consciousness raising, working-through and feedback combined with support for the development and implementation of effective personal or organizational change.

Process. Interaction which involves a number of steps or operations which are linked together in some manner.

Process Clues. Transactions which reveal tactics or disclose the strategy involved in power plays.

Process Group. A group focused on its internal process in order to maintain, promote, achieve or reclaim the orderly existence of the group and is specifically concerned with resolution of the emotional aspects of group life.

Proclivities, Individual. A group member's propensity to express himself or herself in distinctive and unique ways.

Proclivities, Syntonic. An individual proclivity which reinforces group cohesion.

Proclivity, Dystonic. An individual proclivity which is in conflict with the group cohesion or group culture.

Projection. The loading onto another person, group or object the denied feelings withheld by an individual or group member.

Psychological Leader. The most powerful person in the minds of the group members. The personal powers of such a leader are usually exaggerated and on occasion seem to have a mystical hold on the actions and reactions of group members.

Requisite Institutions. Those social structures and processes which match authority and accountability, nurture trust and confidence in working relationships, and provide opportunities for individuals to work to their full capability. Requisite institutions facilitate awareness, trust, confidence, cooperation and collaboration which achieves cohesion and individual well being. These may be designated as pistogenic institutions.

Rescue Triangle. A concept where three basic role positions (Persecutor, Rescuer and Victim) are arranged around a triangle and persons involved in relationships switch from one role position to another in relation to the amount of guilt and resentment felt.

Responsible Leader. The individual who occupies a formal organizational position and is held responsible and accountable for his or her decisions through the formal organizational structure.

Responsibility. A task assumed from the forces within one's self in which joy, reward and satisfaction are the ultimate payoff sought.

Robopaths. Workers in an organization who have become dehumanized so they are actors mouthing irrelevant platitudes, devoid themselves of feeling, experiencing programmed emotions with little compassion, empathy, or sympathy for other persons.

Role. The sociological context of individual behavior as follows:
1. An essential element of the manifest organizational structure.
2. The manner in which a person is supposed to behave in the role assignment made in the manifest structure.
3. Roles derived from splits, projections and collusions which occur within the private structure and are derived from meeting the stroking and time-structuring needs of the membership.
4. An element of a person's script.

Role Assignments. The covert role given to group members which fulfill the stroking and time structuring needs of the membership.

Role Senders. Persons who communicate role expectations to another.

Role Set. The totality of the number of role senders communicating role expectations to a role player.

Scarcity. In a power play that which is perceived to be in scarce supply and is sought through a power play transaction or series of transactions.

Script. A life plan based on a decision made in childhood, reinforced by the parents, justified by subsequent events and culminating in chosen behavioral alternatives.

Scripting. The socialization of children to develop certain parts of their personality while suppressing the development of other parts.

Sentient Group. A group in which the members feel they belong and are safe, to which they feel committed, and from which they derive support and nurture.

Sex-Role Scripting. Child-rearing practices which, among other things, penalize and reward attributes and behavior thought to be desirable or undesirable to the specific sex of the child involved. For example boys are penalized for showing their feelings or expressing their intuition and girls for thinking and doing. Additionally, boys are supported to be tough and unfeeling and girls are supported to be vulnerable and weak.

Strain. Psychological, physiological or behavioral deviation from normal responses in a person.

Strategic Structure. The strategic aspects of the organization involving the higher management processes of an organization which is concerned with developing and maintaining organizational policy, program and goals, responding to organizational survival needs, crucial participation in policy and budgeting support decisions, and developing and maintaining organizational power resources.

Stress. Any aspect of an environment which poses a threat to individuals and groups.

Stressor. An aspect of an environment which produces stress.

Stroke. A unit of social recognition and a fundamental unit of social action.

Stroke Economy. Affirmation and caring attention must be earned. The rules:

1) no strokes may be requested;

2) no strokes may be accepted;

3) all strokes must be humbly received and quickly discounted;

4) strokes may be given only rarely under special circumstances.

Structure. Particular patterns of role relationships within bounded social nets.

Structure Hunger. The need of a group member to have his or her time structured.

Support Group. An ongoing trust group where it is safe to express feelings in safe ways and feel safe and caring support from the members.

Survival, Effective. The ability of a group or organization to do organized work.

Survival, Ideologic. Survival of the group exists only in the minds of its members and ceases to exist as an effective force.

Survival, Physical. Survival of solely the physical aspects of the group or organization where the ideological aspects have lost their vitality.

Tactical Structure. The middle-range of an organizational management arrangements concerned with implementing and coordinating organizational activities and tasks consistent with organizational policy and program commitments.

Task. The expenditure of energy, physical or mental, for a purposeful activity or to the undertaking of action or making an effort to do or make something.

Task Group. A group functioning in work mode where individual energies are devoted to primary tasks.

Termination. An event or condition which occurs when the group is no longer meeting the needs of its members. It may occur through decay, destruction, erosion, attrition or infiltration.

Transaction. An exchange of words and/or gestures which constitute a unit of social intercourse.

Unclear Feelings. Vague feelings carried by a person who is not in touch with the exact substance and dimensions of the feeling but nevertheless experiences discomfort.

Work. That aspect of human activity wherein the individual exercises discretion, makes decisions and acts, in seeking to transform the external physical or social world in accord with a pre-determined goal.

Work Capacity. The distance into the clock-time future up to which a person is capable of organizing projects and acting upon them so as to produce an output.

Work (personal). Activity concerned with learning about one's own inner process, how that process was internalized and how it is expressed in personal behavior and transactions in a family, social or work (employment) setting. Then taking action based on a conscious personal decision to alter one's transactions in accord with previously determined objectives. This is only disclosed through personal growth, awareness, experiential or therapy processes.

Xenophobia. Fear of anything foreign or strange.

BIBLIOGRAPHY*

Adorno, T.W.; Frenkel-Brunswick, Else; Levinson, Daniel J.; Sanford, R. Vevirt. *The Authoritarian Personality*. New York: W.W. Norton, 1950.

Agee, Philip. *Inside the Company: CIA Diary*. New York: Stonehill, 1975.

Anshen, Melvin, and Wormuth, Francis D. *Private Enterprise and Public Policy*. New York: The Macmillan Co., 1954, pp. 136-169.

Ardrey, Robert. *The Territorial Imperative*. New York: Antheneum, 1966.

————. *The Social Contract*. London: Collins, 1970.

Arendt, Hannah. *The Origins of Totalitarianism*. New York: Harcourt, Brace & World, Inc., 1951.

Argyris, Chris. *Integrating the Individual and the Organization*. New York: Wiley, 1964.

————. *Interpersonal Competence and Organizational Effectiveness*. Homewood, Ill.: Dorsey Press, Inc., Richard D. Irwin, Inc., 1962.

————. *Personality and Organization*. New York: Harper, 1957.

————. *Understanding Organizational Behavior*. Dorsey Press, Inc., 1960.

————. *Management and Organizational Development*. New York: McGraw-Hill Book Co., Inc., 1970.

Augur, Helen. *An American Jezebel, The Life of Anne Hutchinson*. New York: Brentano's, 1930.

Bach, George R. and Goldberg, Herb. *Creative Aggression*. Garden City, New York: Doubleday & Co., 1974.

Bakke, E. Wight. *Bonds of Organization*. New York: Harper & Row, 1950.

Bales, Robert F. *Interaction Process Analysis*. Cambridge, Mass.: Addison-Wesley, 1950.

Banet, Anthony G., Jr., and Hayden, Charla. "A Tavistock Primer." In John E. Jones and J. William Pfeiffer, *The Annual Handbook for Group Facilitators*. La Jolla, Calif.: University Associates, Inc., 1977, pp. 155-167.

Barnard, Chester I. *The Functions of the Executive*. Cambridge: Harvard University Press, 1938.

Barnett, H.G. *Innovation: The Basis of Cultural Change*. New York: McGraw-Hill Book Co., 1953.

Barnett, Richard J., and Muller, Ronald E. *Global Reach: The Power of Multinational Corporations*. New York: Simon & Schuster, 1974.

Baum, L. Frank. *The Wizard of Oz*. Chicago, Ill.: Reilly & Lee Co., 1900.

Bell, Daniel. "The Corporation and Society in the 1970's." *The Public Interest*, No. 24 (Summer), 1971, pp. 5-32.

————. *The Coming of Post-Industrial Society*. New York: Basic Books, 1973.

Bendix, Reinhard. "Bureaucracy and the Problem of Power." *Public Administration Review*, Vol. V, 1945.

————. *Work and Authority in Industry*. New York: Harper, 1956.

————. *Max Weber: An Intellectual Portrait*. New York: Anchor Books, Doubleday & Co., Inc., 1962.

Benedict, Ruth. *Patterns of Culture*. New York: Houghton Mifflin, 1934.

Bennis, Warren G. "Leadership Theory and Administrative Behavior: The Problem of Authority." *Administrative Science Quarterly*, Vol. 4 (1959), pp. 260-301.

————. *Changing Organizations*. New York: McGraw-Hill Book Co., Inc., 1966. Now titled *Beyond Bureaucracy* and reissued as a McGraw-Hill paperback edition.

————. "A Funny Thing Happened on the Way to the Future." *American Psychologist*, Vol. 25, No. 7, 1970, pp. 595-608. Reprinted in J.M. Thomas and W.G. Bennis, editors, *Management of Change and Conflict*. Baltimore Md.: Penguin Books, 1972.

————; Benne, K.; and Chin, R., editors. *The Planning of Change*. New York: Holt, Rinehart & Winston, 1961.

————. *Beyond Bureaucracy*. New York: McGraw-Hill Book Co., Inc., 1966.

* Straight news stories used in this text have not been included in this listing.

————, and Shepard, H. A. "A Theory of Group Development." *Human Relations*, Vol. 4, 1956, pp. 415-437. Reprinted in Warren G. Bennis, K. Benne, and R. Chin, editors, *The Planning of Change*. 1st edition. New York: Holt, Rinehart & Winston, 1961, pp. 321-340.

Bensman, Joseph and Vidich, Arthur J. *The New American Society*. Chicago: Quadrangle Books, 1971.

Bentley, Arthur F. *The Process of Government*. new edition. Cambridge, Mass.: Harvard University Press, 1967. First published in 1908.

Benveniste, Guy. *Bureaucracy*. San Francisco: Boyd and Fraser Publ. Co., 1977, pp. 3-26.

————. *The Politics of Expertise*. 2nd edition. San Francisco: Boyd and Fraser Publ. Co., 1977.

Berelson, Bernard and Steiner, Gary A. *Human Behavior: An Inventory of Scientific Findings*. New York: Harcourt, Brace & World, Inc., 1964.

Berle, Adolph A., Jr. *The 20th Century Capitalist Revolution*. New York: Harcourt-Brace, 1954.

————, and Means, Gardiner C. *The Modern Corporation and Private Property*. New York: Macmillan, 1932.

Berne, Eric. *Games People Play*. New York: Grove Press, 1964.

————. *The Structure and Dynamics of Organizations and Groups*. New York: J.B. Lippincott Co., 1963.

————. *Transactional Analysis in Psychotherapy*. New York: Grove Press, Inc., 1961, Ballantine Books.

————. *What Do You Say After You Say Hello?* New York: Grove Press, Inc., 1972.

————. And posthumously under the editorship of Claude Steiner with the assistance of Carmen Kerr. *Beyond Games and Scripts*. New York: Grove Press, Inc., 1976.

Bernstein, Carl and Woodward, Bob. *All the President's Men*. New York: Simon & Schuster, Inc., 1974.

Bettleheim, Bruno. *Love is Not Enough*. New York: The Free Press, 1960.

————. *Children of the Dream*. New York: Macmillan Publ. Co., Inc., 1969.

Bion, Wilfred. *Experiences in Groups*. New York: Basic Books, 1961.

————. "Experiences in Groups." *Human Relations*, Vol. 3, pp. 395-402, 1950. See also Vols. 1, 1948, pp. 487-496; Vol. 2, 1949, pp. 12-22 and pp. 295-303; Vol. 3, 1959, pp. 3-14; Vol. 4, 1951, pp. 221-227.

Blake, Robert and Mouton, Jane F. *The Managerial Grid*. Houston, Texas: Gulf Publ. Co., 1964.

Blanchard, William H. *Aggression American Style*. Santa Monica, Calif.: Goodyear Publ. Co., Inc., 1978.

Blau, Peter M. *Bureaucracy in Modern Society*. New York: Random House, 1956.

————, and Scott, W. Richard. *Formal Organizations*. San Francisco, Calif.: Chandler Publ. Co., 1962.

Blumberg, Stephen K. "The Manager's New Role: Add a Little EVPOSDCORB." *Public Management*, Vol. 59, No. 10, Oct. 1977.

————. "Notes on the Art of Administration." *Midwest Review of Public Administration*, Vol. 14, No. 4, December 1980.

————. "POSDCORB Revisited: Humanistic Guidelines for the Executive." Unpublished manuscript. California State University, Long Beach.

Boguslaw, Robert. *The New Utopians, A Study of System Design and Social Change*. Englewood Cliffs, N.J.: Prentice-Hall, Inc., 1965.

Boulding, Kenneth E. *The Organizational Revolution*. New York: Harper, 1953.

————. "The Role of the Social Sciences in the Control of Technology." In Albert H. Teich, editor, *Technology and Man's Future*. New York: St. Martin's Press, 1972.

Boulton, David. *The Grease Machine*. New York: Harper & Row, 1978.

————. *Conflict and Defense*. New York: Harper & Row, 1962.

Braybrooke, David and Lindblom, Charles E. *A Strategy of Decision: Policy Evaluation as a Social Process*. New York: The Free Press, 1963.

Brown, Lester. "Suddenly, National Security is a Whole New Animal." *Los Angeles Times*, Dec.

4, 1977, Part IV, p. 3.

Bugental, J.F.T. "The Humanistic Ethic – The Individual in Psychotherapy as a Societal Change Agent." *Journal of Humanistic Psychology*, Spring 1971. Reprinted in John F. Glass and John R. Staude, *Humanistic Society: Today's Challenge to Sociology*. Pacific Palisades, Calif.: Goodyear Publ. Co., Inc., 1972, pp. 294-306.

Burns, Thomas and Stalker, G.W. *The Management of Innovation*. London: Tavistock Publications. 1st edition, 1961. 2nd edition, 1966.

Burrow, Trigant, "The Social Neurosis." *Philosophy Science*, Vol. 16, 1949, pp. 25-40.

Caiden, Gerald. *Administrative Reform*. Chicago, Ill.: Aldine Publ. Co., 1969.

Campanella, Tommaso. *The Defense of Galileo*. (translated and edited with introduction and notes by Grant McCollen), New York: Arno Press, 1975.

Campbell, John P.; Dunette, M.D.; Lawler, E.E.; and Weick, K.E. *Managerial Behavior, Performance and Effectiveness*. New York: McGraw-Hill Book Co., Inc., 1970.

Caplan, Robert; Cobbs, Sidney; French, John, Jr.; Van Harrison, R.; and Pinneau, S.R. *Job Demands and Worker Health: Main Effects of Occupational Differences*. Washington, D.C.: Government Printing Office, National Institute of Safety and Health, 1975.

Carroll, James D. "Noetic Authority," *Public Administration Review*, September/October, 1969.

Carroll, John B. and Kerlinger, Fred N., editors. *Review of Research in Education*, Vol. 2. Itaska, Ill.: F.E. Peacock, Publishers, 1974.

Cartwright, Dorwin, editor. *Studies in Social Power*. Ann Arbor, Mich.: Institute for Social Research, 1959.

————, and Zander, Alvin, editors. *Group Dynamics: Theory and Research*. 2nd edition. Evanston, Ill.: Row, Peterson & Co., 1960.

————. *Group Dynamics: Theory and Research*. 3rd edition. Evanston, Ill.: Row, Peterson & Co., 1968.

Cattell, R.B. "Concepts and Methods of Measurement of Group Syntality." *Psychological Review*, Vol. 58, 1948, pp. 48-63.

————. "New Concepts of Measuring Leadership." In Dorwin Cartwright and Alvin Zander, editors, *Group Dynamics*. 3rd edition. New York: Harper & Row, 1968.

Clark, C.H. *Brainstorming*. New York: Doubleday & Co., Inc., 1958.

Cleveland, Harlan. *The Future Executive*. New York: Harper & Row Publ., 1972.

Coleman, James S. *Power and the Structure of Society*. New York: W.W. Norton & Co., 1974.

Collins, Barry E. and Guetzkow, Harold. *A Social Psychology of Group Processes for Decision-Making*. New York: John Wiley & Sons, Inc., 1964.

Colman, Arthur D. "Environmental Design: Realities and Delusions." In Arthur D. Colman and W. Harold Bexton, *Group Relations Reader*. Sausalito, Calif.: GREX, 1975.

————. "Irrational Aspects of Design." In Arthur D. Colman and Harold Bexton, *Group Relations Reader*. Sausalito, Calif.: GREX, 1975.

————, and Bexton, Harold, editors. *Group Relations Reader*. Sausalito, Calif.: GREX, 1975.

Cook, Fred J. *The F.B.I. Nobody Knows*. New York: Macmillan, 1964.

Corwin, Ronald G. *Education in Crisis*. New York: John Wiley & Sons, Inc., 1974.

Coser, Lewis. *The Functions of Social Conflict*. London: Routledge & Kegan Publ., Ltd., 1956.

Crawford, Deborah. *Four Women in a Violent Time: Anne Hutchinson (1591-1645) Mayer Dyer (1591-1660) Lady Deborah Moody (1600-1659) Penelope Stout (1622-1732)*. New York: Crown Publ., 1970.

Crozier, Michel. *The Bureaucratic Phenomenon*. Chicago, Ill.: University of Chicago Press, 1964.

Culligan, Matthew J. and Sedlacek, Keith. *How to Kill Stress Before It Kills You*. New York: Grossex & Dunlap, 1976.

Cummings, Michael S. "Dogmatism and Radicalism, A Reassessment." Unpublished manuscript, Political Science Department. Denver, Colorado: University of Colorado.

Dahl, Robert A. *Modern Political Analysis*. Englewood Cliffs, N.J.: Prentice-Hall, 1963.

Danhoff, Clarence H. *Government Contracting and Technological Change*. Washington, D.C.:

The Brookings Institution, 1968.

Davis, John P. *Corporations, A Study of the Origin and Development of Great Business Combinations and of Their Relation to the Authority of the State.* Written in 1897 and published in 1904 and republished in New York: Capricorn Books, 1961.

Davis, S.A. "An Organic Problem Solving Method of Organizational Change," *Journal of Applied Behavioral Science*, Vol. 3(1), pp. 3-25, 1967.

Dean, John. *Blind Ambition.* New York: Simon & Schuster, Inc., 1976.

Delbecq, Andre L., Van de Ven, Andrew H., Gustafson, David H. *Group Techniques for Program Planning: A Guide to Nominal Group and Delphi Processes.* Glenview, Ill.: Scott, Foresman and Co., 1975.

Deutsch, Karl W. *The Nerves of Government.* New York: The Free Press of Glencoe, 1963.

Diamant, Alfred. "The Bureaucratic Model." In *Papers in Comparative Administration,* edited by Ferrell Heady and Sybil L. Stokes. Ann Arbor, Mich.: Institute of Public Administration, 1962.

Dicey, A.V. *Introduction to the Study of Law and the Constitution.* 8th edition. London: Macmillan, 1927.

Dinnerstein, Dorothy. *The Mermaid and the Minotaur: Sexual Arrangements and Human Malaise.* New York: Harper & Row, 1976.

Domhoff, G. William. *Higher Circles.* New York: Random House, 1970.

_____. *Who Rules America?* Englewood Cliffs, N.J.: Prentice-Hall, Inc., 1967.

Downs, Anthony. *Inside Bureaucracy.* Boston: Little, Brown & Co., Inc., 1967.

Downs, James F. *The Navajo.* New York: Holt, Rinehart & Winston, 1972.

Drucker, Peter F. *The Concept of the Corporation.* New York: John Day, 1946.

Dubin, Robert; Homans, George; Mann, Floyd C.; Miller, Delbert C. *Leadership and Productivity.* San Francisco, Calif.: Chandler Publ. Co., 1965.

Durkheim, Emile. *Suicide.* New York: The Free Press, 1951.

_____. *The Division of Labor in Society.* (1933, reprint) New York: The Free Press, 1961.

Dvorin, Eugene P. and Simmons, Robert H. *From Amoral to Humane Bureaucracy.* San Francisco, Calif.: Canfield Press (a division of Harper & Row), 1972, p. 60.

Easton, David. *A Framework for Political Analysis.* Englewood Cliffs, N.J.: Prentice-Hall, 1965.

_____. *A Systems Analysis of Political Life.* New York: John Wiley & Sons, Inc., 1965.

Eiseley, Loren. *The Unexpected Universe.* New York: Harcourt, Brace, Jovanovich, 1964.

Ellul, Jaques. *The Technological Society.* New York: Alfred A. Knopf, 1964.

Erikson, Erik. *Childhood and Society.* 2nd edition. New York: W.W. Norton & Co., Inc., 1963. (1st edition, 1950.)

_____. *Insight and Responsibility.* New York: W.W. Norton & Co., Inc., 1964.

Etzioni, Amitai, editor. *Complex Organizations: A Sociological Reader.* New York: Holt, Rinehart & Winston, 1961.

_____. *The Active Society.* New York: The Free Press, 1968.

Ezriel, Henry. "A Psychoanalytic Method of Group Treatment." *British Journal of Medical Psychology*, Vol. 23, 1950, pp. 59-74.

Fanon, Frantz. *The Wretched of the Earth.* New York: Grove Press, 1965.

Fayol, Henri. *General and Industrial Management.* Constance Storrs, translator. London: Pitman, 1949.

Fesler, James W. *The Independence of State Regulatory Agencies.* Chicago: Public Administration Service, 1942.

Filley, Alan C. *Interpersonal Conflict Resolution.* Glenview, Ill.: Scott, Foresman & Co., Inc., 1975.

Fink, Stephen L.; Beak, Joel; Taddeo, Kenneth. "Organizational Crisis and Change." *Journal of Applied Behavioral Science*, Vol. 7, No. 1, 1971, pp. 15-37.

Follett, Mary Parker. *Dynamic Administration: The Collected Papers of Mary Parker Follett.* Edited by Henry C. Metcalf and Lyndall Urwick. New York: Harper, 1942.

————. "The Process of Control," in Luther Gulick and L. Urwick, eds. *Papers in the Science of Administration.* New York: Institute of Public Administration, 1937, pp. 161-169.

Fox, Alan. *Beyond Contract: Work, Power and Trust Relations.* London: Faber & Faber, 1974.

Fox, Elliot M. "Eric Berne's Theory of Organizations." *Transactional Analysis Journal,* Vol. 5, No. 4, Oct. 1975, p. 349.

Frank, Howard H. *Women in Organization.* Philadelphia: University of Pennsylvania Press, 1977.

Frank, Lawrence K. "The Need for a New Political Theory." *Daedalus,* Summer 1967, p. 184.

French, J.R.P. and Raven, B. "The Bases of Social Power." In Dorwin Cartwright and Alvin Zander, editors, *Group Dynamics.* 2nd edition. Evanston, Ill.: Row-Peterson, 1960, pp. 607-623.

French, Wendell L. and Bell, Cecil H., Jr. *Organization Development.* 2nd edition. Englewood Cliffs, N.J.: Prentice-Hall, Inc., 1978.

Freud, Sigmund. *Civilization and Its Discontents.* New York: W.W. Norton & Co., Inc., 1961.

————. *Totem and Taboo.* New York: Vintage Books. Copyright 1928 and 1946 by Dr. A. A. Brill.

Friedlander, F., and Brown, L.D. "Organizational Development," *Annual Review of Psychology,* Vol. 25, 1974.

Friedman, Anita. "Mediation." In Hogie Wyckoff, editor, *Love, Theory and Politics.* New York: Grove Press, Inc., 1976, pp. 91-106.

Fromm, Eric. *Escape from Freedom.* New York: Holt, Rinehart & Winston, Inc., 1941.

————. *The Sane Society.* New York: Holt, Rinehart & Winston, Inc., 1955. Reprinted by Fawcett Publications, Inc., Greenwich, Conn.

————. "What Does It Mean to be Human?" *The Revolution of Hope: Toward a Humanized Technology.* New York: Harper & Row, 1968. Reprinted in J.F. Glass and J.R. Staude, editors, *Humanistic Society: Today's Challenge to Sociology.* Pacific Palisades, Calif.: Goodyear Publ. Co., Inc., 1972.

Fuller, R. Buckminster. *Utopia or Oblivion: The Prospects for Humanity.* New York: Bantam Books, 1969.

Galbraith, John Kenneth. *The New Industrial State.* Boston: Houghton-Mifflin Co., 1967.

Galtung, Johan. "Violence, Peace and Peace Research." *Journal of Peace Research,* No. 3 (1969), pp. 167-172.

————, and Hoivik, Tord. "Structural and Direct Violence." *Journal of Peace Research,* No. 1 (1971) pp. 73-77.

Gamson, William A. *Power and Discontent.* Homewood, Ill.: Dorsey Press, 1968.

Gendron, Bernard. *Technology and the Human Condition.* New York: St. Martin's Press, 1977.

Gerth, H.H. and Mills, C. Wright. *From Max Weber: Essays in Sociology.* New York: Oxford University Press, 1958.

Gittell, Marilyn. *Participants and Participation.* New York: Center for Urban Education, 1967.

Glass, J.F. and Staude, J.R., editors. *Humanistic Society: Today's Challenge to Sociology.* Pacific Palisades, Calif.: Goodyear Publ. Co., 1972.

Golding, William Gerald. *Lord of the Flies.* New York: Coward-McCann, 1955 (fiction).

Golembiewski, Robert T. "Three Styles of Leadership and Their Uses." *Personnel,* Vol. XXXVIII, No. 4 (July-August, 1961), pp. 34-45.

Gordon, Thomas. *Parent Effectiveness Training.* New York: Peter H. Wyden, Inc., 1970.

Gross, Bertram M. *The Managing of Organizations,* Vol. I & II. Glencoe, Ill.: The Free Press (a division of Macmillan Co.), 1964.

Guinther, John. *Moralists and Managers.* New York: Anchor Books, Doubleday, 1976.

Gulick, Luther and Urwick, Lyndall, editors. *Papers on the Science of Administration.* New York: Institute of Public Administration, 1937.

Hall, Edward T. *The Hidden Dimension.* New York: Doubleday, 1966.

Hall, Richard. "The Concept of Bureaucracy, An Empirical Assessment." *American Journal of Sociology,* Vol. 69 (1963), pp. 32-40.

————, et al. "Organization Size, Complexity and Formalization." *American Sociological Review*, Vol. 33 (1968), pp. 909-912.

Halperin, Morton. *The Lawless State: The Crimes of the U.S. Intelligence Agencies.* New York: Penguin Books, 1976.

Hammer, Richard. *The Court-Martial of Lt. Calley.* New York: Coward, McCann & Geoghegan, 1971.

Hampden-Turner. *Radical Man.* New York: Anchor Books, Doubleday & Co., Inc., 1971.

Hare, A. Paul.; Borgatta, Edgar F.; and Bales, Robert F.; editors. *Small Groups: Studies in Social Interaction.* New York: A.A. Knopf, 1961.

Harris, Thomas A. *I'm O.K. – You're O.K.* New York: Harper & Row, 1969.

Heilbroner, Robert L. *An Inquiry into the Human Prospect.* New York: W.W. Norton & Co., Inc., 1974.

Herring, Pendelton. *Public Administration and the Public Interest.* New York: McGraw-Hill Book Co., Inc., 1936.

Hersh, Seymour M. *Cover-up: The Army's Secret Investigation of the Massacre at My Lai 4.* New York: Random House, 1972.

————. *My Lai 4: A Report on the Massacre and Its Aftermath.* New York: Random House, 1970.

Herzberg, F. *Work and the Nature of Man.* Cleveland, Ohio: World Publ. Co., 1966.

————; Mausner, B.; Synderman, B. *The Motivation to Work.* New York: John Wiley & Sons, Inc., 1959.

Homans, George C. *The Human Group.* New York: Harcourt, Brace and World, Inc., 1950.

Horney, Karen. *The Neurotic Personality of Our Time.* New York: Norton, 1937.

House, R.J. and Wigdor, L.A. "Herzberg's Dual-Factor Theory of Job Satisfaction and Motivation," *Personnel Psychology*, Winter, 1967, pp. 369-389.

Huse, E.F. *Organizational Development and Change.* St. Paul, Minn.: West Publishing Co., 1975.

Huxley, Aldous. *Brave New World.* New York: Harper, 1932.

————. *Brave New World Revisited.* New York: Harper, 1958.

Inge, W.H. *The Idea of Progress.* Romanes Lecture, Oxford: Humphrey Milford, 1920.

Jacoby, Henry. *The Bureaucratization of the World.* Translated from the German by Eveline L. Kanes, Berkeley, Calif.: University of California Press, 1973.

James, Muriel and Jongward, Dorothy. *Born to Win.* Reading, Mass.: Addison-Wesley Publ. Co., Inc., 1975.

James, William. *The Principles of Psychology.* Vol. 2, London: Henry Holt & Co., 1890.

Janis, Irving and Mann, Leon. *Decision Making, A Psychological Analysis of Conflict, Choice and Commitment.* New York: The Free Press, a division of Macmillan Publ. Co., Inc., 1977.

————. *Victims of Groupthink.* Boston, Mass.: Houghton-Mifflin Co., 1972.

————, and Wheeler, Dan. "Thinking Clearly about Career Choices." In *Psychology Today*, May, 1968.

Janov, Arthur. "For Control, Cults Must Ease Profound Pains," *Los Angeles Times*, Dec. 10, 1978, Part VI, p. 3.

Jaques, Elliot. *Changing Culture of the Factory.* New York: Dryden, 1952.

————. *A General Theory of Bureaucracy.* New York: Halsted Press, John Wiley & Sons, Inc., 1976.

————. "Social Therapy: Technocracy or Collaboration," *Journal of Social Issues*, Spring, 1947, pp. 59-66.

Jaworski, Leon. *The Right and the Power: The Prosecution of Watergate.* New York: Reader's Digest Press, 1976.

Jeffers, Harry Paul. *The C.I.A.: A Close Look at the Central Intelligence Agency*, New York: Lion Press, 1970.

Johnson, Diane. "Heart of Darkness," *New York Review of Books*, April 19, 1979.

Jongward, Dorothy. *Everybody Wins: Transactional Analysis Applied to Organizations.* Revised edition. Reading, Mass.: Addison-Wesley Publ. Co., 1976.

Jun, Jong S. and Storm, William B., editors. *Tomorrow's Organizations.* Glenview, Ill.: Scott, Foresman & Co., 1973.

Jung, C.G. "On Sychronicity." In *The Portable Jung.* New York: Penguin Books, 1971.

————. "The Concept of the Collective Unconscious." In *The Portable Jung.* New York: Penguin Books, 1971.

————. *The Portable Jung.* New York: Penguin Books, 1971.

Kahn, Robert L.; Wolfe, Donald M.; Quinn, Robert P.; Snock, J. Diedrick; and Rosenthal, R.A. *Organizational Stress in Role Conflict and Ambiguity.* New York: John Wiley & Sons, Inc., 1964.

Kahn, Robert L. and Boulding, Elise, editors. *Power and Conflict in Organizations.* New York: Basic Books, Inc., 1964.

Kanter, Rosabeth Moss. *Men and Women of the Corporation.* New York: Basic Books, 1977.

Kaplan, D. "Power in Perspective," in R. Kahn and E. Boulding, editors. *Power and Conflict in Organizations.* London: Tavistock Publications, 1964.

Kaplan, Roy H. and Tousky, Curt. "Humanism in Organizations: A Critical Appraisal." *Public Administration Review* (March/April 1977), pp. 171-180.

Karpman, Stephen B. "Script Drama Analysis." *Transactional Analysis Bulletin*, Vol. 7, No. 26, 1968, pp. 39-43.

Kast, F.E. and Rosenzweig, J.E. *Organization and Management: A Systems Approach.* New York: McGraw-Hill Book Co., Inc., 1970.

Katz, Daniel and Kahn, Robert L. *The Social Psychology of Organizations.* New York: John Wiley & Sons, Inc., 1966.

Kilduff, Marshall and Javers, Ron. *The Suicide Cult: The Inside Story of the People's Temple Sect and Massacre in Guyana.* New York: Bantam, 1979.

Kirschenbaum, Howard and Glasser, Barbara. *Developing Support Groups: A Manual for Facilitators and Participants.* La Jolla, California: University Associates, 1978.

Klein, Melanie, et al. *Development in Psychoanalysis.* New York: Hillary House, 1952.

Kluckhon, Clyde. *The Navajo.* Cambridge, Mass.: Harvard University Press, 1951.

Kohler, Adam Tom. "A Social Systems Approach to Program Evaluation." *Journal of Personality and Social Systems*, Vol. 1, No. 1, April, 1977, pp. 65-77.

Kohlmeier, Louis, Jr. *The Regulators: Watchdog Agencies and the Public Interest.* New York: Harper & Row Publ. Co., Inc., 1969.

Koontz, Harold and Gable, Richard W. *Public Control of Economic Enterprise.* New York: McGraw-Hill, 1956.

Korda, Michael. *Power! How to Get It, How to Use It!* New York: Random House, 1975.

Korman, Abraham K. *Organizational Behavior.* Englewood Cliffs, N.J.: Prentice-Hall, 1977.

Krause, Charles A. with Stern, Lawrence M., Harwood, Richard and Johnson, Frank. *Guyana Massacre: The Eyewitness Account.* New York: Berkley Press, 1977.

Kroll, Morton. "Hypotheses and Design for the Study of Public Policies in the United States." *Midwest Journal of Political Science*, Vol. 6, 1962, pp. 363-383.

————. "Understanding Large Organizations—The Group Field Approach Revisited." *Public Administration Review.* (Nov./Dec. 1976), pp. 690-694.

Laing, R.D. *The Politics of Experience.* New York: Ballantine Books (Random House), 1967.

Lasswell, Harold D. *Power and Personality.* New York: W.W. Norton, 1948.

Leighton, Alexander H. *The Governing of Men.* Princeton, N.J.: Princeton University Press, 1945.

Leighton, Dorothea and Adair, John. *People of the Middle Place: A Study of the Zuni Indians,* New Haven, Conn.: Human Relations Area Files Press, 1966.

Lepawsky, Albert. *Administration.* New York: Alfred A. Knopf, Inc., 1955.

Levinson, D. "Race, Personality and Social Structure in the Organizational Setting." *Journal of Abnormal and Social Psychology*, Vol. 58 (1959), pp. 170-180.

Levy, A.B. *Private Corporations and Their Control.* London: Routledge and Kegan Paul, 1957.

Lewin, Kurt. *Field Theory in Social Science.* Edited by D. Cartwright. New York: Harper, 1951.

Lieberman, Morton and Borman, Leonard D., editors. "Self Help Groups," *The Journal of Applied Behavioral Science*, Vol. 12, No. 3, July-August-September, 1976.

Likert, Rensis. *New Patterns of Management.* New York: McGraw-Hill, 1961.

————, and Likert, Jane Gibson. *New Ways of Managing Conflict.* New York: McGraw-Hill Book Co., Inc., 1976.

————. *Human Organization.* New York: McGraw-Hill Book Co., Inc., 1967.

Lindzey, Gardner and Aron, Elliot, editors. *The Handbook of Social Psychology.* 2nd edition. Reading, Mass.: Addison-Wesley Publishing Co., Inc., 1969.

Lippitt, Gordon. *Organizational Renewal.* New York: Appleton-Century-Crofts, 1969.

————. *Visualizing Change.* Fairfax, Virginia: N.T.L. Learning Resources Corp., Inc., 1973.

Long, Norton. "Public Policy and Administration: The Goals of Rationality and Responsibility." *Public Administration Review*, Vol. 14 (Winter 1954), pp. 22-31.

————. *The Polity.* Chicago, Ill.: Rand McNally Co., 1962.

Loring, Rosalind and Wells, Theodora. *Breakthrough: Women Into Management.* New York: Van Nostrand Reinhold Co., Inc., 1972.

Lupton, Tom. "Best Fix in the Design of Organization." In *Task and Organization*, edited by E. T. Miller. New York: John Wiley & Sons, Inc., 1976, pp. 121-149.

Lyden, Fremont J.; Shipman, George A.; Wilkinson, Robert W. Jr., "Decision-Flow Analysis, A Methodology for Studying the Public Policy Making Process." In Preston P. LeBreton, editor, *Comparative Administrative Theory.* Seattle: University of Washington Press, 1968, pp. 156-157.

————; Shipman, George A.; and Kroll, Morton. *Policies, Decisions and Organization.* New York: Appleton-Century-Crofts, 1969.

McCarthy, Mary Therese. *Medina.* New York: Harcourt, Brace & Javonovich, 1972.

Maccoby, Michael. *The Gamesman: The New Corporate Leaders.* New York: Simon & Schuster, 1976.

McGregor, Douglas. *The Human Side of Enterprise.* New York: McGraw-Hill Book Co., Inc., 1960.

Maguire, John and Dunn, Mary Lee. *Hold Hands and Die: The Incredibly True Story of the People's Temple and Reverend Jim Jones.* New York: Dole Books, 1977.

Maine, Sir Henry. *Early History of Institutions*, 1875, and his *Ancient Law*, 1885. Boston: Beacon Press, 1963.

March, James G., and Simon, Herbert. *Organization.* New York: John Wiley & Sons, Inc., 1958.

Marchetti, Victor and Marks, John D. *The C.I.A. and the Cult of Intelligence.* New York: A. A. Knopf, 1974.

Marcus, Joy. "Intimacy." In Hogie Wyckoff, *Love, Therapy and Politics.* New York: Grove Press, Inc., 1976, pp. 213-220.

Marcuse, Herbert. *One-Dimensional Man.* Boston: Beacon Press, 1964.

Margulies, Newton and Raia, Anthony P. *Conceptual Foundations of Organizational Development.* New York: McGraw-Hill Book Co., Inc., 1978.

————. *Organizational Development: Values, Process and Technology.* New York: McGraw-Hill Book Co., Inc., 1972.

Marris, Peter and Rein, Martin. *Dilemmas of Social Reform.* New York: Atherton Press, 1967.

Marshall, James. "The New Guerrillas: Public Administration in the New Industrial State." Unpublished doctoral dissertation, University of Southern California, 1973.

Marx, Karl and Engels, Friedrich. "On Alienation." Selected from their writing in G. Wright Mills, editor, *Images of Man.* New York: George Braziller, Inc., 1960.

Maslow, A.H. "A Theory of Human Motivation." *Psychological Review*, (July, 1943), pp. 370-396.

————. *Motivation and Personality.* New York: Harper & Row Publishers, Inc., 1954.

————. *Toward a Psychology of Being.* Princeton, N.J.: D. Van Nostrand Co., 1962.

————. *Eupsychian Management.* Homewood, Ill.: Richard D. Irwin, 1955.

May, Rollo. *Power and Innocence.* New York: W.W. Norton & Co., Inc., 1972.

Mayo, Elton. *The Human Problems of an Industrial Civilization.* Boston: Harvard Business School, 1933.

————. *The Social Problems of Industrial Civilization.* Boston: Graduate School of Business Administration, Harvard University, 1945.

Medieros, James A. and Schmitt, David E. *Public Bureaucracy: Values and Perspectives.* North Scituate, Mass.: Roxbury Press, 1977.

Meier, Kenneth J. *Politics and the Bureaucracy: Policymaking in the Fourth Branch of Government.* North Scituate, Mass.: Duxbury Press, 1979.

Menzies, Isabel E.P. "A Case Study in the Functioning of Social Systems as a Defense Against Anxiety." *Human Relations,* Vol. 13 (1960), pp. 95-121.

Merton, Robert K. *Social Theory and Social Structure.* New York: The Free Press of Glencoe, 1963.

————; Gray, Alisa P.; Hockey, Barbara; and Selvin, Hanan C., editors. *Reader in Bureaucracy.* Glencoe, Ill.: The Free Press, 1952.

Milgram, Stanley. "Behavioral Study of Obedience." *Journal of Abnormal Psychology,* Vol. 67 (1963), p. 371-378.

————. *Obedience and Authority.* New York: Harper & Row Co., Inc., 1974.

Mill, John Stuart. *On Liberty.* (1859). Edited by Alburey Castell, Arlington Heights, Ill.: A.H. M. Publishing Co., 1947.

————. "The Subjection of Women." in John Stuart Mill, *Three Essays: On Liberty, Representative Government, The Subjection of Women.* London: Oxford University Press, 1975.

Miller, Eric J. and Rice, A.K. "Individuals, Groups and Their Boundaries." In Arthur D. Colman and W. Harold Bexton, editors. *Group Relations Reader.* Sausalito, Calif.: GREX, 1975, pp. 43-68.

————. *Systems of Organization.* London: Tavistock Publications, 1967.

Mills, C. Wright, editor. *Images of Man.* New York: George Braziller, Inc., 1960.

Mills, Jeanine. *Six Years with God: Life Inside Reverend Jim Jones' Peoples Temple.* New York: A & W Publishers, 1979.

Mills, Theodore M. *The Sociology of Small Groups.* Englewood Cliffs, N.J.: Prentice Hall, Inc., 1967.

Mitchell, William C. *The American Polity.* New York: The Free Press, 1962.

Mooney, James D. and Reily, Alan C. *The Principles of Organization.* New York: Harper & Bros., 1939.

Moreno, J.L. *Who Shall Survive: A New Approach to the Problem of Human Interrelations.* Washington, D.C.: Nervous and Mental Disease Publ. Co., 1934.

Morris, Desmond. *The Naked Ape.* New York: McGraw-Hill Book Co., Inc., 1967.

Morris, Robert and Binstock, Robert H. *Feasible Planning for Social Change.* New York: Columbia University Press, 1966.

Morrow, Allyn A. and Thayer, Frederick C. "Collaborative Work Settings: New Titles Old Contradictions." *Journal of Applied Behavioral Science,* Vol. 13, No. 3 (1977), pp. 448-457.

Morrow, William L. *Public Administration, Politics, Policy and the Political System.* 2nd edition. New York: Random House, 1980.

Muller, Herbert. *The Children of Frankenstein: A Primer on Modern Technology and Human Values.* Bloomington, Inc.: Indiana University Press, 1970.

Nadler, Gerald. *Work Design: A Systems Concept.* revised edition. Homewood, Ill.: Richard D. Irwin, Inc., 1970.

Newsweek, December 4, 1978, "The People's Temple Cult of Death," pp. 38-82.

Newton, Peter M. and Levinson, Daniel J. "The Work Group Within the Organization: A Sociopsychological Approach." *Psychiatry.* Vol. 36 (May 1973), pp. 115-142.

Normanton, E. Leslie. "Public Accountability and Audit: A Reconnaissance." In Bruce L.R. Smith and D.C. Hague, *The Dilemma of Accountability in Modern Government. Indepen-*

dence vs. Control. London: Macmillan, 1971.

Organ, D.W. "Some Variables Affecting Boundary Role Behavior." *Sociometry*, (1971), pp. 524-537.

Orwell, George. *Nineteen Eighty-Four.* New York: Harcourt, Brace, 1949.

Osborn, Alex. *Applied Imagination.* New York: C. Scribner Sons, 1957.

Parsons, Talcott. *The Social System.* Glencoe, Ill.: The Free Press, 1951.

———— ; Bales, Robert F.; and Shils, Edward A. *Working Papers in the Theory of Action.* New York: The Free Press of Glencoe, 1953.

————, and Shils, Edward A., editors. *Toward a Theory of Action.* New York: Harper & Row, 1951.

Peel, Roy V., editor. "The Ombudsman or Citizen Defender: A Modern Institution." *The Annals of the American Academy of Political and Social Science*, Vol. 337 (May 1968).

Peers, William R. (Lt. Gen.) *The My Lai Inquiry.* New York: Norton, 1979.

Perkus, Cathy. (editor). *Cointelpro: The F.B.I.'s Secret War on Political Freedom.* New York: Monad Press, 1975.

Perls, F.S. *Ego, Hunger and Aggression.* New York: Vintage, 1947 and 1969.

Perrow, Charles. *Complex Organizations.* Glenview, Ill.: Scott-Foresman, 1972.

Peters, B. Guy. *The Politics of Bureaucracy.* New York and London: Longman, Inc., 1978.

Peterson, Paul E. "The Politics of American Education," in Fred N. Kerlinger and John B. Carroll, editors, *Review of Research in Education*, Vol. 2, Itaska, Ill.: F.E. Peacock Publishers, Inc., 1974.

Pfeffer, Jeffrey. *Organizational Design.* Arlington Heights, Ill.: AHM Publishing Corp., 1978.

Piaget, Jean. *Logic and Psychology.* New York: Basic Books, 1957.

Plato. *The Trial and Death of Socrates.* translated from the Greek by Benjamin Jowett, New York: Heritage Press, 1963.

Poland, Orville. "Program Evaluation and Administrative Theory." *Public Administration Review.* (July/August, 1974), pp. 333-338.

Pondy, L. "Varieties of Organizational Conflict." *Administrative Science Quarterly*, (May 1969), pp. 499-507.

Popper, Karl R. *The Open Society and Its Enemies.* Vols. 1 & 2. (Fourth edition, revised 1962.) New York: Harper & Row, Inc., 1963 by arrangement with Princeton University Press.

————. "Organizational Conflict: Concepts and Models." *Administrative Science Quarterly*, (Sept. 1967) Vol. 12, pp. 296-320.

Presthus, Robert. *The Organizational Society.* New York: Alfred A. Knopf, 1962.

Price, Charlton R. and Levinson, Harry. "Work and Mental Health." In *Blue Collar World: Studies of the American Worker.* Arthur B. Shostak and William Gomberg, editors. Englewood Cliffs, N.J.: Prentice-Hall, Inc., 1965.

Prouty, Leroy Fletcher. *The Secret Team: The C.I.A. and Its Allies in Control of the United States and the World.* Englewood Cliffs, N.J.: Prentice-Hall, Inc., 1973.

Ranson, Harry Howe. *The Intelligence Establishment.* Cambridge, Mass.: Harvard University Press, 1970.

Redford, Emmette S. *Administration of National Economic Control.* New York: The Macmillan Co., 1952.

————. "Administrative Regulation: Protection of the Public Interest," *American Political Science Review*, Vol. XLVIII, No. 4, Dec. 1954, pp. 1103-1113.

————. *Democracy in the Administrative State.* New York: Oxford University Press, 1969.

————. *Public Administration and Policy Formation.* Austin: University of Texas Press, 1956.

————. *The Regulation Process.* Austin: University of Texas Press, 1969.

Revere, Joan and Klein, Melanie. *Love, Hate and Reparation.* New York: W.W. Norton Co., Inc., 1964.

Rice, A.K. "Individual Group and Intergroup Processes." *Human Relations*, Vol. 22 (1969), pp. 564-584.

Rice, Berkeley. *The C-5A Scandal: An Inside Story of the Military-Industrial Complex.* Boston: Houghton-Mifflin, 1971.

Rich, Adrienne. *Of Woman Born: Motherhood as Experience and Institution.* New York: W. W. Norton & Co., Inc., 1976.

Riedel, James A. "Citizen Participation: Myths and Realities," *Public Administration Review*, May/June 1972.

Rioch, Margaret J. "The Work of Wilfred Bion on Groups." *Psychiatry.* Vol. 33 (1970), pp. 56-66. Reprinted in Arthur D. Colman and Harold Bexton, editors, *Group Relations Reader.* Sausalito, Calif.: GREX, 1975, pp. 21-34.

――――. "All We Like Sheep – (Isaiah 53:6): Followers and Leaders." *Psychiatry*, Vol. 34 (1971), pp. 258-273. Reprinted in Arthur D. Colman and Harold Bexton, editors, *Group Relations Readers.* Sausalito, Calif.: GREX, 1975, pp. 159-177.

Robbins, Christopher. *Air America.* New York: Putnam, 1979.

Rogers, Carl R. and Skinner, B.F. "Some Issues Concerning the Control of Human Behavior, a Symposium." *Science*, Vol. 124 (Nov. 30, 1956), pp. 1057-1066.

Rothlisberger, F.J. *Management and Morale.* Cambridge, Mass.: Harvard University Press, 1941.

――――. and Dickson, William J. *Management and the Worker.* Cambridge, Mass.: Harvard University Press, 1939.

Rourke, Francis E. *Bureaucracy, Politics and Public Policy.* Boston: Little, Brown, 1959.

Rubinstein, Moshe F. *Patterns in Problem Solving.* Englewood Cliffs, N.J.: Prentice-Hall, Inc., 1975.

Russell, Bertrand. *Freedom vs. Organization.* New York: W.W. Norton & Co., Inc.

――――. *Power.* New York: Barnes & Noble, Inc., 1962.

Ryan, William. *Blaming the Victim.* New York: Pantheon Books, 1971.

Sampson, Ronald B. *The Psychology of Power.* New York: Vintage Books, 1965.

Santillana, George de. *The Crime of Galileo.* Chicago: University of Chicago Press, 1955.

Sarason, Seymour. *The Culture of the School and the Problem of Change.* Boston: Allyn and Bacon, Inc., 1971.

Scheider, Thomas M. and Crowell, Laura. *Discussing and Deciding: A Desk Book for Group Leaders and Members.* New York: Macmillan, 1979.

Schein, Edgar H. *Organizational Psychology.* Englewood Cliffs, N.J.: Prentice-Hall, 1971.

――――. *Process Consultation: Its Role in Organizational Development.* Reading, Mass.: Addison-Wesley Publishing Co., Inc., 1969.

――――. and Bennis, Warren G., editors. *Personal and Organizational Change Through Group Methods: The Laboratory Approach.* New York: John Wiley & Sons, Inc., 1965.

Schiff, Ashley L. *Fire and Water.* Cambridge, Mass.: Harvard University Press, 1962.

Schwartz, Eleanor Brantly. *The Sex Barrier in Business.* Atlanta, Ga.: Publishing Services Division, Georgia State University, 1971.

Selye, Hans. *The Stress of Life.* Cambridge, Mass.: Harvard University Press, 1962.

――――. *Stress Without Distress.* New York: J.P. Lippincott, 1974.

Selznick, Philip. "An Approach to the Theory of Bureaucracy." *American Sociological Review*, Vol. 8 (1945).

――――. "Foundations of the Theory of Organizations." *American Sociological Review*, Vol. XIII (Feb. 1948), pp. 25-35.

――――. *Leadership in Administration.* Evanston, Ill.: Row-Peterson, 1957.

Shaw, Marvin E. *Group Dynamics, The Psychology of Small Group Behavior.* New York: McGraw-Hill Book Co., Inc., 1976.

Shils, Edward A. "Charisma, Order and Status." *American Sociological Review*, Vol. 30, No. 2 (April 1965), pp. 199-213.

Shipman, George A. *Designing Program Action – Against Urban Poverty.* University, Ala.: University of Alabama Press, 1971.

Shutz, W. *Joy: Expanding Human Awareness.* New York: Grove Press, 1967.

Silberman, Charles E. *Crisis in the Classroom.* New York: Random House, 1970.

Simmons, Robert H. and Dvorin, Eugene P. *Public Administration, Values and Policy Change.* Alfred Publ. Co., Inc., 1977.

————. "The Washington State Plural Executive: An Initial Effort at Interaction Analysis." *Western Political Science Quarterly*, Vol. XVIII, No. 2, (June 1965), pp. 363-381.

————. "The Role of the Select Committee on Nationalized Industry in Parliament." *Western Political Quarterly*, (Sept. 1961), pp. 741-745.

Simon, Herbert A. *Administrative Behavior.* 3rd edition. New York: Macmillan, 1976 (1st edition, 1948).

Singer, David L.; Astrachan, Boris M.; Gould, Lawrence J.; and Klein, Edward B. "Boundary Management in Psychological Work with Groups." *Journal of Applied Behavioral Science*, Vol. 11, No. 2 (1975), pp. 137-176.

Sirica, John J. *To Set the Record Straight: The Break-in, The Tapes, The Conspirators, The Pardon.* New York: Norton, 1979.

Skinner, B.F. *Beyond Freedom and Dignity.* New York: Vintage, 1972.

Smith, Bruce L.R. and Hague, D.C. *The Dilemma of Accountability in Modern Government: Independence vs Control.* London: Macmillan, 1971.

Smith, Maury. *A Practical Guide to Value Clarification.* La Jolla, Calif.: University Associates, 1977.

Smith, Michael P. "Alienation and Bureaucracy: The Role of Participatory Administration." *Public Administration Review*, (Nov./Dec. 1971), p. 660.

Sneed, Joseph D. and Waldhorn, Steven, editors. *Restructuring the Federal System: Approaches to Accountability in Post-Categorical Programs.* New York: Crane, Rossak & Co.

Sorokin, Pitrim and Lunden, Walter. *Power and Morality: Who Shall Guard the Guardians.* Boston: Porter Sargent Publ., 1959.

Steiner, Claude. *Scripts People Live.* New York: Grove Press, 1974.

————. "Cooperative Meetings." *Issues in Radical Therapy*, (Winter 1977), p. 11.

————. "Cooperation." in Hogie Wykcoff, editor, *Love, Therapy and Politics.* New York: Grove Press, Inc., 1976.

————. editor. *Reading in Radical Psychiatry.* New York: Grove Press, Inc., 1975.

————. "Revised Principles of Radical Psychiatry." *Issues in Radical Therapy*, (Spring 1977), pp. 12-14.

————. "Working Cooperatively." *Issues in Radical Therapy*, Vol. 3, No. 4 (Fall 1976), pp. 22-25.

Swisher, Carl Brent. *American Constitutional Development.* 2nd edition. Cambridge, Mass.: Houghton-Mifflin Co., 1954.

Tannenbaum, Robert and Davis, Sheldon. "Values, Men and Organizations." *Industrial Management Review*, Vol. 10. pp. 67-83.

Taylor, Alfred Edward. *Socrates.* Garden City, N.Y.: Doubleday, 1953.

Taylor, Frederick W. *The Principles of Scientific Management.* New York: W.W. Norton & Co., Inc. By arrangement with Harper & Row. Copyright 1947. First copyright by Frederick W. Taylor, 1911.

Teich, Albert H., editor. *Technology and Man's Future.* New York: St. Martin's Press, 1972.

Thayer, Frederick C. *An End to Hierarchy! An End to Competition!* New York: New Viewpoints (a division of Franklin Watts), 1973.

Thelen, Herbert A. *Dynamics of Groups at Work.* Chicago, Ill.: University of Chicago Press, 1954.

Thomas, J.M. and Bennis, W.G., editors. *Management of Change and Conflict.* Baltimore, Md.: Penguin Books, 1972.

Thomas, Theodore Hubert. "Innovation in Organizational Structure: Normative Implications of Participating Styles." Unpublished manuscript (doctoral dissertation) submitted to the University of California, Los Angeles, Political Science Faculty. Copyright by Theodore H. Thomas (1977).

Thompson, James D. *Organizations in Action.* New York: McGraw-Hill Book Co., Inc., 1967.

Thompson, Laura and Joseph, Alice. *The Hopi Way.* New York: Russell & Russell, 1965.

Thompson, Victor A. *Modern Organization.* New York: A.A. Knopf, 1961.

_____. *Bureaucracy in the Modern World.* Morristown, N.J.: General Learning Press, 1976.

_____. *Without Sympathy or Enthusiasm.* University, Ala.: The University of Alabama Press, 1975.

Thorsrud, Einar. "Democracy at Work: Norwegian Experiences with Non-bureaucratic Forms of Organization." *Journal of Applied Behavioral Science*, Vol. 13, No. 3, 1977, pp. 410-421.

Tichy, Noel M. "Agents of Planned Social Change: Congruence of Values, Cognition and Actions." *Administrative Science Quarterly*, (June 1974), p. 179.

Townsend, Robert. *Up the Organization.* New York: A.A. Knopf, 1970.

Tregoe, Benjamin B. *The Rational Manager: A Systems Approach to Problem Solving and Decision Making.* New York: McGraw-Hill Book Co., Inc., 1965.

Truman, David B. *The Governmental Process.* New York: Alfred A. Knopf, 1960.

Tullock, Gordon. *The Politics of Bureaucracy.* Washington, D.C.: Public Affairs Press, 1965.

Turquet, P.M. "Leadership: The Industrial and the Group." In G.S. Gibbard, J.J. Hartman and R.D. Mann, editors, *Analysis of Groups.* San Francisco: Jossey-Bass, 1974, p. 357.

Ungar, Sanford J. *F.B.I.: An Uncensored Look Behind the Walls*, Boston: Little, Brown and Co., 1975.

U.S. Department of the Army. *The My Lai Coverup: Beyond the Reach of the Law?* The Peers Commission report with a supplement and introductory essay on the limits of the law by Joseph Goldstein, Burke Marshall, Jack Schwartz, New York: Free Press, 1976.

Vickers, Sir Geoffrey. *Value Systems and Social Process.* New York: Basic Books, Inc., 1968.

Waldo, Dwight. *The Administrative State.* New York: Ronald, 1948.

_____. *The Enterprise of Public Administration: A Summary View.* Novato, Calif.: Chandler Sharp Publishers, Inc., 1980.

Walton, Richard E. *Interpersonal Peacemaking: Confrontations and Third Party Consultations.* Reading, Mass.: Addison-Wesley Publ. Co., 1969.

Watters, Pat and Gillers, Stephen, (editors). *Investigating the F.B.I.* New York: Doubleday, 1973.

Weber, Max. *Essays in Sociology.* H. Gerth and C. Wright Mills, editors. New York: Oxford University Press, 1946.

_____. *Economy and Society.* Edited by Guenter Roth and Claus Wittch. New York: Gedminster Press, 1968.

_____. *The Protestant Ethic and the Spirit of Capitalism.* Talcott Parsons, translator. New York: Oxford University Press.

_____. *The Theory of Social and Economic Organization.* A.M. Henderson and Talcott Parsons, translators. New York: Oxford University Press, 1947.

Weinder, B. *Theories of Motivation: From Mechanism to Cognition.* Chicago, Ill.: Markhour Press, 1962.

Weinstein, Deena. *Bureaucratic Opposition: Challenging Abuses at the Work Place.* New York: Pergamon Press, 1979.

White, Leonard D. *The Federalists: A Study in Administrative History.* New York: The Macmillan Co., 1956.

_____. *The Jeffersonians: A Study in Administrative History, 1801-1829.* New York: The Macmillan Co., 1961.

_____. *The Jacksonians: A Study in Administrative History, 1829-1861.* New York: The Macmillan Co., 1963.

_____. *The Republican Era: A Study in Administrative History, 1861-1901.* New York: The Macmillan Co., 1963.

White, Ralph and Lippitt, Ronald. "Leader Behavior and Member Reaction in Three Social Climates." In Dorwin Cartwright and Alvin Zander, editors, *Group Dynamics: Research and Theory.* 3rd edition. New York: Harper & Row, 1968, pp. 326-334.

Whiteside, Thomas. *The Pendulum and the Toxic Cloud.* New Haven, Conn.: Yale University

Press, 1979.

Whyte, William Foote. *Organizational Behavior: Theory and Application.* Homewood, Ill.: R.D. Irwin, 1969.

Whyte, William H. Jr. *The Organization Man.* New York: Simon and Schuster, 1956.

Wilbern, York. "Administrative Control of Petroleum Production in Texas," in Emmette S. Redford, editor, *Public Administration and Policy Formation.* Austin: University of Texas Press, 1956.

Williams, Leonard. *Challenge to Survival.* London: Audre Deutsch, Ltd., 1971.

Wilson, Sloan. *The Man in the Gray Flannel Suit.* New York: Simon & Schuster, 1955 (fiction).

Wilson, Woodrow. "The Study of Administration." *Political Science Quarterly*, 1887, pp. 197-222.

Winslow, John F. *Conglomerates Unlimited, The Failure of Regulation.* Bloomington and London: Indiana University Press, 1973.

Wise, David. *The American Police State: The Government Agencies Against the People.* New York: Random House, 1976.

————. and Ross, Thomas. *The Invisible Government.* New York: Random House, 1964.

Wright, Charles R. *Public Leadership.* San Francisco, Calif.: Chandler Publ. Co., 1961.

Wyckoff, Hogie, editor. *Love, Therapy and Politics.* New York: Grove Press, Inc., 1976.

————. "Equalizing Power in Groups." *Love, Therapy and Politics.* New York: Grove Press, Inc., 1976.

Yablonsky, Lewis. *Robopaths: People as Machines.* Baltimore, Md.: Bobbs-Merrill Co., Penguin Books, 1972.

Yankelovich, Daniel. "The New Psychological Contracts at Work." *Psychology Today* (May 1978).

Young, Michael. *The Rise of Metirocracy.* New York: Random House, 1959.

Zald, M.N. *Power in Organizations.* Nashville, Tenn.: Vanderbilt University Press, 1970.

Zand, D.E. "Trust and Managerial Problem Solving," *Administrative Science Quarterly*, Vol. 17, 1972, pp. 229-239.

Zander, Alvin. *Groups at Work.* San Francisco, Calif.: Jossey/Bass Co., Inc., 1977.

Ziegler, H. and Peck, W., "The Political Functions of the Educational System," *Sociology of Education*, Vol. 43, (1970) p. 115.

Zimbardo, Philip G. "The Human Choice." In W.J. Arnold and D. Levine, editors, *Nebraska Symposium on Motivation*, Vol. 17, Lincoln, Nebr.: University of Nebraska Press, 1969.

INDEX

INDEX OF NAMES

INDEX OF SUBJECTS